Also By Arnold Forster

The New Anti-Semitism (with B.R.Epstein)
The Radical Right (with B.R. Epstein)
Report on the John Birch Society, 1966 (with B.R.Epstein)
Report on The Ku Klux Klan (with B.R.Epstein)
Danger on the Right (with B.R.Epstein)
Some of My Best Friends . . . (with B.R.Epstein)
Cross-Currents (with B.R.Epstein)
The Troublemakers (with B.R.Epstein)
Report From Israel
A Measure of Freedom
Anti-Semitism '47

SQUARE ONE

A MEMOIR
by
ARNOLD FORSTER

Foreword by Elie Wiesel

SQUARE ONE

DONALD I. FINE, INC.

New York

Library of Congress Cataloging-in-Publication Data

Forster, Arnold.
Square one.

1. Forster, Arnold.   2. B'nai B'rith. Anti-
defamation League.   3. Antisemitism—United States.
4. Jews—United States—Politics and government.
5. Jews—United States—Biography.   6. United States—
Ethnic relations.   I. Title.
E184.J5F615 1988   305.8'924'073   88-45424
ISBN 1-55611-104-5 (alk. paper)

Manufactured in the United States of America

10 9 8 7 6 5 4 3 2 1

To Jayne, Stuart, Carole and Charles, their generations
and all who follow, that they may live
free from hatred

Contents

CONTENTS

Preface

This book is not meant to be only about the treatment of Jews by non-Jews or about the Middle East and the forty-year Arab-Israeli confrontation. It is also, I hope, about broader reactions to these issues. For example, when I write about the 1987–88 "uprising" on the west bank of the Jordan River—Judea and Samaria—and in the Gaza strip adjacent to the Sinai desert, the larger relevance of this *"intifada"* is the international community's reaction to the tragic eruption. Similarly people's boredom or exhaustion at hearing more about the Holocaust; a nation electing a president *because* he has a Nazi record; another president arranging a controversial visit abroad that ignores the meaning of the Holocaust; a major American political party raising a presidential candidate to the eminence of second place in its primary electoral contest in spite of his expressed antipathy to Jews and Israel; the United Nations, a consortium of states chartered to preserve peace and security, permitting itself to be used to spread hatred toward some of its own members, with anti-Semitism becoming a means of addressing problems in nearly every area of the globe. In all of these events I have tried to look for underlying motivations. Written from a personal view, the intent has been to probe and measure overt and sub-liminal non-Jewish attitudes about Jews and Israel according to actual behavior and the spoken or written word. The guideposts range from the Ku Klux Klan to the John Birch Society, from the German-American Bund to Nazi Germany, from the Arab boy-cott of Israel to Yassir Arafat's Palestine Liberation Organiza-tion, from the State of Israel to the United Nations, and from Catholic, Protestant and Moslem communities to Jews them-selves. Along the way the tragedy of the late motion picture star, John Garfield, is told at length and in detail as symbolic of community indifference to victimization of Jews. I offer, too, an eyewitness report and analysis of Adolph Eichmann's trial in Jerusalem for Crimes Against the Jewish People as an insight into the world's response to the mass murder of European Jewry. The arrest and conviction of Julius and Ethel Rosenberg for giving the Soviet Union America's atom-bomb secrets are examined, but essentially for the Jewish response to the public's view of the case.

Eyewitness stops are made, too, for close-ups of prominent personalities who played significant roles in the events that un-fold, including Walter Winchell, Senator Joseph E. McCarthy, David Ben-Gurion, David Rockefeller, Zubin Mehta, Walter Mondale and Secretary of State George P. Shultz, along with others.

At the close it becomes persuasively clear, at least to this observer, that a tired truism is too much the unfortunate reality: *plus ça change, plus c'est la meme chose.* Unknowingly we may have been on something of a figurative treadmill away from bigotry over the last fifty years. And only if we face this can more solid and substantial progress be made in the future. At least if I've raised some concern, stirred inquisitive interest, provoked candid discussion and precipitated further search for truth, my effort will have served some useful purpose.

While I've written in the first person, it should be understood that I have been a small part of a much larger team of intelli-gent, informed men and women of the Anti-Defamation League of the B'nai B'rith, with whom I worked in close unity to achieve whatever successes or suffer whatever failures that appear in our attempt to face controversial issues. Errors, exaggerations or understatements, like the opinions expressed, are altogether my own.

For support in the task now completed I am profoundly indebted to May, my beloved wife of nearly half a century, and to my devoted friend and law partner, Bernard D. Fischman, who first suggested to me the need for this book. They both gave endlessly of their time, wise guidance and valuable advice—far beyond what I deserved but surely needed.

—A.F.

Foreword
by Elie Wiesel

Arnold Forster needs no introduction to the American public. His daring initiatives as general counsel and associate national director of the Anti-Defamation League for forty years—the most stormy and also the most exalting years in the history of the American Jewish community—have earned him a well-deserved international reputation.

Arnold Forster, my old friend, also does not need me to preface this magnificent book of memories. But the cause that he defends, that he has always defended, demands that many of us rally to his side.

Throughout his life, Forster has mobilized enlightened public opinion against one of the foremost evils of the twentieth century, or rather, of the last twenty centuries: anti-Semitism. Unmasking hatred, denouncing it, disarming it; such are the goal and strategy of Arnold Forster and his collaborators. Still, in Forster's view, their victories, impressive as they may be, are

15

few. He does not hesitate to recognize that with regard to anti-Semitism, in the United States and in the world, we are back to "Square One." In other words, we must start all over again.

How is one to explain the anti-Semitic phenomenon? Academics everywhere have tried for years to analyze it, to dissect it, to penetrate it. There are those who assign the blame to fanaticism. Others invoke the economic factor: in the Middle Ages the money-lenders, the usurers, were Jews; impossible not to hate them. Then there are those who stress the psychological phenomenon: the Jew represents the *other,* the foreigner. Of course, there are many attempts at explanation: philosophical, sociological, political. Each is valid for a particular period, a particular country, a particular case. None answers the question. The unknown element remains. There is, there always will be an inexplicable aspect of anti-Semitism that resists comprehension.

How does one explain the anti-Semitism of the Fathers of the Church? Or that of a Voltaire or a Wagner? Or that of a Dostoevsky and a Celine? How is it possible to be a great moral thinker *and* the enemy of a community of men rooted in the memory of God? How can one write masterpieces and at the same time propagate hate among one's peers—is it that Jews were not considered peers? How can one in our own country, founded by foreigners for other foreigners, foster ugly and dangerous hatred for men and women because they are of a different color or because they remain faithful to a more ancient covenant?

The hate toward the Jew is sometimes powerful enough to unite men who otherwise would be opponents. Why is this so? Why do groups or individuals who have nothing in common unite when it comes to maligning Jews, reviling them, persecuting them? Why this need to hate the Jew? And how is it that this hatred has survived so many centuries? Surely, anti-Semitism is the oldest prejudice and human-rights violation.

That it has survived is documented brilliantly and chillingly by the author. Anti-Semitism of the right and of the left, communist anti-Semitism, Arab anti-Semitism (no this is not a contradiction, Forster says; and he is right: all are thriving). What is the anti-Zionist campaign, the anti-Israeli propaganda, if not the same archaic hatred in modern dress? Is Forster not correct in warning us that the battle against the enemies of the Jews is far from being won?

Read his book. Even if you are not always convinced that his pessimism is justified, you will be enriched. You will learn things you did not know about Jewish life in the U.S.A. The author's memories of Hollywood (John Garfield, Dore Schary) will make you smile. The book will also make you cry: Forster's last meeting with David Ben-Gurion; his radio broadcasts of the Eichmann trial; his race by car to Brandeis University, where his son had just been assaulted and wounded by a gang of the KKK. Forster not only knows how to explain; he moves you to anger, compassion or laughter. One understands why he made himself take on so many battles in the interest of justice. One also understands how a man with such a passion for truth and memory stood up to a Joseph McCarthy, or a Henry Luce, press empire and all. Here is a fearless man who refuses all compromise when it comes to defending the Jewish people, and through it, all of humanity.

Courageous and lucid, Forster acknowledges that during the Reign of Night in Europe, the American Jewish community did not do enough to come to the aid of the doomed Jewry of the ghettos and the camps. He says it because he believes it, because he knows it to be true even if it hurts to say it. In this book of some four hundred pages, the Holocaust is mentioned only in passing, but the memory of the Holocaust is present on every page. One feels its shadow every time Forster confronts a decision to challenge the racial persecutors and their accomplices.

Have I suggested that this book is somehow pessimistic? If so, permit me to correct myself. Arnold Forster is too active, too energetic, too creative to give in to pessimism. In this book, as in his life, he proves that it is always up to the individual to fight against evil, and that sometimes it is possible even to win. He says it himself: if we are not back to "Square One" it is because Israel exists. He loves Israel, as I do, with all his heart.

He is not embarrassed to say it out loud; and neither am I.

—Elie Wiesel
New York City
June, 1988

1

A Breed Apart

I was taking a violin lesson from a teacher whose name is gone beyond recall. Suddenly, my fiddle's squeaking sounds were overwhelmed by a series of steam-whistle blasts emanating from atop the nearby massive American Bank Note building. My mother clutched my hand and we hurried down three floors to the crowded street below, the music teacher following close behind. There the swirling, moving throng appeared confused and frightened. Actually they were hurrying toward the ear-shattering sound as if magnetized. Within five frantic minutes we moved from the East Bronx corner of Barretto Street and Southern Boulevard to the red-bricked, giant structure on the hill.

A wild thought went through my mind. World War I was being fought overseas, perhaps now it had reached our shores. To a six-year-old, the possibility conjured up dagger-topped helmets on German soldiers brutally crushing us. Such was the stuff of a youngster's nightmares.

The increasing mob crowded the high walls of the fortresslike factory, milling about, pushing and shoving, waiting for an explanation. Then while the piercing noise continued its alarm an accurate explanation spread from mouth to mouth: the steam-whistle was screaming for joy—an armistice had been declared, the war was over.

I did not know at the time that for me and my generation a long war was beginning. Had I been an adult, and aware, the enactment of the Alien and Sedition Act that year might have been a warning signal of the dangers to human rights in the years ahead.

The present, they say, is ruled by the past. Or at least the past is prologue. Consciously or not we are motivated not only by our life's experience but also by our heritage. In a real sense, then, my lifelong struggle against anti-Semitism was also a battle for my mother, father and grandfather, as well as for their values.

As a youngster growing up in the early twenties I well remember coming up against anti-Semitism. At the time it seemed merely adolescent mischief by my peers, not reflecting an attitude shared by the adult world. But to me it still said that Jews were a breed apart, not better, not worse, just different. In spite of the epithets—sheeney, Jew bastard, kike, mockey, Hebe, Yid—I had no sense of Jews being inferior. But it made me feel *afraid.*

The Hunts Point section of the East Bronx during my elementary school years was ethnically mixed—Italian Catholic, Irish Catholic and Jewish. Virtually no blacks. The only blacks I knew personally were two sons of the janitor in our lower-middle-class tenement. Nine and ten years old, we were close friends. Mostly, I think, because we happened to live in the same building.

The Italian neighborhood toughs had ruled that Jewish youngsters, and the infrequent black youth, were not to walk in *their* territory. The Irish were not considered friends either but were "allowed"; the Irish, it seemed, were tough too, and besides, they were also Roman Catholics. We Jews were not exactly namby-pambies either. The battles were with bottles, sticks and rocks. Some of us, on both sides, would bleed. A suture or two on our faces or heads was not uncommon.

A Breed Apart

Still, strangely, in this brawling our group had no sense of belonging to a persecuted minority. Certainly, there never was a feeling of being a long-suffering special group. A child's world is small, and we young Jews did not think of ourselves as outnumbered. We only knew that as Jews we were considered outsiders and therefore unacceptable—but we didn't care. If you had said to me I was a member of a "minority," I would have asked, "What does that mean?" We happened to be Jews and they, stupidly, didn't like Jews.

Still, I don't remember that we even disliked Italians as such. Feared them, yes. Resented the bullies who attacked us. But not as Italians. We didn't transfer individual acts and attitudes to the group. As Rogers and Hammerstein put it, we had to be carefully taught.

But we *were* white-skinned. When I was offered something to eat in the house of a black playmate—summertime I would run in for a cold drink of water; easier than climbing three floors—there was a strange hesitancy about putting a spoon in my mouth, aware that it had been in a Negro's mouth. That's what blacks were called in those days. Negroes. And I would have to overcome a reluctance to take a glass to my lips because it was in a Negro household. I remember actually putting the edge of the glass on my chin under my lip, pouring the water over it into my mouth to avoid intimate contact. How hesitant, too, I was to keep my handkerchief after my black friend used it. I remember his name today although it was more than sixty-five years ago—Ernie Johns. He had fallen and cut himself and I lent him my handkerchief. After it was stained with his blood I threw it away, feeling it was unclean. And these were my friends, and we were allies against common enemies, the Italians and Irish, just a few blocks away. To this day such memories haunt me.

Religious class—five or six benches, and a desk in front of the window in a small store directly across the street from where we lived—was a fairly meaningless chore after school hours. We learned little; the teacher was too busy keeping order with a long wood stick or a broom handle to worry about our studies.

One non-English word, only one, remains with me from that place. I hear it still. *Roo-ik!* In Yiddish it means "Order".

My mother and father were part of that segment of American Jewry that failed to work very hard at being religious. The traditional rules meant little to them. Nor did they flaunt their Judaism: in those years to be a Jew outside one's own circle was to be subjected to discrimination. They were first-generation Americans and they wanted very much to belong. They always thought of themselves as native Americans with solid middle-class values.

But they were Jews in a non-Jewish world. Pop was the "High Holiday" type; those days were just about the only times he attended synagogue. Mom was not even that, although she was consciously Jewish and certainly a product of a Jewish home. Which meant, at least in our early years, mandatory visits to grandparents on Jewish "occasions"—we only had my mother's folks—and a carryover of a few traditional dishes on our table.

One small evidence of how my parents sought to assimilate is the choice of names they made for my sisters and brothers, names considered in those years to be very American: Irwin, Vera, Sanford, Eleanor, Arnold. Not a single Sarah, Rebecca, Abraham or Isaac in our large family. My mother was one of eleven children, most of whom were themselves married with children; not one was named Irving. The style was Leroy and Carol and Alvin and Lester. Seventy years ago!

We did have Seders on Passover, and Pop and his sons went to synagogue on Rosh Hoshanah and Yom Kippur. And while Mom's father was alive the grandchildren were sent to *shul* on Saturday mornings. My father was not there, but Grandpa was, and he insisted we learn to read the prayer book better than we had been taught in Hebrew school.

I remember how Grandpa would take his grandsons—my brothers, two cousins, me—and press us into a reading competition with other grandchildren after services on Saturday to see which of us could get through a Hebrew paragraph better and faster. No one of us could understand a word he was reading, but Grandpa's brood was able to speed through much of a Saturday morning service from beginning to end faster than most of the other youngsters.

We children, of course, were allowed to play outside during the reading of the week's Torah portion, recited in the middle of the morning service. But we never thought much about why we were excused from that segment of Sabbath prayers or from the Yiddish *derusha* (sermon) that followed the Torah reading. Children learn early on not to look gift horses in the mouth.

Maybe I felt more Jewish than memory tells. Perhaps what I'm saying is that I regarded being Jewish as just an ordinary fact of life—not unique or oppressive. We were living in our own little world and, as the old joke goes, "When you're in love, the whole world is Jewish." I recognized an enemy out there but did not think about the why or wherefore, just accepted it. Nor did I consider its deeper implications. We were Americans but different from the others, and they didn't like us because of the difference. But that was it. A youngster of nine or ten doesn't usually comprehend anti-Semitism, at least not its profound and melancholy meaning.

In their final years, and they lived a long time, my folks became affirmatively Jewish, aware and caring about the security of Jews and deeply concerned for Israel, yet still not especially religious. Their feelings of vulnerability when we were children and during the time of the Nazis seemed to have dissolved by the Sixties. Hitler had surely been the reason for their late-developing Jewish consciousness. I was now their main connection to the Jewish State. My own relatively early defiance of anti-Semitism, tinctured later with contempt for the gutter bigot and anger at the tutored hater, persisted and is still alive and burning.

From our third-floor apartment on Barretto Street I could see into the storefront window of the Hebrew school directly across the street, and so I knew whether the pupils had arrived and when it was time to rush downstairs to class. For almost four years I had been one of the unruly youngsters filling five rows of benches in front of our teacher's battered desk. I sat there for an hour four afternoons a week because Mom had decided Grampa would like me to absorb some Jewish training. Her father, an immigrant from Kovna, Lithuania, and an Orthodox Jew, had expected that I as the eldest son would be Bar Mitzvah, and Mom respected his wish. It was also assumed that my brothers would follow in the same path.

The classroom was an almost barren fifteen-by-thirty-foot store between a grocery and plumbing shop. On one wall hung a large shallow wooden box stained brown, a makeshift Holy Ark. A shabby, faded blue velvet curtain hung across its front concealed two small Torah scrolls that were wrapped in shiny white satin covers decorated with gold embroidery. On Friday evenings and Saturdays, and each weekday morning at six-thirty A.M., Sunday at eight-thirty A.M. and at sundown, the classroom was a synagogue. Ten or more old men, or at least they seemed so to me, constituting the traditional religious quorum, gathered to pray. They filled the urgent need of an ever-changing small group of Orthodox Jews in mourning who came to say Kaddish. When they completed their eleven-month mourning period they were rarely seen again at daily services.

It was in this unattractive room at the crack of dawn on a Monday or Thursday morning that I was Bar Mitzvah before going off to class at PS 48. I will never know why the ancient ceremony for thirteen-year-olds was not scheduled for me on the traditional Saturday morning. Pop and Grampa were there, and my two brothers, Irwin and Sandy—Joey had not yet arrived—the only ones I knew in the small congregation except for the familiar face of my Hebrew teacher, who led the prayers.

I chanted the appropriate Hebrew blessing before and after being called to the Torah, from which the week's portion of the Bible is read on Saturdays, a smaller portion on Mondays and Thursdays.

I understood not a word I recited. Nor was I called on to make the usual speech offered today by most thirteen-year-olds who perform this religious rite of passage. Perhaps this was because I spoke only English and their preferred language was Yiddish (which, in the early years of his life my father understood but

24

A Breed Apart

because he did not use as an adult forgot almost entirely). Or maybe I was not called on to speak because in Orthodoxy, in the lower middle class of Jewry in the twenties, Bar Mitzvahs had not yet assumed ceremonial and social importance. They were a religious requirement, a happy time, especially for the adults, but not a party. At the end of the service, however, I was handed a tiny silver cup brimming with wine and the old men gathered around me, their glasses filled with whiskey held high, to wish me a *mazel tov.* For that brief moment I was the center of the service and understood I was being formally inducted into the faith.

Actually the solemn ritual, the way it was conducted, was not an enjoyable introduction into "Jewish manhood" for a young boy. It seemed a strange, severe and uncomfortable experience. No doubt my religious training left much to be desired, yet I still remember how to chant the blessings before and after the Torah reading, and almost in tune. And having long since mastered a fractured Hebrew, I now know and appreciate the meaning of the words I recited by rote that early weekday morning. I also think I felt Jewish even if my "welcome" into "Jewish manhood" was not exactly an impressive moment for me. Or so it seems in hindsight.

My father, good looking and outgoing, always trying to make people laugh, was a lovable character; no great shakes financially but in every other respect a success. He was known to everybody as "Hymie." A manufacturer of boys' clothing, his career was cut short by an illness—cancer and surgery in his mid-forties. But even that did not exclude him from his joy in living. Recovered, he ran for election as a Republican candidate for the New York State Assembly; long service at the local Republican headquarters in a heavily Democratic district had earned him the nomination. No prize; it was a foregone conclusion he would lose, and he did. He spent his remaining years, until age retired him, as a tax accountant.

In 1971, Leonard Lyons, the popular Broadway columnist whose daily anecdotes entertained readers, led off with this:

25

Arnold Forster of the Anti-Defamation League, had a dinner party at his home celebrating his parents' sixtieth wedding anniversary. His father reminded the gathering that on his fiftieth birthday forty-one years ago he fell unconscious, had major surgery and the family was told he had limited time left. He then revealed the secret of his escape from death—"Get yourself a long-term disease, and then be sure to take very good care of it."

Hymie went right on enjoying life until his mid-nineties, and we were all deeply devoted to him. One evening after dinner, free of any pain or complaint, he went to bed, fell asleep and never woke up.

Dora, my mother, was a protective mother hen, not in the ordinary sense but more in the fashion of a street fighter. And she physically matched her personality. Not a large woman but solidly built and firm-featured, she exuded a feminine strength. No one would risk touching any of Dora's kids, surely not when she was around. Never mind what she herself would do to us; at the least, a hard slap when we deserved it. She never struck my sisters, only the boys. And all of us at once worshiped and loved her.

Six headstrong children made it a matter of survival for Dora to hold us in tight rein—what other way could she keep the crowded household together and in some sort of harmony? Born over a spread of many years, the six of us were more than a handful for her. Hymie wanted little, if any, role in bringing us up, let alone in exercising discipline, gladly leaving such unpleasant responsibilities to Dora. A nonphysical person, he would never think to lift a finger to us in punishment, and never uttered an obscenity in our presence. Seeing Mom wing one of us with the palm of her hand, even if it were for an inexcusable infraction, Pop would mutter from a respectable distance, "Your hand should fall off, hitting them!" In this respect he was an absolute pacifist.

While still healing from his surgery, Pop was, of course, home from work. Money was not plentiful, it never had been, and Dora, as usual, was carrying the burden of household chores by herself. We children helped some, but Mom cleaned, sewed, laundered, cooked, saw to our cleanliness, study habits and "intra-family relationships." My sisters, Vera and Eleanor, both older than I, were already in high school. My two younger brothers, Irwin and Sandy, and I attended public school—the Joseph Rodman Drake School on Spofford Avenue, some blocks east of Hunts Point. Joey, the youngest, had not yet come along. Our school principal, Mr. Blum—he had no first name—ran a strict school, governed with an iron hand and insisted, among other rules, that boys wear white shirts, blue ties and trousers.

Sometimes clothing was in short supply in our lower-middle-class home, and Mom didn't always have time every day to do the laundry. I remember one time when we ran short of clean white shirts and Dora sent me to school dressed in a blue sailor suit. In the First World War it was the fashion to dress little boys in imitation naval uniforms. Now, after the war, Mom still kept such outfits in our closets and had no reluctance about us wearing one when it was necessary.

That morning I arrived in class on time and was immediately singled out by the teacher for my navy blue blouse and "invited" to come to the front. Why was I not wearing a white shirt? The soft tone of her voice suggested she knew the answer and did not care much for the rule. I explained I had no clean one. Down to the principal, she said, and again her reluctance came through. He would deal with the problem, she would not. From Mr. Blum there was no reluctance as he told me to go home and come back in a white shirt. My mother's surprise at seeing me back so soon turned to anger when I told her the reason. "Take yourself right back to school," she ordered, "and tell your principal we have no clean white shirts your size in the house."

Ten minutes later I was again in Mr. Blum's office. "My mother sent me back," I shamefacedly told him. "She has no clean white shirt for me."

"You get out of this office right now," he fairly shouted, "and return with your mother."

Half an hour later Dora, with me close on her heels, stormed into the principal's office to announce to the clerk she had come to see Mr. Blum at his request. She was immediately led into the inner sanctum, me following in her wake, still wearing my dark blue sailor suit.

The principal rose from his desk, circled around it to confront my mother and with heavy contempt thundered, "What's the matter, you too busy playing bridge with your lady friends to wash a shirt for your son?"

The resounding slap on Mr. Blum's face could be heard in the outer office. "Now you go get a court summons for me," she said, "and we'll let the judge say whether you can chase my son out of school, deny him an education and talk to me that way because I don't have enough white shirts for him."

Turning abruptly, Mom patted me on the head and instructed me to go back to my classroom. Without another word, she then strode from the principal's office. Mr. Blum stared at me in stunned silence. After a long moment I slowly, tentatively, faced around and walked out without being stopped and went back to my class.

The matter never came up again, and I learned a lesson I never forgot: the imposition of arbitrary, unreasonable rules by one human being on another, an analogue of society's war on itself, always has to be resisted or the despots and bullies will surely win out. It seems life forces usually begin as faint shadows and need years before they begin to take shape. It's in retrospect that we see in sharp focus what once appeared indistinct and unintelligible . . .

Consider Alex Shaw, a gentle, studious youngster who lived on Barretto Street diagonally from our house on the other side of Southern Boulevard. He and I spent much of our idle and study time together, classmates at PS 48, street pals and best friends. Alex's Dad was modestly successful as a wholesale baker, and a glass of milk along with all the cakes we could eat at his house after school was a special treat.

At the age of twelve pink-cheeked Alex and I joined the Boy Scouts together, memorized the oath and regularly attended meetings. It was my first social intimacy with kids of other faiths, and what I remember most was my surprise that "they" were just like us. We were given short pieces of rope and taught ten different knots, although no one explained why it was necessary to know these things—none of us ever mentioned he hoped to join the Merchant Marine, where such knowledge is essential. Hiking was on the agenda too. Conceived to teach forestry, it let tenement kids climb trees and gave an opportunity to consume al fresco meals of hamburgers and franks cooked over open fires while baking potatoes in the ashes—never call them potatoes, they're "mickies," we were told. The most accessible "woods" for hiking, at least the easiest and cheapest for us, were in the Palisades across the Hudson River in New Jersey. A five-cent trolley ride to Dyckman Street took us to the upper reaches of the Bronx. Summertime trolleys in those days were built with rows across, not lengthwise, and had no side walls. Riding them was as much fun as anything in the Palisades amusement park. Another nickel for the ferry to New Jersey on the opposite shore, and with knapsacks on our backs we would set forth.

Of course, these were not woods at all. Five minutes from the ferry slip we would be walking along a wide shoreline footpath stretching for unknown miles northward, a dirt road shaded by steep bluffs towering four hundred feet above us. Led by our tall skinny Scoutmaster, nine or ten of us in our kerchiefed uniforms and World War I soldier hats trudged along the riverbank, covering perhaps three miles until lunchtime. We'd then stop, camp, build a fire, pull tin pans, plates and other such paraphernalia from our backpacks and try to fix an outdoor meal. Some of us brought along canteens filled with warm soda. We amused ourselves tossing stones onto the river, scaling them across the water, or we would climb through the brush above, trying not to lose balance, then slide down on the seat of our pants to the dirt path at the bottom.

This was the kind of day we looked forward to when we set out one perfect Saturday morning. Except this time some of the Jewish kids among us were carrying a sense of guilt—it was our Sabbath or a Jewish holiday, either Passover or Shevuoth, the

29

only Spring holidays. But neither Alex's parents or mine were Orthodox, and so it took only minimum coaxing to gain permission for the troop hike on that glorious spring day.

As before, we set up camp after a two-hour trek, built our fires, put the food to them and sat around munching on charcoal speckled, half-cooked hamburgers. Five of us at each fire, legs crossed on the ground, in a circle, eating, chatting, laughing. Somewhere an unseen climber, making his way through the brush above us, kicked a rock loose and it came hurtling down. Bigger than an oversized fist and with descending force the stone struck Alex on the head, bounced to the ground with a sickening thud. Alex let out a sharp cry, reached to his head and fell backward. Stunned, frightened and hurting, Alex stared vaguely at his blood-stained hand and made no effort to move.

We were all around him immediately, putting cold compresses to his scalp, propping him up, telling him he'd be fine. When he finally sat up the painful bump on his head seemed enormous.

Clearly Alex needed a doctor, and just as clearly he was in no condition to walk on his own to the ferry. The scoutmaster told us tc stay together as we packed up, smothered the fires and got ready to return. But what about Alex? We were in luck—coming toward us in a canoe were two men leisurely paddling along the shore. We yelled out to them about the accident and asked that they take Alex across the river to the hospital near the ferry.

Alex stretched out on the bottom of the canoe, head resting on his knapsack, and the flimsy canoe moved away at surprising speed in the direction of the Dyckman Street hospital a block or two from the Hudson.

Arriving at Barretto Street several hours later, I ran to Alex's house to tell his parents what had happened and found Alex resting on the couch, an oversized bandage on his head. It seemed X rays had revealed only a minor concussion, the doctors had stitched his scalp and sent him home with the usual advice that he take it easy for a day or so.

Three days later Alex died.

A Breed Apart

* * *

I had never confronted death before. Still not yet fourteen years old, I am not sure I really understood its permanence. I remember I couldn't accept it about Alex . . . he still seemed to be there. How could he be dead?

The same day he died we were told there would be a Boy Scout funeral. I had never been to a funeral. Be in uniform when you arrive at the synagogue, we were told. The troop would be walking alongside the casket after the ceremony from the sanctuary to the hearse outside in the street, and then we would be taken to the cemetery to walk again with Alex to his grave.

I did not sleep that night. My friend's death was unimaginable, unbelievable and frightening. But in the morning I had my regular breakfast before setting out for the funeral and I remembered to be careful my scout uniform was in good shape and my shoes shined.

The service at the synagogue is lost to me—I recall nothing about it, not who spoke or what was said. I recollect only my trembling. When the eulogies and prayers were finished I took my place with the other youngsters on either side of the casket and, all eyes on us, marched to the waiting funeral cars. In that short walk I think I came as close to being brokenhearted as a little boy can be. My friend was in the box, and he would never come out.

Family and other mourners milled about outside the synagogue, arranging themselves in available cars. For the scouts there was one of Mr. Shaw's bakery trucks, its doors open. We were told to climb in and sit on the floor, and solemn and silent, we did as we were told. Inside the van with the doors closed, we gradually became aware that above us were boxes of cakes, all *kinds* of cakes and with the most tempting aromas. As the truck rumbled forward one boy jumped to his feet, holding on so as not to topple, reached for a carton, opened it and handed it down. Followed by another and another. Inside each was an assortment of mouth-watering pastries filled with jellies, meringues, cherries, whipped creams. We tore into them. It was like a wonderful dream, and an escape. It was a moving feast.

As the bakery truck slowed down, turned into the cemetery gates and stopped near the burial grounds, we all carefully cleaned cake crumbs and powdered sugar from our faces and uniforms, straightened ourselves and moved over to the hearse. Taking our places at the casket as the Boy Scout honor guard, we walked slowly alongside Alex's coffin to the open grave, all solemn and quiet. And there, as the rabbi intoned the mournful *Ale Male HaRachamim,* I wept.

At the age of seventy-five plus, thinking back on Alex's death, it is only now clear to me how much we children did not comprehend, could not, the loss of a child, its unending tragedy, the pain of the parents, their bottomless grief. No, there was scarcely a flicker of comprehension the day we buried Alex Shaw.

A psychologist might conclude that my full recollection of the dreadful incident suggests that for me it was a most significant childhood trauma, repressed but never gone. Such traumas, it seems, aren't only indelible, they also can germinate values. In my personal history I think Alex's death created an abiding sense of outrage against any and all senseless death.

At DeWitt Clinton High School classwork claimed most of my after-school hours trying to master languages—French for three years, Latin for four. Latin was especially important, I thought, because I had decided to go to medical school after college. My trouble wasn't so much a lack of scholarship as the consequence of achieving a high rating in an aptitude test given immediately on entering Clinton that precipitated me into a small, select class of first-year students who were offered a chance to complete high school in three and a half instead of the usual four years.

For me it was a mistake. It was impossible for me to complete the first year of high school in six months and still somehow master the basics of the two languages I'd selected. I was ill-prepared after only one semester to enter second year study in either subject, and for the next three years I struggled to catch up with four-year classmates and had to be satisfied with barely passing grades in the two foreign languages. It was the Dramatic Society at the end of the class day that gave me a needed outlet. Standing on a stage pretending to be someone you're not is blatantly escapist, and playing the role of a buxom young woman in a harem in Edward Knoblauch's *Kismet* is indisputably total flight from reality, particularly for a healthy sixteen-year-old heterosexual male. I always suspected I was among those chosen to be mute concubines in the play because our drama coach thought he could palm off as voluptuous women us going-to-fat young boys. Bedecked in gauzelike pantaloons with overstuffed, spangled brassieres covering our chests and ladies' wigs concealing crew cuts, our only role was to undulate across the stage onto a bed of oversized pillows and lie quietly without attracting any further attention. That should have told me something. It didn't. Right to the end of high school I continued to play a miscellany of minor parts without attracting anybody's attention or applause.

But my high school theatrical stint included friendship with another student, Julius (Julie) Garfinkel, later to become the motion picture star, John Garfield. Julie was winning enthusiastic admiration on all sides. Less than average height but sturdily built, with a strong smile and full shock of dark hair, he seemed bigger than he was. Pursuing his theatrical preoccupation with fanatic intensity, Julie was considered highly talented by his dramatic faculty and was awarded the lead male role in several plays.

Julie and I became friends when Julie invited me to join a teenage acting group offering amateur performances at a public school auditorium in the Fordham section of The Bronx. Fordham Road from Barretto Street was a twenty-minute trolley ride to its northern terminal at the Bronx Zoo. A five-minute walk and I found myself in the auditorium and on the stage. It was enormous fun from the outset, and for the first time in my life I was involved with other people in an adventure of *my* choosing and experiencing some acceptance for what I was contributing to the joint effort. Birth of ego.

33

What I didn't realize at the time was that my mother was subtly encouraging me in my efforts with The Fordham Players, the imposing name the group had adopted for itself. A long time later, when it was plainly evident that the stage was not my arena, she confessed to me that her secret ambition in the days she labored as a teenage seamstress had been to act on the stage. Going from the sweatshop that was also somebody's shabby living room on the lower East Side of New York, directly to marriage and children ended her dream, as it did with so many other women.

I stayed with the Fordham Players until high school graduation ended the group. Julie had been a second-year student and I was a year ahead of him but we stayed friends, of sorts. We met when he wanted me to know that he had signed up with some laboratory theatre and was working hard to become a professional actor. I was green with jealousy. Not long afterward we were together again. This time he had new acting plans, making application for membership in an actual professional theatre. Hearing that he would be trying for acceptance in Eva LeGallienne's Repertory Theatre on Fourteenth Street, downtown, my envy spilled over.

It was 1930. The stock market had crashed only months earlier and the nation was starting on the long slide down into economic chaos. High school diploma in hand, I labored for a year at an assortment of manual jobs, at the same time attending night classes at City College. But my head was full of thoughts about the stage and Julie's new linkup with LeGallienne's. Well, I was determined to make my way into the world of theatre too. Saving enough to pay for a year's tuition, one hundred forty dollars, I transferred to St. John's University in Brooklyn, signing up for only as many courses as would require three hours of a daily class attendance in the mornings. And once again Mom was encouraging me. My two older sisters were at college and working evenings—Vera as a manicurist, Eleanor in a hosiery shop—and they assured me they would come to the rescue if money ran out. (Both of them went on to become school teachers, in those days a career of esteem for young Jewish women, then called girls.)

Now free each day from lunchtime on, I soon found my way to the Cherry Lane Theatre in Greenwich Village, a place I'd only heard about from friends. I introduced myself to Ivan Sokoloff, the Theatre's director. I told him my ambition. He accepted me, but it had more to do with my readiness to help the scenic designer build stage sets and my willingness to paint scenery. In exchange, though, our wax-mustached director did reluctantly agree to let me try out for some minor roles.

I spent the better part of the first month at Cherry Lane pasting layer after layer of old newspaper onto various plaster gargoyles, then coloring the resulting papier-mâché masks to suit. Sokoloff believed the mastery of pantomime was the road to good acting, and so he used the exaggerated disguises for the actors in plays that he created without dialogue.

My reward for performing the unglamorous job was a sequence of minor parts in month-long productions. In one drama, *Gods of the Lightning,* the story of the Sacco and Vanzetti trial, I had the role of Pete, the bartender. The play was an indictment of the miscarriage of justice in a trial for the murder of a paymaster and his guard in a shoe factory. Charged with the crime were a shoe worker and a fish peddler, Sacco and Vanzetti, both untutored, who went to the electric chair not because of guilt beyond a reasonable doubt but because of their radical affiliations. Every night for a month I stood behind a prop bar polishing beer glasses and silently trying to react to the dialogue of actors lucky enough to have lines to speak. Sanford Meisner and Robert "Bobby" Lewis, both of whom would become important stage directors in New York, played the two central characters. Joey Sawyer, who went on to play tough-guy roles in the movies, was the third lead. I was now a part-time actor, but Sokoloff, who spoke with a Russian accent, did not want to put my real name, Fastenberg, on his theatre program. It wasn't somehow seemly for an American actor, said *Sokoloff.*

Never mind what it wasn't, *Gods of the Lightning* was a

never-to-be-forgotten lesson in injustice, with an impact that helped keep me emotionally tied to victims of hatred and discrimination all my life. I saw Julie only rarely after the Fordham experience; dinner once or twice before his show, coffee with him and others after a performance. Getting caught up in studies, my second thoughts were now to go on with college and then, as planned, to medical school. But when the time came for the actual move it was apparent that acceptance to medical school in the United States was not only difficult for Jews but also perhaps beyond my financial reach. I would no doubt have to study somewhere in Western Europe—Jews were more welcome in medical schools there. I gave up the whole idea. Next best was law, and I took that turn in the convenient direction of St. John's Law School.

But I never forgot that but for religion . . .

As would-be actors have always done, I found other work to fill in the empty hours—and to eat. It was still the Depression. Under the New Deal, Congress had created a Civilian Conservation Corps, a Civil Works Administration and an Emergency Relief Act. None of them exactly applied to someone attending professional school and prepping to be a lawyer.

The theatre, my hopes for a career in it, good friendships with stage people all disappeared as I went my different way from actor friends. Some of them turned out to be respected performers, others prominent directors . . . Julie, of course, became a world-class star of stage and screen. I would go on to the practice of law and the fight against anti-Semitism, which many years later would bring me once again together with Julie—John Garfield—in a tragic episode of American history.

2

The Ugly Phenomenon

In those early years, in the ivory tower of a university, I didn't think much about what was happening in the outside world. The country had sunk deep into the Great Depression, but on campus we felt separate and apart from such upsetting reality. The nation's capital was boiling with a "Bonus Army" parked on government grounds in 1932 demanding payment of Veterans' benefits, and U.S. Army troops summoned to drive them away. Herbert Hoover was turned out of the White House, Franklin Delano Roosevelt moved in, and with him came the bank holiday and the New Deal. Europe was suffering major economic and political headaches of its own. A teacher at the university told us about "disturbing" events in Germany—a Lutheran whose origin we guessed from his Teutonic accent; Western Europe, likely Germany or Austria. The professor's concern, and he discussed it incessantly, was the "disgusting revolutionary movement" spreading across Germany. He talked about its beginnings in Austria. Bully boys, he said, had moved into the political arena, taking over the government, trashing civilized rules of governance and making fear and brute force the coin of the day. We listened in almost detached disbelief.

Our professor's classroom probes of the Third Reich was my initial in-depth exposure to Nazism, and it was happening when most civilized nations, including our own, had only a smattering of ignorance about National Socialism. Like so many others, I too had been unaware.

But while Hitler was seizing power in Europe, American Jews were beginning to sense more and more overt anti-Jewish discrimination. We had long become accustomed to *and* had accepted—in education, housing and employment—sudden outbursts of both verbal violence and organized attacks. Economic hardship was taking its toll. People needed a scapegoat for their Depression miseries.

The ugly phenomenon of active American bigotry increasingly occupied the minds and tongues of Jews. We worried about the persecution of German Jews by the Hitler government that had forced out Von Hindenberg, and we feared a growing contagion in the United States. Most of us, though, were unaware of any American Jewish organization to turn to for guidance. A prominent rabbi here or there seemed alert to the growing calamity, but their public comments sounded confusing. We could seek out one of the Zionist organizations whose names we vaguely remembered but they were preoccupied with Palestine. Few of us had contact with such groups; they appeared to constitute a separate community of mainly foreign-born Jews.

In short, secular American Jews in 1935, the milieu I moved in, were disturbed not only about the rise around us of anti-Semitism but also about not being certain where to turn for meaningful counteraction—if there could be such a thing.

Graduating from St. John's Law School, I accepted a no-pay clerkship in a one-man law office at 401 Broadway, even then a seedy section of Manhattan. Since a year's apprenticeship was a prerequisite to admission to the Bar, I took the job, which also meant I had to have weekend work to supply an extra five or six dollars. The nation was just emerging from the Great Depression and the Social Security Act had just passed into law, providing for old-age compensation. I don't recall, though, having to contribute anything from my meager wages.

My law clerkship offered no real challenge. The practice involved petty collection cases. Between such chores I looked for a better assignment, and found it—a clerkship paying a generous seven dollars a week. The new position was at a successful and moderately prestigious law office located in impressive quarters at 80 Broad Street in the white shoe Wall Street section of the city. Old-timers in law practice may even remember the two senior partners—Enos S. Booth and Harris Jay Griston. Their quarters, occupying an entire floor high up in the skyscraper, opened into a wide, forty-foot-long mahogany-panelled reception area, its walls decorated with large oil paintings, portraits of distinguished-looking if unidentified men. Pushing through two heavy, leather-covered swinging doors, a visitor was ushered into a huge law library. On all four sides were doors opening into individual partners' offices. A corner door led to back offices where I sat, the area reserved for secretaries, law clerks and messengers. Fortunately my immediate superior took his responsibility for law clerks seriously, and I began to learn—researching cases, drafting memoranda, answering court calendars, sitting in on depositions.

I stayed a year until admitted to the Bar at the end of 1936. I was twenty-four years old. Along with another young lawyer in the firm, and an old law school classmate, I opened an office at 38 Park Row near the Brooklyn Bridge. Long since demolished, the old shabby building was across the park from City Hall and a stone's throw from the courthouses. I would have to find clients among friends, particularly those from the theatre world. But few of them knew me as "Arnold Fastenberg," so, drawing up the required legal documents, I changed my name to "Forster." Truth to tell, I was rationalizing the change, since the moniker I chose, adopted by my three brothers at the same time, was not the one with which Cherry Lane Director Ivan Sokoloff had dubbed me. He had billed me as "John Arnold." Too artificial and smooth, I felt.

SQUARE ONE

* * *

I recall an observation of my wife some time ago: "You are a born Jew. But it takes many, many years to become a Jew."

I think it was a minor street incident that was the turning point for me in this metamorphosis. The year was 1937; we were a small group of friends out of law school, five of us, standing in front of the house where my family lived on Fort Washington Avenue. The upper West Side of Manhattan, known as Washington Heights, was ethnically divided by Broadway, which ran up its middle. To its west as far as Riverside Drive, a mostly Jewish community; to the east beyond St. Nicholas Avenue, non-Jewish. And the two were separate, different and hostile worlds in spite of their contiguity.

Our group's small talk that Saturday afternoon was interrupted by a loud but unintelligible chant in military cadence coming from a dozen or so young men marching three abreast up the street in our direction. Their rhythmic shouting ripped through the calm of an otherwise pleasant spring day. They were drawing nearer to us and now we were able to decipher their words: *"One, two, down with the Jew. Three, four, hit 'em in the jaw. Up with Hitler, down with the Jew. One, two, down with the Jew. Three, four . . ."* Over and over again.

When they got to where we were standing, without a word passing among the five of us we stepped off the sidewalk into their path. Fists, as they say, flew. Five young attorneys, we should probably have known better. But also healthy and outraged, ours was a spontaneous combustion. The sudden brawl turned out to be a short-lived free-for-all. No one was too badly hurt. Bystanders had quickly stepped in and the scuffling stopped, to be followed by a long shouting match that brought renewed fists. Now they were outmatched; others had come to help us. By the time the police arrived we five had been joined by so many sympathizers that the Jew-baiters appeared to the cops to be a minority on the defensive. Acting on that misapprehension, and asking few questions, the gendarmes concluded that the five of us in the center of the uproar were the aggressors, the others, victims.

Both groups were ordered up against the building and questioned further. Satisfied the incident seemed nothing more than a harmless street fight—although the police had to be aware of its religious overtones—they separated us, ordering everybody off in different directions and warned us to stay away from each other.

Word of the brawl quickly spread among friends. A few days later a young man, George Brandt, came to see me at my law office. Son of an owner of the Brandt theatre chain, he, too, was troubled by the surge of anti-Semitism and its overflow into street violence. George said he'd heard from a mutual acquaintance about the Ft. Washington Avenue incident, would I meet with a small group of his friends to do something about the situation? What, I asked, would we do? He didn't know. I agreed to meet and offered to invite other young lawyers.

George came with about a dozen friends—young men and women that included several New York City policemen he'd persuaded to join him. I had rounded up several former classmates now practicing law, and together we formed an organization we called *The Junior Guild.* How the name was selected I no longer remember, but I do recall we deliberately chose a nondescript identification. Convening frequent sessions, the group discussed what was happening to Jews in and around the city. We listened to each other's stories about anti-Semitic gangs roaming city subways and beating up Jewish passengers. We met and met, worried and worried . . . frustration building.

Discovering where indoor anti-Semitic meetings were being held regularly and the street corners where violence-inclined gatherings would likely be scheduled, we went to hear for ourselves, went to Columbus Circle in Manhattan to hear the anti-Jewish harangues that were getting to be a nightly occurrence at that prominent city landmark. Columbus Circle appeared the favored place for anti-Jewish organizations to gather, but we estimated thirty-five other such meetings took place every week in metropolitan New York. We heard ourselves called Communists, kikes, Russia-lovers, Hebes, anti-Christians. It was an article of faith at these gatherings to condemn Franklin

Roosevelt for "pushing the country down the road toward Socialism." Controversy over New Deal legislation ultimately held to be constitutional by the U.S. Supreme Court triggered even more intense far-right hostility toward the Roosevelt Administration, the Democratic Party, liberals and Jews, who were said to be the power behind the government. Hitler was right in wanting to wipe out the Jews.

Months attending these meetings gave rise to what we thought might be effective direct counteraction. Having studied the statutory grounds to arrest for incitement to riot, disorderly conduct, breach of the peace, etc., we were at least familiar with evidentiary requirements. Two of our members, both nonlawyers, were assigned to attend meetings along with one of our attorneys. If a speech or the situation warranted it, one was to make a complaint to a nearby policeman and request the immediate arrest of the speaker. The other layman would be a witness. (Nowadays police officers are taught how to avoid civilian-demanded arrests, advising complainants to seek a summons from a court.)

At Columbus Circle, if arrests were made as demanded, our complaining witness and his corroborator would follow the crowd to Night Court, where our attorney would offer to represent the complainant. In those years an assistant district attorney wasn't normally present. Our witnesses were cautioned to testify truthfully, without exaggeration but with a clear understanding of the relevant statutes. Carefully planned, the testimony accurate and honest, it worked. We got convictions, but increasing and well-oriented news coverage didn't stop or even diminish the growth of anti-Semitism. Nor, of course, did it touch the larger problem across the nation.

Looking back, it's clear our small Junior Guild organization, typical of others in many large American cities, symbolized the absence of any meaningful local or national Jewish infrastructure to fight anti-Semitism. While we were witnessing a continuing flurry of corner meetings everywhere in New York City, there were not many groups fighting them the way we were. A handful of organizations, maybe, Jewish War Veterans and a miscellany of others. The simple fact is that even entering the forties, Jewish defense agencies as we know them today were all but nonexistent. Religious institutions, yes. And some Zionist activity, many Jewish hospitals and welfare organizations too. But defense movements, no.

It was also in this period that I met and courted May Kasner. She, a graduate of New York University, was thoughtful, intelligent and well informed. Beautiful to look at, a warm, compassionate and challenging friend. She would question much of what preoccupied me. I would learn in the years ahead that this was her way of testing for truth. Over time, she became my hair shirt; more felicitously, my foil. And it was always helpful.

But at the outset of our friendship May wondered out loud "what kind of a nut" she was getting mixed up with. Instead of inviting her to a movie, a party, a concert or other normal activity, I would escort her to an anti-Semitic street-corner meeting in Columbus Circle or Yorkville, or to a frightening South Bronx neighborhood. Now and then I would vary our evenings, taking her along to a neighborhood intersection where we representatives of *The Junior Guild* set up our own box and flag and made anti-Nazi street-corner speeches. Our presentations were freewheeling, not limited strictly to anti-Semitism; they ranged across the spectrum of what we thought was the broader problem. Any danger signal was worth mention, and danger signs were all around. For example, The Smith Act was adopted, making it a crime to advocate or teach the need to overthrow the government, or belong to a group dedicated to such a purpose. Entirely opposed to Communism, we nevertheless had deep misgivings about the outlawing of mere *advocacy*. Democracy, we argued, was being eroded by methods intended to protect it. Jews were fast learning where their safety lay; democracy was the *sine qua non* of Jewish security.

A close companion at the time was Harold Mashioff, a young rabbi in the Reform Movement, an excellent speaker and a militant activist. We first met at anti-Semitic street meetings, to which, like me, he had been "attracted," and we quickly became good friends. Soon the two of us were setting up a joint soapbox. In New York's pro-Nazi Yorkville, the German quarter, we held our meetings diagonally across the street from Jew-baiting harangues, shouting our message to draw the crowds away from the others and over to ourselves. *Roosevelt is right,* we yelled, *in opposing the Nazis and helping the British against them.* And we reached to put meat on the bones ... The Lend-Lease Act, allowing friendly nations to buy American military equipment without money on the barrelhead, we argued, was the right thing to do. The Allied Powers, not the Axis nations, were our natural friends.

Of course there were some listeners who supported us in these confrontations—members of the Jewish War Veterans, some tough Jewish kids from the Bronx, Brooklyn and the lower East Side, and Christians who could not tolerate the Nazis. Two non-Jews, among others, who joined us deserve a statue in their memory even though their story has disappeared in the layers of time. They were father and son, Catholics, Leo Dalton and his son Harry, a West Point graduate who later lost both legs in action as a Lt. Colonel in World War II. The Daltons, calling themselves *The Yorkville Council,* organized a storefront operation in the mid-Manhattan German-immigrant neighborhood to fight the local Nazis and other anti-Semites. They were our Christian counterparts, also lambasting Hitler and supporting the British while projecting a pro-democratic message in opposition to the anti-Jewish street corner meetings. It was a unique operation and it had an impact on the local, hate-filled street scene. Harry died in the early fifties, still comparatively young, as decent and courageous a human being as I ever met, and loved, in my life. Some years ago I planted a small "forest" of trees on a hill outside Jerusalem, honoring their names and memories.

Late in 1938 one of our complainants in Night Court testified that an anti-Semitic speaker had created public disorder when he shouted to his audience that Jews traditionally "murdered little Christian girls in order to drain their blood for ritualistic purposes." The magistrate, surnamed Olivio, after hearing our evidence decided to dismiss our complaint. Turning to me he said that if I "wanted to stop free speech in Columbus Circle," I should "dig up Christopher Columbus and have him knock the gavel down," because he, the judge, "would not."

The magistrate may have been well grounded in his interpretation of the First Amendment guarantee of free speech and assembly. But my research had persuaded me that the Constitution does not protect "fighting words" that incite immediate violence, even if the violence is immediately prevented by attending police. I was aware of the judge's view that mere advocacy of violence (or so-called fighting words) does not remove speech from First Amendment protection. But it was a matter, I believed, of interpreting the facts.

In any event it was my inexperienced legal view that the constitutional guarantee did *not* protect against disorderly conduct or incitement to riot, which I thought the defendant guilty of, and I wasn't having any of the court's summary ruling. In a voice more vehement than was proper, I suggested to the magistrate that "if the shoe were on the other foot, if the statement complained of had been that Christians spilled Jewish blood for their rituals" the court might be reacting differently. Declaring me in contempt, the magistrate angrily directed that I reappear the following night when he would deal further with me. At the same time he summarily dismissed the charge of disorderly conduct against the defendant.

As I left the courtroom with some friends, a stranger sidled up to me, whispered that I seemed to be in trouble and invited me and the others to join him for a cup of coffee. I accepted the invitation. We sat down at a nearby cafeteria and the stranger, saying only that his name was Bob, asked whether I was a Communist or in any way connected with the Party.

"Why that?" I asked.

"I've seen you many evenings in Night Court with the same small group of followers," he said, "and I concluded that you must be involved as part of an organized activity."

We quickly convinced him that we had no left-wing political

affiliations or orientation, that we hated Nazis and anti-Semites, and that as Jews were determined to stand up to the bastards. And that was all. Sure that we were telling the truth, Bob Greenfield identified himself as a representative of an organization he said was known as The Anti-Defamation League. Explaining that it was an arm of the *B'nai B'rith*, a Jewish fraternal order, Bob added that he was on the New York staff of ADL and had been in the courtroom as an observer.

None of my friends or I had ever heard of The Anti-Defamation League but some of us thought we had heard the name *B'nai B'rith*. Taking a handful of pamphlets from his pocket, Bob gave one to each of us, suggesting we run through it quickly. A primitive sort of fold-over, it summarized *B'nai B'rith* and its ADL. His agency, Bob said, was headquartered in Chicago but occupied a small office in midtown Manhattan in a brownstone building and had some good local people, leaders of *B'nai B'rith*, heading it. How could he help, we wanted to know. Well, said Bob, the *B'nai B'rith* district president in New York happened to be the Presiding Justice of the Appellate Division, First Department, which included Manhattan, and he could take me to the judge for advice.

The next morning I found myself sitting in the chambers of Justice Albert Cohn, a well-known and highly respected jurist in the New York State court system. (Incidentally, Judge Cohn was the father of an eleven-year-old youngster, Roy M. Cohn, the New York attorney who many years later gained notoriety as counsel to the infamous Senator Joseph McCarthy, and who went on to become a prominent but controversial lawyer before falling victim to AIDS.)

As I detailed the story to Judge Cohn he listened with growing distaste. His response was a full-blown lecture on the values of the First Amendment and on the need to behave in the courtroom in a more lawyerlike fashion. Having scolded me for my ill-considered tactics, Judge Cohn then bid me good-day but only after making some careful notes. That night when I reappeared in court Magistrate Olivio asked me into his private chambers, gave me my second lecture for the day on free speech and on proper courtroom decorum and then also sent me on my way.

My gratitude to Greenfield was understandably large, and I gladly accepted an invitation to visit his ADL office. There, over the next few weeks, I met the New York director and other staff, and we talked about the Junior Guild working under the unofficial sponsorship of the League with guidance from Greenfield. It was at ADL that I learned that what was happening on New York City streets, in more or less the same degree, was happening to Jews in other cities. The pro-Nazi, anti-British, Roosevelt-hating, anti-Jewish propaganda was the same. Only the names of patrioteering, anti-Jewish groups and leaders differed. Chicago, Philadelphia, Boston, Detroit, Los Angeles and other metropolitan areas were plagued with gutter anti-Semitism. Jews were suffering a national epidemic of scapegoating. And those active in defense of Jews constituted only a handful of our people. Community leadership, local authorities, government representatives were generally distanced from the street. The press was only moderately interested.

Because I had been devoting so much time to ADL concerns, a year later the director authorized Greenfield to pay me a modest stipend on an ad hoc basis. The assignments I was handling for ADL were precisely what had previously occupied me as a Junior Guild volunteer—getting to anti-Jewish street-corner meetings, reporting what I learned, appearing at sessions of Night Court when anti-Semitic activists were before the bench, running down background about leaders of hate groups. Now I was organizing letter-writing campaigns to congressmen and senators, drafting model correspondence myself. When I finally joined the staff on a full-time basis my arrangement was to work with Greenfield doing fact-finding and "law" work. It was now March, 1940.

How did Jews fit into the socioeconomic structure of the American community and what kind of native soil was being tilled by our professional anti-Semites in this period? By and large, American Jews had already learned to live with the second-class citizenship imposed on them by widespread practices of discrimination. "What can we do about it," they asked, "sue City Hall?" It had not yet occurred to the rapidly organizing Jewish community that we *could* fight, for example, against an anti-Semitic quota system in higher education. Parents of Jewish high school graduates had long passively understood many universities were closed to their sons and daughters. Jewish college graduates recognized and accepted that a majority of the better professional schools, certainly in the fields of medicine and law, were virtually barred to them. As a consequence those who wanted to be well-trained physicians were obliged to find their way to Germany, Scotland and other European nations for their degrees. They were resigned to quota barriers just as they passively recognized that certain resorts and residential areas in the United States generally excluded them for the reason of their faith. Leading holiday hotels in the United States were *Judenrein* as a matter of policy. Jews tolerated the situation, avoiding embarrassment by avoiding such places. Here and there, someone would protest, but Jewish organizations were usually mum on the subject, finding little solace in being publicly coupled with other unwanteds, including blacks, whose problem in this respect was far greater. Jews likewise took for granted that executive jobs in insurance companies, banks and steel companies were mostly the private preserves of Protestants and, in lesser number, Catholics. Even law firms in New York City and across the nation, important and prestigious law offices, infrequently permitted Jews into their precincts. Jewish graduates entering practice either joined Jewish firms or opened their own offices.

During this same period, however, anti-Semitism in the responsible American press—vulgar, blatant anti-Semitism—was, for itself already *de trop.* An isolated newspaper might, if it was considered relevant, nevertheless refer to the religion or color of a man arrested for a crime if he happened to be Jewish or black. At least this practice, along with the vaudeville stereotype that in 1913 had inspired the formation of the Anti-Defamation League, was no longer a problem of consequence by 1940.

But anti-Semitism, treating a person differently only because he is Jewish, in the United States was *not* against the law. It was and is an attitude, a prejudice, a point of view—and as such beyond the law's purview. Thought-control is anathema in a democracy, as it should be. Nor is the Jew's enemy the constitutional right of people to hate us and say so. Our enemy is Anti-Semitism, a disease of the human environment that destroys a healthy climate in which Jews may at least live as equals and perhaps as friends.

3

ADL

The Junior Guild was now an established if informal field arm of ADL in New York, and I assigned its members to cover meetings of such as the KKK, Christian Front and German-American Bund, check backgrounds of anti-Jewish activists, and identify the sources of anonymous anti-Semitic literature. Its name disappeared, but the work of our Junior Guild went on.

When people reported anti-Semitic slurs in a subway car or on a street corner, I would assign a volunteer member to meet with the complainant and prepare an affidavit for counteraction. We were at long last routinely able to record under oath much of the violent anti-Semitism in New York, Chicago, Los Angeles and later, Boston. We knew who was publishing and distributing anti-Jewish "literature," and could now gauge the size and significance of the activity. As thin as our operation seemed—by today's standards, insignificant and amateurish—its fact-finding and counteraction became the heart of the organization and eventually American Jews adopted ADL as its eyes and ears for exposing and monitoring anti-Semitism.

The printed poison pouring out of anti-Jewish movements tended to the primitive and simpleminded. Jews were accused of betraying America. *Scratch a Jew and find a Communist.* The bigots argued if one looked behind "Jewish political positions"— whatever that was supposed to mean—he would discover pro-Soviet, anti-German attitudes. To be sure, most anti-Semites were avowedly pro-German, pro-Nazi. The litany went like this: Americans who attacked Hitler were automatically Communists. Therefore Jews were indisputably Communists. Its very crudeness was one reason for its effectiveness.

In this anti-Semitic drive the German-American Bund played a major role in seeding anti-Jewish sentiment. Its leader, Fritz Kuhn, a German living in the States and operating out of Detroit, was actually on Berlin's payroll. We suspected it then, confirmed it later. Even this revelation, added to many others, didn't seem sufficient to arouse people from their comfortable lethargy. Not enough Americans understood we were facing a national racist calamity that targeted Jews. Franklin Delano Roosevelt tried to raise the level of American consciousness in this and other areas by his Four Freedoms speech, but in spite of that rhetoric history shows that he failed the Jews in their darkest hour. Books now document the sorry truth that throughout the Holocaust Mr. Roosevelt kept the Jewish catastrophe low on his roster of priorities, gave no help to the lame and failing efforts of the Christians and Jews, few and as important as they were, who called on him for aid to the hapless European Jews. Sealed in history is the now common knowledge that he and Winston Churchill, his counterpart in Great Britain, were of one mind—that first the war had to be won, and only then would there be time to pay attention to the plight of Hitler's victims and worldwide anti-Semitism.

Being the League's New York counsel was an outwardly impressive but functionally hollow assignment. It called for me to "do something"—whatever I could think of—about the facts turned up in our investigations. Gathering data about anti-Jewish discrimination and undertaking counteraction was not yet part of the job. Alerting our people to the need to stand up for

51

their equal rights seemed necessary. Antidiscrimination legislation, as we know it today, did not exist.

In the opening years of the forties Jewish organizations could claim only a few meaningful connections in the government establishment—local, state or federal. We lived in a time when one did not talk publicly about a person suffering from cancer, and a similar attitude, and reluctance, applied to speaking openly about anti-Semitism. It was said with perhaps some truth that the New York *Times* felt if it could print an edition without a single reference to the word "Jew" the day was successful. In short, American Jews in Hitler's time had no meaningful structure with which to fight anti-Semitism. What little was accomplished the existing handful of organizations carried out quietly, avoiding publicity and discomforted at the notion of Jews being identified as the butt or cause of public turmoil. Jews were simply not prepared for the private war against them at home in the United States. As fast as the "defense" agencies grew, they were still too little and too late, lacking experience and organization. And, saddest to say, they never did gear up in any substantial or effective way to make a difference in what was happening to their brothers in Germany. Our only excuse is that up until the forties a very large proportion of the Jewish community in the United States was not much beyond being first-generation American with little national muscle. And, tragically, most were fearful of using even what they had.

The Jewish defense "hierarchy" was a mixed bag. Many of our leaders had multiple Jewish involvements and interests; fighting anti-Semitism was the Jewish preoccupation of only a few. But these were men deeply disturbed by events in Germany, worried that Nazism could precipitate a major, destructive wave of domestic anti-Semitism.

During this period anti-Semitism, fanning out in Western Europe from Berlin, was not evident in the American Communist movement. Soviet propaganda had deliberately led many to conclude that the new Socialist society was somehow friendly to Jews. And some Jews were disarmed; most were not, recognizing the intrinsic evil of the Soviet's tyrannical ruling body.

They were not taken in by them or by their political parrots in the American Communist Party. Some concerned Jews were sure anti-Semitism could be attributed, in part, to the Jews themselves, convinced high ethics and exemplary behavior were prerequisite to Jewish security. Jews, they argued, could ill afford lapses in deportment, nor could they risk, as could non-Jews, to have their quota of bad among the good. Incredibly the League established a desk concerned with *Jewish* conduct, and it presented the Jewish community with a roster of dos and don'ts: *Dress Conservatively; Don't be loud in public; In Miami Beach don't wear a mink coat over a bathing suit; Don't flash diamond rings on your fingers.*

This approach to so-called questionable behavior disturbed many of us. We believed it to be rooted in self-hatred or, at the least, in poor self-image. We were convinced, too, that Jewish misconduct was wholly irrelevant to anti-Semitism, an excuse of Jew-haters to justify their malice. Wearing excessive jewelry, being rude, speaking loudly in public, while fairly obnoxious, was and is in no sense a particular Jewish characteristic but rather a bigot's rationalization for his hostilities.

The program to correct Jewish conduct caused a furor among our people and, happily, was soon abandoned. The notion that Jewish manners were even in part responsible for anti-Semitism was rejected in fact and in principle. Jewish leadership was slowly learning.

I had been going with May Kasner for two years, and in the Fall of 1940 we decided to marry. Naturally I wanted to be acceptable to her family, but it wasn't as easy as I'd thought. From the moment I appeared on their threshold May's folks had wondered . . . I was not their type, unable to understand a word of Yiddish. Real Jews spoke a proper Yiddish. But I also happened to be a lawyer and they liked that—if I could make a living.

The Forsters, too, were a puzzlement to the Kasners; we did not "keep kosher." Still, they thought us a nice enough family and decided to make do with me as a son-in-law because their daughter wished it so. On the other hand the Forsters conde-scendingly accepted May's "greenhorn" parents, even though both had arrived in the States more than a half-century earlier, before either was ten years old.

Halfway along our courtship May's folks became uncertain of even my bona fides. When they first met me I was practicing law. Sometime between then and my engagement to their daughter my law practice disappeared. Now, instead, I was working for an organization they had never heard of, and con-cerning which Dun & Bradstreet, Mr. Kasner's credit-rating agency, knew nothing.

A modestly successful fur importer, May's dad was not ready to permit his child to marry into poverty. If his future son-in-law couldn't earn a proper living as an attorney, Mr. Kasner could correct the situation. But I would have to remain a lawyer and not waste time with extraneous activities such as fighting anti-Semitism.

"I've looked into this organization of yours," he said, "and all it's doing is fighting anti-Semitism and Hitler. Anti-Semitism you'll never end—we Jews have learned how to live with it for nearly two thousand years anyway. Hitler will eventually die, just another *momzer,* and that'll solve *his* problem. There's no future in the whole thing. You'll be out of a job before you know it and have to start all over again. Better you should let me put you on an annual retainer in my business."

I declined, and eventually he understood he was wasting words. Besides, May agreed with me and told her father that I had to do what I had to do and it was better that way. I'm not sure she was sure.

For me, the exchange with Mr. Kasner was a self-revealing although minor test. His financial offer might have given me fiscal security in the face of marriage. My income from ADL was substantially less than his alternative. Money just counted little in my decision to be part of the League. Security was not a factor. Fighting anti-Semitism was.

4

Prewar Bigotry

The bigoted organizations that stained the nation from the mid-thirties to the end of the fifties, creating a political climate of racial, religious and ethnic hatred, set the stage for McCarthyism. Casting them from historical memory risks failure to understand the damaging potential of their successors, who, if history teaches us anything, will inevitably crop up in the event of a major economic depression, explosive international tension or an actual war.

Yet the isolationist movement, with its anti-Jewishness, is already too much forgotten. Even the America First Committee, the ultimate umbrella organization of the small hate groups scattered across the nation and a forerunner of the McCarthy movement, is today only a hazy memory to most Americans.

Until just before World War II few if any federal agencies were authorized to cover pro-Nazi propaganda. Most of the data they did possess apparently came from our field investigators and from other private organizations. In my own operations I often used two field men for a single mission—the first, who knew me as his or her employer, the other, covering the same assignment, who worked for us through an outside source and who had no idea whom he or she was reporting to.

Careful as we tried to be, the services of undercover people carried a built-in risk of betrayal. When I suspected a breach of trust but wasn't able to establish conclusive guilt I would take the only safe alternative—sever the relationship. The process went like this: If from our working knowledge an investigator's reports seemed questionable I would assign a second agent to the same investigation without letting either know the other's involvement or identity. In the event their reports were irreconcilable, that triggered verification devices. If I was then satisfied I was dealing with a double agent I simply dropped the culprit—the price for this kind of information-gathering.

In many instances our agents were employed by an outside investigative agency operating as an independent contractor. I could only insist on knowing the background of the men and women brought in to do the work. Many were retired local or federal government investigators, non-Jews as worried about the safety of our democracy as we were. (Jewish agents were not as secure from detection, having to conceal their Jewishness to function effectively. In a sense that created a kind of double jeopardy—hiding one's real purpose *and* true identity.) Just as there were Christians in Germany and elsewhere in Nazi-occupied Europe who sacrificed much, including their lives, to save Jews, so there were many Christians in our own country who were deeply motivated, faithful and willingly jeopardized themselves. Those who weren't volunteers still functioned for a comparative pittance.

The bigots often were found in high places. Congressman Clare Hoffman, for example, was a bitter-end bigot and not alone in the Senate or House. He operated within a hate network that included such as Montana Senator Burton K. Wheeler, Gerald P. Nye of North Dakota, Robert R. Reynolds of North Carolina, Theodore Bilbo of Mississippi, and New York Representative Hamilton Fish. The crisis of war convinced us we should know the nature of the activities of these and other men, what if anything they were putting in writing on official governmental stationery about Jews, how they coordinated with like-minded constituents. In short, whether they were giving aid and comfort, wittingly or otherwise, to the anti-Jewish, pro-Nazi cabal within our borders. It was also important to understand the precise role in these activities of Charles A. Lindbergh, prominent private citizen and American hero for his nonstop, solo flight across the Atlantic Ocean.

Walter Winchell, who by-lined the most popular news-mongering column of the day and was the nation's number-one radio newscaster, had a significant role in the fight against anti-Semitism. Much of the country virtually stood still every Sunday night at nine o'clock when he was heard on the air for fifteen minutes. A sensationalist, psuedopolitical savant and gossip, Winchell prided himself on his hard-hitting exposés. He was a raw, primitive American, proudly patriotic, who used his newspaper column like a sledgehammer. Subtlety was a stranger to his daily compositions as well as to his attitudes about people. Winchell, a Jew, was typical of some among us who suffer a certain vulnerability expressed by its worst victims in the cliché, "underneath, they're all anti-Semitic." Winchell was burdened with this complex although married to June Magee, a Christian lady and the mother of his two children, who, perhaps not surprisingly professed no religious preference.

Yet Winchell never forgot his beginnings—or his Yiddish. Once we had an appointment to go over some column material I'd prepared for him. When we met in midtown Winchell told me a friend of his would be driving us to the racetrack—I had no idea we were going there—and on the way we could talk business, then concentrate on horses. Parked at the curb was a long, yellow, open roadster, in the driver's seat a flamboyantly dressed character right out of *Guys and Dolls*, a ten-inch cigar clenched between his teeth. The two of us pushed our way on to the front seat beside him, Walter in the middle . . . and he introduced me to Mike Todd.

No way was I ready to exchange confidences with Walter within the hearing of a non-Jew I didn't know. I tried to gesture my attitude to Winchell. Whereupon he turned to Todd and in fluent Yiddish said: "This *shmuck* doesn't trust you." Todd answered Walter in Yiddish, and for the next few minutes the two of them continued in the foreign tongue with me feeling like an ass and futilely trying to understand.

A friend of the president and many other influential Americans, and fiercely anti-Nazi, Winchell was immensely helpful in our work. Years into my relationship with him he would tell stories of his visits to the White House, how he shared with Mr. Roosevelt funny yarns, political gossip and confidential intelligence. Our ADL material was a prime source for Winchell's stories about pro-Nazis on the domestic scene, and he became a prominent voice in exposing anti-Semitism, pro-Nazism and later, Radical Rightism, which had its counterpart in the House and Senate. When I found clear evidence of anti-democratic and anti-Jewish activities among Washington legislators I would draft whole columns for Winchell, sounding the alarm in characteristic Winchellese. Within a year I found myself giving the columnist ten to fifteen hours a week of my time, and that continued for about sixteen years, until he unexpectedly turned into an ardent supporter of Senator Joseph McCarthy and I then let our relationship grow cold. (When he died two people attended his funeral—his daughter and a rabbi.)

One day Winchell telephoned to say I would be hearing at his suggestion from a man named Sam Shaw and to see him, which I did. Shaw earnestly insisted he felt a profound need to fight bigotry in Congress. By profession he was a freelance photographer for prestigious national magazines and also a talented painter. In the course of recent assignments, Sam told me, he had met Senator Bilbo of Mississippi and was disgusted by the bigot from the boondocks. Nevertheless he had deliberately developed a "friendship" with the senator in order to learn more about him and then go public with it.

Bilbo was known in his own circles as "The Man," in ours, "The Mouth." Typically, on a "Meet the Press" radio program where he admitted membership in the KKK, Bilbo proudly said, "Once a Ku Kluxer, always a Ku Kluxer." When questioned about Negro voting rights, he grinned: "The best way to keep a nigger away from a white primary in Mississippi is to see him the night before."

"I'm at liberty now," Sam said, and would join the senator, if possible, in Mississippi. The results, he thought, might well prove helpful to our cause. I agreed to finance the risky project, and Sam journeyed to Bilbo's hometown, where it required several months of "hanging around" for him to become part of the senator's home "team," another few months to get close to the most anti-Jewish, pro-Nazi voice in the American Senate.

I was soon receiving a continuous flow of reports about the conduct of the senator against Jews, blacks, the Administration, the "internationalists" and other "dangerous elements," reports that I would rewrite into column-items for Winchell. The senator was beside himself, baffled. A session he would have with intimate supporters on a Monday would be revealed the following Sunday night on Winchell's broadcast. A round-robin, provocative letter prepared for the "eyes only" of trusted supporters among Bilbo's constituents soon appeared in Winchell's column. Sometimes to upset the senator even more I would feed his material to Drew Pearson, the Washington, D.C., columnist and a friend, whose national readership was almost on a par with Winchell's.

Convinced he was surrounded by spies, Bilbo became increasingly angry and worried. Everything vicious he said or did on the subject of Jews, blacks, Roosevelt, the Allies was in the press and on national radio a week later. The senator's anti-Semitism ended when he died of cancer of the mouth.

Our antagonists conducted their own secret operations, including use of spies. I discovered this shortly before I took charge of fact-finding prior to the outbreak of World War II. One of my predecessor's agents in Washington, a trained investigator in his mid-forties and well connected in congressional circles, had been posing as a friend and fan of isolationist, pro-German elements in the federal establishment. Every few days this sleuth would prepare a report of his investigations and forward it to our Chicago headquarters. He was meticulous in recording every last detail about the anti-Jewish activities of extremist, right-wing senators and representatives. Occupied as he was, our man nevertheless found time for a whirlwind courtship and marriage to a woman he met on the Washington circuit. After a brief honeymoon the couple returned to Washington and she moved into his bachelor apartment. At the end of his first day back to work our groom returned home to find his brand-new wife missing along with all her personal belongings—and one of his. A trunk. This was very bad news; unknown to us it had been our private eye's practice to make copies of all his reports and store them in the now-missing piece of baggage.

Shortly after the bride's disappearance Senator Burton K. Wheeler's office sent word to our Chicago office that we had been caught "dead to rights." The documentary evidence of our "spying" activities was all there, said the message, securely in the trunk, and the most would be made of it. Chagrin turned to mortification as we learned our agent's newlywed was actually on the senator's team. Her *blitzkrieg* of a love affair had only been part of her scheme to obtain our agent's confidential records. A long marriage to get what she wanted was made unnecessary by our man's studious habit of retaining copies of his reports. She had obtained everything in one swift stroke, presumably enjoying a kind of bonus in the process.

Before long I was on my way to Washington to share the embarrassing facts with a friend living there in retirement after a lifetime of espionage. He expressed disgust at our carelessness and said he could be of no help. I returned to New York disappointed and apprehensive. A month later a burly truckman appeared at my office in New York and wheeled in the stolen trunk on a handcart, deposited it in our reception room and departed. A hurried search through its contents satisfied me all was intact.

In retrospect I think the best thing that could have happened would have been for the senator to expose the full contents of the trunk. Its documents provided proof that a cabal of professional patrioteers, encouraged by senators and congressmen, was trying to destroy the good name of the Jewish community, its leading citizens and other Americans considered their sympathizers. It revealed that some Americans were so fearful of the Soviet Union they believed Fascism disguised as patriotism was a better way. Senator Wheeler, perhaps agreeing that the material damned him rather than us, never revealed the contents, or his "case" against us.

One "America First" private meeting at a Park Avenue address in New York City was especially instructive. Present were men from the highest ranks in their isolationist organizations. The host was Lawrence Dennis, a well-known propagandist and author of *The Coming American Fascism,* in which he celebrated the advantages of Fascism over "decadent democracy." Proud of his reputation in America First circles as "the number-one intellectual," Dennis had called together a handful of key people, among whom were Montana's Senator Wheeler, Col. Charles A. Lindbergh, Merwin K. Hart, head of the anti-Semitic National Economic Council, and several others of like mind-set.

I received a memorandum about the closed session from our investigator and shared it with selected government agencies—our standard operating procedure. Shortly thereafter I met with several federal officials to discuss the significance of the Park Avenue meeting. We talked about the various participants and their comments, and we recognized four of the attendees as investigators for various governmental and private agencies.

The off-the-record session of isolationist leaders had an unexpected aftermath. After a false start with Merwin K. Hart, Dennis had become associate editor of a newsletter, *The Awakener,* and later the publisher of *The Appeal to Reason,* a newsletter of his own. He was a racist, constantly expressing his outrage at other whites who would willingly socialize with Jews. He also regularly denigrated blacks; they, too, were apparently subhumans, not worthy of mixing with whites. Moving high in business circles, a Harvard graduate, the well-dressed, dignified-looking Dennis was peddling his private hate report to diehard reactionary industrialists—and earning lots of money along the way.

I was determined that the off-the-record Dennis meeting be exposed. Attended by a United States senator along with the illustrious Charles A. Lindbergh and others of similar prominence, it was a gathering to plan propaganda activities stained with hatred, and to determine political positions for the isolationist America First Committee; this was a happening too significant to be kept quiet. I shared the story with Winchell, who immediately printed it. The column-item brought a handful of letters from Winchell readers about his exposé, one of which made a startling claim: Lawrence Dennis' mother, it said, was a black woman and his father was white.

To all appearances, Dennis was white and I doubted the story. But the letter offered leads, including names and addresses, and I arranged for an investigation. The story turned out to be true. Dennis, it seemed, had been demeaning blacks out of self-hatred. I gave the evidence to Winchell, who, careful not to gloat, printed it as a surprising fact. He identified Dennis' mother by name and address and revealed the financial support she was receiving from the publisher. Dennis quickly lost supporters, but the professional bigots in the network struck back: they explained to their followers that Winchell was a Jew. Enough said.

Joseph P. Kamp, the pince-nezed, frock-coated, anti-Semitic chairman of The Constitutional Educational League in New York, had a home in Connecticut that reflected a man of considerable means. On his own payroll for fifty dollars a week, the pamphleteer surely had other means; he was also executive editor of his newsletter, *The Awakener.* He was a close friend with Charles White, president of the Republic Steel Company. In any case he found himself well connected, and used the offices of Michigan's Congressman Clare Hoffman to distribute propaganda, including a pamphlet entitled *Hitler Was a Liberal.*

Kamp's basic theme, repeated endlessly in his writings, was the imminent danger to the United States from the "reds" and "foreign-born," especially those with Jewish names. His obsession with ADL ran a close second, seeing it as a "low racket which promotes hate and breeds intolerance." Kamp had gotten into the bigotry business early on, 1933, and by the forties found himself on a first-name basis with nearly everyone in the far-right extremist movement, from Gerald L.K. Smith, the bigoted fire-and-brimstone preacher, to General Robert E. Wood, chairman of the board of Sears, Roebuck. His propaganda materials could be found in every corner of the anti-Jewish underworld.

So it was not surprising we would want to know as much as possible about his work. Our investigator was adept enough to make himself a good "friend" of Kamp. He had worked for both British and French intelligence and at the outset of World War II had served as an instructor in an American intelligence school.

Kamp either owned a small pleasure boat or had repeatedly been the guest of a friend who did, I no longer remember. My field man was aware Kamp's office-at-home contained material that divulged the identity of his financial contributors, network operations, and domestic and foreign connections utilized in his propaganda work. One day Kamp took off for a holiday on the boat. It seemed an excellent opportunity to our investigator, possessing, as he did, a house key his "friend" had given him. He would move into the subject's house and make photographic copies of Kamp's material. The documents he copied revealed Kamp's mailing and contributors' lists, sources of information, cooperating publications, his network of like-minded propagandists and his correspondence with men and women in the world of anti-Jewish bigotry.

While our agent was preoccupied with duplicating Kamp's revealing files he heard voices at the door and recognized Kamp's as one of them. My man was surrounded by photographic equipment, rolls of film, a miscellany of documents and other paraphernalia. Hurriedly gathering it all together, he shoved the material into a cold furnace in the area alongside the office and climbed into a coal bin.

An hour later Kamp and his companion took off, but not

before entering his office to gather up some papers that apparently he had returned to pick up. Fortunately he found what he was looking for, heard no sounds from the coal bin, and left with his companion.

I don't like to think what might have happened if Kamp had returned to stay. The assurance of my investigator that he knew Kamp's sailing schedule and that it should have kept the pamphleteer away for many more days was no consolation or excuse. What if Kamp had decided to remain overnight or longer? Forget it.

Cameras are traditional weapons in the business of espionage, and obviously field men used by some of us in the forties considered themselves members of the trade in spite of cautionary warnings. So it was no surprise the Kamp caper was repeated by still another field investigator under only slightly different circumstances.

Marjorie Lane, like most of our outside investigators, was not Jewish. Her cover was as an "active member" in several anti-Jewish organizations, mostly women's groups. She came to me before the war through her husband, himself an investigator in the U.S. Immigration Bureau who had used our data and facilities in helping to track down aliens suspected of Nazi affiliations. Her marriage to him ended five or six years into her employment with us, but not before she had sharpened her investigative skills under his tutelage.

Marjorie was an intelligent listener with an almost photographic memory for detail. Her anger at the bestiality of the Nazis was the emotion that fueled her ability to work endless hours against an enemy she was convinced would, given the chance, destroy our country. She was never concerned about pay. Working tirelessly, Marjorie had the ability to get her hands on probative documents of every major anti-Jewish outfit in the areas of her responsibility. Her investigative equipment, self-selected and paid for out of her own funds, included miniature state-of-the-art cameras and a small battery-powered white light fitted on a twelve-inch-high stand. She could snap pictures of eight-by-ten-inch sheets of paper as quickly as they could be set down, pulled away and replaced.

I only learned about Marjorie's array of technical aids when they tripped her up. Marjorie had positioned herself as a volunteer in such extremist organizations as Women For the U.S.A., Women United, We, the Mothers Mobilize for America, Inc., and in the national offices of one major anti-Jewish women's isolationist movement, where she typed, answered phones, met visitors.

This particular day Marjorie came to our subject's office with a valise full of personal belongings she would need for a trip scheduled that evening. It was easier, she said, to stay at the office after hours until time to travel rather than first go home to Queens. No sooner was everyone safely gone for the day when there was a knock on the door and Marjorie was joined by a friend. Opening her suitcase and lifting off a thin layer of clothing, Marjorie and her colleague pulled out her equipment, set it up and began a night of photography. Cabinets were opened, documents lifted out as Marjorie scanned page after page to determine their importance. Stopping only for breath and a cup of coffee every few hours, the ladies suddenly froze in their tracks when they heard sounds at the doors of the outer office. Fortunately Marjorie had double-locked the entrance from the inside and the new arrivals were having trouble with the door, just as Marjorie had planned. Locking the door of the room in which they were working, the two then packed their equipment, replaced papers in the cabinets, climbed out onto the fire escape and up to the roof. I have always wondered what some innocent eyewitness might have thought, seeing two middle-aged ladies, one carrying a valise, climbing up a fire escape at six o'clock in the morning.

Marjorie was an undercover agent for over two decades, until her *seventieth* year. An early victim of high blood pressure, she became totally disabled and was a virtual prisoner in her small apartment. Never on our employee roster with rights to disability, health care or pension, we still took care of her for more than ten years after she became ill. Having a deep respect and affection for this dear lady, I persuaded my own physician, Elias Stoller, to attend and care for her without fee. After her death, a relative sent me a carton of her private papers. Only then did I learn that Marjorie was a direct descendant of a pioneering, prominent American family. My bad memory denies me the ability to honor the name in these pages. But Marjorie would have forgiven me. A great lady.

Among the groups we tracked and investigated were some two hundred and fifty small, hoodlum-type nationalists disguised as political movements. In some cases they consisted of only a few people, sometimes even one man. Such was James True, a writer in Washington, D.C., who declared personal war on the Jews. He had no following, but he received repeated newspaper mention far beyond his newsworthiness because he invented and tried to sell what he called the "kike killer." There was nothing unique about the weapon. The "kike killer" was a kind of blackjack that, used properly and in ample numbers, True claimed, would adequately dispose of Jews. He proposed a smaller model, in color, that women could hide in a purse.

We also were extensively ranged against Klan operations. Then as now there was a variety of KKK organizations—the Black Legion, the Ku Klux Klan, the Knights of the Ku Klux Klan, the Knights of the White Camelia and so forth. Through these we found our way into many chapters of the German-American Bund, which, while operating in a quasi-political arena and careful not to indulge publicly in blatant anti-Semitism on American streets, was in fact dispensing anti-Jewish hatred from Nazi Germany.

Groups operating in an environment of self-created hysteria about Communism got our attention. Their message seemed to register in a major way among Catholics. Not so surprising when one notes that the Soviet Union had targeted the Catholic church as a giant millstone around mankind's neck long before the USSR went after any other religious group. It seemed the Soviets were intent on wiping out every vestige of the Roman Catholic infrastructure in Western Europe and in every corner of Eastern Europe where they believed the church to be playing a significant role they had no comprehension of the depth of devotion of Polish Catholics to their church. In short, the Catholic Church was the first religious organization to find itself in an international confrontation with Soviet Communism, and Catholics were as alarmed about the Soviet Union as Jews were about Nazism.

As a consequence, when Father Charles E. Coughlin of Royal Oak, Michigan, appeared on the scene and combined anti-Semitism with opposition to the Soviets, he attracted millions of supporters to what became popularly known as The Coughlin Movement or more accurately, The National Union for Social Justice. It was essentially a national political organization overflowing with, sad to say, relatively unsophisticated, frightened Christians, mostly Catholic and mostly from the blue-collar or so-called lower-middle class. Coughlin, a silver-tongued orator, claimed he had five million adherents, arriving at this number from his circulation of *Social Justice*, from huge amounts of mail and from such evidence as the five- and ten-dollar bills that were folded into letters of praise for him and his positions.

Father Coughlin had been pro-Roosevelt in the early thirties but split from the president in a dispute not over politics but over the question of silver as a monetary base, thereafter becoming a strong Roosevelt critic. In time, with the rise of Nazism the priest's hostility toward the president moved him into a pro-German stance.

5

Father Coughlin

Father Coughlin's first assault on Jews had been made during the 1936 national election campaign. Supporting the candidacy of William Lemke of Fargo, North Dakota, he attacked Franklin Roosevelt in his Sunday radio broadcasts as a "scab president," a "liar and betrayer" and an "anti-God." In these same programs Coughlin further accused FDR of treason, vilified the British and attacked "international bankers" as the financial angels of political evil, identifying only bankers with alleged Jewish backgrounds or Jewish-sounding names.

In 1938 Coughlin opened frontally on Jews, accusing them of plots to enslave the world and conspiracies to enable Communism to take control of everything. In support of his anti-Jewish attacks he quoted from spurious articles or misquoted from genuine documents. Typically, he identified a 1920 issue of the publication, *American Hebrew,* as his source for: *The achievement, the Russian-Jewish Revolution, destined to figure in history as the overshadowing result of the World War, was largely the outcome of Jewish thinking, of Jewish discontent, of Jewish effort to reconstruct.* But the files of the ADL, which serve to remind me of these items, note that Coughlin simply forged the phrase "the Russian-Jewish Revolution" into the original article, which he used in that distorted fashion and represented it as coming from the *American Hebrew*. In the same year the Detroit priest offered this lie to his radio audience of some five million: *The Central Committee of the Communist Party operating in Russia consists of fifty-nine members, among whom are fifty-six Jews; and the three remaining non-Jews are married to Jewesses.* The facts were that the Central Committee of the Russian Communist Party had almost twice the number of members suggested by Coughlin, and nearly all of them were non-Jews.

Coughlin went on to appropriate Nazi propaganda as his own. "Background of Persecution," a signed article in his *Social Justice* publication, set forth alleged facts that originated in a speech given in Nazi Germany by Joseph Goebbels, the minister of propaganda. Eventually this sort of political anti-Semitism did antagonize important elements in the Catholic Church. The beloved George Cardinal Mundelein in Chicago repudiated the radio priest in Royal Oak as a voice of Catholicism, and *The Commonweal*, a major Catholic magazine of national repute, castigated Coughlin.

Coughlin was not deterred by such criticism. Not so long as he was finding favor in so many quarters and the money kept rolling in. Indeed, his radio and press attacks on Jews increased and his influence grew. Now he was accusing European Jewish leaders of an international plot *not only to cast Hitler into hell but to substitute for the national anthem of the countries concerned, the national anthem of Jewry.* It's difficult to believe that an accusation of hostility toward Hitler could be basis for criticizing Jews in the United States of America 1939. But there it is, in the record, and it gives one a sense of the atmosphere in which American Jews were groping for a friendly hand. Coughlin's hate-filled, anti-Jewish message continued to be spread across the nation, seemingly unstoppable and apparently acceptable to millions until America's entry into the war against Nazism changed the picture. In retrospect one wonders how one American, cloaked in religious garb and holding no political office could have rendered the federal establishment, plus most of the media, along with much of America's respected leadership, powerless to confront him in the court of public opinion. The explanation is that Father Coughlin was by no means operating in a vacuum. There was a vast national coterie of like-minded people and organizations that, together, had deeply divided the country about whom to support in the European conflict and which, German Nazism or Soviet Communism, was the greater evil. Or whether to adopt an isolationist stance that would leave the democratic nations of the world to fend for themselves in the military cauldron that was threatening civilization.

Meanwhile dozens of other anti-Jewish and pro-Nazi groups, some already mentioned, were stirring the pot—the Silver Shirts, German-American Bund, White Guard, National Gentile League, American Nationalist Federation, Christian Mobilizers, Knights of the White Camelia, Ku Klux Klan organizations. These "lunatic fringe" outfits had articulate, clever anti-Jewish fanatics that included Gerald L.K. Smith, Fritz Kuhn, George Deatherage, leader of the American Nationalist Federation, General George Van Horn Moseley, hero and prospective "Man on The White Horse" of the organized hate brigade, Gerald Winrod, the Kansas Jay-hawk Nazi, Laurence Dennis and many more. These groups produced an enormous flow of printed poison—books, periodicals, pamphlets, newspapers, leaflets and magazines, but more disturbing, they were sometimes backed up by cadres of goon squads—forerunners of today's terrorists—who used every kind of weapon from "kike-killer" blackjacks to axe handles for assaulting Jews. The hoodlums banded together under such names as the Crusaders for America, American Nationalists, Citizens Protective League, American Patriots. Other violence-prone groups came together under the rubric of The Christian Front, an umbrella name erroneously regarded by the public at large as *the* organization of Father Coughlin. He did use, support, publicize and praise the movement, but The Christian Front was never a single, coordinated operation under his control. In addition there were local pro-Nazi groups using a miscellany of Germanic titles and disseminating virulent anti-British, anti-French, anti-Soviet and anti-Jewish lies.

The propaganda content of this interconnected, nationwide movement was unadulterated Nazism. The *Protocols of the Elders of Zion* was circulated in the millions along with variations of its basic lie that Jews were at the root of everyone's troubles: *The Jews caused the Depression, Jews dominate the Government in Washington, Communism is of Jewish origin, The Soviet Union is a Jewish inspiration, The Comintern is totally Jewish, The Russian Revolution was Jewish financed, Jewish bankers control the world's commerce, Nazi Germany is the innocent victim of Jews,* ad nauseum. The anti-Jewish agitators argued: *Nazism is the only effective defense against Communism . . . Democracy is a tumor on the body of mankind . . . It makes no difference who wins the war in Europe.* Goebbels in Berlin, the archpropagandist of the Hitler apparatus, was the source of much of the political filth that dirtied American channels of communication.

All this was the background against which Father Coughlin operated, thrived, undermined American unity, loosened the support for our friends abroad and robbed American Jews of what had passed for their sense of security in the United States. Small wonder decent Americans of every faith, Catholics included, were delighted when he was driven into oblivion. His transitory success can only be understood as an indication of how many Americans were undecided about their perceived choice between Joseph Stalin and Adolph Hitler. Pearl Harbor finally pinpointed the real issue for them.

Some Jews, terrified by the growth of anti-Semitism in Hitler's Germany, did honestly believe the Soviet Union offered hope. The USSR, as a propaganda ploy, had allegedly made anti-Semitism illegal. It was said to be the first and only government to do so. Apparently making it a crime succeeded in luring some Jews, along with others, into the international Marxist movement. Also, the Great Depression in the United States had created deep frustrations and pervasive dissatisfactions. Rising unemployment fueled an opposition to lifting immigration barriers against Jews seeking escape from Nazi persecution. Americans were hungry. There were free-food lines for the needy, apple vendors on street corners, many of whom had once been white-collar workers. The Soviet Union allegedly offered a society in which no one would be homeless or hungry. Some American Jews, victims of discrimination in jobs, housing and education, were hoodwinked along with many more non-Jews.

But among the Jews were some intellectual Marxist activists whose boldness unfortunately made the Jewish community appear to be soft on Communism. These left-wing extremists were never more than a minor although highly visible number. The heart of the Jewish community was never fooled, never suckered by Communism; the American-Jewish community, after all, included a substantial first generation immigrant group who had fled Eastern Europe when Communism conquered Russia. The overwhelming majority were firmly anti-Communist. Unfortunately, political primitives among non-Jews failed to recognize the essential difference between Jewish socialists who believed Communism to be a profound evil, and Jewish Communists who maintained a pro-Jewish facade but had totally different goals.

So different from today was the role of many Catholics, especially the Catholic establishment. Large numbers were poisoned with the illusion that if one probed a Jew he found a Communist. The result was a body of Catholic opinion, anti-Soviet and anti-Communist, convinced that Jews were soft on Communism.

(To stem the tide of such hatred of Jews, our defense agencies created so-called educational programs to make non-Jews aware of the loyalty and patriotism of American Jews. Stories about Haym Solomon, Jews in the Civil War, World War I and World War II Jewish heroes and the like. Even to the point of getting out pamphlets after the start of World War II showing the number of Jews serving in the armed forces and the number who died as war heroes. Defensive? Of course. Necessary, in view of popular misconceptions? Of course. Proof of Jewish insecurity? Of course. Did it help? Who knows?)

Typically Father Coughlin's *Social Justice* and other anti-Semitic publications labelled even non-Jewish leaders in the Communist Party as Jews. Professional bigots did not hesitate to charge, for example, that William Z. Foster, a non-Jewish national Communist leader of the day, was a Jew. Reading about some of his alleged activities it was evident, said informed observers, the ignoramuses confused his name with mine. The similarity of our names, even though spelled differently (a small matter to the propagandists), is what gave the professional bigot, Joe Kamp, and subsequently the *Christian Front,* the defamatory notion that I was a Communist. The anti-Jewish press actually accused me of anti-Semitic desecrations committed together with unnamed alleged Communists. A story was fabricated in the early fifties that I had marked up an unidentified synagogue. Once floated, the charge was repeated in anti-Semitic journals until it became accepted bigots' lore. To this day I read in anti-Jewish publications that I once desecrated a Jewish institutional building. All of which made me understand I was a scorned enemy of the American hate-world—a reputation I have always carried with pride.

6

America First

A pro-German movement centered in the Midwest and Northeast was convinced Hitler meant to clean Communism out of Europe. To express support of Great Britain—an empire accused of getting into bed with the Soviet Union—was to find oneself a target for attack. The result was an otherwise unlikely amalgam of anti-Semitic forces: Protestant fundamentalists, who came to it from a Ku Klux Klan sentiment; Catholics, whose anti-Jewishness was born of an anti-Soviet hostility; a native nationalist movement that derived its anti-Semitism from an anti-British hatred. It was this combination that nurtured, finally, an organization calling itself the America First Committee, an umbrella movement. The idea for the organization came from the brain of one Douglas Stuart, a twenty-four-year-old Yale graduate who brought it to the leaders of the hate-Roosevelt contingent. With funding from W. H. Regnery, a successful Chicago entrepreneur, and General Robert E. Wood, Chairman of the Board of Sears, Roebuck and Co., Stuart's idea became a reality.

These and other like-minded men were motivated by a conviction that the country had to be isolationist, that the hundred-

74

year-old Monroe Doctrine was the only correct foreign-relations philosophy. They expressed fear that a growing internationalism was motivating the United States to undertake gigantic financial obligations outside our hemisphere that would eventually bankrupt and destroy us. The end result was an anti-British, anti-French and finally an anti-European position that actually had nothing to do with Jews but that somehow became the tortured basis for anti-Semitic sentiments. Hitler's Jews were the available hobgoblins.

As mentioned, the developing America First movement included such politicians as Montana's Senator Burton Wheeler, isolationist in the first instance and therefore imbued with an intense hatred for President Franklin Roosevelt and a need to oppose anything the President proposed or believed in. Curiously, like Father Coughlin, Wheeler himself began as a political liberal. Yet he eventually became a key leader in what was ultimately an anti-British, pro-German, anti-Soviet, anti-Semitic America First movement. In addition to Wheeler were such as Senator Bilbo of Mississippi, whose bigotry was built on a provincial hatred of Easterners. Others were differently motivated. Congressman Hamilton Fish of New York, for example, was a diehard isolationist, which position brought him into the camp of North Dakota's Senator Nye and North Carolina's Senator Reynolds. They eventually found themselves in the same boat with the pro-Germans and anti-Semites. Charles A. Lindbergh, whose political convictions were puzzling, naive, even weird, joined up early. He never believed Nazism was evil. On the contrary, he regarded it a necessary German effort to staunch the flow of Communism, and he justified National Socialism as a healthy, militant method to liberate Western Europe from economic poverty.

Lindbergh blamed the Jews for most of America's foreign problems and described Franklin D. Roosevelt, the British and the Jews as enemy confederates in an international conspiracy. By his attack in a September 1941 Des Moines speech on Roosevelt, Jews, the British and internationalists for allegedly bringing on World War II, Lindbergh revealed the platform of the

America First Committee. It was in part counterproductive, causing many who had until then been misled by the AFC to turn their backs on it.

Before it withered and died the America First Committee had become the central propaganda weapon for isolationists, pro-Nazis and anti-Semites, and in the process pulled into it many political innocents who genuinely believed that through it they were somehow saving America. For concerned Jews the basic standard of measure in judging people and movements was and is anti-Semitism. This time it led some Jews into a fixed anti-right-wing political position that ignored the questionable forces on the Left.

Within the Right Wing movement were almost all the avowed enemies of the Jews, plus a sprinkling of hardcore American Nazis. While exposing the anti-Semites in the America First Committee, we also attacked the organization for accepting them and for subtly adopting their anti-Jewish positions. Before long, Jews found themselves the target of the entire extremist Right Wing, and some were further enticed to the Left by the line that the Soviet Constitution declared anti-Semitism to be a crime. This, along with the fact that the Soviet Union itself was now fighting Nazi Germany, made Jews and others at least reluctant to attack the Soviets.

In September 1939 Communists in the United States became strangely silent about the Nazis—because Germany and the Soviet Union had signed a so-called mutual defense treaty. It was only after the Nazi-Soviet alliance ended in June 1941 that the USSR became anti-Nazi and their American Communist Party began to campaign against the Nazis. Now they were pleading for the rights of Jews, a sprinkling of whom were persuaded to enter their ranks.

As a consequence organized Jewry seemed to some to be politically warped; it fought anti-Jewish Far Right elements while apparently ignoring the menace of the Communist Left. President Roosevelt himself was under attack by American pro-Nazis. They charged him, too, with treason, denouncing him as a "pro-Jewish Communist." When the Depression first struck the nation President Roosevelt had made a herculean and successful effort to humanize what was regarded as democratic capitalism by methods that so-called conservatives denounced as Left-Wing Socialism. Roosevelt was accused of being part of the international Soviet apparatus, and the presence of Jews in his administration was considered clear evidence that *they* were responsible for its Leftist stance.

David Niles, for example, was a "strategically placed" Jew in the White House according to anti-Semites. Niles, a product of the Boston Democratic Party and an ardent New Dealer was, incidentally, the first nonelected person to hold the powerful position of presidential aide since Wilson's Colonel House. Because he was also a concerned Jew, Niles assumed the role of White House liaison to the Jewish community. Profoundly anti-Nazi and very conscious of anti-Jewish dangers, Niles was a friend to those of us defending against anti-Semitism in the late thirties. I repeatedly went to him with problems and he was always helpful.

There had been a significant number of Jews in the Roosevelt camp from its beginning and in unusual leadership positions as well. The president, who had come out of New York, was close to Senator Herbert H. Lehman and to former New York Supreme Court Justice Samuel Rosenman, both prominent and highly respected Jews. Many of Roosevelt's other political associates were also New Yorkers and they, too, were invited to join him in Washington, creating the impression he was close to the Jewish community and partial to Jewish interests.

This, I am convinced, was the fundamental reason American Jewry mistakenly believed the insignificant rescue measures Roosevelt offered European Jewry were all that was possible. They could not imagine that their friend would abandon their people. In retrospect this much is clear, and it has been said increasingly in recent years: Franklin Roosevelt generally ignored the urgent pleas of American Jews able to get his ear about anti-Jewish developments in Europe. Regretably, most of us did not spend a major effort on European Jewish questions because, as mentioned, during that period of Jewish organizational development the primary concern was not anti-Jewish events in Europe but domestic anti-Semitism. Their emphasis was on fighting against Nazi inroads in the United States. None maintained any meaningful foreign operation. Again in hindsight, this was an enormous blunder by the entire American Jewish-defense infrastructure. It's no excuse that American Jews were without political power, which was the fact in spite of the prominence of Jews around Roosevelt, and of less than significant influence, which was equally true. Nor is it an answer that available information about European Jewry was scant, our organization frail, memberships skimpy. *Whatever* we had, *whoever* we were, we should have stopped much that we were doing as Jews working for security here at home and, based on what was publicly known, given far more of our time, energy and resources to saving our brothers and sisters overseas.

As I write these words I realize I am indulging in some typical Jewish thinking; blaming ourselves for what someone else did to us. The Nazis killed our people while the whole world sat by doing nothing to stop it, and we lay the fault at our own feet for the incomprehensible loss.

In spite of his lip service, President Roosevelt did fail to support the struggle against domestic anti-Semitism. He apparently believed, as I've said, that major international difficulties and acute problems in the economic rebirth of America from its devastating Depression were far more urgent than what was regarded to be the comparatively lesser issue of anti-Jewish agitation. What Jews had hoped to secure from the White House was succor and protection against the ever-burgeoning efforts of native extremists marking Jews as enemies of our country, undeserving of the constitutional right to equality of opportunity—the right to be educated, to work and to play where they pleased. Even the right to live, in some people's eyes. The mores of the day included "establishment" discrimination, which Jews had long been subjected to in resigned silence.

The "institutions of discrimination" was the phrase we used to describe this situation, and Jews now increasingly understood that the thoughtless and deliberate practice of discrimination was central to the expanding virus of anti-Semitism. (In the World War II period we still tried without success to get legislative, judicial or just practical relief through the federal government. It was to come at last in the fifties and the years following.)

It is tragic that the same President Roosevelt, alert to the menace of Nazism, was not equally sensitive and responsive to the increasingly dangerous situation into which Europe's Jews were trapped by that very same Nazism. If he had been, perhaps the West's practice of neglect would not have developed, allowing as it did so many millions of innocents—Jews and non-Jews—to be slaughtered.

7

Retreat and Reemergence

The day World War II was brought to American shores in December 1941 by the attack on Pearl Harbor, the destructive political, ethnic and religious divisions in the ranks of the American people were quickly covered over. Open pro-Nazi sentiment evaporated in the winds of war. After other western and European nations had made clear their support of Great Britain, the United States, under the leadership of President Roosevelt, moved to the side of the Allies against Nazi Germany and the nations in its camp. With Pearl Harbor, our country was now firmly in the anti-Hitler coalition although a substantial segment of the American people continued to harbor pro-German sentiments. The war forced them into silence.

The federal government now moved rapidly, setting up special grand juries to probe for possible crimes committed before the war. Laura Ingalls, a socialite pilot who had dropped antiwar leaflets over the nation's capital, was sent to prison for being an unregistered Nazi agent. Ingalls had been a leading public speaker for the America First Committee, with a lengthy record of anti-Jewish activities. Ralph Townsend, another prominent AFC spokesman, went to jail for failing to register as a Japanese agent. He, too, boasted of a substantial contribution to the anti-Jewish propaganda arsenal. George Hill, a clerk in the office of New York's Congressman Hamilton Fish, was sentenced to six years in prison for perjury in connection with his pro-German propaganda mill operated in collaboration with George Sylvester Viereck, a convicted Nazi agent. Fish had brought the two men together.

By July 1942 grand juries in New York and Washington, D.C., had turned out blanket indictments of Nazi and isolationist leaders. In New York, twenty-six German-American Bund leaders were indicted for evading the draft law. In Washington, D.C., twenty-eight propagandists, a potpourri of extremist nationalists, professional anti-Semites and Nazi-connected activists were caught in the federal net and charged with conspiracy to promote revolution in the U.S. armed forces. Thirty publications were listed as the means through which the defendants carried out the alleged scheme, every one of which was subtly or blatantly anti-Jewish, including Elizabeth Dilling's *Red Network* and William Dudley Pelley's *The Galilean.* Pelley, head of the Silver Shirts, labelled by the prosecuting attorney a "traitor" [who] stabbed his country in the back," was sentenced to fifteen years in prison for a criminal charge unrelated to this "sedition" case. The grand jury identified the America First Committee and Hamilton Fish's Committee to Keep America Out of War among the organizations allegedly used by the defendants to sabotage U.S. Army morale.

There were several superseding indictments in the Washington, D.C., case. The final one accused the defendants of having "unlawfully, willfully, feloniously, and knowingly conspired and agreed together and with each other and with officials of the government of the German Reich and the leaders of the Nazi Party" in a drive to wreck the morale of the American armed forces. After eight months the trial was suspended because of the sudden death of the presiding judge. A mistrial was declared when the defendants refused to proceed with the trial before another judge. Two years later the indictment was dismissed and the case was closed. If the litigation did nothing else, it at least interrupted some of the most divisive activities this nation has ever known.

America's entry into World War II also dealt the final blow to Father Coughlin and his pro-Nazi *Social Justice*. Coughlin's whole commercial structure collapsed along with his newspaper, bringing a sigh of relief to an embarrassed Catholic Church and to an apprehensive Jewish community. The demise of Coughlin's bigoted movement that inevitably followed ended one of the scariest chapters in American political history. It took five months for the Christian Front movement to die after the initial blow. Coughlin's propaganda, until then tolerated by the American public, had been largely ignored by Government authorities who believed themselves stymied by First Amendment protections. But in the view of the authorities once the country was at war, the same disruptive activities amounted to virtual treason. The two blows that delivered the coup de grace to one major element in the pro-Nazi machine came from the Catholic Church itself. In April of 1942 the Archdiocese of Detroit condemned *Social Justice,* declaring it not to be an official Church publication and saying that no one should mistakenly believe the contrary. Only days later federal authorities revoked the paper's second-class mailing privilege, barred it from the U.S. mails and charged it with being in violation of the 1917 Espionage Act for "aiding the enemy" by disseminating Nazi propaganda. President Roosevelt's making clear his attitude to cabinet members undoubtedly was the reason for the Post Office Department's action.

All these steps sealed the doom not only of the newspaper *Social Justice,* but also of Coughlin's Radio League of the Little Flower, his Social Justice Publishing Company and his National Union for Social Justice, all private profit-making ventures. Most of Coughlin's pro-Nazi supporters had taken for granted that they had been contributing to nonprofit operations; it had been common belief that the newspaper was the official house organ of the parish priest's Shrine of the Little Flower and that his radio program was the official voice of the suburban-Detroit house of prayer. Here, too, FDR's views played an important role in the Detroit priest's withdrawal from political activities.

So Coughlin was forced out of public life, and his repeated efforts in the years following to re-create his anti-Semitic cause and reestablish himself as an influential force failed. But in the five or six years of his political heyday Coughlin spread more religious hatred across the nation, did greater damage to the American democratic fabric, softened up a larger segment of the populace to the blandishments of pro-Hitler propaganda than any other zealot on the national scene in the period immediately preceding World War II.

But the war only temporarily silenced the professional bigots. Pearl Harbor had destroyed the rallying point—keep the U.S. out of war—that organized isolationist and anti-Semitic forces had been using to win respectability and support. When the war ended they looked for new issues to keep alive their nationwide anti-Jewish movement. Now, though, Jews were spoiling for a fight . . . were angry and reacting to the Holocaust. And having come to civil rights maturity during the war period, Jewish leaders had at long last learned the dangers of silence, and finally understood how to fight against if not eliminate anti-Semitism.

A resurging Ku Klux Klan, while not comparable in size to the nineteenth century or the early twenties Klan, nevertheless had between twenty and thirty thousand members. One Klan leader, Lycergus Spinks, announced his candidacy for governor of Mississippi, vowing to put the blacks and Jews "in their place." He received only 1.5 percent of the total vote. But that a blatant bigot could campaign as a Klan candidate immediately after the war created shock and disappointment. Until then Jews and many others had naively believed that with the military defeat of the Third Reich, Americans had positively learned the evil of blatant anti-Semitism—and there were times when I was among those naive ranks. So the sight of a Klan leader running for public office obviously meant that, naivete aside, many either forgot why Americans fought and died—or never learned.

When Spinks aired his views over radio, we decided we would no longer passively ignore his attacks, a position we might have taken in the late thirties. On the contrary, now we would institute open legal action along with press releases and refusal to sit still in the face of a klansman advocating his own election by defaming Jews. But the legal step was not directed at Spinks. I proceeded against the radio station that was involved, interpreting existing laws to mean that because broadcasters were *licensed* by federal authorities they were not in the same category as newspapers, which were entitled to First Amendment protection. I prepared a petition and submitted it to the Federal Communications Commission, arguing that the airwaves are a means of communication the use of which is authorized on condition that it be in the public interest. Violation risks loss of license. FCC regulation of station owners based on statutory grounds, I said, is a constitutional restriction on unbridled speech, and therefore we have a right to seek relief from its abuse. Radio speeches of the Spinks character aired by a licensed station, I said, violated the public-interest obligation and put the license in jeopardy.

Additional complaints were filed with the FCC about other stations that permitted the Spinks style of inflammatory comment. We won a number of cases, lost more. In some situations station owners backed away from giving their microphones to professional bigots after we complained to the FCC. At other times they fought us even while learning that allowing hate-mongers the use of their facilities was to risk their licenses.

On balance this was a victory. Sometimes the station would offer time on the air to respond to an attack made on Jews. We would turn it down. Engaging in a debate with professional bigots was granting them legitimacy. "Equal time" or, more accurately, "time to reply" under the Fairness Doctrine was not and is not the answer to bigotry. Unreasoned hate is a sickness that should not be given the respect of a debater's response. There is simply no way to answer invidious generalities—lies—about "the Jews." To try is to dignify. Actions speak louder than words.

Retreat and Reemergence

* * *

Dealing with prewar, patrioteering anti-Semites in the postwar period was more of the same except that propaganda
themes were slightly modified. But now American Jewry was
better prepared; we had won our spurs. Each bigot had to be
handled on his own terms, depending on the degree of his
blatancy and the level of his target audience.

Upton Close, for example, had begun his career as an undis-
tinguished radio commentator with the old Mutual Network,
then attracted attention to himself by incorporating the anti-
Jewish propaganda of the day into his program. In his diehard
isolationism he had fought displaced-persons legislation and
proclaimed the United States to be insane. His recurrent basic
theme was still the all-Jews-are-Communists fabrication. Close
was an angry bigot—most of them are, of course—who, having
achieved a certain notoriety, had established himself as a "news
analyst" on a network of independent radio stations across the
country, winning the support of such active isolationists as
Charles A. Lindbergh, General Robert Wood of Sears, Roebuck
and Merwin K. Hart of the National Economic Council. Hart's
clever, patriotic approach was to successful industrialists, still
warning them their businesses and style of life were threatened
by Jewish influences. A New Deal hater, he had favored Spanish
fascism and trumpeted his distrust of American democracy.
Hart could continue to point to the similar views of an Upton
Close on radio as corroborating proof. Colonel Lindbergh had
been a "lay leader" in the movement, clearly gulled by the
Nazis; his reputation had only been sullied, not destroyed, by his
wartime views. General Wood, a millionaire businessman and
large contributor to the old America First, understood commercial enterprise better than geopolitics. He had no change of
heart.

Among enthusiastic Hart supporters also having great wealth
had been the Lamont and Irenee Dupont brothers of Wilming-
ton, Delaware. They remained supporters. Other prominent
businessmen found in the same coterie of big contributors to the
stable of extremist propagandists, included Howard Pew, the oil

tycoon, and E.F. Hutton, the Wall Street broker whose name still partially adorns a leading brokerage firm. It should be added that the financial support of tainted causes from these prominent citizens should not reflect adversely on the major corporations they headed, at least without evidence of corporate involvement, and there was none of that. These anti-British isolationists, many of them multimillionaires, had apparently been seduced into believing a hidden enemy, consisting of liberals, Jews and communists, were part of an international conspiracy that included the British, the Soviets and the Democratic Party. Their views remained unchanged.

Our technique now was to make available to all the media, to the Congress and others, biographies of the "pros," with detailed accounts of their extremist propaganda and their relationships to named financial angels. We provided comprehensive reports on the so-called respectable propagandists as well as on the gutter bigots.

Among the worst of the latter was Gerald L.K. Smith of the Christian Nationalist Crusade, who even during the war had continued to rabble-rouse among a benighted element of the population. He now argued for the complete and absolute social and political segregation of the Black and White races, and insisted the American people were held in slavery by the Jews. Smith proved to be a transparent fraud, constantly pleading poverty. Although highly successful with his followers, Smith's religious enterprises were a pseudopolitical racket carried on by a very professional Protestant Fundamentalist. Smith was the earliest of the genre that had discovered sham-religious bigotry to be a lucrative operation. Whipping up his supporters in "tent" meetings, he built a national organization with tens of thousands of followers. Three decades of raucous hate-mongering made his crackpot Christian Nationalist Crusade a fixture on the American scene. Incessant invective against Jews, Zionists, liberals was so uncontrolled, and so repetitive, the responsible media mostly ignored him. But the rewards continued to be ample for spending time talking against Blacks, Communists, Israel, Internationalists and Jews.

The suave Joe Kamp carried on the same propaganda much less vulgarly under the cover of his Constitutional Educational League. His favorite enemies were still the "reds" and "foreign-born," but they continued to take second place to ADL, which month in and out he characterized as a "fountainhead of malicious information that promotes hate, breeds intolerance, fosters suppression and boycott, and engages in defamation of the vilest sort."

Kamp's main financial source in the immediate postwar period remained Charles White, President of Republic Steel. Like Merwin Hart, he also had sympathizers in the Congress, counting, as mentioned, Clare Hoffman, the Michigan solon. To prove his loyalty, Hoffman dropped a bill into the hopper of the 81st Congress, making it a federal crime to be "a member of or participant in the activities of the un-American, subversive organization known as the Anti-Defamation League." Violation could result in "imprisonment for not more than five years." His proposal, of course, went ignored. The Michigan congressman also helped Kamp and his professional cohorts by frequently placing their propaganda output into the Congressional Record, thereby allowing it free postal distribution. Even Gerald Smith's bilge was not below Clare Hoffman.

We had anticipated a postwar resurgence of organized hatred against Jews. Signs that professional bigots who had loitered quietly during the fighting were once again going all-out confirmed our fears. The anti-Semitic groupings now spread word that freedom in America was in mortal jeopardy unless ubiquitous Jewish influence could be brought under control. Fortunately our investigative operations had continued through the war. In its aftermath the country was busy brushing itself off, trying to rebuild a peace economy. People were preoccupied with straightening out their disrupted lives. Few were in a mood to worry about a hate-brigade reformulating its propaganda to fit the new geopolitical circumstance.

My mind went back to the group of defendants in the aborted sedition case in Washington, D.C., wondering what had become of them. The answers would be a key to our near future problems. Our investigators went to work. Forty-one men and women had been indicted, representing a fair cross-section of the professional anti-Semitic leadership which, before the war, counted its followers in the millions and reflected a movement laden with bigotry. On completion of the survey in December 1947, we knew that except for those few who had quit the business or had been deported, gone to prison, retired for age or died, all were back at their propaganda stands. A typical few:

C. Leon De Aryan, publisher and editor of *The American National Weekly,* whose every issue normally contained anti-Semitic diatribes, had become increasingly vicious and was now reprinting the writings of professional hate-mongers. Gerald Smith's *The Cross and the Flag* was his favorite source.

Elizabeth Dilling, author of the rabidly anti-Jewish *Red Network* and anti–B'nai B'rith *The Octopus,* was now publishing the *Patriotic Research Bureau Bulletin* and had intensified her frenzied writings.

Charles B. Hudson, publisher and editor of *America In Danger,* fervently endorsed by World Service, official Nazi propaganda agency, was going full blast. His central theme: the earth's ills are attributable to the "International Jewish Conspiracy."

Court Asher, publisher of the weekly *X-Ray,* Indiana KKK mobilizer, described by Life magazine in 1942 as a "half-literate, ex-bootlegger," now proclaimed his circulation to be at an all-time high.

Gerald B. Winrod, publisher of the Defender, an anti-Catholic, anti-Semitic monthly magazine, maintaining missions in Puerto Rico, Cuba and Liberia, was constructing a new church and office building in Wichita, Kansas, while turning out anti-Semitic materials and broadcasting bigotry over Mexican radio stations.

And there were the far more sophisticated organizations that had grown up on top of the literary gutter. In short, after the war we were back where we had left off when Pearl Harbor impelled the authorities to try to stop the native "subversive" movement from further activity. It seemed light years away from the Columbus Circle street-meetings presided over by the political hoodlums of the Christian Front. The struggle was now with divisive, pervasive attitudes capable of serious damage to the quality of our democratic fabric. Fortunately the Jewish community pretty well matched the opposition's experience and know-how. Unfortunately anti-Jewish hatred could still get out of hand. Truth to say, it was more frequent than I cared to imagine, and in two particular instances I was its target.

One day a pair of FBI agents announced they had uncovered a plot against me that was hatched in Virginia. A wealthy, professional bigot, a small-time pamphleteer whom I had exposed, had hired a pair of gunmen to come to New York and blow me away. The men from the Bureau assured me they had the conspirators under careful surveillance and were certain they could abort the murder plan. Before it could materialize, they assured me, they could make arrests of the would-be killers on gun-possession charges. But, in the meantime, would I please be thoughtful enough to disappear from home and office for about a week, allowing no one know my destination, just in case the hired hoods gave the FBI the slip? Later I learned the would-be culprits were apprehended after boarding a train in Washington, D.C., bound for New York and me. Both were relieved of unlawful firearms and indicted for the possession violation.

The other occasion was considerably more discomforting. New York city detectives informed me they had been advised by federal authorities that a team of Arab assassins had arrived in New Orleans from the Middle East. The visitors carried a hit list of ten prominent Jews who were marked for elimination and I, said the police, was on the honor roll. It was necessary, according to headquarters, that whenever away from home I be accompanied by a bodyguard until the danger passed. Pressing the detectives, I learned their facts were severely limited; they did not have the identification of the Arab gunmen, just the skimpy details they had shared with me and others on the list of intended victims. I had no choice, they insisted, but to accept the bodyguard arrangement; if anything were to happen and the police, aware of the plot, had failed to take necessary precautions they would be held accountable and possibly exposed to civil liability.

So I submitted. My wife and I were now a threesome from morning to night, seven days a week. Each morning, a plainclothesman would meet me at the house and we would drive a different route to the office. In the evening the same thing home. Restaurant meals required a separate, nearby table for my armed guardian, who had to be strategically situated in the room. An evening at someone's home meant an extra guest, a stranger whose presence had to be explained. One day I suggested to the friendly officer his efforts in my behalf were a waste of time. If someone wanted to kill me, I said, he could surely take careful aim from a nearby rooftop with a telescopic lens on a rifle and fire as I entered or left my office or home. Bang! No more me.

Oh no, he insisted, it's no waste at all. While it was true I could be shot, the murderer himself, he said, risked a real chance of getting caught or even killed. Oh.

My work was bringing me together with prominent personalities, making my plainclothes protector an even more awkward presence. At other times he served as an equalizer, making some important people think me important.

I met Dore Schary for the first time because of my involvement with Winchell. The tall, well-built writer-producer-director, beardless but with the face of a young Lincoln, was then head of a major motion-picture studio, an imposing figure on the Hollywood scene who had never hesitated to express his ideals through his work. Over a period of twenty years he moved up to directing motion pictures and then onto producing assignments. Bringing Laura Hobson's best-selling exposé of anti-Semitism, *Gentlemen's Agreement,* to American movie audiences, was Dore's bold, innovative and daring use of the entertainment medium to fight anti-Jewish bigotry. His successful Broadway play, *Sunrise at Campobello,* the story of Franklin Delano Roosevelt's struggle to overcome the disability of infantile paralysis, which Dore wrote, directed and produced, also a blockbuster movie, made him famous.

What brought Dore and me together in the early forties was what happened at a working session at NBC's old Blue Network studios in New York. Winchell was preparing to deliver his weekly fifteen-minute staccato newscast to millions of listeners. I was in the studio with him, one of a small group who helped gather usable broadcast material. Some of us were always there before the actual program, contributing to the final touches to Winchell's script. Reading through his draft that night I came to an item reporting a rumor that had reached Winchell to the effect that Dore Schary, the Hollywood head of MGM Studios, was studying to convert to Catholicism. I knew Schary at the time only by public reputation, primarily from newspaper stories. But their sum indicated that he was a concerned American Jew living on the West Coast. Comments he had made on issues of Jewish interest, motion pictures for which he had been responsible, positions he had taken regarding our people and their problems all seemed to reflect a man ardently involved in his faith. So Winchell's item about Schary seemed strange to me; just didn't sit right. I asked Walter whether he was sure of his facts. He had the story on good authority, he said.

But I was worried. "How about pulling it out and giving me a chance to check it on the Coast?" I suggested. "No loss if you hold the thing for a week or two. Nothing missed and we'll be sure".

Winchell was agreeable. Next day I wrote a letter to Schary in Hollywood telling him I had been asked about the truth of the rumor that he was studying to convert to Catholicism. I would appreciate, I wrote, any comment he cared to make so that I could respond accurately to inquiries. Almost by return mail came a reply from Dore that, in effect, told me politely but firmly to mind my own business and not intrude on his privacy.

Of course he was right, the matter was personal, private, none of my business. Worse, I had been only half-truthful; I had no rumors, only the Winchell item. I answered Schary, telling him that Winchell had been about to report the rumor on his broadcast and had delayed it pending a report from me. I explained the reason was my suspicion about the story's accuracy, adding that I would report back to the columnist only that I had been unable to nail down the facts.

Within days I received an answer: "Will you find it in your heart to forgive me?" Dore wrote. "You wanted to help me and all I did was be impatient and hurt you. Of course, the rumor is false. Before I could become a good Christian I would have to become a good Jew and I am still working on that."

It would be several years before our paths crossed again. In 1948 it almost did but not quite. ADL's annual meeting that year was scheduled to be held at the Ambassador Hotel on Wilshire Boulevard in Hollywood. An intermittent correspondence had developed between Dore and me, usually about issues of the day touching on Jews. At the planning session for the meeting it was suggested by Alex Miller, one of our top staff, that Dore would make an attractive speaker and that I should extend the invitation. He accepted.

We all flew to the Coast for the gathering, and I looked forward to meeting Dore face-to-face for the first time. But on the day of the dinner his mother died and he immediately flew East. He had, though, prepared a speech for the affair and asked an old friend to read it for him—Leonard Spiegelgass, a prominent Hollywood writer.

Leonard apparently neglected to go over Dore's manuscript before mounting the podium. He walked right into it, innocently reading aloud Dore's thoughts about Israel: "There are fast Zionists, there are slow Zionists." Spiegelgass declaimed, "and there are half-fast Zionists." The audience roared as poor Leonard, startled, looked up in bewilderment.

In the years that followed, Dore became increasingly active with us. When he left MGM and moved to New York he became more deeply involved in our work, and in 1963 was elected our national chairman, contributing much to ADL's liberal, pro-Israel image.

A stickler for principle, Dore created havoc at an ADL meeting when a question came up about honoring President Richard

Nixon. In the 1940s we had paid a tribute to President Eisenhower at our annual convocation, and we did the same for Presidents Kennedy and Johnson. Until President Nixon's term of office.

In ADL ranks Mr. Nixon was anathema long before Watergate. We regarded him a reactionary, untrustworthy right-winger who had failed to support most civil rights causes. But Mr. Nixon had been very helpful to Israel, and this also carried weight among Jews. When the proposal to honor Nixon was made at the meeting, and when after discussion the members appeared ready to approve it, Dore got to his feet and recited the unhappy Nixon record. He ended by declaring his opposition to the invitation.

Many in the room, even some who agreed with Dore about Mr. Nixon, believed it would be offensive not to invite the president in light of our past practice. The issue was joined, and it appeared Dore was going to lose. At that point he employed a strategy, possibly an unfair tactic but one which I privately admired and, in fact, joined with. Dore announced that if the League extended the invitation he would resign. In a job I loved, I echoed Dore along with several others. On that threat, the impeccability of which I'm not too sure, the committee tabled the Nixon invitation . . .

It was the end of June 1980 when I telephoned my secretary from Florida to check mail. A brief note from Dore was addressed to both Bill Fitelson, another longtime friend, and to me:

Dear Bill and Arnie:

Here's a rough outline of things that should be in my will with both of you named as executors. I know it's rough, but at least it says most of the things I want outlined in the Will.

I appreciate so much your willingness to do me this final favor and if the Lord reveals his secrets that we are not supposed to know until we move on from this earth, you can be sure I'll be eternally grateful to you.

Attached to the missive was a memorandum detailing Dore's last wishes, including precise instructions for his funeral. He wanted a private religious burial—a plain pine box in accordance with Jewish reigious ritual and a rabbi to officiate—and afterward a memorial service open to friends, with music and suggested speakers.

I hung up and telephoned Dore at his New York apartment to bawl him out although I knew how much he was suffering with cancer. His housekeeper answered the phone and told me that Dore had passed away during the night.

The private service was as he wished it, the memorial as exact as we could make it. His son Jeb, Bill Fitelson, Leonard Spiegelgass and I, among others, spoke our eulogies. I told of the Winchell incident of thirty-two years before—the false rumor of Dore's plan to convert to Catholicism—and I wept as I talked. Bill read parts of Dore's final instructions to the two of us, including the very last sentence: "All in all, my life has been a good one, full of gifts from God, family and friends. Forgive me my errors. Know that I loved all of you."

And so back to the immediate postwar period.

Walter Winchell and I were lounging in the upstairs private quarters of Sherman Billingsley's now defunct Stork Club on East Fifty-second Street in Manhattan. It was the spring of 1945, well past midnight. We were listening to a West Coast radio commentator's blow-by-blow description of the day's events at the San Francisco Opera House. The mammoth facility had been taken over for an international assembly of statesmen, diplomats and politicians of varying importance, all laboring to give birth to a United Nations.

Winchell, handsome, white-haired, always dapperly dressed in blue serge suits, was still the most prominent newspaper columnist of the day, now syndicated in over six hundred papers and reaching an estimated fifty million readers. His Sunday night fifteen-minute radio newscasts were listened to by an estimated equal number. Although Hitler's war had ended, Winchell remained apprehensive about anti-Semitism under an

94

aggressive, effectively tough demeanor. For a quarter-century he was a dominant personality on both radio and newspapers.

We first met in 1941 when I brought him a copy of a letter Henry Ford had written to us disavowing anti-Semitism and repudiating certain native anti-Semitic movements. Ford had underwritten the distribution of *The Protocol of the Elders of Zion*. Winchell read the Ford letter on the air as a major scoop and it became front-page news. Winchell wanted more, and I was there, ready with additional anti-Nazi material. The relationship would last sixteen years.

After the war I was convinced that the creation of a new world organization dedicated to permanent peace and civilized international conduct was at long last a realistic goal.

"It's actually happening," I said to Winchell. "One big world body for the protection of all mankind. And *maybe* the end of two thousand years of persecution of Jews. Some permanent good out of the war after all."

"Wrong on two counts," snapped Winchell. "The war was not fought to save mankind or its Jews but to stop the Nazis from taking control of the whole damned planet. Two—nobody on earth, no matter how well-intentioned or powerful, can eliminate religious bigotry. Or any other kind of human hatred."

Rejecting Winchell's cynicism, or realism, I insisted that civilized man had finally had it with war. For the first time we had all seen close up for ourselves the unspeakable horrors that a near Armegeddon had wrought on so many millions. Nor could it be forgotten that the nations of the world had passively permitted the slaughter of unknown numbers of Jews simply because they were Jews. (We still did not know how many.) Or the numberless other noncombatants killed only because they— Gypsies, Communists, labor leaders, dissidents, et al.—had gotten in the way of the so-called master race's plans for "cleansing" the world's population. "Racial and religious bigotry, and its particular offshoot, anti-Semitism," I naively concluded, "are dead for the foreseeable future."

How wrong I was.

* * *

95

The ADL had expanded. Jewish organizations for the first time had reached out beyond their own members for additional funds to finance defense work. League branches were now operating in Miami, Atlanta, San Francisco, Boston and elsewhere. Before the end of 1946 ADL's headquarters had moved from Chicago to New York.

It was at this time that our National Director, Dick Gutstadt, showing increasing symptoms of exhaustion, was diagnosed as suffering from abdominal cancer. He died within a year and Ben Epstein was named in his place. I was appointed Associate National Director and General Counsel. We were to be a team that would last thirty-seven years—until Ben's death in 1983.

Ben and I stepped into these new roles in 1946 while still in our early thirties. Which indicates how rudimentary the Jewish community's organized defense structure was at the time. How else to explain the appointment of two comparatively raw young men to head up the best organization Jews were fielding to combat anti-Semitism? And this at a time in American history of great danger to Jews. It also helps explain, but not justify, the failure of any effective American Jewish effort to rescue their imperiled brothers in Nazi Europe.

The postwar objectives of the combined forces of racist hate were a reaction to liberal changes now being attempted in American communities. Blacks were among their targets. Bigots opposed the abolition of the poll tax, fighting to stop Blacks from voting where the poll tax had been eliminated. They tried to block the enactment of fair employment practice laws. Courts were urged to resist inroads on the validity of restrictive land-ownership covenants. Campaigns were launched to frustrate unionization while prominent Catholic and Jewish labor leaders were charged with leading the country toward socialism.

With this kind of action-propaganda created by White extremists, KKK cells inevitably found it easy to reestablish themselves in every large southern community from Virginia to Texas. Elmo Roper, the opinion pollster, warned that "the Klan

Paula Ben Gurion, Israeli Prime Minister's wife, chats with May Forster on the veranda of the Gali Kinneret Hotel, on the Sea of Galilee (on Lake Tiberius), April 1953.

Arnold Forster confers with Israel's first Prime Minister, David Ben Gurion, in April 1953.

Jewish children buying bread in Jerusalem's Old City, April 1953.

Elderly Jews chatting in Jerusalem's Old City, April 1953.

Aged, blind Jew in
Old City, Jerusalem,
April 1953.

Orthodox Jewish chil-
dren in the religious
quarter (Mea Shearim)
of Old City, April 1953.

Stork Club conference preceding Walter Winchell's regular Sunday evening radio broadcast, May 1946. Left to right: Walter Winchell, the author, Attorney Ernest Cuneo, and Winchell's publicist Ed Wiener.

New York Governor Thomas E. Dewey and New York Supreme Court Judge Jacob Grumet congratulate author on the publication of *A Measure of Freedom*, his best-selling exposé of bigotry, April 1950.

U Thant and Adlai Stevenson join the author and his wife in sharing speaking honors at ADL's Inaugural dinner at the New York Hilton, April 1965. *(Photo: Mike Zwerling)*

Dore Schary and author share the platform at New York dinner in honor of ADL Chairman Sam Dalsimer, June 1969.

Jackie Robinson and the author (above), speakers at a
February 1967 dinner. *(Photo: Whitestone Photo)* Jackie
Robinson chats with the author and ADL executive
Philip Bershad at a Civil Rights dinner, October 1954
(below).

Team of lawyers who drafted the Anti-Boycott Legislation, at its signing by President Jimmy Carter in the Rose Garden of the White House, June 1977. Left to right: Maxwell E. Greenberg, ADL Commissioner; Hans Anger-mueller, General Counsel, Citibank; Vincent A. Johnson, General Counsel, General Electric; John E. Hoffman, Jr., Sherman & Sterling; author; Jerry Kandler, General Counsel, Dupont; Ambassador Max Kampelman, ADL Commissioner.

Arnold Forster confers with Vice President Walter Mondale; ADL Chairman Seymour Graubard is in the background, June 1977.
(Photo: The White House)

Author chats about the Middle East with Secretary of State George P. Schultz, Palm Beach, February 1988. *(Photo: Lucien Capehart Photography)*

was on the way back all over the nation, once again targeting minorities and trade unions." It was the first manifestation of unrestrained Klan resurgence since Pearl Harbor, with the hooded order again able to boast a national membership of more than twenty thousand. They resumed cross-burnings, Klan Konklaves, defacement of stores and physical violence on blacks.

It was this situation some years later, in the early fifties, that brought Jackie Robinson and me together. The first black player to the break the color barrier in major league baseball, he had heard me speak at a civil rights dinner, phoned and asked to meet. Jackie asked searching questions about fighting anti-Semitism. Satisfied that we Jews were on to something effective, Jackie helped intensify our cooperative relationship with black civil rights groups, determined that they use our techniques. In his speeches about racism, it became his custom to quote me by name on ADL methods, adding that when blacks succeeded in creating a duplicate operation for themselves, they would at long last be on the road to racial equality. And he worked hard to make it happen, but unhappily it wasn't, and isn't, all that easy—for blacks or Jews.

Yet the Klan would not succeed. Thousands of Black GIs had returned home from overseas, where they had left buried large numbers of their buddies. The anger returning veterans felt at the bigoted reception given them was shared by millions of Americans. So the Klan's numbers dwindled to a quarter of the strength the hooded order boasted in the immediate postwar period, and it has remained that way since.

Other racist anti-Jewish organizations did better. Within a year after the Axis surrender, various sleaze groups were busy replenishing their ranks—The Commoner Party of the United States, the Columbians of Georgia, the American Gentile Army, the Constitution Christian Party, the German-American Veterans Group, the Christian Frontier, the America First Committee and many more. The anti-Semitic press was once again disseminating its hate sheets throughout America. A gaggle of nationalistic Fundamentalists, the forerunners of today's elec-

97

tronic preachers who so oppose a woman's right to choose abortion and favor censorship, were tearing at the walls separating church and state and working to "Christianize" the United States government.

World War II, it seemed, had been only a temporary defeat for America's bigoted extremists. Significantly, even in those years the Fundamentalist ministry exhibited a sharply reactionary political orientation. They denounced the New Deal and attacked as socialist the international efforts to attain lasting peace. Now they were distorting the findings of the Pearl Harbor Inquiry in an effort to besmirch American participation in the war. They defamed our wartime allies and automatically blamed Jews for America's new troubles. In retrospect it's clear the bigots were planting propaganda seedlings for the emergence in the next decades of the political growths that came to be called the Radical Right and McCarthy movements.

Meanwhile clandestine propaganda was being disseminated by a newly established Arab propaganda movement, reflecting the efforts of the Institute of Arab-American Affairs and the League for Peace with Justice, among others. As yet these Arab groups hadn't made frontal attacks on Jews. But because these forces, with their malevolent attitude toward Jews in Palestine and their supporters abroad, avoided invective and the too-brazen lie, they were *more* dangerous. Covertly they did not hesitate to stimulate anti-Jewish sentiments, using notorious Jew-baiters to front for them. Jewish leadership at long last accepted the concept of fighting back openly, in our names, not hiding behind rationalizations to justify keeping our counteraction secret. The notion that anti-Semitism was somehow unintentional was becoming a thing of the past, a sea change in American Jewish life.

One had to be blind not to see the political pattern of organized anti-Semitism. Bigoted extremists and anti-democratic attitudes once considered beyond the pale in a responsibly free society were now tolerated in silence. Typically, a syndicated columnist's clear defense of an avowed anti-Semite imprisoned for sedition brought no objection from the public at large; an open effort by a United States senator to pass legislation in behalf of pro-Nazis ordered deported precipitated no community revulsion; syndicated newspaper articles by a prominent anti-Semite were received by the reading public with no sign of protest.

These 1947 findings of American apathy to anti-Semitism were long forgotten when, twenty-seven years later our best-selling book, *The New Anti-Semitism,* reported the very same kind of situation to be of "recent origin."

"New" was, unhappily, old.

8

Teenage Anti-Semites

Although our time and efforts were now mostly directed toward political, anti-Jewish manifestations across the entire country, a troubling situation in New York City momentarily turned my attention back to my old neighborhood in the northern section of Manhattan.

The street battle involving my law school friends in 1937 had appeared at that time to be an isolated attack. By the mid-forties such incidents had become common. The rampant religious hostility resulting from organized and intensive anti-Jewish propaganda had infected whole sections of the American population. In Washington Heights there were at least ten or eleven synagogues and Jewish institutions. Periodically one or another of them was smeared with swastikas, daubed with anti-Semitic epithets, vandalized, set afire or otherwise desecrated. Gangs of teenagers roamed streets looking for Jews to mug. The property damage and personal assaults brought a flood of complaints to me from local Jewish leaders and parents of victims pleading for help and insisting the police were unable or unwilling to stop the attacks. Desk sergeants, I was told, would listen to the sto-

100

ries, record them on the police blotter, promise to investigate and promptly forget them. My files were crammed with reports of such events, yet police captains advised me their squad cars failed to notice the incidents. Unless complainants could identify culprits, little would be accomplished.

I launched a community-wide investigation, calling on a small volunteer contingent and assigning it the various complaints pouring in from Washington Heights. I needed affidavits from eyewitnesses, follow-up on hearsay, photographs of desecrations plus whatever could be learned about suspects and motivations.

Six weeks later I had an impressive documented record that included evidence that Protestant churches had also been vandalized. Experience had taught me private meetings with the police authorities were a waste of time. Only a community-wide furor would bring results. Convincing evidence that the culprits were Catholic youth complicated matters. Centered for the most part in and around parochial schools, they would go on forays, damage Jewish buildings, assault younger Jews while shouting racist obscenities, then go back to the safety of their own precincts before the police arrived. The only way to get the whole community involved was to call a press conference, something I'd never done before. Victor Reisel, a young but experienced newsman and labor columnist on the New York *Post,* was a friend of mine, he would know, I thought, and could guide us.

When I called him, Victor listened and asked: "How many affidavits do you have? Read some of them to me so that I can evaluate the newsworthiness of your stuff. Name the parochial schools. How many incidents that have been documented? Which synagogues? Who were some of the victims—names, addresses, ages?" I told him all of it.

Victor then proceeded to explain how a press release was framed and a conference conducted. He suggested several victims attend and he said be sure to attach copies of affidavits and photographs to the statement prepared for the media. Set the conference at eleven A.M., in ample time for the evening pa-

101

pers. This would also give the morning papers an opportunity to check out the story. We should also make an oral presentation and be ready to answer questions.

I followed Reisel's instructions. Sending him an advanced set of papers, all the documents, I talked with him about the whole business in the early morning, then called in the press and radio. Opening the meeting, I distributed the documentation, made a brief presentation and called for questions.

The New York *Times* reporter was the first to raise his hand. His words stunned us: "I don't understand why you called this conference," he said. "What we've just received, I've already read in full, written by Victor Reisel in the first edition of this morning's New York *Post.*" He held up the newspaper. On the front page were black headlines telling about our exposé. Chuckles around the room. Nevertheless, although Reisel had scooped them, the newspapermen were interested, and our documentation convinced them that almost every temple and synagogue in Washington Heights had been damaged in the previous three months.

We also got across that the incidents weren't confined to Washington Heights. They had also been discovered, we said, in Staten Island and other boroughs of the city. Most of the vandalism was the work of teenagers who roamed the streets assaulting Jewish children. The attacks had assumed a uniform pattern. If an accosted youngster admitted to being a Jew, a bad beating followed. The New York *Times* man asked sharp questions, demanding details, which fortunately I was able to supply.

Next day the *Times* front-paged our findings and other New York papers followed. Network radio gave our press release. Catholic authorities quickly issued angry denials. Police officials visited my office with requests for documentation and promises to crack down. But Police Commissioner Lewis J. Valentine, reacting to our charges, told the press that "anti-Semitism is always a problem in a large, heterogeneous city such as New York," adding that police measures would be taken "if and when necessary." Police inspectors in charge of the Washington Heights area publicly insisted that our reports were exag-

gerated. "Things are very calm and collected in the neighborhood," one said. "We have received only a single report of
anti-Semitism."

But our statement did prompt the disclosure by New York
City's Commissioner of Investigation that, at the request of
Mayor LaGuardia, his department had been "conducting a city-
wide investigation into all cases of anti-American and anti-Semitic vandalism called to the department's attention" during
the last year. The mayor made an appeal for citizens to join the
City Patrol Corps and thereby perform a patriotic service.

Within weeks after the press conference it became clear we
had been right in making public the Washington Heights problem. Jewish leaders were now meeting with local Catholic officials. An understanding was reached and we embarked together on what thereafter was to become what I think was
perhaps the first meaningful, municipal, interfaith effort of its
kind. (It would be an overstatement to suggest that this well-
intentioned joint effort corrected the sharp hostility demonstrated in local Catholic-Jewish confrontations. The effort may
have helped, but the deeply imbedded differences did not disappear until long after the end of World War II.)

The press conference had been effective. The news stories
had helped bring some public awareness. But something ran-
kled. I telephoned Victor Reisel to say he had embarrassed me
and to ask why he had betrayed my confidence and our friendship in breaking the story in advance of our press conference?

"Listen, buddy," said Victor, "unless you explicitly tell a reporter that what you're sharing with him is off the record, *it is
not.* Besides, it was a helluva story and it's my business to get
it first and get it right. Don't complain, the entire front page of
my paper blared out your story, and you're a hero to the Jews
of New York."

My days as an innocent in dealing with the press—friends and
enemies—were over.

103

9

Israel

From the unusual tone of my associate's voice I could tell that something important was up. Hearing him shout from his nearby room for me to join him, I hurried in. "Israel has declared itself a sovereign nation . . ." There was neither elation in his tone nor a smile on his face.

"Great, wonderful, wonderful!" I said.

He looked at me as if I were stupid and shook his head. "Are you crazy? It's premature. It'll embarrass Washington. It can only mean trouble."

I was not crazy, and it was not premature. Israel's re-creation was two thousand years overdue. In other respects my friend was right; perhaps for reasons different from those he perceived. It *would* be trouble, indeed, longtime trouble, but the price, as it turned out, for a Jewish State. Yet definitely wonderful.

I'm not sure either of us realized on the fourteenth of May 1948 what a massive change the new state would make in our own personal and professional lives, let alone its far more awesome meaning to all Jews, especially those who would be living there. In one stroke the leaders of the Jewish Agency—a self-created international Jewish group speaking for Palestinian Jews—had changed the world for all Jews. The brief exchange with my associate had touched only on timing, not the wisdom or the rightness of the decision. His foresight and fuller understanding was what caused his concern. With little knowledge of the subject I could not anticipate Israel's future, but I knew how I felt.

My personal and very emotional response to the reappearance of the Jewish State was always a source of wonder to me. With no background in Zionism or attachment to any of its institutions, or to Palestinian Jewry, Israel's declaration of independence brought me a sense of belonging that is inexplicable, except in near-mystical terms. That was and is a sufficient explanation for me.

Like it or not every Jew was automatically related to the Jewish State—although some of the more timid, hiding behind their insecurities, expressed initial dislike of the notion that Jews had created their own nation. Most of us, though, understood the relationship deep inside ourselves and in our minds. I think we also realized that, in their hearts, American non-Jews recognized our tie to the new state, even while knowing that we, of course, remained Americans.

Inevitably, Jewish defense agencies would change from America-centered to a concern with the new foreign nation as well. This didn't occur quickly or harmoniously, but the anti-Zionists in the Jewish leadership never stood a real chance of preventing it.

Curiously, the same associate who had such doubts about timing in the creation of the new state not long thereafter brought me together with important Israeli representatives stationed in the United States. He was also the one who encouraged my first cooperation with them, which led to friendships that would involve me so deeply in Israel's life. First I met Reuven Shiloah, a dear and gentle man with a razor-sharp mind who, I believe, held at the time the highest intelligence post in the United States. Then there was a young man like myself, Teddy Kollek, Ben Gurion's aide-de-camp, and also Memi diShalit, a politically

105

wise, public relations member of the early Israeli heirarchy.

These three had excellent contacts with the American establishment, not only within Zionist leadership but also at the nation's capital. None of those relationships, however, could give authoritative answers to their many questions about domestic elements hostile to the new Jewish State. And it was important that they knew the organized sources of hatred for Israel. Who better to turn to than the Anti-Defamation League, which by 1948 was recognized at least within the Jewish community as a most effective fact-finding apparatus. Happily for me, mine was the desk in charge of that responsibility. As you've seen, like most American Jews I was a spontaneous supporter of Israel the day it was born, in spite of knowing little if anything about the infant nation or its people and politics, let alone its language.

If my taste for unending war on anti-Semitism was ever in danger, something I can't conceive, there was now an added cause to spur me on, one that stirred profound emotions within me while generating a deeply satisfying exhilaration. It was also the basis for newly found relationships and friendships.

Short, barrel-chested Paddy Chayefsky, Purple Heart veteran of World War II, was a genuine chunk of Americana, born and bred in the same lower-middle-class Jewish precincts of New York City as I, although a decade later. Molded in that milieu and with similar experiences, it was not surprising that we grew up with similar reactions, attitudes and hopes. Fiercely intense about anti-Semitism, angry and impatient with it, we were equally obsessed with the urgency of fighting the disease. When Paddy died in 1981 at the age of fifty-eight, we had known each other for nearly thirty years, having first met about Israel's birth pangs. He praised my full-time involvement in the Jewish struggle, and I was in awe of his genius as a playwright, his intensity as a Jew and his ability to translate his feelings into prize-winning plays and motion pictures. *Marty, Middle of the Night, Gideon, The Hospital, The Tenth Man, Network,* et al., each raised him higher on the ladder of literary recognition while revealing his passion for the underdog, his hatred of the corrupt, his hopes for mankind—hopes that were diluted only by a deeply rooted cynicism.

Paddy reserved his razor-sharp pen in behalf of Jewish rights and the State of Israel for his private life, but gave it much of his spare time. He would say the Jews were an "endangered species", and manifestly his love for Israel was integral to his Judaism. Injustice of any variety outraged him. Racism was stupid; bigotry, thickheaded—all Paddy's very personal code, part of his being Jewish. And being a Jew was a great source of pride to him; he *enjoyed* being Jewish.

Habitually, Paddy would pick up a telephone and without preliminaries explode in pungent language—his hallmark among intimates. In sentences studded with worthy Anglo-Saxon, he would demand to know what I was doing about this "sunnuvabitch anti-Semite" or that "f—— anti-Israel outrage." But having so unburdened his fury, he then also came on with constructive advice. And he could be eloquent about the political dishonesty of the United Nations, the intransigent enmity of the Arabs and the anti-Israel prejudice of some of the press and television.

Paddy's anger took him to Israel several times in a futile search for stories that would transform Mideast reality into art and make his point for the world. Once he made the trip to research a kind of detective story he had in mind about life on the West Bank. Together we visited police stations, prisons and villages in the Administered Territories. Ultimately he abandoned the project because, he said, "it trivialized the Israelis, and the little nation could not afford that luxury."

Just after the Yom Kippur War in 1973 Paddy phoned to propose we organize a handful of knowledgeable experts into a think tank to consider ideas and actions from day to day to counteract the false images generated by Israel's enemies. For seven years and until he fell desperately ill with cancer, he was a faithful participant in that effort, responsible for the content of many full-page ads that appeared in newspapers across the country, messages that reflected his profoundly sensitive understanding of Jewish and Israeli heartaches.

At the funeral service overflowing with prominent people, Paddy was eulogized by a small number of intimates, including Arthur M. Schlesinger, Jr., Sidney Lumet, Herb Gardner, Bob Fosse, and Rabbi Joseph Sternstein. Fosse, who preceded me to the pulpit and had long been frail—major heart surgery—knew, as did Paddy, that time was running out for both of them. Standing in front of the coffin, Fosse talked of their long friendship, of the agonizing vigil at Paddy's bedside and how they joked that the survivor would do something special in his eulogy for the other. "I hope none of you here with us will misunderstand," he said. "But I made him a promise and I must keep it." With that, he moved back from the pulpit and broke into dance. Stopping suddenly, Bob buried his head in his hands and sobbed violently. Most of us in the chapel wept with him. Paddy would have applauded.

10

Counterattack

The hush-hush approach to fighting anti-Semitism was dead.

ADL's Annual Dinner was May 15, 1948, the place was the Waldorf Astoria and the chairman for the evening was Herbert Bayard Swope, preeminent public relations man, advisor to presidents and member of the nation's social elite. Having settled on the dramatic approach, it only remained for us to decide who to people our *Blueprint for Democracy* with and how to present it. Staging wasn't too difficult. A darkened auditorium, three speaker's stands, on either end of the dais and one in the middle. A tiny concealed spotlight at each lectern catching the face of each participant as he appeared out of the darkness to say his piece and when finished stepping backward and disappearing into the blackness. Yes, theatrics.

Edward R. Murrow agreed to be our centerpiece, the narrator. Elmo Roper, highly respected social scientist and pollster, would offer findings about domestic bigotry. Ben Grauer, famed radio commentator, said he would be pleased to describe the contribution of radio to the American way of life. We added Franklin Roosevelt, Jr., for an upbeat political presence and declaration. And for the American soldier's point of view, there was Harold Russell, the handless veteran famous for his role in the movie, "The Best Years of Our Lives."

Someone suggested we should invite an actor to speak for motion pictures and the legitimate theatre, and the name John Garfield was mentioned. A good possibility, someone added, because he was now living in New York. Could any of us reach him? Heads turned to me, since I was friendly with Irving Hoffman, who was popular with stars of stage and screen and a columnist for The Hollywood Reporter, the industry's trade magazine.

I did not mention my relationship with Garfield in the long ago when he was my school friend, Julie Garfinkel. After all, that had been twenty years ago, I thought to myself, and even our names had been changed since then. I couldn't be sure the famous actor would even remember me. I said I would ask Hoffman to help.

Several days later Hoffman phoned to say Garfield had accepted our invitation but on condition that we replace a pair of theatre tickets for the same May 15 evening, tickets he had worked so hard to get for *South Pacific,* the Broadway musical. That would be easy, I assured Irving. "Write to Julie," he said, "and give him the details."

That day a letter went to Garfield in which I spelled out the program for the evening, told who the others would be in the *Blueprint,* and added we would prepare a suggested narration that he was, of course, free to edit. Within the week I sent Garfield a draft of our proposed script . . .

My phone rang and Garfield introduced himself. The statement was fine, he said, and he had no changes. But had I managed to get his substitute theatre tickets? I assured him he would have them soon. (It didn't cross my mind that Julie would recognize my voice. He said nothing. For some reason I'm not sure I understand I didn't mention the old relationship, maybe afraid he wouldn't remember who I was and it would be embarrassing. Still, I hated the idea of talking to him and not reminding him.) He said he would arrive after dinner and only in time to perform.

A week before the affair I sent Julie the final script with a note about the staging and that we didn't think a rehearsal was necessary. He telephoned anyway for further details. I suggested he come to ADL's hospitality suite in the hotel and I would escort him down to the ballroom floor and through the backstage maze. He could wait there until the lights were dimmed and then find his seat on the darkened dais.

I waited alone for him in the hospitality suite on the eighteenth floor while dinner was being served in the ballroom. A knock on the door. He strode in, looked at me, shoved out his hand and said, "Hello, I'm Garfield."

We shook hands. "Welcome," I replied, "I'm Forster." We stared at each other for a moment, neither of us showing any sign of recognition. I could not tell whether he recognized me, but I waited for a sign. My mind was made up. If he said nothing, I wouldn't either. Probably false pride. Then he asked politely whether he was late, no more. Assuring him he was not, we walked to the elevator and rode to the ballroom floor.

Julie asked the obvious questions, with no sign of any real interest in my answers. What was the size of the audience and how had it all been going so far? A thousand guests, I told him, and all was running very well. I led him through dimly lit backstage twists and turns, wished him good luck and watched him find his seat out front.

The evening was a great success. The audience greeted each participant with generous applause and finished with ovations. It was an exciting, emotional performance. Several days later I sent a letter of appreciation to Julie, enclosing a pair of ducats for *South Pacific*.

Less than three years later I was to meet Garfield again, but under very different and much changed circumstances.

11

The Anti-Eisenhower Crusade

By 1952 a wave of political paranoia had moved across the land, proving that once again a substantial segment of Americans could be more afraid of human rights than of Marxist threats. The anti-Communist eruptions contained the same wrinkle—anti-Semitism. The newly grown hysteria reflected itself, among other ways, in the enactment of the McCarran-Walter Immigration Act, closing America's doors in violation of the spirit if not in law of our traditionally generous immigration policy. Jews still in Europe with bitter memories could not adjust and wanted out. The fears stirred up by the propagandizing of Senator Patrick A. McCarran and Congressman Francis E. Walter created legislative barriers to keep "European" refugees from entering. It was fairly obvious that the doors were being shut because the survivors of Nazism who were seeking a haven in the United States were primarily Jews. Surely a warning of danger ahead.

But the warning was recognized by a relatively small number of Americans. Moving into the new decade, the assortment of professional hate-mongers that had reemerged in 1946 had coalesced into a full-blown anti-Semitic network. In their bizarre

112

cosmogony of anti-Communism, President Eisenhower, who had coordinated his responsibilities as a World War II general with Soviet armies, was damned as a member of the so-called International Communist Conspiracy. And when he ran for the presidency that year the now well-reorganized extremists attacked Eisenhower in a campaign shockingly ignored by the leadership in both major parties as well as in other responsible elements. Intent on defeating the former Supreme Allied Commander of World War II, leaders of the hate network banded together even before attempting the selection of a "viable" candidate of their own. They created a third party composed of the resurgent anti-Jewish, lunatic anti-Communist fringe, thereby frightening Republicans, worrying Democrats and scaring the American Jewish community.

Indeed, they were the first to inject anti-Semitism into a presidential election through a third-party structure. True, these were not a respectable element nor a generally accepted political unit. They were extremist, political zealots. But an anti-Jewish national campaign carried on by a quasi-political organization supported by many small groups with patriotic-sounding names, working toward their frightening goals and seemingly part of a normal election process made an ominous picture. If one were an aware Jew in the United States one had to be worried. More so because Americans, generally, took the ominous development in stride, not stopping even to hand the bigots a figurative back of the hand.

The anti-Eisenhower crusade included nearly every identifiable anti-Jewish organization. Typically, The Minutewomen of USA, a pseudo–anti-Communist outfit that had opposed America's role in World War II, like many others of similar mentality, considered the great war hero a dangerous captive of Communism. Failure to strike back set the ground for what followed. After Eisenhower's election came the John Birch Society, a major disruptive political force that eventually counted millions of members with a budget to match. The Society took its name from John Birch, an American soldier killed by the Chinese toward the end of World War II. He had been an anti-Commu-

113

nist, it was said, who after his death somehow came to the attention of Robert Welch, founder of the Society.

Living in Belmont, a small town outside of Boston, Welch enjoyed a good income from the family's successful candy business, leaving him free to pursue his primitive political philosophy. Interestingly, his family wanted no part of him or his public activities.

We were startled and concerned by the phenomenal growth of the Birch Society. Its central philosophy: an international Communist conspiracy included Americans in government controlled by the Eisenhower Administration in concert with the Jews.

The John Birch Society was made up of ordinary but naive citizens plus some influential Americans who also believed incredibly wild charges about the alleged Communist takeover of the U.S. government. The Society's main membership, from the extreme right wing spectrum of American politics, was carefully if sometimes only obliquely anti-Semitic. It would deny its anti-Semitism, and appeared offended when charged with bigotry. Yet its propaganda materials were often transparently anti-Jewish. Examining the roster of its membership one found a goodly number of anti-Semitic elements from America's racist groups had insinuated themselves into the organization. Klan members who moved into its ranks concealed their Klan identity. Other joiners from the vast pool of the politically lunatic camouflaged themselves in various patriotic organizations that were cooperating in Birch work. More than a few senators and congressmen gave at least indirect moral encouragement.

One of the Birchers' top paid leaders in its early years, and a key professional on the staff, was John Rousselot, who later became a California congressman. Quietly supportive in its declining period was another congressman, Laurence McDonald, from Atlanta, Georgia, a passenger among those killed in 1983 when the Soviet Union knocked a North Korean 747 out of the sky. On his death, McDonald was revealed to be a leader of the Society in Atlanta.

Ben Epstein and I put together books on the Radical Right,

one of them dealing exclusively with the John Birch Society. They did provide much of the background information for the effort to make the John Birch Society anathema to the American people, which eventually happened.

Robert Welch died in 1985 in his eighties, apparently somewhat senile. Toward the end his mental confusion evidently caused internal problems among those charged with trying to make sense out of his paranoid notions. Welch's death brought a major change in the character of the organization—to the relief of many observers. The Society was obliged to abandon many of its early extremist ideological attitudes. In existence to this day, although quite changed, the organization is of little concern any longer to Jews or others. But the impending sociopolitical disaster that our country was to suffer because it had failed effectively to repudiate right-wing extremism was *not* turned aside by the decline of the John Birch Society.

12

Joe McCarthy Plays Poker

The man who dominated the political scene in the chaotic fifties was, of course, the junior senator from Wisconsin, Joseph E. McCarthy. McCarthy should be understood not only as a man and a senator but as an expression of powerful anti-democratic forces in the American body politic. It was not just what he did or said that gave the senator his significance—it was the savage reponse of the tens of millions of people who *believed* him.

People love spectacles. Senator McCarthy substituted senate hearings for the Roman Colosseum festivities. He staged gladiatorial games to tremendous roars from his followers, and his hearings had no more to do with justice than the outrages perpetrated at the Colosseum had to do with real sport.

The senator, having initiated a brutal spectacle, had to keep the show running, and like the impresarios of the Roman arenas he searched the provinces for victims. Any victim would do. His objective, in the end a compulsion, was to keep the show—and its attendant hysteria—going. The traditional association of Jews with human freedom, combined with the anti-Semitic poison that had been insinuated into the American bloodstream, made

116

Jews an almost defenseless McCarthy target in this time of political hysteria.

My own experience with Senator McCarthy began with George Sokolsky, the reigning potentate of anti-Communist journalism in America, who was much more than a Hearst columnist. He served as advisor to Hearst officialdom about the political Left, a sort of father figure to younger like-minded writers and a mentor to certain prominent politicians fixated on the Soviet Union as an instant threat to the United States.

I first met Sokolsky in the late forties, just after the Hearst press printed a sensational report charging Franklin D. Roosevelt and so-called international Jewish financiers with participating in a worldwide Communist conspiracy. The story was based on fraudulent documents from questionable overseas sources. Before that incident was closed by front-page apologies in all Hearst newspapers, we were privately informed by Hearst officials that the "exposé" had been sent out over its wires at the instruction of Marion Davies, the ex-actress and William Randolph Hearst's mistress. The piece was distributed to the Hearst chain, it was explained, on a weekend when nobody in authority was around, and at a time in Mr. Hearst's life when he was no longer able to concentrate on journalistic details. Miss Davies, allegedly with no one's approval, had approved the release of the story directly from San Simeon, the castlelike home on the California coast she shared with the legendary publisher. Because San Simeon was the source, it was assumed down the line that Mr. Hearst himself had approved the release. At least that was what they told us. I confess that the notion has occurred to me that Mr. Hearst's reputation was being protected by his underlings at the expense of Miss Davies, of whom, it was no secret, Hearst officials were not especially fond.

In any case, Jews exploded in anger at the false accusations. My telephone rang. It was George Sokolsky, speaking on behalf of the Hearst Corporation, to introduce himself. A dreadful mistake had been made, he suggested, and he had advised his people that they ought to meet with ADL officials to discuss a

117

solution. Would the League be agreeable, and could I help set it up?

We invited other Jewish organizational leaders to accompany us, and a large and friendly meeting with Hearst officials followed. We came away from it with a good working relationship with the heads of the newspaper empire. In the years that followed, wherever we found ourselves at odds with something in the Hearst press, we could sit across a table to iron it out. The League also received a generous annual contribution to our work.

This was the background when some years later in late November of 1951 the phone rang again with Sokolsky on the other end. Senator Joseph McCarthy, said the columnist, had become increasingly disturbed by the growing misapprehension among Jews that he was anti-Semitic. Mr. McCarthy, he added, would welcome an opportunity to meet with appropriate League officials to clarify the situation, since he considered himself free of religious prejudice. In an aside Sokolsky assured me this was so. Could I be of assistance in putting a meeting together as I had in the Marion Davies matter?

Sokolsky's call posed a sensitive problem. Most in ADL believed McCarthy was continuously violating the constitutional rights of individuals. Many thought him to be anti-Jewish, others worried that he might be, while a handful were still reluctantly willing to give him the benefit of the doubt. Yet after careful deliberation we unanimously concluded that ADL had an obligation to meet and hear out the senator, otherwise we would be open to criticism if we were to charge him at some future time with anti-Semitism—something we had not yet done—without having given him a chance to be heard when he requested it. After all, it had been our policy to meet with all but avowed professional bigots—leaders of the Klan and such—when we were asked for a face-to-face meeting by people complaining they had been falsely charged with anti-Semitism. A United States senator, no matter our preconceptions of him, was entitled at least to the same courtesy and fair treatment.

I returned Sokolsky's call to tell him that ADL was agreeable to meeting with the senator but only on one condition—that the session be off-the-record, not be used in any way by the senator, and nothing be released publicly about it except by mutual consent. No problem, said Sokolsky, proposing a dinner meeting in a midtown New York hotel where he, personally, would be the host; a private suite where we could talk comfortably in a relaxed atmosphere. Agreed.

Representing the ADL were its National Chairman, New York Supreme Court Justice Meier Steinbrink, Henry Schultz and Edmund Waterman, both highly regarded members of our National Commission, Ben Epstein and myself.

We arrived at six o'clock, prepared to spend as much time as needed. In the vortex of the national controversy about the menace of domestic Communism, into which the Jews had been unfairly dragged, this meeting could be of great significance and consequence. As counsel to the League I was asked to state our case at the appropriate moment.

Introductions were made all around and Sokolsky opened the session by repeating what he had told me: Senator McCarthy was disturbed by growing rumors that he was an anti-Semite. He wanted to dissuade Jews who believed him bigoted. He hoped the Anti-Defamation League, the nation's acknowledged Jewish organization in matters of this kind, would listen to his views, question him if necessary and conclude that he was a man of goodwill.

A waiter appeared to take orders for drinks, and the senator used the interruption to smile, engage in banter and small talk. Our side was virtually silent and stiffly formal, as if to signal that the matter at hand was too serious for mindless chatter. "Aw, come on, fellas," urged McCarthy. "I've had a tough day, a tough week, a tough month. Let's relax and talk like friends."

The waiter quietly rolled in a small bar stocked with assorted whiskies from an adjoining room where a table was set for dinner. The senator called for a double scotch. Most of the others ordered drinks. Sokolsky did not. Ben and I did not; we had rules for ourselves in these kinds of situations and they precluded risking a careless tongue loosened by alcohol. But the social break gave me the opening I was waiting for. As the group settled back I spoke up:

"You should know, senator," I began, "that to our knowledge you are correct about the attitude of many Jews. They believe you are, in truth, less than friendly to our people. They come to their view by the number of professional anti-Semites you have allowed yourself to be surrounded with, and with whom you have cooperated in political propaganda. Although you yourself, so far as we know, have not been guilty of anti-Jewish pronouncements, the conclusion is your actions demonstrate that in fact you are bigoted. If you are unaware of the message you have been sending out, you are a victim of your own insensitivity. If you know what you are doing, it's a worse problem."

The senator was surprised but held himself in check. He had not expected this kind of candor. Still smiling, seemingly affable, he called for another double scotch, inviting the others to join him, while asking me, please, to document with specifics what I had just charged. As I talked, Sokolsky became visibly angry and made no effort to hide it. I pretended not to notice.

In the next fifteen minutes I summarized our case. Admitting that what I had asserted could be labelled an accusation of "guilt by association," I stressed there was scarcely a professional American anti-Semite who had not publicly endorsed the senator while supporting his every action. Yet there was no evidence, I added, of his rejecting these people or their praises, an obligation he could not escape as a public official. On the contrary, he had repeatedly gone out of his way to utilize their less blatant materials in his speeches and writings, thereby indirectly endorsing their views. His staff had frequently been seen publicly in their company, I said, and the League was able to document that some of his employees had more than once been involved in some very questionable political shenanigans. He himself, I pointed out, had actually graced the platforms of notorious propagandists who often barely skirted the edges of religious prejudice.

I then named Upton Close, an example of a well-known radio bigot, as one propagandist whose material had been approvingly inserted into the Congressional Record by the senator. I specified other examples of cooperation McCarthy had extended to this professional anti-Semite.

Because the Senator asked for specifics, I continued with additional documentation. I spelled out for him the role his own office's investigators had played in scandalous anti-Semitic attacks on the respected and honored Mrs. Anna Rosenberg when President Truman named her assistant secretary of defense. I identified one of the senator's staff as a man who had traveled to New York with a "leg man" for Fulton Lewis, Jr., another radio commentator widely considered to be a clever and subtle anti-Jewish bigot. And I said that we knew the purpose of the trip was to seek documentation for the case against Mrs. Rosenberg from one Benjamin Freedman, an affluent, self-hating apostate Jew who had spent untold thousands of dollars purchasing, reprinting and disseminating widely the anti-Jewish materials produced by the nation's worst professional anti-Semites. I told, too, how the two men, the one from Fulton Lewis' office, the other on the senator's staff, had carried a letter of introduction to Freedman from Gerald L.K. Smith, one of the most notorious bigots in the United States.

When I paused for breath McCarthy interrupted to explain that with his heavy, overwhelming responsibilities he simply was unable to keep track of all these small matters, or to catch up with staff errors, or to issue denials to the press about his allegedly questionable relationships. The others in our group picked up the argument.

Sokolsky caught my eye, nodded for me to follow him and walked into the bathroom near the foyer. I followed. He was almost apoplectic. "How dare you, are you crazy? Have all you people gone mad? He's an important American senator. I asked you here to make peace with him—not to declare war. You've got to go back there and calm things down. Build friendships, not more walls."

"George," I said, "you invited us here to discuss this subject. He himself suggested we tell him why he is suspect by so many Jews. He was the one who asked for this meeting. He demanded to know why Jews thought badly of him. If you didn't want facts and candor you shouldn't have arranged this. You shouldn't have expected anything less." I turned and walked back into the meeting.

Ed Waterman, trying to stop what had now turned into an argument, asked all to allow him to ask the senator a question. Looking at McCarthy, who was still drinking scotches, he said: "Senator, tell me what you think you are doing in America. Tell me if you think you are good for America, never mind the Jews."

McCarthy was now ever so slightly in his cups, just on the edge but certainly not drunk. Instead of responding, he suggested tempers were short all around. Wouldn't it be better, he asked, to stop at this point and have dinner? The waiter thereupon took the orders but told us that dinner wouldn't be served for some twenty minutes. "Tell you what," said the senator, speaking to Henry Schultz, "you play cards, Henry? Gin Rummy? I'll play you a couple of games while we're waiting."

"Okay," agreed Henry, more, it seemed to me, not to ruffle the senator any further for the moment. "I'll play you one game, he said, one game only. And for a single dollar."

"You're on," replied McCarthy, picking up the telephone and ordering a deck of cards to be sent up fast as possible. Within minutes they were brought in, and with the rest of us watching, the two men played a game. In five minutes it was over. Henry had won. McCarthy drew a single bill from his wallet, held it out to Henry, paused and asked Schultz, "Would you like me to autograph it for you, Henry?"

"No thanks," Schultz said quickly but good-naturedly. "First, it's against the law to mutilate American money," he said, "and then, your signature on the bill will make it counterfeit."

Everyone laughed; we were all relaxed and dinner was ready. The conversation at the table seemed far less acrimonious even though it continued to involve the senator's relationships with questionable elements. Now we were trying to establish a bridge, although neither side softened its position. Off the subject, Sokolsky treated us to a dissertation on the difficulties of exposing Communism in America, with millions of citizens, he said, sucked into it by "commy blandishments."

McCarthy talked of his ideas and plans for the future and declared, for the first time in the long evening, that he intended soon to speak out publicly against anti-Semitism and anti-Semites. He would, he assured us, be more careful in the future not to permit himself to be used by the bigots or tarred with their brushes.

Dinner lasted well over an hour, during which we all roamed the political spectrum, the tension and animus having dissolved in the good food although we remained apart in our views. The senator had drunk his way through the evening but showed no real signs of its effect; he was, as they say, a man able to hold his liquor. Someone reminded the assemblage that both sides had promised a ground rule that the session was off-the-record. At the end we all agreed there was no need at this point to release any public statement about the meeting. We all bid McCarthy and Sokolsky good night with thanks for dinner and for the opportunity to exchange views and left the two of them in the suite.

About a week later the story of the meeting broke in the press, subtly distorted to give a false impression of what had occurred, and we "brilliant" ADL leaders at last recognized that we had been had. *The Capital Times* of Madison, Wisconsin, led off its front page report with: "An attempt by U.S. Senator Joseph R. McCarthy to establish a better relationship with the American Jewish community on the eve of his candidacy for reelection is revealed in an investigation made today by the *Capital Times.*" Analysis of the remainder of this news dispatch and others that followed satisfied us the senator himself had leaked the fact of the meeting. Interviewed, he told *The Capital Times* that "a number of things bothering some of the fellows were discussed" in a four-hour session that was "most profitable," and that he hoped other senators could join in similar sessions. McCarthy added that he had told our group he "has many friends among the Jews and that he resented the attempt that had been made to brand him as hostile to the Jewish people."

To make sure readers would be led to believe that the Anti-Defamation League did not regard him as an enemy, McCarthy revealed to the reporter that "the evening ended in a friendly game of gin rummy at which he lost two dollars to a League official." Perhaps I had been unaware of how his drinking had actually affected Senator McCarthy. Apparently he had been seeing double when he played that game of gin with Henry Schultz. How else explain his statement that *two* dollars had changed hands?

It was to be expected that sections of the press would pick up the story from Wisconsin. Readers everywhere were led to believe that ADL had concluded Senator McCarthy was innocent of anti-Semitism. Several daily newspapers and many Anglo-Jewish weeklies editorially accused us of wrongly allowing ourselves to be used by McCarthy. The New York *Post*, an ADL publishing friend, printed a particularly sharp attack on the League for giving the senator a lever to raise his level of political respectability.

McCarthy won the skirmish; he had used us effectively. Our public response to his violation of confidentiality did little to undo the damage. ADL leadership would allow us to say to the press only that at Sokolsky's intervention we had sat down with the senator to give him an opportunity "to present information regarding his position on issues of interest," that we met, dined with, talked to and heard the senator's "detailed description of his activities in recent years," that it was part of our responsibility to sit with government officials who wanted to discuss matters related to our interests, that the talk was informal, the meeting involving no "commitments on either side nor any endorsement of the senator's political activity."

Many months later Henry Schultz, as chairman of ADL, released a statement to the press analyzing McCarthy's political antics, charging him with doing our country a great disservice and suggesting there was little reason why Americans, Jews included, should put any confidence in the man. It remained for Ben Epstein and me, in early 1956, four years later, to spread on the record fifty-six pages of detailed charges against Joe McCarthy, effectively an anti-Semite, in a book called *Cross-Currents*.

13

The Rosenbergs

The impact of the lie that Communism-is-Jewish was so powerful that few non-Jews were surprised to learn two people named Rosenberg were identified as a part of the Communist spy apparatus. Worse, the mere indictments were satisfactory evidence to many that Father Coughlin and all the others back in the early forties had been absolutely correct—Jews were at the center of the American Communist movement. The federal charges against the Rosenbergs "proved" the truth of the lie that if you scratched a Jew you found a Communist.

The Rosenberg case played itself out in the fifties. Most Jews were profoundly disturbed when Julius and Ethel Rosenberg, husband and wife, were indicted by the government, accused of giving atomic secrets to the Soviet Union. Named along with them was a close relative, David Greenglass, Ethel Rosenberg's brother, and others. All Jews.

After an initial silence to evaluate the situation, the Leftist movement announced that the Rosenberg indictment was sheer anti-Semitism, and its leaders organized a crusade to be carried out across the United States. Speakers thereupon reached into Jewish communities everywhere in an effort to convince Jewish audiences that the indictment had to be fought to protect Jewry in the United States.

The response of the major national Jewish defense agencies, almost without exception, was to get in touch with local Jewish federations, synagogues and temples, Jewish community councils and other Jewish bodies cautioning them that Communist sympathizers had instituted a propaganda campaign and would be attempting to use Jewish platforms to urge protests against the Rosenberg "injustice."

ADL participated in the joint effort but avoided any prejudgment before and during the trial, taking the position the defendants were innocent until proved guilty. The others did the same. Refusing to presume in the absence of convincing evidence that the case was inspired by anti-Semitism, we all also reserved judgment on that score. Needless to say, most Jews hoped it would clearly develop that anti-Jewish bigotry was not a factor *and* that the Rosenbergs would not be found guilty. We were sickened by the whole spectacle, and frightened by the potential impact of the trial.

Our central concern was twofold: to counter efforts of anti-Semites to make bigoted hay out of the Jewish backgrounds of the defendants, and to prevent the case from being used by Communists for their own political purposes.

But our approach was not altogether accepted. The indictment of the Rosenbergs and our efforts to prevent a harmful fallout created a schism in the Jewish community. Jewish defense agencies were attacked by troubled Jewish voices contending the charges against the defendants could be rooted in anti-Semitism. These elements welcomed an opportunity to hear the arguments and resented the advice coming from Jewish organizations.

Our response was that all should, of course, hear both sides, but not under Jewish auspices. The Rosenbergs were indicted as Americans, not as Jews, we said. And we argued that by opening a synagogue or other Jewish facility as a meeting place for a Communist-sponsored campaign, those who did so were simply confirming in the minds of many that Jews were soft on

Communism, that the malignant accusation had, in fact, a basis in truth.

After the Communists' pro-Rosenberg campaign ended, the intramural Jewish controversy it had provoked made it evident the Jewish establishment generally had not welcomed the leftist intrusion or its spokesmen. This provided proof enough for some Christians that the Jewish community, as represented by religious Jews and others who belong to Jewish social centers and the variety of organized Jewish entities, had not been hoodwinked by the Communists. Moreover it was affirmation for some non-Jews that Jews, as such, had been defamed by anti-Semitic propaganda based on the poisonous notion all of us were Communists.

What can't be avoided here is the admission that Jewish defense agencies were themselves prompted more by fear and insecurity than principle in urging Jews to avoid allowing extreme left-wingers to utilize their facilities. It perhaps indicates the extent to which we were all terrorized by the frightening smear that Jews generally were Communists. And it demonstrated the general public mood of the time as well as the insecurity of the American Jew during that period.

Despite all our efforts there was an unfortunate fallout from the finding of Rosenberg guilt. The death sentence made for a continuous front-page story that lasted several years. The execution of the husband and wife illogically convinced millions of credulous Americans that the conventional wisdom was true—if you stabbed a Jew he bled political red. The facts, it was said, were now clear. Here were Jews found after fair trial to have been at the very center of a subversive conspiracy, to have given an awesome scientific secret to a foreign enemy, the Soviet Union, for military purposes. What more did one need to know? To primitives across America the conviction of the Rosenbergs and the continuing campaign of their supporters long after their deaths confirmed the accusations of the professional anti-Semites operating across the country. The damage the propagandists did to Jewish reputation was incalculable.

* * *

The Rosenbergs

Like so many others, Jew and non-Jew alike, I suffered deep pain when the Rosenbergs were executed. Had anti-Semitism been behind the indictment? Jews were among those who played major roles in the case, on the investigatory and prosecutory levels. The government lawyers were mainly Jews, as were the supporting witnesses for the prosecution. The federal judge, Irving Kaufman, who tried the case (and who has been pilloried relentlessly since the day the trial ended) is a respected, practicing jurist and Jew with a record before and after the case that is sound and liberal.

Did the case go forward from its inception because of the anti-Semitism of the day? Was it precipitated by and did it move ineluctably toward its verdict of guilt because of widespread anti-Jewish prejudice nurtured for so many years by the very bigots we had fought so hard to defeat? Although the national atmosphere was poisoned with hatred for Jews, the court record contains persuasive evidence supportive of the court's finding of guilt. But books have been written charging the evidence with having been falsified. Do these accusations contain truth? Don't ask their readers; responses depend on preconceptions. Books have been written defending the honesty of the evidence, too. For those who come to the subject innocent, books alone cannot provide definitive answers. The truth went to the grave with the defendants.

On June 19, 1953, the Rosenbergs were put to death. With the perspective of time, and measured by the sentences given out to the many other convicted spies since the Rosenberg years, the immutable punishment they suffered does seem remarkably excessive.

14

Swastika Epidemic

Anti-Communism with its anti-Jewish ingredient had to take its toll and it did. A synagogue bombing today in an American city would generate no special excitement or newspaper headlines. Occurring with persistent frequency in recent years, as such violence has, American sensibilities are now numb to these abominations. For many Jews, too, such acts today produce little more than momentary expressions of shock, then are quickly forgotten.

But back in the winter of 1951, the Holocaust still fresh in mind and Jews sure even a brazen professional anti-Semite would hesitate to emulate Hitler's storm troopers, word of Florida synagogue bombings was upsetting front-page news. In rapid succession in Miami, rifle shots had pierced a Jewish Center during a membership meeting, a second synagogue was severely damaged by a dynamite explosion, at two others several sticks of explosives were discovered just in time, while a Black housing development, a school building, hotel, cemetery and even a police station were the targets of similar racist violence. Miami Jews were profoundly shaken. ADL national leadership urged its National Director and General Counsel—Ben

Epstein and me—to fly to the southern city, meet with local authorities and satisfy ourselves everything possible was being done to arrest the culprits and prevent a repetition. Fairly certain that we could do no more about what had happened than other observers, but equally sure we could not convince our leadership of this, we agreed to make the trip.

I should not have.

In the long span of time since those early synagogue bombings, we have had plenty of opportunity to study the phenomenon—the character of the culprits, their motivations and the extent of the senseless damage they cause. Over the thirty-seven years since Miami, episodes of anti-Jewish outrages, including bombings, vandalism and other related types of damage to Jewish institutions, add up to thousands. Between then and now there was one nine-week period nine years after Miami, in 1960, when this kind of desecration and destruction erupted in overwhelming number, striking Jewish communities across the United States, Western Europe and Latin America. The "swastika epidemic," as it came to be called, began with an incident Christmas Week, 1959, in Cologne, Germany, and apparently triggered the wave in our own country. Before it subsided the following March we counted more than six hundred such cases. Synagogues, Jewish Centers, well-known Jewish residences, schools and even retail stores were among the targets. Anti-Jewish dabbings were the prime feature of the ugly phenomenon.

Expert observers disagreed about the number of incidents that could be charged to professional anti-Semitic groups and how many were likely the work of unrelated individuals or juvenile gangs. Nor was there accord on the conclusion of some specialists that the rash of "incidents" in the nine weeks was the consequence of imitative behavior. It was noteworthy that despite the worldwide character of the attacks, ADL investigators failed to turn up evidence of an international conspiracy. But there was little doubt in our minds that the flood of occurrences reflected a widespread underlying anti-Jewish hostility reaching from the Atlantic to the Pacific.

Research showed the perpetrators were primarily youths between the ages of thirteen and eighteen. When they were caught their explanations hardly if ever touched on anti-Semitism. However inane their vandalism, they were shrewd enough to deny bigotry. While their parents tried to portray the desecrations as mindless pranks, the misdeeds for us were patent evidence of anti-Jewish feelings. What they proved, tragically, was that anti-Jewish prejudice was in the very fabric of the American community.

Once the epidemic ended we found ourselves again counting domestic attacks on Jewish property in the earlier numbers—the low hundreds each year. For reasons I no longer recall, perhaps because we simply yet lacked the foresight, while the League did keep comprehensive records of reported desecrations or other damage to Jewish religious institutions we did no statistical analysis of the data until 1979. Since then this is the history: in 1979, 129; '80, 377; '81, 350; '82, 829; '83, 670; '84, 715; '85, 638; and '86, 594.

The year 1987 showed a national increase of 17 percent over 1986, in actual count 694 incidents of anti-Jewish vandalism and desecrations including 10 arsons and bombings. The largest number occurred in New York with 207 such outrages, followed by California with 62, a disturbing increase in that state of 121 percent over the previous year. These 1987 figures do not include 324 additional incidents of anti-Semitic physical assaults, personal threats and harassments. Add to all of this the countless unreported attacks, likely many times more than the known numbers, and only then does a truly accurate picture of the situation begin to take shape. Fairly shocking. Yet there was no great reaction across the country: Americans had become inured to this kind of unspeakable violence.

Observers who would deny that such data prove the presence of widespread anti-Jewish attitudes need to answer some questions. How explain the insistently large number of incidents and their geographic spread? If not bigotry, what does cause this behavior? Where did these young people learn to hate? They weren't born bigots, didn't pluck their hostilities out of the air or, acting alone, invent the idea all over the place at the same time. They learned it in the world around them, and therefore the blame must logically be laid at the doorstep of the American people themselves.

Entirely different, of course, is the damage inflicted on Jewish religious institutions by young, neo-Nazi "skin head" groups operating in Chicago, San Diego, Los Angeles and Miami, and by professional bigots operating out of Klan organizations or its various offshoots. Here are terrorists, American style, who are obviously poisoned with anti-Semitic hatred requiring a totally different social therapy. The Miami bombings, for instance, were of that character; professionals were discovered to be behind them.

I said earlier I should not have made the trip to Miami. Looking back, it is hard to believe I went. The kindest view is that my visit was unforgivably thoughtless, and my preoccupation with Jewish defense work little excuse for the trip. Miami happened when our son, Stubs, was past his fifth birthday and May was about to give birth to Jayney. The start of my wife's labor, the doctor said, was anyone's guess. We were both happy about the coming event but somewhat concerned because of our bad experience with the first baby. It was in this circumstance in my personal life that the Miami bombings occurred.

An old reliable friend, Julian Koock, was perfectly willing to assume my filial responsibility—the traditional role of getting one's wife safely to the hospital when the time comes. Which he did, and Jayne was born a healthy and bright little beauty— which she still is—Julian performing his job to its completion, taking May and our new baby home when the hospital signed them out. But I was not there with my wife at a major, difficult moment in her life—if only to hold her hand. I missed the joy, too, of being with her and the baby from the first moment.

Home from Miami, my mistake only vaguely beginning to penetrate, it remained for my discerning mother to offer an unforgettable reprimand. Was I married to May or to my work? Did I have a greater responsibility to my job or my wife? With such poor judgment in my personal life, how reliable was my professional insight? May wryly commented: "I have always understood Arnold's needs. In this case I was appalled by his priorities." Her words still linger in my conscience. It was a guilt never buried, a lesson never forgotten.

15

David Ben-Gurion

By the beginning of 1953, five years after I first met my Israeli friends, it was clear to them that my heart was in the right place and that I didn't balk at trying to respond to Israel's expressed or unspoken needs. It was also clear that neither Ben Epstein nor I knew a great deal about Israel and certainly nothing first-hand. Yet we were still working hard in its behalf.

One obvious way for our new friends to correct the gap was to invite the two of us to visit Israel. Because there was little likelihood that our American-centered agency that had yet no major pro-Israel program would care to underwrite the substantial cost of the journey, Memi deShalit and Teddy Kollek suggested we go as guests of the prime minister. To our delight, we were also told our wives were welcome to come along.

Four weeks in Israel cemented us to the Jewish state. The Epsteins and Forsters were, no question, swept off their feet by the country and its people. It's hard to remember now how undeveloped the parched desert was, how treeless the stony hills, how enthusiastic and proud its pioneers were of their new state, how cohesive its people. The pride and achievement was infectious as we walked through the only cement plant they had built in their entire country, their one pencil factory, the single soapworks, the new campuses in their college and university system, the last a national project evidently regarded as of basic and overriding importance.

Food in the new state was strictly rationed; two eggs a week for each inhabitant and rarely red meat regardless of one's position in the country's power structure. As guests, our small party was privileged to be served eggs and other scarce dishes in hotel dining rooms. We quickly learned to invite others to our meals whenever possible, making certain to order what was allowed to us and pass it to friends.

Our hosts had laid out the red carpet—car, driver and guide included. Of course, after the two young Israelis assigned to us got over the shock of our youthful appearance, we all quickly became fast friends; before our arrival they assumed that the heads of the national Anti-Defamation League had to be middle-aged.

The week wasn't out when Shimshon Arad, our native-born British Army–trained guide from the Foreign Ministry, at the suggestion of his wife Bela invited us to his father-in-law's home for dinner; his own place presumably inappropriate for "company." Bela's father had been in the land for many years and was already an old *Halutznik,* a pioneer; he could afford to receive his daughter, son-in-law and friends at home for a meal.

The older Israeli was rough-hewn. He did not bother to wait until dinner was over before castigating American Jews and his own government. The combination of the two, he fiercely insisted, would ruin Israel before it got a chance to grow up. "American Jews, pouring their money into the Jewish State, and our government doling it out to newcomers makes it too easy, spoils them. Let them do it the hard way," he fairly shouted. "The way we had to do it. It made men of us. You American Jews will make mice of the new immigrants." Son-in-law Shim smiled benignly but pleaded with his eyes for us to understand. Bela supported her father.

It was April, and Passover was to begin during the second week of the trip. Thoughtfully our hosts had arranged for the

four of us to attend a small family Seder at the Jerusalem home
of Isaac Halevi Herzog, the Chief Ashkenazi rabbi of the country. We could not believe our good luck. Dressed to the nines,
at least by Israeli standards, we cautioned our driver to let the
four of us out a block or two short of the rabbi's home in order
not to be seen riding in an automobile on the first night of
Passover. We did not know the custom in Israel but were taking
no chances and walked the rest of the way.

As we reached the entrance to the rabbi's home, a car pulled
up to the curb and out stepped two couples obviously also heading for the Herzog residence. It seemed natural to introduce
ourselves. And so we met Chaim Herzog and his younger
brother, Yaacov. Chaim, on holiday leave from the Israeli Embassy in Washington, D.C., where he was serving as Defense
Attaché, had already completed a term as Israel's Military Intelligence Chief. Yaacov would become advisor to Ben-Gurion
during the 1956 campaign, and the main architect of Israel's
relationship with the Vatican. Chaim introduced himself as
"Vivien," a nickname laid on him in the British Army by his
Irish officer who had trouble properly pronouncing "Chaim".
Yaacov said he was called "Jackie" by friends.

The only other guest for the Seder, a visitor for the holidays
like ourselves, was the Grand Rabbi of Ireland, and old friend
of the Herzog family from their former days in Ireland.

The Seder service was a delight. Ben and I were invited to
lead portions of the recitation and I hated myself for having
taken Hebrew school so lightly thirty years earlier. Correct and
traditional but informal and lighthearted, the reading of the
Jewish escape to freedom from Egypt was interrupted from
time to time by pertinent asides from those around the table.
Jackie was brilliant, showing a vast knowledge of Jewish history
and current events that he blended to the Passover holiday,
making its story politically relevant in ways I'd never thought
about before. His erudition made the others of us feel ignorant.
Vivien's intermittent comments, on the other hand, were brief
but cogent and equally wise. For both of them the Haggadah
story signalled the prophetic Jewish return to Jerusalem, and

they were so obviously proud to be part of it. The Passover service seemed for them a very personal celebration of the fulfillment of the prophecy and of the freedom it at long last brought to persecuted Jews. No other religion, it was pointed out, so celebrated the principle of freedom.

During that three-hour ceremony we four visitors learned more about the inner drives of the original Israeli leadership than at any other discussion we had during our stay. Primary was the prayerful return at long last to the Jewish Holy Land. The Jews of Israel had coalesced and were motivated as one. Theirs was a mission, not a goal. What had happened to the Jews in the Holocaust was never to happen again. Although not the original stimulus for the birth of the nation in 1948, it was nevertheless a central purpose of the new state. That and the certain knowledge that they would rebuild firmly on the ashes of recent Jewish events, so that the world would know Hitler had failed, and God would know that the Jews, the People of the Covenant, were fulfilling their promise to Him. They were bearing witness to His existence.

An amusing note to that Passover Seder at the rabbi's home: During the after-dinner portion of the service the gentle snoring that bubbled through the long white beard of the Grand Rabbi of Ireland lent a touch of earthiness to an otherwise esoteric experience.

We became friends of both brothers. Fourteen years later Jackie was named Director General of the Office of the Prime Minister. By then I was doing my "Dateline Israel" radio broadcasts and he appeared on my microphone to explain why his country was refusing to negotiate the question of Jerusalem with the Arabs. He made a most persuasive case that by every count—religious, historical, political and military—no Israeli government worthy of the name could consider the Arab conditions for peace—the geographic diminution of Israel or elimination of Jerusalem, and remain long in power if it did.

Still young, Jackie seemed destined to reach the highest political heights. It was not to be. In his prime, not long after our broadcast, he became ill with what seemed an undiagnosible disease and died in 1972. Authoritative reports after his death suggested it had been a brain malignancy.

My friendship with "Vivien" Herzog has lasted to this day. At my radio microphone three or four times over the years after he was appointed his country's ambassador to the United Nations we also did a national half-hour television program for "Dateline Israel." Vivien's topic was the need for the strongest possible military defense of Israel; a tiny nation, he said, surrounded by overwhelmingly larger enemy nations, trying at the same time to lift itself up by its very small bootstraps. And thank heaven, he added, for the support of America. Vivien's elevation many years later to the presidency of Israel caused no interruption in our long relationship.

The next afternoon we set out to the north for the highlight of our visit to Israel. David Ben-Gurion had sent word that he would like us to stop by at his vacation retreat and visit with him for a few days. The prime minister and his wife, Paula, were staying for the holiday at the Gali Kinneret, a modest little hotel on the shore of the Sea of Galilee. It was out of season for the lakeside resort and the inn was empty except for the prime minister and Mrs. Ben-Gurion, his entourage, some housekeeping staff and the four Americans from the Anti-Defamation League.

It has never stopped being a wonder to me that Epstein and Forster, comparatively young men with no particular records of accomplishment and surely with no pretensions of importance in the American Jewish community, were regarded as worthy of the invitation. Apparently Israeli officials misconceived us to be of sufficient authority and influence to warrant being virtual house guests of the single most important figure in the Jewish nation. Or maybe we were a revealing measure of their dim view of the American Jewish establishment. But there it was, under the same roof with the Ben-Gurions, relaxing from the arduous tourist tasks traditionally imposed on first-time visitors to Israel, and scheduled to confer with the head-of-state.

We arrived too late in the evening to meet the prime minister and Mrs. Ben-Gurion; they had already retired for the night. But we were told we would have breakfast with them on the veranda at eight A.M. It had been a long day and we were glad to be shunted off to bed.

At eight sharp in the morning we were introduced to Paula and David Ben-Gurion, who obviously had much earlier finished their meal and were having a second tea. The informality of the introductions and the conversation that followed would have misled a bystander into believing we were a group of lifelong companions. Ben-Gurion, short, heavy, an unruly bush of prematurely white hair a dominant feature; she, unpretentious in a house dress, open and direct. Paula talked about the mundane problems of Israel and asked about mutual friends back in the States; we talked about the excitements and pleasures of our visit. Evidently she was a mixture of plain housewife and overprotective nurse, who took her responsibilities seriously but not herself. Her seeming simplicity enabled Mrs. Ben-Gurion to ask blunt questions or candidly tell people when they should go home to let the prime minister get some rest. An honest and direct woman.

Breakfast finished, Paula invited our wives to stroll the premises with her. It was her sign—no doubt sexist but traditional in diplomacy—that we men were to be alone for serious talk. So far it had only been the enjoyable superficialities. The prime minister got to it quickly. Would we two please describe to him in full detail the work of the Anti-Defamation League, its *raison d'etre*, the nature of our leadership, organizational successes, failures and future plans.

Ben and I were experienced in making joint presentations. We spoke eagerly, with conviction, pride and enthusiasm. It was easily a forty-minute statement, the two of us tossing the ball back and forth.

Ben-Gurion listened intently, cutting in only to ask a question here or there. We spelled out problems we thought Jews faced in the United States, the role they played in government, business, in the media, in the professions. Describing the barriers that limited Jewish opportunity in education, employment and housing, we spelled out how we had been fighting those restrictions, and we told some harsh truths about organized anti-Semitism in America. A listener could have been led to believe that Jews in the United States were burdened with a minor kind of second-class citizenship—which would have been correct—but we ended on an upbeat note of achievement and change.

When we finished, the prime minister took a deep breath and said, "So if all the Jews in the United States were to pack up and come here, you wouldn't need an Anti-Defamation League, and you would save yourselves a lot of hard work."

I have no clear memory of how we fumbled our answer to *that* one. But moments later Ben-Gurion got to his feet, sighed, and said he had some reading to do and promised to see us later in the day. He disappeard and we went to find the ladies.

We did not see Ben-Gurion again until the following day, again at breakfast. There he was, with Teddy Kollek, a member of his staff, at his side taking notes. "Good morning," all four of us said at the same time as we settled into chairs.

"Boker tuv," replied the Prime Minister. "You ought to be able to say it in Hebrew if you plan to remain Jewish," and adding gently, "did you sleep well?" Without waiting for an answer, he turned to Ben and me: "How much do you think you will be able to achieve with your Anti-Defamation League? And will it make a great difference?"

"Only the future will tell," said Ben, "but surely it won't hurt."

"It might be worse without us," I added.

"How will you know?" the prime minister persisted. But then, relenting, he quickly added, "Never mind. What you are doing is important. Don't stop. But if you do, come and settle here."

He then returned our touristy compliments of the day before, lecturing us about the joys of being Jewish in Israel. He was clear that to succeed, the Jewish State needed the sympathy if not the support of the Western world. It was equally clear that he regarded Israel an integral part of the West but expected that with the passage of time and the return "home" of Jews from everywhere, the State would develop a character uniquely its own, a mix that would make it truly Near Eastern. His phrase— *What it was in the time of the Bible.*

The German nation owed the Jewish State an enormous debt, he said, and he had no reluctance stating they should repay it with reparations of every kind. I asked the prime minister if he didn't think that in accepting large sums—the cost of an Israeli railroad, for example—from the former Nazi nation he was sullying the memory of the millions of Hitler's Jewish victims. "If they were able to speak from the grave," he replied, "our Jewish people would tell us we must do everything to make sure our state grows strong. So that it will not happen again. If we don't we betray their memory. A homeland for the Jews is an answer to Hitler."

Itzhak Navon, today a member of the Israeli Cabinet after a stint as president of Israel, and a beloved leader of his country, was staying at the hotel with the Ben-Gurions, part of the entourage. Newly installed as the Prime Minister's "political adviser"—a rather impressive title for what I suspected at the time must have been a somewhat lesser responsibility—Navon was more a young political aide.

Each in our fortieth year, Ben and I were somewhat older than Itzhak. He was kind enough to extend a welcoming hand, spending some of his free time with us, explaining, informing, teaching the enthusiastic strangers something of his country. It is not unique in the Jewish State for a visitor to become fast friends with an Israeli even before knowing how to spell his name. And that's the way it was with Itzhak and us four. Paula, too, extended herself, and before the visit was over we were treating each other like members of one small family, on a first-name basis. All except Ben-Gurion, whom we addressed as Mr. Prime Minister—out of respect, not because he seemed to want or expect it.

Across the lake was Kibbutz Ein Gev, the first home in Israel of Teddy Kollek, who had by then already gone on to be part of the Ben-Gurion government team. A music-and-dance festival was scheduled at the kibbutz and visitors were welcome with tickets. Shimshon Arad easily arranged for them before taking off for home for a few days.

After dinner as we set out for Ein Gev, Itzhak Navon offered to drive us there in his jeep. We were delighted. Paula then invited herself along, and we were even more delighted. The jeep took us around the lake to the kibbutz. Walking down a wide path to the big canopied amphitheater, I said to Itzhak that there were six of us and we only had four tickets. "No problem," he said, "I'll sneak in and Paula will simply explain she is Paula Ben-Gurion, the wife of the prime minister."

May interjected, "But couldn't anyone claim to be Paula Ben-Gurion?"

"No one else would admit it," Itzhak chuckled.

After the concert Itzhak turned his jeep over to another member of the prime minister's staff, and a police launch took the six of us home across the lake. In twenty minutes we were on the dock and then the path to the hotel. It was near midnight, everything had been closed up and most lights were out. We entered the lobby and were beginning to say our good nights when Paula asked if we would like some tea and cookies before retiring. Seemed like a great idea. "Fine," she said, "we'll all come to my quarters and I'll boil up some water." Opening her door carefully, Paula turned to us and warned, "Let's be quiet. Ben-Gurion may be asleep."

Tiptoeing into a very large room, we saw a cot bed in the far corner, and in it Israel's sleeping chief of state. Stopping dead in our tracks, the four of us started to back out. "Come in, come in," insisted Paula. "He's snoring and won't wake up." We begged off, whispered our good nights and backed out of the door.

The third and final chat with the prime minister the next morning was actually an amiable cross-examination of Ben and me. Ben-Gurion was hungry for information about the attitudes of the American non-Jewish community and of the United States government itself. How confident could Israel be of continued support from across the Atlantic? Under what circumstances could the Jewish State *not* depend on American loyalty? Who were Israel's major enemies in the United States? Our responses were reassuring. We, at least, had faith.

Between our arranged activities at the lakeside hotel we had found time during the visit to spend with various members of the prime minister's staff, listening and asking questions, and we went away convinced more than ever that the Israeli ship of state was in most competent hands. David Ben-Gurion was singleminded to the point of obsession about building Israel, a thoroughly balanced and convinced zealot. Our deep respect and regard for Israel's founder and statesman, David Ben-Gurion, never waned.

16

The Garfield Case

A star of stage, screen, radio or television could be stopped in his professional tracks by the floating of a rumor he had been seen at a Communist gathering, or that *The Daily Worker* had praised him for extracurricular political activities. Sidney Lumet, a television director of extraordinary talent, was under suspicion and summoned to explain himself because a player in a TV drama he directed had been charged with left-wing affiliations. Shirley Temple was the actress under the gun for suspicious activities, which, it later turned out, happened before her *tenth* birthday. Edward G. Robinson, Gene Kelly, Katherine Hepburn, Lena Horne, Richard Conte, Paul Henreid and countless others found themselves named in the files of the House Committee on Un-American Activities because a West Coast Communist newspaper reported their names had appeared in a leaflet supporting a rally sponsored by the liberally oriented Progressive Citizens of America. The House Committee on Un-American Activities, dubbed by cynics "the House Un-American Activities Committee," held the PCA to be a "demonstrably Communist-front" operation, adding, "When the Communist Party's newspaper says you're "in there pitching on

145

the side of the common man," it doesn't mean you're a rank and file member of the Democratic Party. It means something else."

What that "something else" was supposed to be had been left to the imagination of the reader. But imagination was sufficient to cause those named in the report to be called to account for their activities, and they had better have convincing explanations. In case after case after case.

Albert Dekker, well-known character actor of stage and screen, and a loyal American who could trace his ancestry to the Civil War, was proud of his heritage. A resident of Hastings-on-Hudson in Westchester County just above New York City, Dekker lived in the original home of Admiral Farragut. He liked to remove a wide and long hardwood plank from his living room floor, cut it up into many pieces, fashioning each in the shape of a serving platter, then polish, shine and varnish them for distribution as gifts to friends.

Dekker's problem was that some years before he returned east from a Hollywood film career he had interrupted his acting roles to serve as a California state assemblyman. While in the legislature, among other "suspicious" deeds, he had been master of ceremonies at a function for American Youth for Democracy, an organization the House Committee on Un-American Activities dubbed a cover-up for the "Young Communist League."

Dekker counterattacked and fought hard, denying Communist sentiments or affiliation. Denying without proof of purity was a mortal sin in the eyes of zealot anti-Communists. By the time he found his way to me, Dekker was unable to secure work in Hollywood or on the New York stage. He told me that although he was not Jewish he believed the League was morally obligated to help him; he had been defamed. I helped arrange performing dates for dramatic readings at *B'nai B'rith* lodge meetings across the country. We became good friends, and soon he was referring others who found themselves in similar blacklisted circumstance.

Many prominent film personalities were simply gullible

146

Americans lost in the intricacies of international politics. I won't dwell on each of them; the stories are too similar. But some had unique aspects. Judy Holliday, for example, comedienne of stage and screen, visited me, talked of her difficulties, received some suggestions and departed. I never studied her record and I never heard from her again. But some years later George Sokolsky informed the Un-American Activities Committee that I had sent her to him for guidance. I don't recall that, or the outcome.

Lee J. Cobb, the burly and brilliant star of *Death of a Salesman* and other fine films and plays, stopped by one summer day at my Fire Island home in Ocean Beach, New York, introduced himself and without telling me who had suggested he see me mentioned he was having more and more difficulty finding roles. It was clear to him, he said, that those who were turning him down for work were not candid about why. Their explanations were patent camouflage; evidently his real problem was political, not the alleged unsuitability for the roles he wanted.

I volunteered to help, offering to bring him together with activists in the anti-Communist movement. But I warned him that to win their help he would be obliged to answer questions about his past political activities. I could offer him no advice on this matter of conscience. But he would have to say outright whether he was or had been a Communist. Those were the rules he would have to play by, and he would have to decide for himself whether he was willing to do so.

Cobb went away without revealing anything about himself and I never saw him again. About a year later, in June 1953, the press reported his appearance before the Un-American Activities Committee, where he admitted former Communist Party membership, the price for permission to return to work as an actor. I deliberately played no role in persuading Cobb—or anyone else who came to me in trouble—to bare his secret; that was not my way. My concern was with actors or actresses, many Jews among them, who had been unfairly condemned and blacklisted without credible cause. Or who had attempted to make peace with the forces of McCarthyism only to be rejected

147

by the hysteria of critics. It was never my place to suggest to a blacklist victim that he or she reveal personal political history as the price of rehabilitation.

Larry Adler, the harmonica genius, was a case in question. He came to see me at the suggestion of his former stage partner, Paul Draper, a leading dancer and choreographer of the thirties and forties. After one session Adler learned from me I could not be helpful. He arrived at my desk with a large chip on his shoulder. Convinced he was a victim of anti-Semitism, he heard that I was sympathetic to blacklisted performers and might be helpful. He sat with me for an hour or two, emotionally recited his constitutional rights and demanded to know whether I would arrange an appointment for him with Francis Cardinal Spellman. Why that, I wanted to know. Because, said he, the root cause of his trouble was among certain elements in the Catholic Church who were the heart of the McCarthy Movement. They were responsible for what was happening, for the destruction of civil liberties in our country, for the deprivation of the right to work if one did not agree with the political majority. And he wanted the opportunity to explain this to His Eminence and ask him to help stop it before democracy was destroyed.

I declined to help in this fashion and he left unhappy. Many years later, from his permanent residence in England where he had become an expatriate, Adler publicly attacked me for suggesting that he submit himself to anti-Communist professionals who would help him recant. No truth whatever in his charge; his memory had betrayed him. The irony is that Larry Adler, at some point in his long, unsuccessful struggle against the black-listers, took an oath that he never was a Communist. And likely this was true. In any case, how sad for our country to have lost him and his musical genius; part of America's punishment for not having effectively rejected McCarthyism sooner.

In March 1952, it was almost four years since my letter of appreciation to John Garfield for his participation in ADL's *Blueprint for Freedom*. Now, again, he was on my mind. While my brief encounter with him at the Waldorf had been long forgotten, at the same time I was, of course, aware of the whisperings about Julie being trapped in the McCarthy hysteria. My days were preoccupied with the McCarthy movement and its tragic fallout on theatre and motion picture people. I never tried to analyze what exactly motivated me to move into that particular blacklisting aspect of the McCarthy campaign. If I had turned my back on the blacklisting problem because it had no clear anti-Jewish quotient, no one in ADL would have raised questions. I guess maybe my own lifelong attraction to the stage and desire to be part of those who were in that world had something to do with it.

It was gossiped in motion picture circles that John Garfield was on the Hollywood blacklist and finding it almost impossible to secure acting roles. As I would soon learn from him directly, he had not made a movie in nearly two years, although his last, *He Ran All the Way,* had been a blockbuster. In those two years Julie had appeared in some inconsequential summer stock and been featured briefly, nine weeks to be exact, in a revivial of *Golden Boy.* For his role, he was paid eighty dollars a week, minimum equity scale. This for an actor who had earned hundreds of thousands a year, today's equivalent of millions. It was not a lack of talent. John Garfield was a brilliant star of stage and screen. He was out of work for political reasons . . .

The switchboard operator rang to say there was a Mr. Garfield on the phone. A moment later: "Arnold, this is Julie. I must see you." He didn't say, "This is John Garfield" or "This is Jules Garfield." Only, "This is Julie."

"What's up?" I said in a false matter-of-fact tone, then added as if I had heard from him only the day before, "How are you?"

"I'll spell it out when I see you. Sam Shaw thinks you can help me." His voice was low, dead serious–sounding and worried. "Sam offered to phone you. I told him never mind, I'll call you myself, that the two of us have known each other a long time."

We made an appointment for the next morning at my office. Sam must have told him something about my current activities, probably to persuade him to see me. And Sam probably also told

Julie more, such as that my name had once been "Fastenberg" just as his had once been "Garfinkel." Sam was like that. Perhaps he had touched a button in Garfield's head, switching on a light about a relationship Julie had long forgotten. The only other possibility is that Julie had played a game with me at the ADL dinner four years earlier. Except what would have been the point? (In the days that followed and until his death three months later, neither Julie or I ever mentioned to each other his Waldorf appearance or the relationship of our high school days, and I never learned the answer to that mystery.)

Julie walked into my office precisely at nine the next morning. Our receptionist went into mild shock when she recognized the star. A moment later we met in the corridor as I walked from my office to welcome him. "Glad to see you, Julie," again as if it were an everyday occurrence. He mumbled something to the same effect.

Julie was different now, no longer the chesty young lion exuding confidence, older than his thirty-nine years. For the next two hours it all poured out. He had done everything possible to clear his name, he said; had told the House Committee on Un-American Activities all there was to tell, had "eaten shit" all over the place. Bitter, feeling humiliated, he said he couldn't remember who they all were. "It hasn't done me a goddam bit of good," he added. "Nobody believes me."

As he talked Julie sounded, by turn, strong and fighting mad, weary and resigned. But always impatient and frustrated. He had used the best lawyers, had followed purportedly expert advice, had reached out in many directions and was now, in desperation, coming to me because Sam had told him I had succeeded with a handful of others who had been in his situation. Maybe I could perform a miracle.

I explained to Julie how I'd been approaching the problem for others before him. My role was different, I said, from that of other lawyers, public-relations experts, press agents and the like, all paid people who had acted in behalf of prominent movie and theatre figures accused of being Communists or active sympathizers. I came to it *pro bono,* from an agency that was chartered to defend against defamation, that had a reputation for reliability and accuracy and that had stepped into this situation because McCarthyism had both the smell of anti-Semitism on its edges and the appearance of outrageous unfairness in an area of human relations that was of concern to us.

We agreed to meet again when Julie would bring his entire file for my study. And we conferred frequently after that. It was essential that I know everything he had done politically—how and why. A game plan was needed, one with no holes, and one that would stand the most searching scrutiny. Surely it would not be easy to turn Julie's problem around. As he said, he had already tried everything.

I spent hours with Julie's documents spread out before me and asked endless questions. The more I probed, the clearer it was that John Garfield, world-famous actor, was inexcusably hurt by the wave of irresponsible anti-Communist charges and paranoia rolling across our nation, drowning an untold number of other equally gullible but innocent liberal Americans. It appeared to me that Julie's political and professional involvements, spread over a twenty-year period, were overwhelmingly on the non-Communist, pro-democratic side. At the same time he had without question time and again in these efforts joined paths with some undoubted Communists.

We now had to win acceptance for Julie's stated position from the newspaper contacts I described, and the corroborative evidence of his innocence. And we had to go public, all out, with an anti-Communist position. I asked Nat Belth, ADL's chief press representative, to join me in our efforts, and we became a threesome.

Julie laid before us a two-inch thick document, "Statement about John Garfield." It had been drawn up by his attorneys Louis Nizer and Sidney Davis and submitted to the House Committee on Un-American Activities when he appeared before it the previous year. It was an impressive, persuasive and carefully detailed account of his political and professional activities bearing on his attitude toward Communism. The formal presentation opened with the statement he had released when he first had been subpoenaed to appear before the Committee: *I have always hated Communism. It is a tyranny which threatens our country and the peace of the world. Of course, then, I have never been a member of the Communist Party or a sympathizer with any of its doctrines. I will be pleased to cooperate with the committee.*

This unequivocal declaration was followed by a second affirmation that he was not and never had been a Communist, actually or ideologically, in fact or in sympathy, always a liberal and loyal American with no divided allegiance, a registered Democrat who had contributed liberally to the party and actively campaigned for its candidates with the exception of his support of Wendel Willkie, Republican presidential candidate.

Julie documented these statements beginning with his attacks on the Nazi-Soviet Pact back in 1939. He then set out a distinguished record of *pro bono* civilian service with the armed forces in World War II, entertaining in dangerous war zones, visiting every base in the Caribbean area at the request of General George Marshall and travelling more than forty thousand miles in doing so.

The statement went on to tell how Julie helped organize the Hollywood Canteen, raise $600,000 for Veterans Hospitals, sell countless hundreds of thousands of dollars worth of War Bonds and make speeches to more than a million Americans in behalf of the war effort.

Julie also revealed he had tried to enlist in the army as a private but had been turned down as an overage married man with two children; that he had given blood innumerable times and that he had once almost been killed when an exploding shell missed his moving jeep outside Cassino, Italy and then again while flying in an army transport that lost an engine on a flight from a Portuguese base to Marrakech in Morocco. He spelled out attacks on him by left-wingers for his crossing picket lines in motion-picture labor disputes and his support of the right-wing Screen Actors Guild on which he served for six years. He told of his substantial contributions to various Catholic charities, navy relief, Red Cross drives, Disabled American Veterans,

Salvation Army and many more. Hardly the stuff of a Communist or sympathizer. To insure no misunderstanding over what he stood for, Garfield then listed citations that had been levelled against him, each suggesting the possibility of sympathy with Communism, and convincingly explained away each one.

Incredibly, none of this helped. Every explanation was rejected, mostly because of a single response he gave to the House Committee on Un-American Activities when he was on its witness stand being questioned under oath at a closed hearing: *He swore that to his knowledge he had never met a single Communist in Hollywood.* This solitary statement, made in a moment of great apprehension when already unnerved by the destruction of his career and wounded by false accusations of disloyalty, was his undoing. Several days afterward the committee leaked to the press that it was seriously considering forwarding the transcript to the U.S. Department of Justice to examine it for a possible perjury indictment. My subsequent inquiries about this during my research into the various aspects of Julie's blacklist status revealed that the committee almost routinely sent records of testimony of many Hollywood personalities to the Justice Department. I also learned from friends in Justice that Garfield's matter "was never even near any indictment."

So this was the nub of his problem—his oath that he had never met anyone that he knew was a Communist, and the rumor of his possible indictment. We decided on a course of action to persuade two or three of my newspaper contacts in the anti-Communist movement that Garfield was not a Communist sympathizer in spite of the endlessly repeated charges to that effect, and that his pro-democratic record was so ample and substantial that minimal fairness required he be allowed to resume his career.

We agreed on two other simultaneous approaches. Julie was to accept public, noncommercial appearances that would confirm where he stood politically, and he was to write an in-depth article, setting forth how he had been sucked into contributing to some Left Wing causes that were tainted with Communism. The key to the proposed article, its underlying assumption, was to be that Julie was naive and careless, never troubling to look closely or ask probing questions about the political orientation of men and women who had sought contributions or the use of his name for what seemed worthy causes.

I had no difficulty in persuading Victor Riesel, the anti-Communist labor columnist, that Garfield was an extraordinarily gullible liberal or at worst, a political fool. A side trip convinced Frederick Woltman, Pulitzer Prize–winning anti-Communist columnist for the Scripps Howard newspapers, of the same thing. He promised to write about accepting Garfield as a good American.

Riesel thought we ought to involve columnist George Sokolsky, the potbellied sage to both Senator McCarthy and the House Committee on Un-American Activities. Sokolsky agreed to receive Garfield and listen to him. Riesel and I went with Julie to Sokolsky's apartment on New York's West End Avenue, where we spent several hours. When Sokolsky seemed to approve what we were doing, we left to prepare clarifications of Garfield's positions and previous answers on the subject of his questioned record. Sokolsky promised us he would assure everyone of Garfield's bona fides if we followed through.

In the meantime I okayed Julie's public appearances at an April 30 "Fourth Birthday Party for Israel" at Ebbets Field, sponsored by the Israel Anniversary Committee, and at a Hunter College student rally where he attacked Communism. Several days later we had him at a Waldorf luncheon sponsored by the Home and Hospital of the Daughters of Jacob. All the while Victor Riesel was spreading word in the ranks of the anti-Communist forces that John Garfield was *not* a Communist, not even a Communist sympathizer. Just one big damn fool who carelessly permitted himself to help unworthy Left-Wing causes and unwittingly allowed his name to be used by politically sophisticated, camouflaged Communist sharpshooters.

The groundwork was being carefully laid for Julie's big public article that would once again repudiate and denounce Communism, but which would, for the first time, explain how he had been lured into being used. The path to professional reaccept-

The Garfield Case

ance would be eased by a new visit to the FBI, when Julie would answer questions that had been left open the last time around. Several weeks later, in April, accompanied by his counsel Sidney Davis, Julie performed this chore, apparently with satisfying results. He came away elated with the way things were going.

Toward the middle of April the job of writing the article that Julie was to sign was completed by Belth and myself. Julie had worked long and hard on it with us. Entitled "I Was a Sucker for a Left Hook," we decided to offer it to Look magazine, the picture publication that also carried popular articles and was, at the time, the only serious competitor of Life magazine in the field. "Shap" Shapiro, vice president in charge of circulation, was a very close friend. He agreed to submit the piece for publication. But toward the end of April it was rejected by Bill Lowe of Look's editorial department as "slick, nonspecific and a special plea." At my suggestion Shap asked for reconsideration and I agreed to go back to the writing desk with Julie. Lowe said he would "take a look at a better job," but he was "not very confident about the prospect." It was a setback that turned Julie glum again, but he was willing to stay with it.

When John Garfield's wife Robbie learned he was working with me on a proposed article for a national publication, thereby helping clear his name, she was upset. Apparently Julie had told his wife the approach he was taking in the piece. On any grounds, Robbie had no cause to be upset with Julie for what he was trying to do to extricate himself from the blacklist. Apparently, though, she resented my efforts in his behalf because she thought I was letting him surrender to the blacklisting gang.

Robbie, according to Julie, refused to understand his need to make some accommodation. She did not want him to bend to the knee before those she regarded as contemptible and detestable McCarthyites. She said so to Julie. The argument that followed was so heated that Julie packed a bag and checked into the Warwick, a quiet semiresidential hotel in mid-Manhattan. It was clear to me from some of his remarks that his staying away

155

from home was a temporary matter. Julie said little about the argument during the frequent sessions at my home, but one day he left early, explaining he was going home to pick up his young son David to take him bike riding in Central Park.

On Monday, May 19, Julie telephoned to say he could not meet me during that day. He arrived, instead, at 9:30 in the evening and worked with me way past midnight. He was back at my desk midmorning Tuesday for an additional eight-hour session, all involving a revision of his article that he hoped would satisfy the editors of Look. He left before nightfall. I never saw him again.

In the news stories about his sudden death, the press said that on Monday evening he joined some cronies at cards—it had to be after he left me at midnight—and played until dawn Tuesday. According to Iris Whitney, an actress friend Julie had recently turned to for advice, he telephoned her in the early evening on Tuesday, apparently just after leaving me, and the two of them went to dinner at Luchow's, the legendary turn-of-the-century German restaurant on Fourteenth Street in Manhattan. If the press was correct, it would mean Julie went without sleep for thirty-six hours before he met with Miss Whitney.

Iris Whitney went on to tell the police that Julie became ill at dinner and couldn't finish his meal. She persuaded him to walk back to her nearby Gramercy Park apartment to rest. She knew about his previous heart attack and was obviously worried.

That first attack had been seven years earlier in 1945, and the press at the time reported Julie had collapsed on a tennis court in Beverly Hills. While working with him on his blacklisting problem he mentioned the reason for his collapse. Shooting a difficult scene for a movie, he explained, had taken the better part of a day because the actress playing opposite him repeatedly blew her lines. His role, he said, was that of a prizefighter, and the script called for him to be working out on a punching bag while having a dialogue with the leading lady. The repeated takes left him tired but not so weary as to stop him from going directly to the tennis court from the studio.

His doctor later told him he had "torn a muscle in his heart," a damage that would be permanent but not necessarily disabling. I have no way of knowing whether he correctly repeated his physician's diagnosis, but I do know that in the news reports after Julie's death the story of his collapse at tennis was slightly different from what he had told me. The press had it that playing the role of a prizefighter, Julie was doing a rope-skipping scene while chatting with a little boy who flubbed his lines again and again, making endless "takes" necessary.

In any case, when Iris Whitney returned with Garfield to her place he stretched out on her bed and went to sleep. Iris told police that in the morning she got up from the couch in her living room and went to wake Julie up. Unable to arouse him, she immediately phoned his physician, who arrived quickly, examined Julie and pronounced him dead. It was ten A.M. Wednesday morning.

Even in death Garfield was denied relief. Journalism's McCarthyites picked over the anti-blacklisting actions of his final days, distorting Julie's efforts to vindicate himself. When the press asked me a day or two after Julie's death what I felt about Garfield, I said: "We went over his record pretty minutely and I was satisfied that Garfield had never been a member of the Communist Party. He was guilty of two things—of loving people and of being naive. For his naivete, he paid with his reputation." And, I sadly add, with his life.

17

"The Goddam Jews in New York"

Early in 1954 the late Herman Edelsberg, ADL's longtime liaison to the federal establishment, and I were discussing office matters at lunch in the dining room of the Carrol Arms Hotel, an old-world favorite eating place for Washingtonians that has long since disappeared. A waiter stopped at the table to hand me a business card. "It's from the gentleman sitting in the far corner," he said. The scribbled message asked simply that we join his table when we were finished eating. It was signed, "Joe".

I turned, searching the room, and spotted Senator McCarthy lunching in a far corner with Roy Cohn and Howard Rushmore. Cohn, still in his twenties, was already prominent as the Wisconsin senator's counsel on his Permanent Subcommittee on Investigations. A quick-witted young lawyer, Cohn's involvement with McCarthy disturbed many of his friends. Always nattily dressed, ever ready with a sardonic remark and an expert at razor-sharp repartee, Cohn made good newspaper copy. In New York legal circles it was thought by many that his father, Albert Cohn, a prominent New York appellate division judge, was uncertain about his son's career. Although proud of Roy's involvement and prominence in vital issues of the day, Judge

Cohn worried about the much criticized legal tactics that seemed the hallmark of his son's and McCarthy's investigations. Yet the judge was careful about his comments even among acquaintances. Most knew of his great respect for the First Amendment. I remembered the judge lecturing me for what he regarded an abuse of an anti-Jewish agitator's constitutional right of free speech.

Sitting with McCarthy and Cohn was Howard Rushmore, a member of the senator's subcommittee staff after leaving the Communist Party, and now a syndicated Hearst columnist. I already considered Roy Cohn a bad boy, a sentiment that had gotten me into a sharp tiff with a dear friend for taking exception to his nominating Roy for membership in the ADL's highest body. Cohn was a lawyer who should have known better, I thought, than let McCarthy ride roughshod over constitutional rights. He could have kept the senator from mistakes that hurt many innocents and damaged Jewish reputation in the process. Roy was among a small handful of men who manipulated the senator for their own private war on left-wingers and, truth to tell, the senator seemed to have no real understanding of the forces at play around him.

My objections to Roy, no secret from him, kept Roy out of the Anti-Defamation League, something he bitterly resented at the time, prompting him to tell Winchell we had rejected his application because he was "too anti-Communist." That slander confirmed what I thought about Roy. It mattered not at all to Cohn that two years earlier Epstein and I, director and associate director respectively of ADL, had written a book, *The Troublemakers,* that contained a serious attack on the Far Left. The volume, released under the aegis of the League, exposed the infiltration of Communists into the Civil Rights movement, charging they had intruded for ulterior political purposes. It scorned, too, Communist propaganda that held Capitalism responsible for racial and religious discrimination. (The distrust Roy and I felt for each other would last until his death.)

Now, here in the restaurant, I wondered how I'd be treated by him. Seeing me looking in his direction, the senator gestured hello and I nodded, indicating we'd be over shortly. I had not seen or talked with McCarthy since December 1951, more than three years earlier, when we had that counterproductive, "poker game" dinner with him and George Sokolsky. But in the meanwhile the senator had built himself enough of a record to convince me he was bad medicine. Not that the League itself, although recognizing the evil in the man, had yet become sufficiently resolute to attack McCarthy frontally. We were suffering from the same fear of him and his destructive, national movement, that affected so many others. ADL had been treading cautiously about him while demonstrating its opposition to his frenetic crusade. It was not until 1956, when Ben Epstein and I released our book, *Cross-Currents,* that we openly attacked McCarthy himself.

Shortly before our book, the League had spoken up in a lead article in our organization's bulletin over the signature of Henry Schultz, our national chairman. The subject was the disturbing tendency sweeping across our country toward blind and indiscriminate hatred for those with whom one disagreed. It pointed to the widespread practice of Americans extracting from each other a "new form of loyalty oath which does not express loyalty to the nation, but to the society of 'againsts.' " The trend toward conformity was "stultifying" it said, and could be "murderous." The article was critical of McCarthy, but omitted pinning the label of anti-Semite on him.

As Edelsberg and I now walked toward the senator's table in the Carrol Arms restaurant I could not guess what the reaction would be. Reaching the table, we exchanged greetings. Cohn's opening remark to me was, "How are all the goddam Jews in New York?"

"Fine. I had dinner with your father last night," I said, annoyed by his wisecrack, especially in front of non-Jews.

Senator McCarthy, holding a clipping from a magazine, asked whether I had seen the story accusing him of being a homosexual. In his hand was an article about a party attended or given by the senator in a Milwaukee hotel room in which a waiter, according to his reported affidavit, said he had witnessed obvious homosexual conduct among the guests. I had seen the piece.

"You're supposed to be a smart PR man," began the senator, handing me the tearsheet. "What would you do about this libel if you were I? Ignore it? Tell them off? Sue?"

I looked at McCarthy and said with a straight face, "Well, Joe, I don't know the facts. What did happen that night?"

He grinned. "Why, you son-of-a-bitch," he said, chuckling. "I'll bet you were the source for the story."

"Honest injun, Joe, I wasn't."

"Listen," said the senator, turning almost serious. "I can prove I once slept with three different women on one weekend. That would make my case, wouldn't it?"

"No. That might prove only that you're a degenerate." I grinned.

"I'm convinced you gave those bastards the story," McCarthy shot back at me, not, I believe, quite meaning it. "Suppose I call them up and convince them the story is a phony," he suggested. "Wouldn't that be good? Shouldn't I?"

He had opened the door for a tired old joke I was not above using. "Joe, if you succeed with the editors," I replied, "next edition the headline will be 'Senator McCarthy Denies He's a Homosexual'. So go ahead and fight it if you want another damaging story on the subject."

Some months later I heard that investigation revealed that the waiter who had prepared the accusing affidavit had spent time in a mental institution. But I don't know how true that story was, either.

Three or four days after the McCarthy meeting in the hotel restaurant my attention was drawn to Drew Pearson's nationally syndicated column, "The Washington Merry-Go-Round." In it was the colloquy between Cohn and me about "the goddam Jews in New York." Reported accurately, just as it happened, I guessed Herman Edelsberg was the source for Pearson. I had not given Pearson the item and, surely, none of the others would. Both of us were good friends of the columnist and we each fed him material. Next afternoon my phone rang and Roy Cohn was on from Washington, D.C. "Arnold, did you see the Pearson paragraph?" he asked, his voice very earnest.

"Yes, of course."

"I would like you to answer a question honestly," said Roy. "When I made that remark about Jews, you knew I was kidding, didn't you? I was making a funny, wasn't I?"

"Roy, are we talking for the record?"

"I don't know," he said quickly. "Do you have a recording machine going?"

"You tell me first," I answered, adding that I could not imagine an intelligent Jew making the reported remark with any seriousness, only in bad taste, even if in jest.

The truth is neither of us was recording the conversation, and neither believed the other was. I think.

18

Subpoenaed!

In 1956, a little more than four years after Garfield's death, my efforts in behalf of blacklisted actors came back to haunt me. McCarthyism was still tearing the country apart. The Fund for the Republic, financed by a Ford Foundation grant, had been established as an educational institute in the field of civil liberties. Progressive in nature, it undertook to conduct a study of blacklisting in the motion picture and radio-TV industries. John Cogley was selected as the director of the project and assigned to write the resulting report.

For more than a year a large staff of reporters and researchers collected evidence and information in an effort to answer troubling questions about blacklisting—did it really exist? If yes, how did it begin, who carried it out, who were its victims? Was "clearance" possible? If so, by whom and through what procedure? And who were all the players? Inevitably during the course of the fund's investigation Ed Engberg, a keen investigative reporter working close with Cogley, would be pointed in my direction by the suggestion that I might be a worthwhile source and likely sympathetically disposed. A correct evaluation and I was interviewed at some length.

Early in July 1956 a report, written by John Cogley, executive editor of *The Commonweal,* was issued and hit its mark, squarely on target. The impact shook up those in the private sector—Hollywood, the stage, journalism, radio and television circles—who were depicted as part of a loose national network of blacklisters. The report also nettled the House Committee on Un-American Activities, which was bitterly criticized for its role in the blacklisting drive. The committee's chairman, Francis Walter (D. Pa.), and his staff were infuriated at the charge that a combination of zealots, striking indiscriminately at Communists, sympathizers, well-intentioned liberals and total innocents, damaged or destroyed the careers of many of the most talented artists in the entertainment world.

Cogley described in depth how the blacklist was built up, the basis on which its accusations were published in books, pamphlets, reports and studies that listed the "guilty" together with their achievements and alleged political misdeeds. His report went on to describe the "security clearance system" by which accused performers, writers and directors were rehabilitated or assigned to the dustbin of unemployables. And Cogley hung much of his case, at least in its "clearance" aspect, on an unnamed "public relations expert" whom he quoted in explaining precisely how the rehabilitation process worked and who were some of its engineers. Among other participants tagged by Cogley's unidentified source were George Sokolsky, Victor Riesel and Frederick Woltman, the Pulitzer Prize–winning reporter of the Scripps-Howard newspapers. This is how he reported the comments:

A New York public relations expert who has guided more than a dozen once-blacklisted performers to the "right people," explained his role this way:

"If a man is clean and finds his way to me the first thing I do is examine his record. I look particularly to see if it includes charges that he is a member of the Communist Party. I want to find out if he is 'clearable.' Once I am convinced that he is

164

not a Communist, or if he has been a Communist, has had a change of heart, I ask him whether he has talked to the FBI. If he hasn't, I tell him the first thing he must do is go to the FBI and tell them everything he knows. I tell him to say to them, 'I am a patriotic citizen and I want you to ask me any questions you have in mind.'

"Then I find out where he is being blacklisted—where it is he can't get work, who in the industry is keeping him from working, and who outside the industry has made him controversial. If, for instance, I find it is the American Legion, I call one of the top Legion officials and tell him this man has come to me for help and says he is innocent. The official may say to me, 'Why, this guy has forty-seven listings and I know people who say they don't believe him.' But I say, 'I'm going to have him make a statement.' Then, when the Legion guy gets the statement and has read it, I call and ask him for a note saying he is satisfied by the statement. He will usually say, 'I won't put anything in writing but if anyone is interested have him call me.'

"Somewhere along the line I may find George Sokolsky is involved. I go to him and tell him that the Legion official thinks this boy is all right. If I can convince Sokolsky, then I go to Victor Reisel, Fred Woltman [New York *World-Telegram* and *Sun* staff writer] or whoever else is involved. When I've gotten four 'affidavits' from key people like these, I go to Jack Wren at BBD&O and to the 'security officer' at CBS.

"I wait a few days, then I telephone Wren. He may say to me, 'You're crazy. I know fifteen things this guy hasn't explained.' I ask him, 'What are they?' and he says, 'He didn't come clean.' So I send for the guy. He comes in here and he moans and wails and beats his head against the wall. 'I have searched my memory,' he will say. 'I have questioned my wife and my agent. There's not a thing they can remember.'

"I call Wren back and he says, 'When your boy is ready to come clean I'll talk to him.' In that case we've reached a dead end. My boy has been cleared but he can't get a job. I know cases where victims have sat around eight to ten months after 'clearance' before they got work.'"

A second possibility, the "clearance" guide pointed out, is that Wren will say, "I think you're right about this boy, but what do you want from me? I can't hire him." In that case, the public relations man said, the victim has to find a friend who is casting a television show and is willing to put him on the air to test his "clearance." If the attempt backfires and protests come in, the guy is through.

"Last of all," the guide said, "there is the possibility that Wren will pick up the phone and call a casting director or producer and say, 'Why don't you give Bill a part in the show?'" Once the blacklisted performer appears on a CBS television program, it is notice to the industry and to all the producers that he can be used.

The public relations expert concluded: "A guy who is in trouble, even if he has a good case for himself, will stay dead unless he finds someone like me who can lead him through the jungle of people who have to be satisfied. He has to persuade these people one by one. Usually he finds his way to a lawyer and that comes a cropper, or he finds a public relations man or press agent who doesn't have the confidence of the 'clearance men,' and he's only wasting his time."

I recognized the essence of the statement as mine. Surely I had said much of what was set forth. Not all of it and not in the exact words, even if Cogley did use quotation marks. It was Engberg's best memory plus his interpretation of what I meant, and fair. Pervading my statement but lost in the written synopsis was my carefully expressed overall attitude—that fundamentally we were dealing with blackmail, utilizing the only possible approach to save the professional life of the victimized artist, and that the entire process was disgusting but inescapable. I had frequently compared it to negotiating with a kidnapper; refuse and you lose your child. Cogley had telescoped the interview so that the statement was imprecise with respect to my attitude but substantially accurate with regard to the facts.

The press immediately urged that Robert M. Hutchins, President of the Fund for the Republic, produce the unnamed expert on whom the report had relied for its central thesis on "clearance." Mr. Hutchins refused, insisting it was entirely proper to withhold the identity of his confidential sources. John Cogley took the same position. I had exacted from his field investigator a pledge of confidentiality as the source of the information.

I am sure Hutchins and Cogley would have respected my confidence had they been pressed to the wall, so to speak, by the House Committee on Un-American Activities. But I couldn't keep silent in the face of their dilemma and the consequent damage to their credibility if I didn't speak up. At the same time, unfortunately, there was an underlying attitude reflected but not articulated in the remarks attributed to me that I considered inaccurate. I did not believe that Woltman or Reisel, on whom I had relied in some degree, were bad people. If I'd thought so I would not have sought out their help. My contacts in this area were small in number, and the names recited were the names I had used in the Fund For The Republic interview.

I sat down and got off a letter for publication to Woltman. Among other things, I wrote: "Although I do not consider myself a 'public relations expert', I recognize some material . . . as things I told an interviewer . . . I would be sorry if this particular section of the report were misinterpreted . . . I was visited by an interviewer for the project because of my long interest and that of the Anti-Defamation League in the whole problem of Communism, in the dangers of subversive activity and in the need to protect innocent people from invasion of their civil rights and civil liberties . . ."

Within a day or two, all I had written to Woltman was carefully set forth by him in his syndicated newspaper column, and John Cogley no longer had the problem of keeping his secret. Both of us were thereupon subpoenaed to appear before the Committee. So were Sokolsky and several others who had been named in the Cogley Report. Complaining that his health prevented a trip to Washington to appear before the Committee, Sokolsky instead sent a long and detailed letter. In it he denied there was any such thing as a "clearinghouse," adding that his efforts had only been "rehabilitative." He noted that roughly three hundred Hollywood people were able to return to work because of the kind of efforts he had made. Commenting on the Cogley Report itself, Sokolsky wrote: *"Reference is made to Victor Reisel, Fred Woltman and I (sic) acting together. This never happened, except that Victor Reisel came to my home one day with John Garfield. Just before he died, Garfield was preparing a statement in Arnold Forster's office, which he told me would show the relationship of Charlie Chaplin to Communist recruitment in this country."*

The Chaplin item was news to me.

For a week before the hearing, the press was filled with stories about the Cogley findings and the resulting attacks on him and the Fund for the Republic. Preparing to testify, I anticipated a thorough cross-examination about the Garfield matter. I thought it natural only because of the many press reports immediately after Julie's death telling about my role in the preceding months in the attempt to salvage his career.

It did not happen. Perhaps the reason the Walter Committee avoided the Garfield matter when questioning me was a little noticed paragraph in the Cogley Report quoting Richard Nixon, then a United States senator and a favorite of the Walter Committee. He had made a name for himself early on in the McCarthy era, playing a leading role in the anti-Communist campaign. Cogley represented Nixon as saying that "any number of actors suffering from unfavorable rumors were eager to appear before the Committee." But only three, said Nixon, were called, *"although the Committee had no proof of Communist Party membership, past or present."* The three were Edward G. Robinson, Jose Ferrer and John Garfield. Robinson, said Nixon, requested the hearing but Garfield and Ferrer were subpoenaed because they had been "the subject of considerable interest on the part of private organizations."

When the Woltman column first appeared, the press, of course, played large the discovery of the unnamed public relations specialist. My anticipated testimony would seem, to all intents and purposes, the key to the fundamental truth of the Cogley Report that both a blacklist and a clearance committee existed; flattering, to say the least, in face of all the denials.

168

Subpoenaed!

When I was identified in the press stories as general counsel to the Anti-Defamation League, some of ADL's leaders were immediately nervous for its reputation and about my involvement in the hearings. Most of our leadership, however, took the story in stride, not unhappy that ADL was revealed as an agency trying to help Americans who allegedly had been unjustly defamed. League laymen were overwhelmingly anti-blacklist and anti-McCarthy.

Before Cogley's appearance, Chairman Walter told reporters that the Cogley study "levels very grave charges against organizations and persons in the entertainment industry who have fought the Communist conspiracy." A spokesman for the House Committee told the press that his group wanted to find out whether "Forster is the unnamed public relations expert who is quoted extensively in the report about his experience in arranging for the 'clearance' of artists falsely suspected of pro-Communist leanings."

Cogley's subpoena called for him to appear and testify the day before my scheduled appearance. He now had no reason to hesitate about naming me as the so-called public relations expert. On the contrary, he had a perfect right to do so because I had publicly disclosed my identity. Before he left for Washington, Cogley paid me the courtesy of a phone call to tell me he was planning to share my name with the Committee. I told him to go right ahead, that he was completely free to do so.

Committee Chairman Walter received me on the stand as a witness he anticipated would be friendly and helpful. Together with his committee counsel he quickly took me through the preliminaries and the story of my efforts to help actors, and then reached the subject of clearance. The congressman was very pleased when I made it clear, under oath, that I did not believe those I had named as newspapermen helping me were enemies of civil liberties. I said they "were doing good, not evil." At that point, Mr. Walter thanked me and added, "You have confirmed our suspicion that this (Cogley) report isn't worth the paper it's printed on. I don't think there is a blacklist—"

"I think there is, sir," I contradicted, almost interrupting him.

"I define blacklisting as the denial of employment to a man on grounds other than merit without first letting him be heard." Chairman Walter was not pleased. He had anticipated I too would deny a blacklist existed. I went on: "This is a dreadful thing, the blacklist. If the Fund for the Republic report results in this kind of hearing, in public discussions across the country, if it does nothing else—regardless of its accuracy or inaccuracy on any point—I think it will have performed a great public service."

The chairman could not get me off the stand quickly enough. In his hurry to end my testimony before I did any more damage he muttered, "I think you are absolutely right, I thank you very much for appearing here today, good day."

Responding to press questions outside the Committee Hearing Room, I said the blacklist, to my knowledge, was the creation of a cabal of extremist self-styled anti-Communists using their cause to deny their victims the right to earn a living for having allegedly radical political views. Newspaper headlines the next morning made it evident the hearings had boomeranged. I had testified to the accuracy of the pervasive suspicion that an organized blacklisting operation actually existed on a national scale, the Committee's insistence to the contrary notwithstanding, as we lawyers say.

The Cogley Report on Blacklisting had come through unscarred. Official congressional testimony was now clear on "Blacklisting in the Movies, Radio and Television." It was a fact and a tragic calamity that no longer could be denied. This was the payoff I'd waited almost a decade for. Not a payoff to me personally; a payoff to all those who suffered blacklisting's cruelties, and to the band of courageous men and women who determined that history should depict McCarthyism as having been an American aberration rather than a traditional characteristic. I slept well that night in the nation's capital.

The irony of the McCarthy movement—blacklisting was only one facet of it—is that Senator McCarthy provided a marvelous smokescreen for the Communist Party International. The whole Communist propaganda apparatus trumpeted his every excess to the whole world every day. The civilized world was more revolted by McCarthyism than by Communism. Senator McCarthy provided the Communists with the greatest protective camouflage, one which their propaganda machine would never have been able to develop by itself. Senator McCarthy also paralyzed whole segments of American society by casting terrible suspicion among government agencies and foreign allies. No corps of Red agents could have accomplished so much.

Going through folders on the subject of blacklisting I came on a letter by Ed Engberg written a quarter of a century after Cogley's and my appearance before the Walter Committee. It was published in the February 1981 issue of *The Commonweal.*

Santa Barbara, Calif.

To the Editors: Like Michael Harrington (review of Naming Names, Dec. 19), I collaborated heavily in the getting up of the facts for, and in the writing of, the Fund for the Republic's report on blacklisting. I agree that Victor Navasky "has all the main facts right" as I know them and that, indeed, his "moral and political analysis is quite compelling." However, in the rush for medals and the chance to swap tales with the Veterans of Moral Anguish of the 1950s, one ought to pause to give thought to others who wrestled with their consciences, often with a good deal more at stake than we diarists and scriveners working under the well-endowed auspices of a safely established foundation.

I think, for instance, of Arnold Forster of the Anti-Defamation League. Navasky describes with care and sympathy the ADL's and Forster's response to the agony-inducing choice conjured into being by McCarthyism and the moral failure of politics and business "leadership." He does not recount, because he had no occasion to discover, that Forster was also the study's deep throat, so to speak. Without his help, I don't know that we should ever have been able to break out in the detail we did the hidden, jerry-built system that had been devised for the purgation and "clearance" of blacklisting's victim.

I was pointed to Forster by Philip M. Klutznick, then a Chicago-area real estate developer of generous and liberal vision, a force in Cook County politics and most recently com-

171

merce secretary in the Carter administration—a man, in short, who had little to gain except in the long run, and then not to himself, by giving me his cooperation. Forster, in turn, told me in detail how the clearance system worked, who the players were, how they worked, and why, in his shrewd judgment, they did what they did. It cost him an appearance before HUAC in which, under the circumstances, he committed himself quite honorably . . .

. . . Apart from the theological debates which seem to occupy the Old Left nearly as much as they do the New Right, we owe them a great deal—not the least for keeping alive a vision of that which we might become. This is only to add a bow, too, to the Arnold Forsters and Phil Klutznicks and Eugene McCarthys of the bedeviled fifties. And yet, look where we are.

Our next book, *Cross-Currents,* helped create a permanent record of our attitude and activities about blacklisting. The deadly headlines instigated by McCarthy and his counsel, the ambitious Roy Cohn, we wrote, caused irreparable harm to individuals and gave the country the impression that the defense establishment was loaded with disloyal American Jews. We nailed that lie. Another part of the book concentrated on specific cases of McCarthyism, citing major situations in which the movement had targeted numerous loyal Jewish-Americans, accusations later proven to be totally false.

Cross-Currents covered much more. It hit the bookstalls in 1956, shocking many "insiders" and numerous Americans out of a complacency that had resulted from the military defeat of Nazism and from some encouraging domestic progress in civil rights. The book documented the activities of many individuals on the fringes of national politics, and of some who functioned at the international level. It showed how these activities set up currents that disturbed the mainstreams of harmonious human relations, and exposed the fact of a worldwide anti-Jewish web. Another section of *Cross-Currents* focused on the resurgence of neo-Nazism in West Germany and on the ineffectual methods of the postwar German leadership in countering it. A third section examined the Middle East—its hatreds, tensions and dangers. The groups responsible for endangering peace there were named and numbered. There were the hard-line Arab nations disagreeing with their "moderate" Arab counterparts, fighting each other for territory and power yet achieving unanimity against the common Jewish enemy. Except for Egypt and some other slight shifts in alliances since that time, the big powers are still using their military muscle in the area's political game. As of this writing, nothing much has changed since then with respect to as the prospects for Middle East peace. It remains a volcano, at times seemingly cool on the surface, but boiling beneath and ever threatening to erupt at any moment.

19

"Danger on the Right"

By the mid-1960s we were deeply committed to fighting against a broad spectrum of racial and religious prejudice. No longer parochially oriented, our concerns stretched to Blacks, Catholics, Chicanos, American Indians and others. Yet our primary involvements reflected the impact of world events upon Jews anywhere and everywhere. But our major efforts weren't on the old concerns of our predecessors, who had been preoccupied with anti-Semitic stereotypes or harmful jokes told on the stage about Jews, or with newspapers that in reporting the commission of a crime described the culprit as Jewish while offering no similar information if the subject was not. And our attention to anti-Semitism was no longer limited to organized anti-Jewish bigotry but rather to the wider prejudice against Jews.

Racial and religious discrimination in the United States had become "pervasive and as dangerous as a plague in medieval times." An embedded discrimination had wrecked careers, invaded schools, tainted industry, corrupted leaders of our society, damaged the economy and, in this measure, infected every corner of our public and private lives. That it was a national

scandal was the essence of our new book, published in 1962—
Some of My Best Friends . . . A most outrageous illustration of
the quota system involved Emory University's dental school in
Atlanta, Georgia. The excuse one of its officials offered for barring Jews as dental students was that "they suffered a congenital
failure of digital dexterity." In plain English, the man was saying
Jews were physically unable to use their fingers as deftly as
non-Jews. This slight case of lunacy, incredibly, was offered by
a so-called professional educator.

The widening spectrum of our discrimination concerns saw
its parallel in our involvements in political bigotry. Of the several books Epstein and I did on the Radical Right, our 1964
study, *Danger on the Right,* had an obvious impact on the Birch
Society. Shortly after its publication the book was denounced by
the Radical Right's Man on a White Elephant, Barry Goldwater,
the senator who had been named the GOP's presidential hope-
ful. Goldwater said our book was "propaganda," and his anger
created national attention that helped make the book a best-
seller. The senator had shot himself in the foot.

Danger on the Right was an attempt to cauterize the nation's
Right Wing by forcing the separation of the genuine conservatives in its fold from the anti-Semitic and anti-Black bigots who
infested it. Several of the organizations and people we named
in the book protested they were not anti-Semitic. But ours
wasn't a study of anti-Semitism; rather it was a document expressing concern that the Right Wing had become captive of a
bigoted movement, a situation that could invite a national catastrophe. We were explicit that if they shook out the bigots we
would be content—in retrospect a bit preachy-cheeky on our
part, to say the least. But it worked. We made clear our view
that the Far Right would represent a perfectly legitimate political position so long as it remained untainted by anti-Semitism;
otherwise we exercised our right to criticize as forcefully as we
knew how.

Danger on the Right was dedicated to the memory of John F.
Kennedy. In a speech he never delivered, the late president

175

eloquently capsuled the mud-slinging problem of the day. Two paragraphs of that speech prepared for delivery in Dallas, Texas, on November 22, 1963, included:

> There will always be dissident voices heard in the land expressing opposition without alternatives, finding fault but never favor, perceiving gloom on every side and seeking influence with responsibility. These voices are inevitable . . . But today other voices are heard in the land. Voices preaching doctrines wholly unrelated to reality, wholly unsuited for the sixties, doctrines which apparently assume that words will suffice without weapons, that vituperation is as good as victory and that peace is a sign of weakness.

The conservative, William F. Buckley, Jr., and this writer have rarely seen eye-to-eye on most matters over the last three decades. And from time to time our differences have led to sharp criticisms of one another. The reasons should be clear to any reader who has reached this far in our story.

Under the name Neal B. Freeman, whoever he was, Buckley published in a September 1966, issue of his National Review a two-page piece entitled "Guide to Unsatisfactory People." (I can only imagine what the original title was before it reached the desk of the magazine's libel counsel.) Freeman's effort consisted of photographs of thirty-two faces identified as those of prominent people presented to subscribers for their "reading displeasure." A thumbnail caption about each was intended to be devastatingly clever. Sprinkled among left-wingers and an assortment of off-beat characters were such as the late David Susskind, William Fulbright, Robert Goulet, Drew Pearson, Ed Koch, Mark Hatfield and Yours Truly. Reserved for me was this snappy line: *"Arnold Forster,* whose every activity we are watching very, very closely."

The thinly veiled threat National Review directed at me was not a surprise. Especially in light of our publication of *Danger on the Right.* After all, we did devote twenty tough pages in the book showing Buckley to be a full-fledged member of an extremely conservative movement that perhaps witlessly encouraged Radical Right elements with supportive political rhetoric. Our study blamed Buckley for serving as a kind of ideological bridge between leading Radical Rights tinged with anti-Semitism and his own more respectable wing of the Far Right that was not.

But Freeman's labored derision failed as an answer to our documented analysis. *Danger on the Right* was written at a dangerous moment in American life. Anti-Semitism poisoning its philosophic baggage, the Radical Right was becoming a threat to the democratic fabric. Unless stopped in its tracks it could cause irreparable damage—our major reason for writing the book.

We respected Buckley's central position in molding National Review, his monthly literary creation, into an opinion journal of political consequences. But we trusted that its acceptance as such carried a responsibility to reject a mindless overlap with the Radical Right or a role as fellow-traveler. In the parlous sixties, Buckley's allowing that to happen we believed to be a political indulgence or luxury the nation could ill afford. Especially from a molder of public opinion who already had the good sense to issue a devastating denunciation of Robert Welch. (Likely, Buckley felt he had no alternative but to repudiate the founder of the Birch Society when Welch denounced democracy as an instrument for demagoguery and a "perennial fraud." He also could not ignore such a gem as this from the pen of Robert Welch: "President Eisenhower is a dedicated, conscious agent of the Communist Conspiracy.")

In *Danger on the Right* we made the point this way: "Buckley is too smart to accept the Radical Right mythology that the Communists are already in operational control of the country. Nor does he think the United States has been sold out by presidents who have been part of the Bolshevik conspiracy. What Buckley believes ails the United States in its domestic and foreign policy is liberalism and its seeming blunders. What Buckley calls liberalism, Founder Welch of the Birch Society call Communism, and the only essential difference is that Welch thinks the United States has been degraded by traitors, while Buckley thinks it's been degraded by blunderers . . ."

Buckley, we felt, was less forthcoming about the John Birch Society itself. In editorially repudiating Welch, he declared that the Society included "some of the most morally energetic self-sacrificing and dedicated anti-Communists in America."

With such significant disparities in political outlook between the Birch Society and Buckley, it could only be cause for regret that a perceptive and discerning conservative would lend his rhetoric to movements that supported causes and slogans of bigoted, radical origin. Our research for the book showed Buckley to be changing from an aging boy wonder of extreme conservatism—he was only thirty-nine at the time—to a major and respected figure on the American Right. But in the process he was sitting at the same rallies and applauding the same ideas as the Radical Right, sometimes making common cause with them even while sincerely avoiding their flirtation with anti-Semitism and ignoring their conspiracy-theories of American history.

It is worth noting that in the twenty-odd years since we released our findings, Robert Welch now dead, the John Birch Society has shed itself of its former anti-Semitic characteristics. In the same period Buckley, about whom we wrote in our book "he was no anti-Semite and will have no truck with anti-Jewish bigotry", has built a proper wall between himself and the politically lunatic conspiracy views of the Birch organization. Maybe *Danger on the Right* accomplished more of its purpose than we thought.

20

Nightmare: *In which it Hits Home*

The street lamp just outside our New Rochelle home reflected the blanket of white on the front lawn through the foggy library window. The trees were laden with clumps of snow, and tire marks scarred the snow on the street. It had been coming down heavily all evening, and the icy December 1965, night seemed colder, our home warmer. I was deep in a lengthy analysis of Mideast political events, waiting for the eleven o'clock news while our thirteen-year-old Jayney slept soundly. May, at her regular Thursday evening bridge game, was enjoying herself fifteen minutes away in Eastchester. Why she would go out on a night like this escaped me.

I grabbed the phone before the startling ring ended, trying to keep it from waking up our daughter. "Hello, is this Mr. Forster? "I am Dr. Frank speaking here at the hospital in Waltham, Massachusetts, near Brandeis University. I'm sorry to be calling you but . . ."

The next seven hours were an unforgettable nightmare. My chest began thumping as the doctor told me in calm tones that our son, Stubs, had been injured; how badly he didn't know yet. Stubs, he said, was discovered by a passerby some hours before, lying unconscious and badly bruised in the grass alongside a road on the Brandeis campus. Medical tests were being performed at the moment to determine the extent of his injuries but the results hadn't been determined. No, it was not an automobile accident, the doctor went on. Seems the boy was badly beaten by a gang of men, the Waltham police were investigating. You'd better come right away. Tonight. He hung up.

My tightly controlled voice on the phone call to May did not prevent her panic. She asked for details I did not have. In ten minutes, as Jayney finished dressing, May was at the door. She broke into tears, sobbing quietly as she packed a small bag after hearing the few details I could offer. The three of us bundled into heavy coats, mufflers and gloves and within minutes were driving on the Hutchinson River Parkway headed for Boston.

As the car wheeled along the icy slick highway we rode in anxiety-smothered silence. May kept brushing away tears. A bewildered Jayney, sitting alone in the rear seat, stared out the snow-covered window into the black night. Leaning forward, straining to see the road, I remember I kept muttering, "the sons of bitches, the sons of bitches."

After a long silence, Jayney spoke up. "Dad, why'd they beat up Stubs? Did he do something wrong?"

"They went after him, Jayney, because he's my son, your brother."

"Why, what'd *you* do?"

"I defend the Jews."

"Did the Jews do something wrong?"

"No. We're pretty much like all other people, some good, others bad. Of course some Jews are no good but that isn't why they dislike us. That's the excuse. It's because they think we're different, they think of us as strangers in their world. Some say we get what we deserve because in biblical days, so they were taught, Jews killed their Christ. Others are jealous because they think we're smarter and more successful, which is stupid. Frustrated people often need somebody to hate, to blame for their problems, and it's easy to pick on the Jews. But not all Christians do that. Not most."

180

"Is this going to be the way it is when I'm grown up?"

"Jayney, I used to think when all people have what they need, what every human being is entitled to, things like food, a decent place to live, freedom, a fair chance to improve . . . that it would stop. I don't think so anymore. Too many people have bad streaks in them—jealousy, anger, things like that. Jews will just have to keep on defending themselves . . ."

Jayney was silent again.

And I worried that I had been woefully inadequate in my answers to her terribly important questions.

My mind went back nineteen years to August 1946 when Stubs was born at Doctor's Hospital in Manhattan. May, twenty pounds above her normal weight, had been miserable and relieved at long last to be going into the hospital. August of 1946 had hardly begun but we were already in its dog days. It was midmorning when she trundled, heavy and swaying, through the maternity entrance. I held her by the elbow, as much to comfort as to help her, and carried the traditional overnight bag filled with pretty nightgowns, two light robes and an assortment of toiletries. May was scared but also excited. There was also some concern. Our fears had not been turned aside by the assurances of Dr. Freed, the obstetrician in charge, that this time was not like the last; all the right signs were evident and May would be having a normal healthy baby. Four years earlier he had made us no such promise, but at that time we didn't take notice. May and I realized how different this moment was from the earlier one. Four years before, no sooner had the nurse prepared May for bed than Dr. Freed suggested he and I go to his office several floors below. Innocently I had followed him, on the way asking the questions most expectant fathers put at such times. It wasn't until he had sat down at his desk opposite me, spun around in his chair and put an X-ray picture on the frosted glass hanging on the wall that I sensed something unusual. In the jumble of his medicalese I slowly began to understand he was telling me May would have her baby live but there was *no* chance it could survive very long; hours at most. Some sort of congenital heart defect, he said. And while the baby could live inside the mother with her help, it could not make it alone. His words were swallowed in my panic. The doctor made it clear there was no guesswork involved in his awful diagnosis, nor was there a chance of the outcome being any different from his grim prediction. Go back to your wife's room, he advised, and try to appear cheerful. "Smile to her and after a little bit we'll take her to the operating room, where I will force labor—which has already begun but not enough—and take the baby."

I felt cold. My whole body shook. I nodded and found my way back to May's room, eyes glazed and worrying about being able to carry off the lie. At least no need for that concern; she was sweating, in acute pain and totally involved with what was happening to her. She of course had no idea about the problem and paid no attention to me. As they wheeled her out I followed down the corridor and kissed her on the forehead before she disappeared into the elevator. Minutes later, walking in Central Park I began to cry but then managed to get control of myself. For two hours I wandered aimlessly on the paths and across lawns, two hours, then was back at the hospital at May's bedside. She was asleep.

The doctor had been right back then. But this pregnancy was different. Dr. Freed had sailed all smiles into May's room, examined her, made small appropriate jokes, the kind he had obviously told many times, and told me to relax. Calling for an orderly to take May down to the delivery room, he left us before the attendant arrived. May followed in minutes and I sat down in her room to wait. An hour or so later May was back, still sedated, her belly flat. The nurse explained where I could go to see our child. Scurrying down the hall, I stared through a glass wall into one of a row of cribs to see a tiny, wrinkled, beet-red gargoyle face topped with stringy yellow hair.

We named our baby "Stuart William" after nobody at all, only because we liked the sound of it. Then we immediately dubbed him "Stubs" because, even to us, the formal monicker we had just laid on him seemed too pompous for an infant. My father later complained that we had "spelled the baby's true name inside out," insisting it should have been "Menachem Mendel," after his own departed father. When Stubs was called to the Torah for Bar Mitzvah thirteen years later, my father saw to it that Stubs was summoned in Hebrew just that way, with the added phrase, *ben Avieh,* son of Arnold. To his last days pop never called Stubs anything else but Menachem Mendel . . .

My mind raced on, oblivious that I was driving on a dangerously wet highway. Now it was 1951, Stubs was only five, fourteen years ago . . . We were spending the summer at our beach house on Fire Island off Long Island's Atlantic shore. My youngest brother Joey, then in his late twenties, wiry and athletic but slight, was our weekend visitor with his wife and baby. It was a full household—Stubs, myself, May pregnant with Jayney, our housekeeper and guests. We were all at the beach enjoying the sun and cooling ocean winds. I stood up, took my little blond-haired boy by the hand and walked him into the shallow water. Joey followed along. Standing knee-deep, we liked the cold water lapping around our legs. Saying he would give Stubs a ride, Joey bent down, lifted the boy up onto his back and started forward. Joey's arms were behind him, holding my son firmly. Stubs had clasped Joe around the neck. "Where are you going?" I asked Joey.

"Just a little way. Don't worry. I got him tight."

"No, don't . . ." Joey didn't hear me. Before I could protest further Joey was up to his shoulders in the waves, Stubs hugging him tight around the neck. The waves got higher and heavier. As one broke, Joey ducked under to avoid getting its full force, disappearing with Stubs. Seconds later he was up on the other side of the wave but Stubs was no longer with him, no longer to be seen. My heart sank. I ran into the water, dove into a wave, came up swimming in the direction of Joey. My years as a lifeguard, arranged in heaven, made it near-automatic. I could see my brother swirling, splashing, searching.

In the time it took me to reach Joey I'd made a decision. If I didn't find Stubs under the water I would keep swimming out into the ocean until I could go no further. If my son was gone I was determined not to go back to shore. There was no question about it. I knew I would keep going.

Reaching Joey, I surface-dived toward the bottom, able to see nothing because of sand stirred up by the pounding waves. I groped around under the water blindly, frantically. My head struck my son's small body. In an instant I was on the surface holding his head above the water. Moments later I carried him on shore, a frightened little boy but otherwise fine . . .

I realized now, driving the car, that in the years since I had more than once sat up in bed at night, sweating, reliving those terrible moments. Still not over its horror, I knew then I would never succeed in blotting the incident from memory.

The last time I saw him Stubs sported a blond beard and a contagious grin. As I strained in the dark to see the road ahead, blinded by the snowflakes in the glare of my headlights, I'd once again been reliving the agony of that day on the beach. And the same sense of fear, and futility, overwhelmed me. "Sons of bitches," I kept muttering. Little Jayney, more aware than I knew, said nothing.

It was a slow, dangerous ride all the way. In good weather the trip would have taken about three hours but in the snow and sleet it took more than five. A cold dawn touched the winter sky as we slowed into the parking lot in front of the Waltham Hospital and stepped out into the wet snow. The three of us hurried toward the entrance. In a minute an attendant in the lobby ushered us down the corridor, where we met the physician in charge. "How is he?" I blurted out, not waiting to be introduced.

"Well, that depends on whether his liver is damaged and how badly," came the disembodied voice of the doctor.

I feared the worst. The blood drained out of my head, the room began to spin and I started to sink to the floor. The doctor and orderly grabbed and held me up. Steadying myself, I asked the doctor please to repeat what he said.

"It's not all that bad," he assured me. "The boy took a heavy pounding. They punched him unconscious. But he's young. Nineteen, right? And unless the X rays show some serious internal injuries he'll be all right."

The doctor had no details of the assault; we would have to see

184

the police later in the morning. "In the meantime," he suggested, "peek into your son's room for a minute if you want. Don't be frightened by his swollen face. It's black and blue but that will pass. He's sleeping. Then you three get some sleep."

We did not recognize Stubs.

Later in the day the police told us they suspected a Klan gang. The culprits had muttered something about "quieting your father down a bit. Change his mind. Get him off it." The police had no specific leads but were "working the area," trying to locate and question known local KKK hoodlums . . .

The police never caught the guilty ones. Stubs spent a week in the hospital recovering from the beating. His liver, thank heaven, had not been severely damaged. Three or four times in the next weeks and months I phoned the authorities but they had nothing to tell me.

That was the end of it. Stubs returned to his classes. But I knew he had paid the price for my public attacks on the Klan. Whether he worried about another attack in the three years he was at Brandeis I'll never know. He did not talk about it and we never asked him. But as long as I live, the picture will never fade in my mind of him being held, arms pinned by a brute standing behind him while the others take turns smashing his face, stomach, and chest and spitting obscenities at him about his father. I shiver now just thinking about it—even though he is a mature physician, a successful internist with a little blond boy of his own.

21

Adolph Eichmann

By May 1960, Israel had established an international intelligence agency that with increasing need for it and much actual experience had become an effective worldwide operation. Among tasks assigned its operatives was the hunting down and capture of leading Nazis who had escaped the Allied net, especially those discovered after the war to have been primarily responsible for carrying out the "Final Solution"—the murder six million European Jews. Many had escaped the American, British, French and Soviet armies when the combined Allied forces overran Germany and Nazi-held territories. Following the Allied war-crimes trials, the Jewish State was intent on capturing and punishing hidden anti-Jewish culprits for "crimes against humanity."

Among those sought was Adolph Eichmann, former SS Obersturmbannfuehrer, wanted for carrying out Hitler's hideous human liquidation program. He was the Nazi who had selected Cyclone-B gas to kill Jews otherwise not hanged, shot or starved to death. Disappearing when Germany collapsed, Eichmann had become the prime target of Israel's international search.

According to never ending rumor, Eichmann was turning up

from week to week everywhere in the world. Actually, after his escape from Europe, Eichmann lived in Argentina for twelve years before the Mossad nabbed him. He had arrived there in August 1948, his family following after him in 1954.

Among other Israeli intelligence operations, the Mossad—an acronym for the Hebrew name of the undercover service assigned to operate abroad—constantly sought leads from reliable governments and from other contacts and sources.

I was a source. Now and then the Mossad would be tipped off that a wanted Nazi criminal was allegedly hiding somewhere in the United States. Word of it would sometimes reach me. I would undertake a preliminary rundown to corroborate the report. Before Eichmann was caught I probably chased down a dozen rumors about him, none resulting in anything worthwhile.

I can't recall whether it was Eichmann or Martin Bormann who was the suspect in question, but I once received word he was living in Brooklyn and masquerading as a teacher in a Hebrew School, a Talmud Torah. I started a probe—wasteful, as it turned out to be—to determine whether the man fingered was actually a Jew and rabbinical teacher.

Simon Weisenthal, operating out of Vienna, is a well-known, one-man research effort intent on uncovering fugitive Nazis. He has not, as far as I know, released any list of Nazi criminals apprehended as a result of his work although he has done well in keeping the public's eye on the subject of prominent escaped Nazis. For this he is widely honored. His more recent endorsement of Kurt Waldheim's candidacy for president of Austria gives pause in estimating the self-avowed Nazi hunter.

Sometime early in 1960, based on whatever facts, Weisenthal concluded that he knew where Eichmann was. In Japan, he believed. To verify his suspicion Weisenthal needed additional funds. According to my source then high in the Israeli government, the celebrated Nazi-hunter flew to Jerusalem to see Prime Minister Ben-Gurion, there to share with the Israeli leader his purported information. Weisenthal requested financing from the Israeli government. Ben-Gurion checked with the

Mossad and decided against financial assistance. Weisenthal then released a story in Israel saying in effect that the Israeli government was refusing to help capture Eichmann.

Only a short time before, the Mossad had itself located a Ricardo Klement in Buenos Aires who it believed to be Eichmann. The first clue that led the Mossad to the Argentine came from a blind German, non-Jew, living in the Andes region of the Argentine in a small town called Tunuyan. He offered an address for Eichmann from which the Mossad traced the suspect to his Buenos Aires residence. The Israeli agents then dug up a second clue—immigration records of Eichmann's wife Vera. To confirm their finding, they surreptitiously photographed "Mrs. Klement" and sent the results home. One of her pictures was then mixed with ten other photographs and shown to two men who had known Mrs. Eichmann in Germany. Both picked out her picture.

But they were still not sure. The problem was in the Israeli intelligence agency's local biographic notes on Klement. They disclosed he was the father of one son—Eichmann had three. Buenos Aires municipal records recorded Klement as the second husband of Adolph Eichmann's widow. For herself, Klement's wife had spread word in the neighborhood that she was Eichmann's widow and that three of her four children were Adolph's. The fourth, she said, was the son of her new husband, with whom she was now living. So while Israeli investigators thought they had fairly good cause for believing their man was indeed Eichmann, they were not ready to pick him up without absolute confirmation.

At the same time the Israeli undercover team worried that if the man was indeed Eichmann he might learn of the report in Israel about Weisenthal's claim. While the Viennese Nazi-hunter said he knew the German criminal's whereabouts, he did not reveal the place. The Mossad therefore was afraid that Eichmann could conclude his Argentine hideaway was compromised. If so, he might run. At that point the checking had to be stopped—it might boomerang—and the Mossad team considered capturing Klement and interrogating him to make sure he was Eichmann. If they turned out to be wrong, they would simply release him.

The suspect was living in a suburb on a far edge of Buenos Aires and working in a factory on the opposite side of the city. Each weekday morning he would stroll a block to board a cross-town bus, ride through the city and stop a short distance from the factory, reversing the procedure in the evening. Daily, like clockwork, the Mossad investigators followed the man from his home to the bus, across town to the factory and back.

Soon after the Weisenthal story broke in Jerusalem, "Ricardo Klement" stopped on his way home from work at a florist shop. He took home a bouquet. It was March 21. The Israeli under-cover men immediately checked the Argentinian records of the suspect, his birth and marriage dates, his wife and children's birthdays. None matched the date of the flowers.

The investigators simply could not understand why Klement would take flowers home at that time. It took some doing, but after a short while the Mossad came up with Eichmann's vital statistics as recorded in Germany. The date of Eichmann's marriage to this wife matched the date of the flowers—March 21!

The former Nazi SS officer had changed his family's name, the marriage records, et cetera. But he had failed to realize that to maintain his cover he should have brought flowers to his wife on the changed date. The Mossad was now convinced they had the right man.

Various descriptions of how the Israelis picked up Eichmann and took him to Israel have been made public but the version told to me soon after it happened, and verified as recently as May 1987, by Rafael Eitan, the agent who headed the capturing team, is surely the most authoritative. Incidentally, as recently as April, 1988, Eitan told me that he thought Weisenthal be-lieved Eichmann to be hiding in Saudi Arabia, not Japan.

Abba Eban was Israel's foreign minister at the time. It was announced he would visit Argentina to participate in the cele-bration of a national holiday, and the Argentinians were most

pleased to have him present. Eban flew in on an El Al plane
made available to him ostensibly because there were no commercial Israeli flights to the Argentine.

The aircraft was now sitting at the Buenos Aires airport waiting to fly Israel's foreign minister to his next destination. The
Mossad agents, three of them, arrived and parked their automobile on the street between Eichmann's house and the intersection where he usually stepped off the bus that brought him from
his factory job. Other agents were waiting nearby should they
be needed.

Standing at the parked car, its trunk open, the men were
fussing with tools, apparently fixing a flat tire. As Eichmann
came abreast of the automobile, an agent reached out and
seized him. They grappled. The two others joined in, one
quickly smothering a handkerchief over the German's mouth.
Inside the car, Eitan told Klement to "please be quiet or you will
be dead." They were the first words spoken to the captive and
said by Eitan in German, as a test.

If the allegedly Argentinian-born prisoner understood them,
it would be corroboration of sorts that they had the right man.
Eichmann responded in German that he would obey and was
as compliant as a drugged pig. He actually put his head in
Eitan's lap on the ride to the safe house so that he would not be
seen outside the automobile.

Driven into a private courtyard and taken into the safe house,
Eichmann was held prisoner for nine days. While being kept
there Eichmann revealed the very characteristic which he was
later to use in his trial as a defense against the crime charged.
He claimed he was just a cog in a much larger machine who
simply carried out orders and had no choice to do otherwise
except on pain of death. Now in the safe house he repeatedly
assured his captors that he would do exactly as he was told, that
he could even be relied upon to go to the airport alone, unas-
sisted, without running away, if that's what they wanted. When
arrangements were completed for his departure Eichmann was
given an El Al steward's uniform to wear, was administered a

190

sedative in his arm in order to insure he would not become violent on the way to the airport.

The embassy called the Argentinian police to report that one of the El Al crew was quite sick and had expressed a desire to be taken home. Could the department please arrange a police escort for the trip to the airport? The El Al plane was still sitting on the tarmac near a runway, ostensibly waiting for Abba Eban to finish his business.

The police could not have been more friendly or helpful. They arrived, sirens blew and Eichmann, involuntarily playing his assigned role as a very ill diplomat in an Israeli uniform on his way home. The gate guards had been notified, and with the assistance of the police the semidrugged Nazi was helped onto the El Al plane, which promptly headed for Israel.

Abba Eban was still sitting in Buenos Aires awaiting his departure time when Adolph Eichmann came fully alert in the plane. Soon the world learned Israel had kidnapped a major architect in the Nazi mass murder that killed nearly six million Jews.

Such was the description of the snatch, given to me in Jerusalem soon after it occurred. A few of the details were reported some years afterward in a book written by the late Moshe Pearlman, a prominent Israeli figure. At the time, however, Jerusalem revealed only that Eichmann was captured in the Argentine and flown aboard an El Al plane to Israel.

Many years later, in 1985, Peter Malkin, one of the three Israeli undercover men who captured Eichmann, visited New York and I lunched with him. He confirmed much of what I had originally heard that was confirmed later by Eitan but with this slightly different twist: As they were getting ready to leave the safe house, Malkin said, he dressed Eichmann in a "uniform," made him feel important, persuaded him to agree he was leaving the Argentine voluntarily, and walked him aboard the airplane. I have no way of knowing whether for the record Peter was alibying Eichmann's kidnapping as a voluntary trip by the Nazi.

* * *

Eichmann's seizure, forced flight to Israel and quick indictment for crimes against humanity precipitated a great outcry
around the world about the methods employed to bring him to
justice. Critics argued the charges against him were based on
acts committed before Israel existed and relied on a statute
enacted after Israel was created—a statute that made Eichmann's misdeeds criminal only after their commission, a statute,
furthermore, that directed itself in Israel to activities that had
taken place in Germany and not Israel. So it was argued that the
prisoner was being subjected to an *ex post facto* law adopted by
a government of a nation for a crime allegedly committed elsewhere and before the nation could be its victim. The Jewish
State, said the critics, was in gross violation of international law.
The Argentinian government expressed irritation and immediately filed a formal protest with Israel.

In the worldwide debate many American Jews felt a sense of
unease. They were sure Israel would be damned for the alleged
illegal capture in a foreign land. But Israel had no intention of
backing down. It would proceed as planned. Its local statute
called for the death penalty—singularly drawn for the kind of
crime Eichmann was charged with. In no other instance is there
capital punishment in Israel.

Some civil-liberties advocates argued an Israeli hearing would
not be a genuine trial. They said it would be a judicial circus, a
kangaroo court in which Eichmann would not have a chance of
being judged fairly. The Israelis, critics claimed, had already
found him guilty and in their own minds had already sentenced
him to death. It remained, they said, only for the Jewish judges
to act it all out in a mockery of a court proceeding.

The international controversy sent a shiver through most
Jews everywhere. Seizing Eichmann and carrying him off to an
Israeli prison without the knowledge or approval of the Argentinian government, while a magnificent exploit, did not sit well.
Some insecure souls, having lived through the Holocaust, were
deeply concerned about the impact of adverse public opinion,
afraid the charges about the scheduled trial would turn out to

be accurate. And inevitably, they thought, it would incite increased anti-Semitism.

The negative reaction to the Nazi murderer's capture suggested the need to counter the potential danger to Israel's reputation, and we decided on a major educational campaign as a preventive remedy. The trial would not begin for another year.

At a board meeting called to consider the subject was Samuel O. (Shap) Shapiro, circulation manager of Look magazine, which had some fifty radio stations under contract for a daily fifteen-minute broadcast. Using a variety of human-interest stories, the program was an effective promotional activity for the magazine, and Shapiro thought it might also prove useful to us.

Suggesting I be sent to Israel to cover the trial, he argued that as a lawyer, writer and public speaker I should be able to tape interesting stories around the case. I might even be able to show that the proceeding was not a kangaroo court, and also demonstrate that Israel provided the same protections that Western society guaranteed to defendants in criminal cases—the right to counsel, to cross-examine and, in this case, help in finding witnesses.

Shap promised that if I were to send back worthwhile tapes he would arrange their broadcast on his network of stations. Jumping at the opportunity to attend the trial even though I had never written or delivered a scripted radio broadcast in my life, I flew to Jerusalem and proceeded to tape programs for several weeks.

The Look syndication people had made clear they did not want so-called "hard" news of the trial from me. There would be plenty of reporters in and around the courtroom every day reporting the trial testimony and rulings. They wanted only soft background stories—explanation, analysis, anecdotes, vignettes. Feature material or information others did not report.

On the other hand I preferred facts to back up what we anticipated would be the truth—that in spite of the unusual circumstances of the case, the Israelis would conduct the trial according to accepted Western legal principles.

I wrote and recorded a daily fifteen-minute report about what was happening in and around the courtroom, and reactions in Israel to the trial testimony. For me every day in court was like attending a funeral. At times I wept openly during the proceedings, as others did. There was a temptation when court recessed in the evening to wash my hands like an orthodox Jew coming back from a cemetery after a burial service. Sometimes while recording my statement in the hotel room I would weep just speaking my prepared script.

As the facts that were brought out at the trial reached the Israeli public, young people began to wonder what sort of stock they themselves came from. What kind of cowards were these European Jews who apparently went so passively to their deaths in the camps? Why didn't they fight back? Why did so many go sheeplike to slaughter? They talked openly about their disillusionment, and to their elders it was a strange and most unexpected reaction.

To make matters worse, Hannah Arendt, the respected German-born Jewish sociologist with predetermined notions about the conduct of European Jews caught in the Holocaust, was covering the trial for The New Yorker magazine. Her book, *Eichmann in Jerusalem,* published in 1961, had stirred up bitter controversy with its claim that Jewish leaders throughout Hitler-occupied Europe had virtually betrayed Jewry. Arendt's thesis was not quietly accepted by American Jews, although her writings had enormous impact in many quarters. It was her opinion that European Jewish leadership, in a vain effort to save its constituencies from the Nazis, was too submissive, and in many cases actually turned in Jews and Jewish records. By their passive attitudes and actions, she believed, Jews had contributed to their own destruction.

The young people in Israel were hearing from court witnesses as well as reading sad and terrible stories about how many innocent Jews went to their deaths. With Arendt telling how German and Polish Jewish workers participated in roundup procedures, one could well understand the reactions of some young Israelis.

194

Gideon Hausner, the trial prosecutor, demonstrated that Jews in the ghettos of Poland and elsewhere did not have much more than rocks and sticks. A glass bottle filled with kerosene became, he proved, the only instrument of attack or defense. That was the best the Jews could find to resist Nazis firing cannons from tanks.

Hausner put a linguist on the stand to read the testimony from a Nuremberg trial record of an eyewitness to a mass execution on October 5, 1942, in the Ukrainian town of Dubno near the Polish border. The eyewitness, Herman Friedrich Graebe, a managing engineer, had been hired by a construction company to oversee the renovation of buildings on the grounds of the slaughtering. The Nazis had been killing 1500 Dubno Jews daily and 5000 more remained to be liquidated. Speaking softly, the linguist read the statement: "There were huge mounds of earth of about 30 meters long and 2 meters high. In front stood several lorries of the people guarded by armed Ukrainian militia under the command of an SS man. All the captives had yellow stars on the backs and fronts of their clothing so they were recognized as Jews. I heard rifle shots, one after the other, behind one of the mounds. At the order of the SS man who held a riding whip, men, women and children of all ages climbed down from the lorries to undress and separate their clothing according to shoes, outerwear and underwear and place them in designated places. I saw a pile of shoes, maybe 800 to 1000 pairs—large stacks of clothes. Without yelling or crying these people undressed, stood together in family groups and kissed, made their farewells and waited for the signal of another SS man who stood at the mound, also with a whip in his hand. During the fifteen minutes as I stood by the mound I heard no complaint or pleas to be spared. I watched a family of eight people—husband, wife of about fifty years old, with their children, one eight or ten years old, as well as two grown-up daughters of twenty to twenty-four years old. An old lady with snow white hair held a one-year-old child, sang to him and tickled him. The child was squeaking with delight. His parents watched with tears in their eyes. The father held the hand of a boy about ten years old, speaking to him quietly. The boy struggled with his tears, the father pointed a finger to heaven, stroking the boy's head and seemed to be explaining something to him."

Hausner asked the witness to go on. It was so painful I hardly remember what followed. The hushed courtroom learned that the witness watched the father lift the boy on to his knee, point high in the sky, holding the little boy's attention with his words, talking to him without stopping. Moving a little closer, he could hear the father saying to his son: "That's where you and I are going. There, up there in the sky—to heaven—there it's clean and warm and smells nice and there are good things to eat, and you will see again everybody you love, your friends, momma, me, our family."

Listening, my mind went to the SS commander and Hausner's concern about the young people of Israel. The SS man must have wondered . . . What kind of cowards are these, the Jews? Why didn't he try to strike me or any of us with his fists? Why didn't he hit out at somebody, anybody, even if only to protest. Instead he accepted quietly, without struggle. Cowards, they're all the same.

Led by Hausner, the witness had tried to make clear to the deadly silent courtroom—silent except for an audible sob—how much strength it took for that father to make the last few moments of his son's life on earth calm and assuring; how, rather than let the boy watch and hear people wretch and scream and bleed and die, that father was protecting his son from the agony, giving him a momentary comfort. The courtroom spectators understood.

By interrogating the witness in that fashion Gideon explained a good deal to the judges and, more important, to the skeptics of the world, sent them a message, helped them understand what had actually happened in Hitler's Europe twenty years earlier. And answered Hannah Arendt.

When I taped what I'd written about this testimony for my radio program I cried as I talked into the microphone. Years later when my colleague, Abe Foxman, and I were on the tarmac at the Tel Aviv Airport at four o'clock one morning we reacted the same way as we witnessed and recorded the landing of one of the earliest airplanes filled with Soviet Jews to arrive in Israel. Jews coming home at last. Many bent down and kissed the concrete as they stepped off the airplane.

After preparing weeks of Eichmann trial programs I returned to New York to find that radio stations across America were using my recordings. They sensed something different in the tapes, a firsthand report with a candidly pro-Israel point of view. Many of the radio stations asked whether I would like to make more programs from Israel—about life in the Jewish State. It would be some five years before I got around to working out the details necessary for undertaking that assignment in a series called "Dateline Israel."

I was reporting on the Eichmann trial in April of 1961 when I got a letter from May. "Why," she wrote, "have men proceeded from one mass slaughter to another? Consciously or unconsciously, they do many monstrous things. So let's imagine a vast amphitheatre in the middle of the Gobi Desert reaching miles up and seating every living person except those on the floor of the arena. Each seat has a telescope giving full view of those below. In the arena's boxes are seated the heads of all the governments. A huge electric furnace of 3500 degrees is burning and from one side come the people of Auschwitz and Buchenwald and other extermination camps. One by one they advance in single file until soldiers of the various nations push them into the furnace, one at a time. Singly they come—little boys, little girls, the aged and the others. Each is pushed into the oven. But some do not die. Horribly burned, they stagger out the other end, unrecognizable. If that were to happen, such a cry would come from the throats of assembled humanity as to break the wall—I hope.

"But such a cry would be only the beginning of consciousness, not the full consciousness essential to stop a plague of human hatred. In other words, the beginning is that Dr. Jekyll must face his mirror and recognize Mr. Hyde. After that, there is hope. I hope . . ."

May's words were a reaction to the trial reporting, including my radio stories—what she called "the beginning of consciousness." She was right, of course. Humanity's cry was barely audible in the aftermath of the Final Solution. I heard no echo of it at the trial, nor did I see any smashed walls, and my omission, as with others', reflected it. But she couldn't accept hopelessness.

This is part of what she heard from me over the radio waves:

April 12, 1961:

The trial is off to an intelligent start, at least with respect to the reaction of the communications people and their needs—there are literally hundreds of them from across the world—to the manner and conduct of the trial.

The security arrangements seem a little excessive—compulsory frisking each time one enters the court compound no matter they are accredited reporters from the press, wire services, radio and TV networks, newspapers and magazines, and no matter how often they come and go each session. I just can't see the newsmen working for UPI, Life Magazine, CBS, et al., trying to light a fuse under Eichmann. They all seem, however, to take the practice in good spirits.

There is always coffee, essential to reporters, and also cakes and sandwiches. The pressroom looks pretty much like a city desk in any metropolitan newspaper. In addition to coffee, there is orange juice—a standard Israeli drink—next to many typewriters, alongside ashtrays filled with stinking cigarette and cigar butts.

The three judges are physical counterparts of Hollywood screen judges. Almost stereotypes. They speak in calm quiet tones, in Hebrew, of course. Spectators who don't understand the language sit, as do the reporters, with head sets to hear simultaneous translations. The prosecutor also talks in measured tones, as does Eichmann's counsel, Dr. Servatius.

In other words, up front is a conservative appearing, sophisticated, intelligent, highly civilized court proceeding. This kind of demeanor impresses. Those on the bench and at the prosecutor's table outdo the British in terms of reserve, decorum and dignity. It has made a favorable impact upon the working reporters; extremely important. . . .

April 15, 1961:

On trial for his life, Eichmann has been charged with deliberate slaughter of millions of human beings. Everything about the case appears extraordinary: the crimes with which he is charged, the conditions under which they took place, the method of his apprehension, the site of the trial and the trial itself.

These extraordinary circumstances focus world attention upon the proceedings in the Beit Ha'am, the converted courthouse in Jerusalem. They have already raised questions and charges quite as strange as the facts surrounding the Eichmann case.

Israel believes it has the right to try Eichmann. Certain lawyers, including some friendly to Israel, question the legal precedents. But except for segments of the hate press no one defends Eichmann or seriously questions his guilt. Only the legalities and ethics come up for discussion. But the debate is so heated, basic facts are often forgotten; people sometimes talk as though Israel and Jews generally—not Adolf Eichmann—were on trial.

Many questions about the case have been raised in the months preceding the trial. The first came the instant Prime Minister David Ben-Gurion announced in May 1960 that Adolf Eichmann had been caught and would be tried in Israel for his role in the mass murder of Jews under Hitler. How had be been tracked down and where? How had he been brought to Israel?

Then came second questions, more vexing ones about the legalities, ethics, the political and historical wisdom of the trial. Why try a man fifteen years after he had committed a crime? Why should Israel, a country founded more than a decade after the crimes were committed, have the right, not Germany, to try him? What could the trial possibly accomplish—except satisfy a desire for revenge? Why not let sleeping dogs lie?

The questions were serious and I tried to learn some answers.

The purpose of the trial? Israel stated the trial's purpose was to alert the world's conscience to the fearful consequences of totalitarianism. The most terrible, Israel said, is genocide. Its chief victims in modern history—although not the only ones—have been Jews.

Israel also believes that the generation that has grown up since World War II does not fully understand the dangers inherent in an authoritarian society because the full horror of Hitlerism has not yet been brought home to them.

One thing is clear: The Eichmann trial will cause much personal anguish for many Israelis; more than 300,000 of them lost at least one immediate relative to the Nazis, and the testimony will reopen deep personal wounds. But the government has concluded it is important the world be reminded of Nazism's horrors. The hope is that the trial will serve as an effective educational weapon to assure it never happens again.

Israel knows that to be effective the trial itself will have to be fair, legal, and just. And it is determined that it will be—and without a spirit of vengeance.

Israel is against capital punishment. The prime minister and his government indicated their feelings on the subject: both made clear Israel is not interested in punishing Eichmann for punishment's sake. Ben-Gurion added it is impossible to avenge the murder of six million humans simply by punishing one of the culprits; there can be no fit punishment for a person guilty of the crimes charged to Eichmann, nor would his death give any satisfaction. But death will be mandatory if Eichmann is found guilty of genocide.

Until just before the trial, there was no statute in Israeli jurisprudence providing for a way to carry out a death sentence. The genocide statute, enacted in 1950, failed to say how the death penalty was to be administered. Legislation had to be enacted specifically for the purpose; it provided for death by hanging.

The persistent fact of Israeli life is that capital punishment, especially hanging, is regarded as unethical and even contrary to Talmudic Law. Everywhere in Israel religious scholars, philosophers, prominent lawyers seem to be in accord that capital punishment is wrong—even for Eichmann.

Everything at the trial in Israel seems strangely different from what we normally expect in a criminal proceeding in America. In the States, juries decide whether defendants charged with murder live or die. In Israel there is no jury system. In its place is a panel of three judges.

More than 400 news correspondents crowd the courtroom and corridors. Videotapes of the proceedings are available to broadcasters from anywhere in the world to assure equal access to all. As correspondents gather from everywhere to talk in hotel lobbies, coffee shops and outside the courthouse in the warm Jerusalem sun, one hears the reservations about the trial evident in the minds of many.

To appreciate the answers of the Israelis, one must remember the background of the case—what happened from 1943 to 1945—at least as seen by the average person in Israel. It was a time, they say, of madness. Standards of morality, law and civilization were reversed. Nazi gangsters and hoodlums were in control and it was state policy to massacre and plunder. Wrong was right, the innocent were guilty, murderers were decorated as heroes.

In short, the crimes of the Nazis transcended the ordinary limits of human understanding, certainly transcended the crime anticipated in ordinary codes of law. This difference between Nazi genocidal crime and all other kinds of crime known to mankind was understood at Nuremberg, where the judges had to revise their thinking to cope with the cases before them. At Nuremberg not everyone agreed as to what the law should be. There were no precedents. It is easy, therefore, to understand why some aspects of the Nuremberg laws were criticized by lawyers and laymen who believed that conventional legal principles were violated.

The same thing is happening in Jerusalem. Criticism comes particularly from those unable to grasp the magnitude and unprecedented nature of the crimes charged. The answers of Israeli spokesmen sometimes satisfy, sometimes not.

The prosecution is not impeded by the question of kidnapping. The government takes the position that many nations have pursued similar action in apprehending criminals. In our own country American courts apply the common-law principle that they cannot be concerned with the *manner* in which a defendant is apprehended.

A leading case at home had this to say on the subject: "The power of a court to try a person for a crime is not impaired by the fact that he had been brought within the court's jurisdiction by reason of a forcible abduction. Due process of law is satisfied when one present in court is convicted of crime after having been fairly apprized of the charges against him, and after a fair trial in accordance with constitutional procedural safeguards. There is nothing in the Constitution that requires a court to permit a guilty person rightfully convicted to escape justice because he was brought to trial against his will."

Another question in the corridors is why wasn't Eichmann legally extradited? Once having captured Eichmann, it is argued, Israel should have petitioned Argentina for his extradition since both Israel and Argentina are members of the United Nations, and the UN has, on occasion, appealed to member nations to extradite and surrender war criminals.

Again, the legal issues and the moral issues run into each other: Argentina has long been a haven for Nazi war criminals, and for such crimes never honored an extradition request. The West German Government sought the extradition of such war criminals as Karl Klinghofer and Dr. Joseph Mengele, but its requests were rejected. The Israeli Government made the point that, in view of Argentina's past position and the absence of an extradition treaty, there was no basis for believing that an extradition request would be honored.

Lawyers point to the writing of Hugo Grotius, the founder of modern international law. Grotius rejected a nation's right to furnish asylum to criminals. A community, he said, may be held responsible for harboring those who have done wrong elsewhere; the responsibility consists in either punishing or surrendering the guilty party, especially when such crimes affect human society at large.

Another argument heard around the courthouse: Wasn't Israel trying Eichmann under an *ex post facto* law? An *ex post facto* statute is a law that makes an act criminal after the act itself had been committed. True, it is outlawed in American jurisprudence. But the *ex post facto* concept is American, based on the idea it is unfair to compel a man to stand trial for a deed which he could not have known was a violation of law when he committed it. Obviously, this concept cannot apply to murder; no one needs formal notice it is morally, legally and ethically wrong to kill another person without justification. Further, the *ex post facto* concept is not a principle of international criminal law, only of some nations' laws. Finally, Eichmann is before the court under a statute based upon international penal law as enunciated in the Nuremberg trials and in the Genocide Convention.

April 18, 1961:

  By what right did Israel claim jurisdiction over Eichmann?

  Some observers contend Eichmann's crimes were committed in Europe and should have been tried there. None of the crimes alleged against him, they argue, was committed in Israel, which, in fact, was not in existence as a state at the time.

  The Israelis answer: The territorial principle was never absolute, even in the United States or the United Kingdom, where it originated. Douglas Chandler, an American who broadcast throughout the war for Nazi Germany, was tried and convicted for treason in the United States although his crimes were committed in Germany.

  Israel points out that no rules of criminal jurisdiction exist to resolve such cases of conflict. For example, they say if West Germany had wanted to try Adolf Eichmann—which it did not—it would have no more right to do so under international law than Israel. In that case, there would be no way of deciding which country had the better jurisdiction.

Shouldn't Eichmann have been tried by an international tribunal?

Many who ask this suggest that Israel should have contented itself with being prosecutor, rather than judge; instead of trying Eichmann, it should have taken the matter to the United Nations. The United Nations, they argue, could then have created a special tribunal to judge Eichmann under the Nuremberg principles affirmed by the UN General Assembly in 1946.

The Israelis respond there is little likelihood the United Nations would have recreated a special international court, similar to Nuremberg or Tokyo, in order to try Eichmann. The fact is, they add, the UN General Assembly twice rejected proposals for a permanent international criminal court. The plain fact is no such court exists and neither Eichmann nor his lawyer, nor any government, suggested one.

Can the trial be fair? Hasn't Eichmann already been prejudged and found guilty?

Those who ask hold that Eichmann has in effect been condemned by the head of the Israeli government. In the United States the same accusation is also levelled in countless magazine articles, books, television and radio programs. Mr. Ben-Gurion, it is said, did not hesitate to refer to the prisoner as "the man who killed six million Jews," and to Eichmann's victims as having been "murdered."

Israel answers matter-of-factly that neither Ben-Gurion nor world opinion is going to pronounce legal judgment in the Eichmann case. Israel is a democratic state, they say, and its judiciary, as in the United States, is an independent branch of government, not subservient either to the executive or legislative arms of the state. Eichmann's guilt or innocence, they conclude, will be determined by an Israeli court solely on the basis of evidence before it.

I think it is obvious the Israeli court is not unbiased. No three Israeli judges could believe that Nazism was a good thing. And no Israeli court could have anything nice to say about it. Just as any court anywhere—in the United States, Israel or elsewhere—is prejudiced against murder, so are Israeli judges. The question will be, *Is Eichmann guilty as charged?* The issue is *not, Is Nazism a crime?"*

The question is asked whether the charges under which Eichmann is being tried are by themselves proper charges. A segment of opinion heard in and around Jerusalem hotels believes Eichmann should have been charged with genocide and not with "Crimes Against the Jewish People."

The essence of law, these critics argue, is that a crime is committed not only against the presumed victim but against the community as a whole. By charging Eichmann with having committed crimes against Jews alone, the Israeli Government implied what he did was not a crime against non-Jews or against society in general. The Nuremberg trials, it is stressed, were based upon war crimes, whether committed against Jews or non-Jews and equally crimes against international law. The Israeli indictment was therefore out of keeping with the trend of modern law in defining a crime in terms of the religion of the victim, rather than the nature of the criminal act.

The Israelis counter by pointing out that the charges against Eichmann list fifteen counts; four based upon crimes against the Jewish people, seven for crimes against humanity, one for a war crime, and three for belonging to Nazi organizations. Thus, Eichmann was in fact being tried for his crimes against non-Jews as well as Jews. And to identify one group as the victim of the genocide did not minimize the crime or deny that other races, religions and nationalities were equally its victims. *All* acts of genocide, they insist, remain crimes against humanity.

By indicting and trying Eichmann for "Crimes Against the Jewish People," did Israel not arrogate to itself the right to represent all Jews? There is little basis in fact for the accusation. The law under which Eichmann was indicted related only to genocidal activities committed between 1933 and 1945. The statute in question made it absolutely clear that it applied to no other acts against the Jewish people.

One day during the trial I asked an Israeli passerby on the street in front of my hotel what he believed was the pur-

pose of the Eichmann trial. "Justice," he said, "to achieve justice . . ."

April 20, 1961:

At long last, sixteen years after the Allied powers won World
War II, Adolf Eichmann, the man identified by his fellow Nazis
as the originator and executor of the master plan to exterminate
every Jew in Europe, is on trial for his life. For many days a
library full of the Nazi atrocities perpetrated on millions of
innocent men, women and children has been recreated in the
courtroom. A haunting and dreadful picture has been drawn
from eyewitnesses, victims and the carefully kept Nazi documents themselves.

The horrors charged against Eichmann are so immense and
ghastly as to be incomprehensible to the normal mind. For the
purposes of the trial there has been brought back to life, so to
speak, the gruesome symbols of death in Hitler's Europe: Extermination centers sprinkled across the continent and surrounded
by electrified wire fences. Death camps filled with torture cells,
gas chambers containing false shower heads to fool trapped
victims, subterranean execution rooms for wholesale shooting of
nonmilitary prisoners, crematory furnaces capable of incinerat-
ing thousands of victims daily, and factories for boiling human
beings—to turn them into soap. All this, and more, is charged
to Adolf Eichmann as the indictment against him is documented, and as evidence accumulates from extermination
camps with names like Auschwitz, Buchenwald, Ravensbruck,
Treblinka, Belzek, Wolzek.

Listen, from the mouth of an expert eyewitness, an important
Nazi who was himself involved with Eichmann, who admitted
he killed, as he said Eichmann killed, was guilty, as he said
Eichmann was guilty: On January 3, 1946, fifteen years earlier,
SS Captain Dieter Wislicheny took the stand in Nuremberg. He
had, he said, worked in the same office with Eichmann, had
been one of his chief assistants, his personal representative in
Slovakia, Greece and Hungary in carrying out the Final Solution.

Lt. Col. Smith Brookhart, assistant trial counsel for the United States was examining the witness:

"In your official connection, did you learn of any order which directed the annihilation of all Jews?"

"Yes, I learned of such an order for the first time from Eichmann in the summer of 1942. About seventeen thousand Jews were taken to Slovakia as workers. Eichmann assured the Slovakian Government that these Jews would be humanely and decently treated in the Polish ghettos. This was the special wish of the Slovakian government, which later expressed the desire that the Slovakian delegation be allowed to enter the areas to which the Slovakian Jews were supposed to have been sent. I went to see him in Berlin. Eichmann had given an evasive answer. I pointed out to him that abroad there were rumors to the effect that all Jews in Poland were being exterminated. I pointed out to him that the Pope had intervened with the Slovakian government in their behalf. I begged him to permit the inspection. Eichmann told me that this request to visit the Polish ghettoes could not be granted under any circumstances whatsoever. In reply to my question, "Why?" he said that most of these Jews were no longer alive. I asked him who had given such instructions, and he referred me to an order of Himmler's.

Col. Brookhart asked, "Where were you at the time of this meeting with Eichmann?"

The witness: "This meeting with Eichmann took place in Berlin in Eichmann's office. Eichmann told me he could show me this order in writing. He took a small volume of documents from his safe and showed me a copy of a letter from the chief of the security police in the S.D. The gist of this letter was roughly as follows: 'The Fuhrer orders the Final Solution of the Jewish Question. All Jewish men and women who are able to work are temporarily exempted from the so-called "Final Solution" and used for work in the concentration camps.' "

Lt. Col. Brookhart: "Any question asked by you as to the meaning of the words 'Final Solution' as used in the order?"

Wislicheny: "Eichmann explained to me what was meant by this. He said that the planned biological annihilation of the

Jewish race in the Eastern territories was disguised by the wording 'Final Solution.' "

Again, Brookhart: "Was anything said to you by Eichmann in regard to the power given him under this order?"

Wislicheny: "Eichmann told me that he personally was entrusted with the execution of this order. He had received every authority from the chief of the security police. He himself was personally responsible for the execution of this order."

Lt. Col. Brookhart: "Did you make any comment to Eichmann about his authority?"

Wislicheny: "Yes. It was perfectly clear to me that this order spelled death to millions of people. I said to Eichmann, 'God grant that our enemies never have the opportunity of doing the same to the German people.' In reply to which Eichmann told me 'not to be sentimental. It was an order of the Fuehrer's, and would have to be carried out.' "

Later on in the testimony, to tie it down conclusively, Lt. Col. Brookhart asked Wislicheny: "When you say the Jews taken to Auschwitz were submitted to the 'Final Solution', what do you mean by that?"

Wislicheny: "By that I mean what Eichmann had explained to me under the term 'Final Solution'. That is, they were annihilated biologically. As far as I could gather from him, this annihilation took place in the gas chambers and the bodies were subsequently destroyed in the crematoria."

In short, Eichmann was no mere soldier carrying out military orders. His was a far greater role. And Wislicheny's testimony established beyond any doubt that Eichmann recognized it . . .

April 22, 1961:

It has been eminently clear from the beginning of the trial that the defendant, charged with the most horrible crimes the mind of man can conceive, is receiving a fair trial. The three judges, all of German-Jewish background, are court models of disciplined fairness. Yet they are not, in the deepest recesses of their hearts, neutral. Impossible. Who can be neutral about the bestial murder of six million innocents? However, they are clearly determined to abide strictly by accepted court rules of fairness. These judges are in the Western tradition.

The court is most considerate of defense counsel. They seem to be leaning backward in favor of Eichmann in some of their rulings. For example, permitting Dr. Servatius to object to the introduction of documentary evidence, demanding that it be expunged from the record although it had previously been admitted into evidence with no objection from him. This could not be done in the courts of the United States.

This does not mean that the prosecution itself, or that any of the three judges lacks trial experience. They are fair but firm, quiet-spoken but self-assured, even-tempered but principled. Yet it must be that these men see Adolf Eichmann not only as a man accused of unbelievable crimes but as a living symbol of a malignant disease that killed millions. The putrefaction that was Nazism needs the cold impersonal precision of a surgeon to lay open properly for all the world to see.

To know the horrible record is to understand some of the mail that came from people in scattered countries. Letters from victims, from families of victims and others who witnessed the crimes charged to Eichmann. Letters from Christians and Jews. Some of them ask for the privilege of being the executioner when the time is at hand to take the prisoner to the gallows. A preliminary analysis of the international mail that has arrived at the office of the Israeli prime minister from the United States, Israel, West Germany, France and England shows: Of those expressing clear opinions seventy-two percent spoke in congratulatory terms. Less than two and a half percent of the mail was condemnatory. Many wrote that the crimes were too terrible even for capital punishment. Others opposed the death penalty for religious or moral reasons. But the largest number expressed the conviction that when the trial was done and the record established, if the proof of guilt is conclusive and judgment is rendered accordingly no useful purpose will be served in permitting Adolf Eichmann to live any longer.

These extreme reactions arise from the nature of the defendant's crime. Adolf Eichmann persisted in slaughtering Jews and others long after it was clear that Hitlerism and all it stood for was doomed. The collective sense of shame, which reflects itself in the mail pouring into Israeli government offices, comes because civilization is being reminded of something it prefers to forget: that when Jews most needed a place of refuge, a haven, the world closed its doors, leaving them to be dragged off to the concentration camps and gas chambers.

Men guilty of far lesser brutalities than Eichmann have been shot, hanged or otherwise summarily put to death. Israel's method of a genuine trial, controlled by strict rules of evidence, in the presence of the world's press, is a sign of civilized conduct. It is because the three men sitting in judgment of Eichmann are so conscious of their responsibility to do justice that we in the courtroom in Jerusalem find them to be so protective of the defendant's rights. They are trying this case against Adolf Eichmann under laws new to mankind. But the countless murders with which the prisoner is charged are also crimes new to mankind. It is a civilized consequence to meet new problems with new laws. This trial of Adolf Eichmann is the least the world deserves . . .

April 30, 1961:

The winter rains are over in Israel and as the warm sun shines down on Jerusalem, prelude to a long dry spring, summer and fall, there is great tension in the air. One hears many tongues from many lands, and they are all targeted on one person, Adolf Eichmann, the Nazi extermination boss on trial for his life after breaking loose from an American prisoner-of-war camp in occupied Germany and successfully hiding for fifteen years.

Before Eichmann was finally apprehended in the Argentine he had kept undercover for three years in a small village in Lower Saxony about 120 miles west of Berlin, living as a lumberjack, using the name Otto Henninger. In 1950 with the help of the Nazi underground he went from this north German village across Austria into Italy through Rome, stopping in Geneva.

There he was given false papers, a fraudulent passport and a ticket for a ship to Buenos Aires.

For twelve years he lived safely in the Argentine until finally he was apprehended by an expert squad of Israeli operatives, some of whom had spent time in one of Eichmann's concentration camps or had witnessed one of his own family killed by Eichmann's murderers.

One of the main reasons for this trial, which inevitably is tearing open so many deep wounds for so many people in Israel, is the government's wish to teach its own young and the youth of the world the evil of Nazism and to remind the rest of us what an incredible price had to be paid by humanity to rid the earth of Hitlerism.

Does the world want to be reminded? Is the trial of Adolf Eichmann here in Israel an effective method? One can already get a small idea of the reaction to the historic hearing being conducted here in Jerusalem. Members of the press are normally keen observers. Hundreds of them are gathered here in the Holy Land from many nations. I polled some of these reporters and of one thing I am sure, there are many different attitudes toward the Eichmann trial in Israel. On one score there is unanimity—all agree that the prisoner deserves to be tried and punished if guilty.

A number of newspaper and TV reporters here from our own country were among those who raised questions about the manner in which Eichmann was brought to Jerusalem, and about the propriety of a trial in Israel. Increasingly these American reporters are learning that international law does not support their position. On the contrary, it seems to uphold the morality of the capture, the legality of the trial.

Reporters from behind the Iron Curtain insist the Nazi war criminal should have been tried in a Soviet satellite nation—Poland, for instance, where they say a major portion of his crimes were committed. They are angry, too, because they are sure Israel will not have the "courage" to execute Eichmann. Of course they believe there is no question that he should be hanged. If you talk long enough to these reporters from Communist countries you learn that what they really want is to try Eichmann themselves in order to whip West Germany and Israel with Soviet propaganda—West Germany because they believe it still Nazi-ridden, and Israel because they regard it a tool of Western capitalists.

The French people, according to their representatives here in Jerusalem, feel differently. Bravo the Israelis! they cheer. What a capture! What brilliance! took guts, courage, know-how! The Israelis caught him and they should have. These French reporters say that the Israeli Embassy in Paris has been deluged with letters from Frenchmen who suffered under the Nazi occupation, asking for the privilege of tightening the noose around Eichmann's neck when the time comes. Of course, these reporters add, there are some among the French who are worried by the trial—men who collaborated with the Nazis and who are fearful their names may be spoken by some witness in the trial.

Reporters from Germany are volubly anti-Nazi, expressing great satisfaction that Eichmann is on trial in Israel but hoping the world will remember that not all Germans were Nazis and that present-day Germany does not resemble the Third Reich in any respect. On this score, it must be admitted, the Adenauer government record is excellent. But these reporters whisper there are Germans at large today, free and comfortable citizens in their homeland, shivering in their proverbial jackboots lest Eichmann or some prosecution witness name names, including theirs, in telling the whole ghastly story.

As for the people of Israel, one finds varying reactions. The youth who were born here, the sabras in the colleges and universities, consider Nazism to be history about which they are eager to know more. Some of the comparatively recent immigrants from Asian or African countries, or the *Cochin* from India, had heard little of Hitler or Eichmann. However, old-time Palestinian Jews and others from Europe who left before Hitler or who came afterward from his concentration camps regard both Adolfs to be cast in the same mold. For them, there is no question about the historic justice of the trial. They sum it up: Eichmann was a wanted Nazi war criminal for sixteen years. No murderer should escape punishment because he illegally flees to hide in another country. It is the law of civilized nations that the method of bringing a suspect into a country for criminal trial is of no interest to the court. Eichmann was wanted in Nuremberg for war crimes specifically against the Jewish people, to whose total destruction he was personally assigned. No other country can provide a larger body of witnesses against Eichmann since there are more concentration camp survivors in Israel than any place else on earth.

The capture of men who harmed Jews was not part of the Jewish struggle for independence. That effort was fired not by vengeance but by a burning passion for freedom and national self-expression, and by a wish no longer to be the helpless victims of pogrom and massacre. But the mood and spirit engendered by Israel's statehood made an impact on Israeli agents, prompting them to search for Eichmann and bring him before a court of justice. I can only believe that if Israel did not exist, Eichmann would still be at large . . .

May 2, 1961:

The French and British press were impatient with the extended time the prosecutor, Gideon Hausner, used in justifying to the court the propriety of a trial in Israel. He took two days. Hausner was, I think, trying to establish to the satisfaction of the world that this trial in Israel was justified.

Servatius introduced a hundred-page memorandum arguing against the court's jurisdiction. There is a very healthy respect for his ability as a "public relations" lawyer. In addition to legal skills, he obviously knows how to play to the grandstand, which in this case is the world. Servatius believes the cause of Eichmann as a defendant is gone, that he is through, that nothing Servatius can do will save him. Servatius is trying instead to defend Germany.

Defense counsel wants to strengthen contemporary Germany's reputation by saying to the world the Third Reich was in the control of a German minority. Obviously, he is going back to live again in Germany after this trial. If he does not succeed in saving the good name of West Germany, his life at home could be a troubled one. There have been some here who believe that Servatius deliberately made application for legal fees from the West German government to defend Eichmann, knowing in advance that he would be refused. In this way he enables the West German government to disassociate itself publicly from the defense of Eichmann and from anything that was Nazi. Hausner is regarded as a very competent, thorough, undramatic lawyer. Many attending the trial think he is the right kind of personality to represent the State.

The three judges have won the approval of most of the newspapermen spending time in the courtroom. The judges are relaxed, not stern yet not weak. They show Servatius every courtesy, frequently leaning over backward to express regret that they must call for this, that or the other kind of proof from him. They completely ignore Eichmann in his glass cage. They rarely even look in his direction. The defendant, for his part, confines himself to watching his own lawyer when Servatius is speaking, or sometimes looking up at the three judges when one of them speaks. Only infrequently does he turn in the direction of the reporters, diplomats, other observers or the spectators...

May 5, 1961:

By 1961 David Nichol had been foreign correspondent for the Chicago *Daily News* in Europe for nearly twenty years. Headquartered in Bonn since the Nuremberg Trials in 1946, Nichol is now in Jerusalem covering the Eichmann case. I took advantage of the presence at the trial of this authority on European affairs, with this exchange:

"You were in Berlin in the 1940s. Were you an eyewitness to any of the atrocities now being described in the courtroom?"

"In Berlin, we didn't see much direct evidence of the tragedies that are talked about here in this trial. We did, of course, see SS men in black uniforms all over the place and we were very aware of the restrictions which were being placed on the

Jews. They had already lost most of their property and most of their civil rights."

"Were you ever in a concentration camp?"

"Yes, I went into Maidanek, one of the big extermination camps, which is included in the indictment against Eichmann. It's near Lublin in Poland. We went in there just two or three days after the Soviet army had taken the area. The camp hadn't been cleaned up yet. I've never seen anything so ghastly in all my life. There was such a litter of decaying bodies."

"What's your reaction to the way the trial is being conducted?"

"The Israel authorities are, if anything, being too meticulous. There was a long legal argument at the beginning of the trial to establish the jurisdiction of the court. Obviously this is making a record for jurists in establishing the rights to try this man."

"Does the elaborate courtesy of the judges toward the defendant and toward his counsel strike a strange or curious note?"

"No, I'd expect that from any decent court which respects the principles of justice. I remember at the Nuremberg trial the judges were very precise and correct in their approach to the top Nazi leaders who were on trial there."

"What is your overall reaction to the way the trial is being conducted by the Israeli prosecutor and the court?"

"I was here last summer for three weeks just after Eichmann had been captured and I talked at great length with people in the Israeli Department of Justice. I left convinced then that Eichmann was going to get as fair a trial as possible—at least as fair as every other Nazi war criminal got at Nuremberg."

"What was the feeling in Germany before you left there to cover the trial?"

"There, Germans were very upset. They were afraid and with good reason. They knew that all the stories of the wartime horrors were going to be retold, as they certainly have been. The Germans themselves hope that this would once and for all clear away some of the bad atmosphere that has existed."

"Do you think it will have a therapeutic effect on the German people themselves?"

"There's a big program underway in Germany itself to round up the people who were involved in these things. The Germans at the Nuremberg trial were preoccupied with just being alive, finding food and a place to live. Their own system of newspaper and radio was so undeveloped at that stage, that they really don't know much about the Nuremberg Trials."

"Do they seem to have a sense of guilt now about the Hitler period, in the face of the Eichmann trial?"

"It's difficult to find anybody who admits that he was actually a Nazi, but in private conversations people feel pretty badly about this. I was talking with a German correspondent the other day and he said, 'Even though I wasn't physically in Germany during Nazism, I can't help but feel awful.'"

"Are you familiar at all with the feelings of the people in East Germany, the people under Soviet domination?"

"Every time we go to Berlin it is possible to go to East Berlin. We cannot travel into Eastern Germany as such. But we can listen to their radio and talk to the refugees who come out at the rate of five hundred or so daily. We read their newspapers and I think it is correct to say that we are somewhat familiar with what they feel."

"Is there any difference in feeling between the East and West Germans with respect to the Eichmann trial?"

"The East Germans never admitted that they had any responsibility for anything of this sort. The East Germans refused to have anything to do with the restitution agreement with Israel. They haven't even been very cooperative about setting up this trial. They have wanted to intervene but to intervene for their own purposes. The East German Communist regime is trying to use the Eichmann trial to destroy the West German government and Chancellor Adenauer."

"Do you think West Germany will be harmed in its relations with the nations of the world as a result of these months of hearings against Eichmann?"

"Oh, sure they'll be harmed. But I'm not sure that it's necessarily a bad thing in itself. Germany since World War II was first terribly pushed aside and hated by everybody. Then as the Russians appeared, everybody began to make friends and agreements with Germany. Perhaps it's a result of some of these things that both the Germans and ourselves will have a sound healthy approach to each other. . .."

May 7, 1961:

Debate is on full blast in the corridors and press rooms of the Beit Ha'am, the community center converted into a courthouse. The West Germans are fearful it will serve but to poison the free world's attitude toward themselves. The East Germans are sending home dispatches designed to accomplish exactly that purpose. The Soviets see the entire affair as an Israeli political effort to justify its own, by Soviet lights, unfortunate existence. And the Israelis see it as monumental ironic justice.

Strange to say, there are nations, and they are not few, who are learning via the Eichmann trial for the first time the whole story of the Nazi effort to wipe out the Jewish people. The Japanese people, for example—part of the Axis powers during World War II—occupied with their own battle front, blocked from German sources, were kept in the dark by their own government censorship. They never had the opportunity to hear the ghastly truth. The people of the new African nations were also mostly unaware of the story. And then, of course, the youth of the world who were too young to read or understand.

It is not enough, say the Israelis, that there were Nuremberg trials following the defeat of the Third Reich and that the world learned something of the gigantic Nazi horror. The Nuremberg Tribunal conducted war crimes trials only. The Eichmann trial, they point out, is not a war crimes trial but a genocide trial. Germany had a policy of anti-Semitism from the very inception of Nazism in 1933 that eventually led to the mass murder of Jews. The program of extermination, they explain, was separate and apart from the military killing in World War II, and irrelevant to the reasons that inspired Hitler to start that war.

The Eichmann indictment itself, the basis for the ongoing

trial, say the Israelis, contains fifteen separate counts and only one is a war crime as such. Some of the other counts do touch on Eichmann activities during the conduct of the war, but they are not the gravamen of the indictment. The essence of all the counts are Eichmann's misdeeds against Jews. The evidence which the Israeli prosecutor is busily submitting to the court and making part of the permanent historical record does not concern the facts of the war crimes presented at Nuremberg.

For the first time, eyewitnesses, victimized Jews are now testifying in depth. There will be an effort to show the permanent effect of Hitler's extermination program on the Jewish people, the dire demographic result. In short, the complete Nazi program for the wholesale destruction of an entire people is being laid bare before the world, under oath and with incontrovertible evidence. And an accounting of the impact is being placed in the permanent records of mankind.

When we understand this purpose, say the Israelis, we will be able to comprehend more clearly their attitude in insisting that Eichmann stand trial in their land. No longer is it a story of all Nazi crime and of World War II. This is the special, additional, particular Nazi crime against the Jews of Europe and, if Hitler could have made it so, the Jews of the world.

Israelis are unanimous that the world must learn the dangers of opening the floodgates of religious prejudice. They know the meaning of anti-Semitism. Only their children are shocked by what they are reading in their newspapers, hearing from the courtroom and learning from parents who share their personal experiences.

One finds a significant unanimity when he asks the average man in the street what he would like done with the prisoner if, when the trial is over, a guilty verdict results. "What to do with Eichmann? That's easy," they say. "Take him around Israel. Let him see it all. Let him see the smiling faces and the healthy bodies of our youth. Let him see the orchards and the concert halls, the fertile farms and the cities. Let him know that we have rebuilt stronger than ever despite his efforts to wipe us from the face of the earth."

They know the suggestion is fantasy. But they are expressing their great pride in what they have accomplished for themselves in the short span of thirteen years. They feel a quiet satisfaction in the knowledge that they have re-created a decent life for themselves even while remembering the sense of utter hopelessness in Hitler's Europe . . .

May 8, 1961:

Standing in front of the courthouse is the noted author, Meyer Levin, whose best-sellers include *The Old Bunch* and *Compulsion.* Mr. Levin, who discovered the diary of Anne Frank in Europe and brought it to the United States, where he turned it into a literary symbol of Jewish courage, is attending the trial as an observer. I probed his reactions. "What is the meaning of the Eichmann trial to the people of Israel?" was my opening question.

"It has not only a modern but an ancient meaning. Eichmann is the symbol of every mass murder in the entire history of the Jewish people. He is Haman, who tried to destroy the Jews in the time of the kings of Persia, the event we celebrate every year at the time of the festival of Purim. He is the Spanish Inquisition. He is the personification of evil in the human spirit—and not only to the Jews, of course. He is the evil that pervades the world, that brings wars, that brings prejudice, that brings hatred between people. To extricate the essence of this evil and to show it to the world is really the object of this trial."

"You think the trial has a universal meaning, a special meaning for Jews and for Christians?"

"It has just as universal a meaning and just as special a meaning for Christians and Jews as does the Bible."

"What will be accomplished by the long recital of the entire ghastly story?"

"The education of the world, if it would only listen. The object has in great measure already been accomplished. Since the capture of Eichmann, there has been more written, spoken and discussed about the Holocaust, about the destruction, the genocide, of the Jewish people in Europe than there has been in the entire period since the war. It has brought to light the whole issue as never before, and that is an educational effect the world needed."

"Wasn't the world already treated to this story at the Nuremberg hearings?"

"No. The Nuremberg trials were a much more complicated war-crimes presentation. There was the fact, the feeling, that the victors, in a sense, were punishing the vanquished, that it was a court made up of victors. Incidentally, that really wasn't true, it was a fair court. Here, too, of course, with the trial in Israel, people may say that there is an element of revenge. But the effort in this situation is to bring out almost in a scientific way, almost in a medical way, even in this long drawn-out fashion, the whole mechanism of mass murder. That was not done at the Nuremberg trials, except in a general sense. On the whole, the genocidal plot escaped in the specific trials of personalities at Nuremberg."

"What should be reported to the American people about what is happening here in Jerusalem, seven thousand miles from them?"

"They should be told to listen and pay heed to this example of how the human spirit can be driven to take part in mass destruction while rationalizing its cruelties by saying man can no longer control what he does, that man is only a cog in a machine. I studied the Eichmann materials over a period of years. Working on elements of this story ever since, as a reporter in the war, I was practically the first to enter the liberated concentration camps to find out what had become of the Jews. The world has to see that man still must be master of himself, that each individual still must retain his responsibility for his own moral behavior, that we must not accede to the view that we are only cogs in a machine, soldiers who have to carry out the most inhuman orders under any circumstances; that we must return to the view that each man is the master of his own soul and responsible to mankind and to God for his behavior and not only to his immediate commanding officer."

"What will be the outcome of the trial so far as Eichmann is concerned"?

"It's of the least importance what happens to Eichmann. The great importance is what happens to humanity from now on. Eichmann is only a specimen of a very unfortunate and very bestial type of humanity, and his fate doesn't concern me at all."

"Have you talked with any of the American reporters at the trial covering it for home?"

"Yes."

"Tell me their general reaction to the trial."

"On the whole they think it is over scrupulous, that the court is leaning over backward to provide the utmost latitude of argument for Eichmann's counsel; that there is a scientific exactitude and calm about the way in which the presiding judge and his two colleagues examine the case and that the court proceeding is remarkably cool and unprejudiced in its atmosphere."

"In the immediate years after World War II, Mr. Levin, you spent many months trying to bring the diary of Anne Frank to the attention of the world. You did it successfully and the book publication had a tremendous effect. How would you compare the impact of the current trial of Eichmann with the impact of *The Diary of Anne Frank?*"

"They are different sides of the same coin. There has been comment recently from some psychiatrists that the diary showed that people in a tragic situation might tend to hide, might not take the line of resistance that they should. This trial, the other side of that coin, shows the persecution, the drive that they were under, how it was almost impossible to do anything but try to hide . . . We have here in Jerusalem in these very days a Memorial to the Martyrdom of the People who were in the various concentration camps and we also have a Memorial to the Fighters of the Warsaw Ghetto. At the very last, of course, there were uprisings and efforts at resistance, but the material being produced at the trial shows how virtually impossible it was to stand up successfully against the tremendous machine of destruction of Hitler's operated by people like Eichmann . . ."

May 9, 1961:

Sitting in the courtroom of the Beit Ha'am day in and out, listening to the trial of Adolf Eichmann, his life at stake on charges of "Crimes Against Humanity" and "Crimes Against the Jewish People," the observer learns why Israel sought so long and so hard to find and capture the Nazi who had been in charge of the liquidation of all Jews, and why this little nation has insisted on putting him on trial before its own judicial tribunal.

To the people of Israel, Adolf Eichmann is the living personification of Nazism.

When Dr. Servatius urged on the court that it should release Eichmann and permit him to return to the Argentine because, in the attorney's words, "Eichmann is no longer a menace to civilization, that with the end of the Third Reich his client had resumed his former role as a peaceful law-abiding citizen; that with the downfall of the Hitler regime the defendant freed himself from his oath of loyalty to it"—in making his plea Dr. Servatius missed the point of the trial. If his argument were to stand up, every one of the high Nazi war criminals at Nuremberg could have gone scott free by the simple device of saying that he had finally abandoned Nazism.

But that is only a superficial answer to Dr. Servatius. Substance is this: Adolf Eichmann is a symbol of a Nazi government that bathed Europe in Jewish blood after an incredible decision to exterminate every last Jew. The Israelis, after nearly two thousand years, now have their own government, their own state, and they have captured the man primarily responsible for the liquidation of millions of their kinsmen less than a generation ago. This new state is intent upon seeing to it that the world never again is drowned in the blood of the Jewish people. It is a universal danger. Civilization, Israel says, has made Jews the barometer of its own mental health, its sanity. When the world goes berserk, on a murderous rampage, inevitably the Jewish people are among those victimized.

The prosecutor has offered into evidence for the court to consider, a history of the last thirty years. Once before, Mr.

Hausner has said, Jews tried to warn the world that its collective life and freedom was in jeopardy. From 1932 until the explosion in 1939, an unprepared Jewish community pleaded in vain for the society of nations to recognize the grave danger. The prosecutor has reminded us that in November 1938, the time of the infamous Crystal Night, Chaim Weizmann, later Israel's first president, speaking from London while the synagogues in Berlin were burning, said to the world: "Today it is the temple of the Jews in Berlin, tomorrow it might be Westminster Abbey."

And so it was—in 1941 the great blitz came to London in the Battle of Britain, and before World War II was ended forty-four million human beings had gone to their graves in defense of freedom. Among them were six million Jewish noncombatants, deliberate victims of organized pogroms.

Only days ago the ashes of thousands of Jews which had been buried temporarily in 1950 in a casket on a hillside in Israel were lifted up, carried in their container and interred in a tabernacle on Memorial Mountain in the Judean Hills of Jerusalem. Two hundred yards away in the Yad Vashem, the Memorial Archive of Nazi Atrocities, are two letters. Both bear Adolf Eichmann's signature.

The first letter is to the German Foreign Ministry, dated February 8, 1943, in which he objects to an exchange of five thousand Bulgarian Jewish children for German prisoner-of-war soldiers. The transfer of the five thousand children to Palestine, he complains, would irritate the Arabs. The second letter, dated June 22, 1942, notified the German foreign ministry that in August trains will be available daily to deliver Jews to Auschwitz, a thousand to a train. The list includes forty thousand Jews in Occupied France, forty thousand in The Netherlands, and ten thousand in Belgium. "None is able to work," adds Eichmann, "and none is a citizen of the United States, Great Britain, Central or South America . . . I hope you can have nothing to say against my actions," Eichmann concludes.

The Israeli prosecutor here in the Beit Ha'am will likely suggest that perhaps Eichmann's superiors in Berlin in fact had no objection. But what nonsense, he must then add, to argue that this man is now a harmless, law-abiding citizen.

I talked to an Israeli, David Shaltiel, who fled Germany in 1933 only to return some years later as a secret emissary to bring children out through the Jewish underground. In silence, from his hiding place, he watched nude Jewish girls run down public streets at the bayonet points of laughing Nazi soldiers. David cried quietly as he saw from another hideout mothers being torn apart from their children and herded into cattle cars for the crematorium. Then caught, he spent three years in a concentration camp. Before escaping, David saw Jews kicked by jackbooted Nazis into large trenches which quickly became mass graves as machineguns sputtered into bellies and faces.

This man said to me: "We know that the trial will not bring back a single child to life . . . will reunite no family separated by death . . . will wipe out not one moment of suffering . . . will free no concentration camp survivor of the nightmares which are his legacy from the Nazis. But they put yellow badges on us. They robbed us of our dignity. They took our souls from us. They killed us like animals. They ground us into dust.

"Never before," he added, "have we brought our persecutors to judgment. Always others have held the trials, made the record and decided the punishment. Now, finally, we are doing it ourselves. This will help restore our dignity, give us back our souls. By the trial of Adolf Eichmann here in Israel we are telling the world that never again will Jewish blood be free for the spilling."

In the 1948 War of Independence General David Saltiel commanded the Israel Armed Forces in the successful battle for Jerusalem.

May 10, 1961:

As the trial of Adolf Eichmann gets deeper into the twelve-year history of Germany's Nazism, Israel's passionate desire to see justice done and the reasons for it become crystal clear.

But justice to whom? To Adolf Eichmann, the man charged with "Crimes Against Humanity and Against the Jewish Peo-

Recording Israeli Air Force Chief Ezer Weizman for Dateline Israel radio broadcast, at Tel Aviv's Defense Ministry Headquarters, July 1979.

Prime Minister Golda Meir interviewed for Dateline Israel program, at her desk in Jerusalem, May 1973.

On location in Israel for Dateline Israel radio series, July 1970.

Director Sam Elfert with the author photographing a page from the original Anne Frank diary during the July 1978 filming of *Avenue of the Just*. Holding the diary is one of the original employees, Mr. Meip, who hid the family in the attic.

Author interviews Otto Frank (above), father of Anne, in Basel, Switzerland, during the July 1978 filming of *Avenue of the Just*. With director Sam Elfert (below) and members of the TV crew, sketching out the concentration camp scene for the film.

Co-authors Epstein and Forster present a copy of *The New Anti-Semitism* to Prime Minister Itzhak Rabin and his wife, Leah, November 1974.

Thanking Menachem Begin at an ADL leadership session with the Prime Minister. Left to right: Arnold Forster, Nathan Perlmutter, Maxwell E. Greenberg, and Kenneth J. Bialkin, June 1979.
(Photo: Rachamim Israeli)

Mayor Teddy Kollek and the author share an outdoor press conference in Jerusalem, June 1979. *(Photo: Rachamim Israeli)*

Prime Minister Yitzhak Rabin discusses the Middle East with Milton S. Gould and the author in New York, November 1985.

The author interviews Israel's President Itzhak Navon at his Jerusalem residence, July 1978. *(Photo: Ross Photo)*

Yosef Tekoah (center), Israel's Ambassador to the United Nations, and the author share the speakers platform at a Ben Gurion University dinner in New York City, October 1982.

Author interviews Prime Minister Golda Meir for TV program in Jerusalem on the occasion of Israel's 25th Anniversary, May 1973.

Prime Minister Menachem Begin chats with the author in Jerusalem after completing Dateline Israel radio interview, June 1979.
(Photo: Rachamim Israeli)

ple"? To the Nazi butchers who were his partners in an incredible mass murder? Not at all. Israel's profound desire is to see justice done to the six million Jewish dead who went to their graves simply because it was decreed by the Third Reich that there was no room for them on God's earth.

In short, the prosecutor has made clear that he is the attorney for the dead, not the living. Further, that unable to make ethnic distinctions in the matter of mass murder he represents not alone the Jewish dead but all those innocents who were slaughtered by the Nazi extermination machine.

In his revelations Gideon Hausner, the Israeli prosecutor, has put into the indelible pages of history a role of honor of thousands of Christians who died violently by Nazi torture for their vain efforts to put a stop to the subhuman extermination program. In his very opening address, as only one example, he pointed to a priest sent to a concentration camp by Adolf Eichmann personally for daring to plead publicly against the cruelties under which the Jews were being crushed.

The central issue of the trial is the crime against six million Jews. This is the difference between the tragic story being told in Jerusalem and the many trials that were conducted by the Allied powers in Nuremberg. This is why the state's attorney concentrates on Eichmann's special responsibility for the annihilation of Jews. This is why he points out that the crimes for which Eichmann is now on trial began years before the Third Reich precipitated the Second World War. This is why he has brought out the whole tragic story of anti-Semitism from the beginning. The crime, he has said, was not the result of "a momentary passion," or "a darkening of the soul" but of a calculated decision by a mighty criminal conspiracy involving thousands of participants.

In this context the history of anti-Semitism from its inception becomes relevant to the trial of Adolf Eichmann. It is the backdrop against which hideous anti-Jewish outrages were conceived and perpetrated. And as they are recited by witnesses, one's blood goes cold while the mind rejects that it could have been reality.

Of what is Eichmann guilty? asks Israel. And the state's attorney answers: "True, we know of only one incident in which Eichmann actually beat to death a Jewish boy who dared to steal fruit from a peach tree in the yard of his Budapest home. But it was also Eichmann's word that put the gas chambers into operation. He lifted a telephone and railroad cars departed for extermination camps. His signature was the seal of doom for many tens of thousands. He had but to give the order, and at his command the troops routed Jews from their neighborhoods, beat and tortured them, chased them into ghettos, stole their property. Then, finally, after torture and pillage, when everything had been wrung out of them, when even their hair had been taken, they were transported en masse to their slaughter . . . Then the corpses were of value. Their gold teeth were extracted and wedding rings removed.

"And so Eichmann must bear the responsibility for it all," concluded the state's attorney, "as if it were he who with his own hands knotted the hangman's noose, lashed the victims into the gas chambers, shot in the back and pushed into the open pits every single one of the millions who were slaughtered. Such is his responsibility in the eyes of the law and such is his responsibility according to every standard of conscience and morality."

Now it is clear that the personal crimes of Adolf Eichmann were also the actual criminality of an entire government. His accomplishments in human destruction were at the same time an accurate record of the successful Nazi effort to obliterate six million Jewish people. The two crimes are inextricably interwoven.

So, Eichmann is not on trial alone here in Jerusalem, not sitting in the chair of the accused by himself. With him in the courtroom, unable to escape responsibility, is every grown man who lived in Hitler's Germany who failed to cry out against the inhuman Holocaust. Who were they? The prosecutor has named one: Adolf Eichmann.

On January 30, 1933, President Paul Von Hindenburg gave the rule of Germany over into Hitler's hands. Did he know, asked Gideon Hausner, did he know what he was doing to his people and to the world? The answer was clear, said the prosecutor. After swearing in the members of the new government, Hindenburg added, "And now gentlemen, forward with the help of God." Germany did indeed stride forward, Hausner concluded, toward war, horror and shame.

Will Israel's passionate goal of justice for the Six Million be attained? The only justice that can be won for the dead is that it be inscribed in the pages of history of mankind. A memorial built not of stone, not of words, but of unforgettable grief. If civilized society remembers forever in shame what it permitted to happen in the twentieth century, Israel will have succeeded in coming as close as it is possible to winning justice for those who are today but a memory and a few ashes in a hillside.

For days on end—as the Israeli prosecution, one flight above this press room here in the Beit Ha'am, puts into the trial record in the case against Adolf Eichmann the whole gruesome story of human destruction—spectators, newsmen, diplomats and other observers sit in stunned silence. They are simply aghast at what they are hearing. Eichmann, too, sitting impassively in his glass cage, seems to listen as carefully as the others.

There is no laughter among the spectators in the corridors and halls during the court recesses. And here in the press room itself—filled with longtime newspapermen, radio and TV reporters, a group that rarely takes itself seriously, men who normally develop a fund of cynical wisecracking jokes about their assignment and the people they are covering—here, too, there is no laughter, no fun, no joke-making.

The prisoner sits in the dock in the courtroom upstairs, listening carefully to every word that is being spoken, showing no emotion. He rarely reveals even a reaction to what is happening. Either Adolf Eichmann is a hardened, disciplined soldier with such complete mastery of himself that he is able to hide his feelings of regret or remorse—if, indeed, he has such feelings— or else he remains the arrogant, unrepentent, unregenerate Nazi capable of crushing to death a little hungry boy who had stolen a peach from a tree in his garden; a man who will be reached by nothing, even his own death.

Several historical truths seem for the first time since the fall of the Third Reich to be unfolding, facts which are not generally known: in many quarters of the world the impression has been that most of the six million Jewish victims of Adolph Hitler and Adolf Eichmann went to their deaths in resignation, submission and defeat. This, the prosecutor is now showing, obviously bears little resemblance to the reality. The Jews of Nazi Europe went down fighting, according to the documented evidence in the hands of Gideon Hausner, the prosecutor, who this very moment stands before the court upstairs in this building, adding to the sworn record the whole courageous story.

The Warsaw Ghetto, one of the greatest tales of human bravery and endurance in all of history, it now appears, was only one of many similar heroic if tragic episodes. There were the ghettos, too, of Vilna, Bialystock, Lodz—none less awe-inspiring than any other in its record of resistance. In all of these barbed-wire, makeshift walled-in prisons Jews fought practically with their bare hands against heavily armed, highly trained storm troopers who outnumbered them a thousand to one. The enemy was a jackbooted, Hitler-poisoned, Nazi bully. The ranks of the Jews were made up of small children, pious old Jews and young women. The majority of the able-bodied men among the Jews had been the first to be seized before they knew what was really happening and before they could organize themselves to fight back.

The world turned its back, until almost the last hour when six of Europe's seven million Jews had been turned to ash. But now it is clear that perhaps a million of those Jews were killed resisting the Nazi conquerer, fighting back against Hitler's juggernaut, dying *not* on their bedraggled knees but on their blood-soaked feet.

Another item new for history's dark pages, and not well known before this trial of Adolf Eichmann began here in this courthouse in Jerusalem: the Nazi extermination organization had devised a *special* program for the liquidation of Jewish children. Haphazard information available until now had led the world to think that the Nazis had routinely included chil-

228

dren among all other victims. Not so. For the children there were special arrangements. Nor am I now referring to the 140 Christian children who were slaughtered by Eichmann's storm troopers when they leveled Lidice in retaliation for the assassination of Reinhard Heydrich, the Nazi security chief.

But let's take it from the court records, I quote Gideon Hausner:

"Eichmann dealt personally with the deportations from France, and his representatives went to Pierre Laval to bargain over the expulsion of the Jews. His stewards forcibly separated children from parents, the mothers holding onto their offspring and begging the butchers to leave them together. At the end, no more than four thousand children between the ages of two and four were left. As early as August 14, 1942, an aide reported to Eichmann, and informed the Auschwitz Camp Commandant that the deportation of children had been started."

Listen to a description of how these children arrived in a concentration camp in Europe:

"The children would arrive at the camp packed in buses guarded by policemen. They would be put down in the courtyard surrounded by barbed wire, guarded by a platoon of French gendarmes. The police and the gendarmes, hard people not usually given to emotion, could not hide their abhorrence over the task they were compelled to carry out. On the arrival of the buses they would begin to remove the children and lead them in groups to the hall. The older ones holding the hands of the smaller children, or carrying them in their arms. They did not weep—the children. They walked terrified, disciplined, miserable and complied with the order like a flock of sheep, one helping the other."

Listen to how they were deported from the camp: "On the day of deportation they would be awakened at five o'clock in the morning, irritable, half asleep, most of the children would refuse to get up and go down to the courtyard. The volunteer women would have to urge them gently, patiently so as to convince older children that they must obey orders and vacate the halls. On a number of occasions the entreaties did not help, the children cried and refused to leave their mattresses. The gendarmes would then enter the halls, take up the children in their arms as they screamed with fear, struggling and grasping each other.

"The halls were like a madhouse. The scene was too terrible for even the most hardened of men to bear. In the courtyard they would call out the names of the children, one by one, mark them off in the register and direct them to the buses. When the bus filled up, it would leave the camp with its cargo. Since many children remained unidentified and others would not answer to their correct or assumed names, they would include them in the convoy to make up the necessary number.

"Each convoy consisted of five hundred children and five hundred adults chosen from the camp prison. Within a period of about three weeks, during the second half of August and again in the first part of December 1943, four thousand children just made into orphans were transported in this fashion inter-mixed with adult strangers."

This, then, is Adolf Eichmann, the man who answered to the court only days ago, when asked whether he pleaded guilty or innocent to the charges against him: "Within the spirit of the indictment, I am not guilty."

This from a man who made it his business to murder children.

May 11, 1961:

Standing with me in a quiet corner of the courthouse where Adolf Eichmann is on trial for his life is Dr. Melvin Tumin, associate professor of sociology and anthropology at Princeton University.

"Dr. Tumin, do you have any reaction to the trial?"

"I am extraordinarily impressed with the seriousness, the de-corum and the quiet with which the proceedings are being conducted, impressed especially in view of the fact that there in the glass box sits a man who unquestionably was responsible in large part for the murder of six million Jewish people."

"Is there a special reason for your attendance at the trial or did you come here out of personal curiosity?"

"Curiosity is not quite the right word. I have a deep personal interest in the trial, being a Jew. I also have a professional interest because I am about to start a study of anti-Semitism in several countries in Europe. One of the important ingredients of this study is intimately connected with the trial. I am worried at the degree of forgetfulness that I observed among people all over the world with regard to what happened under Adolph Hitler and under Adolf Eichmann. I am also very interested in the extent to which the Jewish people of the world, and especially of Israel, have managed to make such a remarkable adjustment after that Holocaust."

"Dr. Tumin, you recently completed a summary and evaluation of all available data on anti-Semitism in the United States covering the last thirty years. Do you relate your findings to the Eichmann trial in any way?"

"One of the important findings of the summary research is that very little is known about the causes of anti-Semitism, except that anti-Semitism seems to appear under very different circumstances and at very different times for very different reasons."

"Then what is the value of this trial? If the causes of anti-Semitism vary greatly from country to country, how do you expect the particular lesson of this case to be helpful?"

"In two ways. It serves to remind us that mankind can become beastly toward itself if we are not extremely careful about the conditions under which we live. Secondly, it reminds us that because the causes of anti-Semitism seem to be so diverse, we must always be prepared for its appearance. Anti-Semitism can arise unless we are extremely careful about the form and organization of our society. This trial is a symbolic reminder to the world that this can happen at any time."

"Can you tell me whether any changes have occurred since 1945 to lead you to believe that what happened in the thirties and forties with Hitler's Third Reich cannot ever happen again?"

"I see no reasonable basis for assuming that under the 'right' circumstances this could not happen again. There is continuing evidence of plenty of Nazi sentiment still left throughout the world."

"If the educational values in trials such as this one have no effective counter-purpose with respect to anti-Semitism, what is the answer to the age-old problem of anti-Jewish hatred?"

"There is no answer in any final sense about hatred among human beings. What makes it possible for human beings to live with each other in decent ways, whether they be Jew or Christian or Moslem, is democratic organization and a fair chance at a decent life for all. It must be made possible for them to find their own ways in life without their having to take out their misery and suffering on others."

"You looked at Adolf Eichmann in the courtroom upstairs. Did you have any personal reaction to him? Did you see in him anything special?"

"My first reaction is that this simple-looking individual could not be responsible for the monstrous Holocaust. He looks like an assistant professor in a remote university. He is neat and orderly. But then I noticed what some others have noticed—that he almost does nothing, is granitelike. He never moves. He never seems to blink. His face seems to undergo no changes. He rarely uses his hands. I have come to the conclusion that inside, at least, this man is, for the first time in fifteen years, enjoying himself. He is once more back in the limelight. He is Adolf Eichmann, the great mass murderer of Jews, a task to which he apparently was dedicated with great devotion fifteen and twenty years ago. Of course I can't prove that he is enjoying it but it's very difficult for me to understand the immobility and the impassivity of that man unless he is now once again playing the role of the superman in which he believed so deeply twenty years ago."

"When he was asked by the presiding judge to answer 'guilty' or 'not guilty' to the charges against him, he responded, 'In the spirit of the indictment I am not guilty.' Dr. Tumin, in your judgment does that curious language convey any special attitude on the part of Adolf Eichmann?"

"Yes, I think it conveys from him and from many others like

him an effort, an attempt, to use extremely formal, legal devices to excuse themselves from great moral indictments of which I think they stand guilty. The resort to the legalism of 'in the spirit of the indictment,' is an effort to say that the indictment is by some curious legal standard improper and that therefore he is not guilty because of the legal impropriety. I happen to think he is wrong on both counts—that the indictment is legally proper and that he is morally responsible, whichever way you cut it."

"One more question, Dr. Tumin. What is the value of this trial in 1961 in your judgment?"

"I will repeat. The value of the trial is that it will keep alive in the forgetful conscience, and in the dying memory of the world, the most important event of the last twenty-five or thirty years, namely the Nazi Holocaust . . ."

May 12, 1961:

We are nearly at the end of the trial of Adolf Eichmann. Enough has been revealed, put into the record and been expressed by those here in Jerusalem watching the trial, for an interested observer to be able to form some tentative conclusions about the findings of the court, the meaning of the evidence and its impact thus far on civilized nations.

These things are clear: Eichmann has gotten a fair trial in the sense in which we in the United States talk of a fair trial—expert defense counsel; a prosecutor who avoids, at every cost, any semblance of browbeating; a presiding judge who is scrupulously careful about observing all the rules of the evidence; all the protections afforded by Israeli law to any prisoner before the bar. In this respect the Eichmann trial proceeding in Jerusalem is similar to the trials we in the United States have traditionally been accustomed to under constitutional rules.

Second, it seems clear that the jurisdictional criticisms which were heard from some quarters regarding the manner of Eichmann's capture, the propriety of conducting the trial in Israel, the concept of charging him with crimes under a law which was adopted in 1950—five years after the destruction of Hitler's

Third Reich—these and other such criticisms have dissolved in the flood of documentation showing that the defendant was not only officially responsible for carrying out the mass destruction of Jews but that he personally derived great emotional satisfaction in perpetrating some of the most atrocious crimes ever committed by man against his fellow man.

For example, when the Norwegian government tried to save its own Jewish citizens, Eichmann flew into a great rage. The idea of Jews escaping the crematorium was unacceptable to him. Though no superior of Eichmann's required it, he insisted on deporting eight hundred of the total one thousand Norwegian Jews. Twenty-one came out alive. When the Danes in Denmark brought off a miniature Dunkirk in stealing its Jews away from Eichmann by boat in the dark of the night, the defendant was insane with fury.

Third, most people have become convinced that the weight of international law and the decisions of the highest courts in the nations of the free world, including the United States, is on the side of Israel with respect to its right to try Eichmann under a law copied from the Charter of Nuremberg, a legal tribunal created by the Allied powers to try Nazi leaders for their war crimes.

Then, too, civilized society now seems satisfied about the fundamental morality and justification of the trial.

Several other points have been established. One, Adolf Eichmann was not at all a simple clerk, a civil servant fulfilling an assignment. He was not only a government bureaucrat in overall charge of a human extermination program. Much more. He was a willing, even eager director of the mass slaughter. He went far beyond the call of duty time and again in his thoroughness in trying to obliterate Jews from the face of the earth. He had a personal mania and drew great inner satisfaction from the incredible slaughter. No simple soldier he, just taking orders.

Two, it appears from the evidence that there were great heroes, Christian and Jew alike, in the countries occupied by Hitler; men and women, indescribably heartbroken over the

234

bloodbath, who themselves went to violent deaths in their sometimes successful, more often frustrated attempts to save some of the victims of the terror.

Such a man was Roaul Wallenberg, a Swedish diplomat in Hungary, a Christian who worked to save thousands of Jews, who used his diplomatic status and a printing machine to turn out false citizenship papers from his own homeland for men, women and children who otherwise would have gone to the gas chambers.

The importance of Wallenberg—about whom we have heard much as the evidence unrolled against Eichmann—is symbolic. Alone, he saved tens of thousands of human beings. Europe did not need the monumental might of millions of soldiers of the Allied powers to stop the slaughter. It only needed a thousand Wallenbergs.

And the obvious question poses itself: If Wallenberg could do it, where were all the others? As the Israeli prosecutor has said, men are still asking themselves how it is possible, how could it have happened? In short, this trial has already pointed a finger of blame at those outside of Germany who sat on the sidelines until too late.

Which brings us to the third tentative conclusion about the need, the meaning and the value of this trial: it was and is necessary. The man, Eichmann, and the system of human destruction for which he stood, inevitably had to come before the bar of justice. This was a crime far different from the war crimes of World War II and it needed a different and separate hearing before the world.

Its meaning is clear in every page of the tragic testimony. Its value? It is a worthwhile lesson to the living. It cannot rescue the six million dead—but it can help them to rest quietly in their graves. To them, what can be said is in the province only of poets. Even Gideon Hausner, the man who has given thousands of hours trying to find the right words to describe what happened, turned to the poetic voice of a mother in the terror whose husband had been taken off to the Ponar concentration camp, and offered her words to the court:

Quiet, quiet, my son, let us speak softly,
Here grow the graves
Which they that hate planted.
Here are the paths.
The roads lead to Ponar,
There is no way back.

Father has gone, never to return.
And with him the light.

Quiet, my son, my treasure.
Let us not cry in pain.
In any case, we have wept;
The enemy does not understand.
The sea has limits and a shore—
This, our suffering
Is limitless,
Is endless.

Israel is saying that the suffering of Jews, of mankind, must not be limitless, must not be endless. It is saying that never again in the history of civilization should a repetition of the Holocaust be permitted. Never again.

This is Arnold Forster in Jerusalem.

22

Dateline Israel

Taping my daily report on the Eichmann trial had been a traumatic experience. This may have been why I waited five years before accepting the offer to make other radio programs in Israel for broadcast in the States. Nineteen sixty-eight saw the completion of my first twenty-six fifteen-minute interviews to be distributed to some fifty U.S. radio stations. Nearly two decades later, when I discontinued "Dateline Israel," after taping nearly 500 programs, it had more than 400 radio outlets plus sixteen television programs broadcast over national networks.

Designed to project an image of Israel as a living democracy, Western-style, "Dateline Israel" hid none of Israel's blemishes, inevitable in any twentieth century society. There was no effort to portray Israel as better than other democracies—different but not better. I did keep a careful eye out for interviews that might provide insights on the quality of life in the young Jewish state and on its national *raison d'etre*.

The Music of Thereseinstadt revolved around Joza Karas, a Czech-born musician I met on an El Al airliner to Israel. Chance seated us together on the long flight to the Mideast. A professor of music at the University of Connecticut, Karas was now enjoying American citizenship. I spoke of my preoccupation with anti-Semitism and Nazism, and he revealed his recent successful search for sheet music composed by inmates at Thereseinstadt, the concentration camp in Czechoslovakia. I remembered the Nazi camp as a Hitler hellhole turned by the Germans into a showplace for visitors to see how humane was the treatment meted out to Jewish captives. Part of the camp's camouflage was a makeshift orchestra of inmates who performed as the price of a temporary delay of the trip to the gas chambers. Rounded up like cattle from Nazi-occupied territories, most concentration camp victims had arrived without even a toothbrush and only the clothes on their backs. Of course, they had no musical instruments. These had to be provided by the Nazis from their confiscated loot. And there was no sheet music.

On a return visit to his native Czechoslovakia, Professor Karas told me—he, a Christian who migrated to America unable to withstand the stench of Nazi Europe—that he had heard an incredible story from local friends. Jewish composers in the camp, they said, had written their own music for the orchestra but were careful to bury the documents in camp grounds before going to the death chambers.

Karas said he had known about the orchestra at the camp. The possibility of the existence of the music took him back to Thereseinstadt, if possible to find the hidden treasure. Within a year he located what had not been destroyed, and now was on his way to share the documents with Israeli archivists.

Arriving in Jerusalem, I arranged to tape the professor's story for inclusion in my "Dateline Israel" series. After it was broadcast the account was picked up and turned into a television presentation.

The uninterrupted Jewish presence in the Middle East for more than four thousand years was another chronicle I came on after meeting Professor Michael Avi Yonah. A prestigious Jerusalem archeologist, Avi Yonah traced Jewish history for me, proving its continuity with artifacts recovered in archeological digs. Still another interview spoke of an important Israel contribution to medical science, and was spelled out by two young

scientists from the Weizmann Institute at Rehovoth. They outlined a simple method, the first of its kind, for determining the
presence of leukemia in the human body almost from the onset
of the disease.

It was October 6, 1973, the Day of Atonement, holiest day of
the year for Jews, and Egypt had levelled a surprise attack upon
Israel. Jews the world over, believing the new state might well
be brought down, feared an end to their dream in our time. But
the Yom Kippur War ended six days later in an Israeli victory—
which many thought to be a miracle. Reason enough for an
interview with Israel's chief Ashkenazi rabbi, Shlomo Goren,
who, anyway, was on my "Dateline Israel" list. And his dual role
as the Israeli armed forces chaplain made it particularly appropriate.

The rabbi, a slight man with a well-trimmed beard and unruly
hair, whom I had not met before, received me in his study. The
appointment had been fixed by the information section of the
foreign ministry. The rabbi's housekeeper served tea and cookies while we chatted, a convenient device for creating a rapport
likely to assure a better interview. As we began to get ac-
quainted I prepared the recording equipment, plugged in the
microphone and attached one to each of our lapels.

For openers, to acquaint listeners, at my request Rabbi Goren
talked about his background and told of his responsibilities as
chief of chaplains. I probed the levelling impact of a civilian
army filled with young men of families from every part of the
world with vastly different backgrounds. Yes, of course, he said,
it was assumed to be an orthodox Jewish army. Every last one
of them hated killing but understood his unavoidable duty to
protect hearth and family. Every male soldier, to be sure, was
given *tfillin,* the phylacteries worn each morning by Orthodox
Jews at prayer. And, the rabbi added, along with a uniform each
soldier was also issued a pocket-sized copy of the Old Testament.

"How do you explain Israel's victory in six short days?" I
wanted to know. Rabbi Goren looked at me, his eyes crinkling

with a secret. Suddenly he raised an arm and pointed a finger skyward, jabbing it to the heavens. Needless to say his gesticulating did not register on the tape, so I volunteered, "You point to the sky, Rabbi. Does that mean you believe the Good Lord had something to do with it?"

"Something to do with it? *All* to do with it. He *made* it happen," and his eyebrows rose almost to the top of his forehead.

"Do you really know that?"

"It's in the Bible and very clearly, too." Reaching to a shelf in back of his chair, the rabbi produced a small, cloth-bound copy of the Old Testament. "This is the Bible we give every soldier," he said, flipping through its pages for the confirming paragraph. He then read a sentence or two aloud from Leviticus 26:6,7 in which the Lord promises the Jews that "a hundred of them shall give chase to ten thousand," and that their "enemies shall fall before [them] by the sword." With no small stretch of imagination, the excerpt could conceivably be interpreted as a prophecy of a Jewish victory forecast to occur at some unknown future time and place. And it broadly matched what had happened in the Six Day War.

The interview over, we chatted again as I wrapped up the recording equipment. The small military copy of the Old Testament sat on the desk between us. I looked at the rabbi and asked whether it was an extra volume and, if so, could I possibly have it to take home.

"Gladly", said the Rabbi. "But, why would you want a copy of the Old Testament?"

"It would be a real joy to give it to my father, Rabbi," I replied, "and it would give him great pleasure if you would autograph it to him".

"Happily." Rabbi Goren smiled. "But why would your *father* want it? You are not Jewish."

"Of course, I am."

"Then why," he said, looking at me straight-faced, the faintest twinkle in his eyes, "have I been so polite to you?"

There it was, joking about the sense of insecurity always felt

240

in the presence of a non-Jew by so many Jews everywhere. The impact of timeless hostility.

In the summer of 1974 I did a radio interview with Zubin Mehta, famed conductor of the Israel Philharmonic Orchestra long before he was selected for a similar assignment by the New York Philharmonic. The Indian-born maestro was scheduled for a concert that included Verdi's *Requiem* to be performed at Manger Square outside the Church of the Nativity in Bethlehem. Singing with the orchestra were Robert Merrill, Martina Arroyo and other prominent opera stars.

Before the concert began I arranged to meet Mehta alone in the Grotto below the church, where it is said that Jesus was born. There, microphone live, I probed his feelings on the exciting occasion. Mehta, a Parsi by religion, and I, a Jew, were both deeply moved. At the intermission I interviewed Merrill and Arroya, and also taped the concert itself to use for background music.

Years later, in the summer of 1982, when Mehta had become the Israel Philharmonic's conductor, the orchestra and he consented to my doing a television film telling his and the group's story. I flew to Israel to record and interview orchestra members and conductor on tour through Israel and at concerts performed in the Frederick Mann Auditorium in Tel Aviv. I had not seen Mehta since the Bethlehem concert. Meeting him at the hall in Tel Aviv, I extended my hand, asked did he remember me, recalling the radio interview in the Bethlehem Grotto. The maestro looked at me for a long moment. "Well, I remember Jesus," he said, "but I'm not so sure about you".

Weeks later when we finished the assignment, Zubin and I were good friends. The television program even won us an Emmy in June 1983, given for outstanding achievement in the performing arts by The Academy of Television Arts and Sciences. Three years earlier "Dateline Israel" had won us our first Emmy for my film, "Avenue of the Just."

In making "Avenue" I travelled with a camera crew across Europe, the United States and the Mideast, locating and interviewing Christians in former Nazi-occupied nations of Europe who had risked their lives to save Jews. Able to find some of the victims they rescued from death, we recorded the stories and put the victims together on film with their saviors. Each of the Christians had been a guest of the Israeli government, seeing the country for a month, and honored at a tree-planting ceremony on the Avenue of The Righteous Gentiles. Bronze plaques bearing the names of these heroes are set under the trees along a quiet path on a hill in Jerusalem leading up to the Yad Vashem, the Israeli memorial to the Six Million dead.

In a race against time, Israel's search for such Christian heroes continues, its difficulties compounded by the characteristic modesty of these people who rarely speak of their selfless deeds. During a 1986 visit to Poland five years after completing the "Avenue of the Just" film I luckily succeeded in finding Jozef and Stefania Macugowski, an elderly farm couple in their mid-seventies, living an hour away from Crakow. Forty-five years earlier, during the Nazi invasion of Poland, these two hid Zahava Burack, a Westchester neighbor of ours, from the German invaders.

Zahava, not having their correct name or address in Poland, had been trying for seventeen years to locate the Macugowskis. She was a child in hiding; her home during World War II was a dirt dugout for potatoes under the floor of their farmhouse. Zahava, age eight, her two sisters and mother and father lived for two-and-a-half years under the ground in the covered trench that was too narrow to accommodate five human beings. Only days after Zahava and her family crowded into the gravelike pit, their bodies crushed against each other twenty-four hours a day, the farmhouse was taken over as a local headquarters by the invading Nazis. The Macugowskis were kept on by the occupiers as servants. When the Germans were away in town each night the young couple would bring to the hideaway leftover scraps of food, water to clean away body lice and skin sores, and to lift out human waste.

I phoned Zahava from Poland and gave her the Macugowskis exact whereabouts. She immediately arranged for the aged couple to fly to Westchester, the start of an extended holiday. In New York they were given new clothes and a dinner in their honor attended by five hundred guests—and then left on a trip across the country, courtesy of Zahava, to see how Americans live. Before this book reaches the reader, the Macugowskis will have been on their way to Israel for a tree-planting ceremony at the Yad Vashem and a month as the Jewish state's honored visitors. Then they will go back to Poland with arrangements of supplementary support for as long as they live.

One will find the Macugowskis' name inscribed on a plaque under a tree on the Avenue of the Just.

23

The Patriarch

In November of 1970 May and I called on David Ben-Gurion in his book-lined study at his Tel Aviv house a block from the sea. The occasion was a taping for "Dateline Israel" to talk about the state of the Jewish nation in its twenty-second year. Our visit lasted nearly two hours, chatting, coffee and cake, and recording. But he had time now. And Paula was no longer there to chase away visitors. A stroke had taken her nearly three years before.

It was now eighteen years since May and I first had the opportunity for a conversation with Ben-Gurion. After the 1952 meeting at the Sea of Galilee our encounters with the "Old Man" had depended more on chance—in the Knesset corridor, sometimes at private gatherings where we hastily exchanged greetings and a comment about current issues. He would always inquire good-naturedly: "You still at it, saving Jews from the anti-Semites?"

The bushy-browed, white-haired leader, the last of the giant statesmen of the thirties and forties, was now on the political sidelines in retirement. But judging from his more recently quoted statements about international events, it was evident Ben-Gurion continued to watch the global political parade *and* its impact on Israel. Engaging him in quiet discussion about current events, as I did, and then formally interviewing him revealed the still sharp mind and intellectual skills of the old master statesman. He asked whether I was busy with a new book, and that surprised me, never imagining he knew that much about my activities. "If you've read anything I've written," I said, fishing for a compliment, "tell me whether I should continue."

"You write books about anti-Semitism, that I remember," he said. "But if I did read them I don't remember."

The old fox had seen through my question and used a sledge-hammer. But then he softened the blow by adding, "It's important to fight anti-Semitism but it never ends. Not even a strong Israel will make a true difference in the *galut.*"

The world outside Israel, the *galut,* was my turf, and I had written that an Israel *would* make a difference. I like to believe that he at least glanced through some of what I had put to paper even if he thought naive what I had written.

The tiny microphones were now pinned on each of us, and the interview began. The years had not dulled Ben-Gurion's insights, nor his Johnny-one-note concern with the need for Jewish immigration to Israel. His response to my question about how he judged the outcome of his own sixty-year dream of a Jewish State: "It's not all I hoped for, I wanted so many things. First, peace, then, at least a half million Jews living here".

This brought him to "the early days" of the European Jews in Palestine and of Petach Tikvah, which he said was the first village settled by the pioneers. Ignoring the efforts of my assistant, Abe Foxman, fiddling with recording dials to insure fidelity, Ben-Gurion in the middle of the recording session turned to May. "Do you know the meaning of the two words, *Petach Tikvah?*"

May, conscious he was wearing a live mike, simply wagged her head in the negative. She feared ruining the interview with such an interruption. But her answer did not satisfy the old leader. "You should learn Hebrew," he pressed. "That's part of being Jewish. Without it, when you come here to stay it will be harder". After a pause: "So why don't you answer me?"

She still said nothing, just smiled. He then turned to me to resume recording, and offered what seemed a puzzling non sequitur: "The State has not happened yet." But then he added, "First of all, we need a minimum of another five or six million Jews. Now we have only two and a half".

Eager to get from the former prime minister his opinions of some contemporaries vis à vis Israel in its formative years, I lumped Churchill, Roosevelt, Stalin and DeGaulle together in one question. "Why do you combine these four men?", he demanded. "They were not a team." He then spoke highly of Roosevelt and Churchill and defended DeGaulle. Stalin was an enemy.

I suggested that DeGaulle's comment during the Six Day War that "Jews were domineering" seemed to hint of anti-Semitism. Ben-Gurion corrected me: "It was not during the Six Day War. It was in several speeches afterward. And I wrote to him about it and DeGaulle answered, "On the contrary, I meant what a spirited people the Jews were".

Did he believe Israel should surrender any captured territories to the Arabs to achieve peace? Ben-Gurion's answer: "If there's a possibility of peace, we should give back all the territories with two exceptions—Jerusalem and the Golan. If you have been to the Golan you understand why I add it".

"What do you think are Russia's long-term goals in the Middle East?"

"I doubt that they themselves know. Russia is neither a democracy or even less a Communist country. It is a mixture of Stalinist and Mussolini regimes. Russia's ambition is to rule the world."

Ben-Gurion's capsule views of several American presidents was revealing. Truman was "the best"; Eisenhower was "a friend"; Kennedy was "a good friend," Johnson was "a very good friend." He refused to evaluate Nixon, who, he pointed out, was the incumbent president and therefore not to be characterized by him.

"How long before peace will come to the Middle East?"

"I hope we will have it in ten or twelve years. It depends on Russia. The Arabs will have to abide by Russia's will".

What message did he have for the Jews in America? "Three things", he said. "Tell the Jews to teach their children three things. The Bible in Hebrew, Jewish history and the Jewish language".

He fooled me there, not mentioning emigration to Israel.

Two years later, in the summer of 1973, we saw Ben-Gurion again in Israel. We had been going there, twice annually, sometimes more to record "Dateline Israel" programs and to visit good friends. Our Israeli intimates, answering their phones, were never surprised to hear May's voice or mine on a local call. "Dateline Israel" was six years old and the only regular radio feature that reached the United States about life in Israel. It was being broadcast over hundreds of radio stations from coast to coast and in several other English-speaking nations.

Ben-Gurion was an increasingly sought-after subject for interview by the media because he had become a world figure of impressive vintage. Most of his contemporaries had passed on. This somehow rendered him in many minds an especially authentic source, an original participant. Surely his long years at his nation's helm had determined much of its history, and his involvement was deep in Israel's quarter-century of armed truce, a condition repeatedly interrupted by shooting wars. Although Ben-Gurion was no longer granting interviews to journalists, I was determined to see him to record another talk.

Now eighty-seven, Ben-Gurion was still shuttling between his modest desert shack at Sde Boker in the Negev and his house in midtown Tel Aviv, a block from the sea. Today both are landmarks, museums of his work and life. This particular month he was in Tel Aviv, and although his secretary vaguely remembered me, he tried to discourage an interview: "The Old Man is very tired . . . not quite up to it . . . involved with matters of his own history."

I tried to assure him I would be gentle, brief, and easy. "He would enjoy my visit with him," I told the secretary, trying to make him believe my motive was not only selfish. Immodestly I added, "He always does." Finally the secretary gave in and without checking with Ben-Gurion scheduled an appointment and told me when to appear.

The guard at the front entrance of the small Tel Aviv residence on the street now known as Rehov Ben-Gurion had obviously been told we were coming. He admitted May, Abe Foxman and me into the house and BG's secretary led us up the creaky stairs to the study. There he was, sitting in a stuffed easy chair, a book in his lap. I was shocked at his appearance. Taking turns shaking his hand, we each said our names, and each received an impersonal acknowledgement.

His once chubby cheeks were now drawn, hollow, almost to the point of emaciation. His trousers were much too big for him. Loosely fitting dentures clacked when he talked. While Abe set up the recording equipment and pinned microphones on us I tried without much success to sustain a conversation. It was evident why his secretary had tried to dissuade me from the interview. And I regretted my insistence. Now, though, I had to go forward. Knowing this would surely be my last talk with him—in fact, it was the last formal interview of his life—I solemnly reached out with grand questions: "Mr. Ben-Gurion, when you first came to Palestine did you believe you would actually live to see a State of Israel created?"

Honesty increases with old age: "When I came to Palestine," he said, "I believed that we would get only a few thousand Jews in Israel, and they would build a small number of settlements".

"Now that the state is twenty-five years old, how does the reality, the actuality, compare to your dream?"

"It's not the fact that it's a state", he said. "The question is how many Jews you have." The former prime minister was back at his traditional pulpit. Thereupon he embarked on a rambling recitation about the several *aliyahs*—migrations of Jews to Palestine—from Europe, and the difficulties each arriving wave suffered under the British and Arabs. I pulled him back to the present: "How would you resolve the Arab claim to Jerusalem, something that troubles the world greatly?"

"The Arabs", he said, "cannot claim Jerusalem because Jerusalem was never an Arab state. The world knows that this is the State of the Jews. This *state*, not *the* state, because there are many Jewish states. But this is the state—Jewish land and Jewish State—not any other people. Christians may believe in Jerusalem but it is not their thing. It is not what it is for Jews."

A little garbled, perhaps, and somewhat inarticulate; the decay of age was showing but his message came through. I moved to the subject of the Occupied Territories: "How large, geographically, do you think Israel should be, what boundaries?"

The old man switched right back to his single track: "Boundaries are not especially important but the number of Jews is. I believe that we must have at least seven, eight million Jews in Israel. Then we'll have a Jewish State."

I changed the subject to Arabs: "A million Arabs in the Occupied Territories are slowly being absorbed into Israeli life and its economy. Is that good for this country?"

"The Arabs", he answered, "were here a few hundred years. They're entitled to live here. They ran away before the state was proclaimed . . . by order of the Mufti . . . But the Arab who lived in Israel is entitled to live in Israel."

I wondered to myself what the extremist Rabbi Meir Kahane of the anti-Arab Jewish Defense League, ever talking about deporting all Arabs, would have you say had these statements of Ben-Gurion actually been broadcast. I said nothing about Kahane. Instead: "What about the attitude of France?"

The question moved him to comment on Israel's mid-fifties invasion of the Sinai Desert—along with England and France— undertaken to punish Nasser's Egypt. He grumbled somewhat incoherently about the move being misunderstood, then came sadly telltale signs of deterioration. He could not remember the name "Egypt," confusing it with "Lebanon." He could not recall the name "Sinai Desert."

I felt like a thoughtless intruder imposing on the fading old gentleman with my petty conceit of a radio program. When, in answering the next question, the phrase "Mediterranean Sea" was beyond his memory reach, I knew he had run out and that I should stop. But he went on, groping for words, haltingly, trying to communicate. I did not want to cut him short. He talked about another country but then, frustrated, confessed he could not remember its name. I knew he was thinking of China, but I did not say so. In the pause I quickly put a closing query, and then only to be sure he did not suspect I was giving up. I already knew we would never use the tape for a broadcast. "Mr. Ben-Gurion, I asked, "what do you think the future of Israel will be?"

"The future of Israel depends on two things," he said. "It's rather one thing but it's two different things. We need another five, six million Jews, and we have got to conquer the desert."

It was an obvious final question and, it worked. Perhaps I should have anticipated his answer. Ben-Gurion was not a complicated man. What was on his mind he voiced and always it related primarily to his beloved Israel. No matter the question, he always came back to it. It cannot be denied that making Israel happen was his sole self-appointed purpose in living. A unique Israeli whose place in world history will endure.

Some have been critical of Ben-Gurion's obsession, claiming he carried out his life's work during the worst of times for Jews. He failed, they said, to pay proper attention to Holocaust victims. Perhaps it is a blemish that Ben-Gurion's long-range interest in a new nation was so profound and all-consuming it actually blinded him somewhat from the more immediate need to save Europe's Jews from Hitler. It may be true, as it is also alleged, that to achieve have his goal he turned himself into a headstrong, single-minded Zionist who allowed nothing to block his drive to re-create a Jewish nation. It has even been written that Ben-Gurion was a heroic public figure who shamelessly neglected his wife and children in favor of his zeal for a Jewish State. Yet it was because he was all this and much, much more, that Ben-Gurion succeeded in his life's work. *Israel exists.*

Obsessed, myself, with the problem of anti-Semitism and what happened under the Nazis—a charge, incidentally, frequently directed at me—I should be among the first to criticize Ben-Gurion's alleged default concerning Hitler's war on the Jews. More so, because the Holocaust was the ultimate anti-Jewish tragedy of our century, if not of all Jewish history. But the ultimate tragedy, if Ben-Gurion had *not* been obsessed, would have been the destruction of the dream of a Jewish State or of the Jewish State itself. The fulfillment of that dream is to his credit and glory. Who am I, or others, to criticize?

Not many months after this last interview, in November, 1973, they laid this Lion of Judah to rest at Sde Boker, his home in the Negev that he loved so much.

24

Arab Boycott

It is a mistake to assume that Americans who play the Arab boycott game against Jews and others trading with Israel are necessarily anti-Semites or hostile to the Jewish State. The evidence indicates that mostly they are businessmen driven by greed. The same exemption from bigotry cannot be extended to the countries composing The League of Arab States. This coalition boasted a twenty-two-year history of anti-Jewish and anti-Israel discriminatory activity. Before the Jewish State, The Arab Boycott Committee, created and controlled by the Arab League, concentrated on a single target—the Palestinian Jewish community. Representing twenty-one Arab nations, the Committee then undertook to investigate companies they believed Jewish, Zionist or related to the Jewish Agency, the leading organization that offered to represent and act for the Jews of Palestine. If confirmed, such companies were blacklisted. The purpose, simply put, was to prevent normal growth of the *Yishuv*—the Jewish community of Palestine—and to keep it from securing any kind of major foothold in the Holy Land, a name the non-Jewish world generally used for Palestine.

In 1952, four years after Israel declared itself a state, the well-financed Arab Boycott Committee enlarged its operations to extend its impact world-wide, using boycott activity as a three-pronged weapon: imposing the boycott, a form of economic warfare; publicly boycotting Jews, a propaganda device; intruding itself between Israel and the rest of the world while explaining the justice of its case, the Committee's political agenda. The Arabs were carrying out a tri-partite boycott. Primary boycott—Arabs refusing to trade with Israel; a Secondary boycott—Arabs refusing to trade with anybody doing business in or with Israel; a tertiary boycott—American companies refusing, at the insistence of the Arabs, to do business with companies doing business in or with Israel.

Early on, the Boycott Committee set forth its prohibitions in a formal memorandum distributed to small and large companies across the free world: "It is prohibited to own factories, assembly plants, or any commercial agency of any kind of product in Israel. If you grant to the Israelis the use of your name, patents, licenses, or franchise the manufacture of your product to them, you go on our blacklist. If you have a recognizable interest in an Israeli firm, grant technical or consultative services, take membership in an Israeli Chamber of Commerce anywhere in the world, you go on the Arab blacklist."

The Committee employed a number of tricky devices. A favorite was to mail questionnaires to major American companies it knew had no intention of doing business with Israel—companies that did no exporting or importing—asking them whether they were trading in or with Israel. Most questionnaire recipients routinely fell into the trap of responding innocently in the negative. The Committee now possessed a basis on which to include the respondent in a privately circulated roster of business enterprises reporting no commercial relations with the Jewish State. This was meant to show the force and legitimacy of the boycott. The Arabs were not disturbed that cataloging an American company in this manner could cause it serious business losses in the United States. American customers trading with a concern so cataloged frequently resented the reported participation in the Arab boycott. To get off the roster some victimized corporations offered to trade with the Arabs—an extra dividend for the Arabs.

Then there were firms that actually were trading in the Arab world while refusing to do business in Israel. But they did not wish the fact to become known lest they be criticized for supporting only the Arab side. The Arabs were clever enough to avoid publishing their names.

When the boycott appeared by the mid-fifties to be achieving some success I set up an investigative procedure to learn the who, what, when and where of Arab boycott activities within American borders. It was important to know to whom the Arabs were reaching out and what Boards of Trade or Chambers of Commerce were complying with boycott demands. The Arabs had arranged for such trade organizations to certify that a member signing a contract to do business in the Arab world was not also doing business with Israel. Chambers of Commerce were routinely furnishing the requested certificates and also answering Boycott Committee questionnnaires.

Early on we met with the New York Board of Trade—the equivalent of chambers of commerce in most cities—to question the propriety of its handling certificates of compliance for the Boycott Committee—certificates attesting that members were not trading with Israel. Listening to our story, the Board reconsidered its practice and instructed the staff to discontinue participation in the Arab procedure. Other boards and chambers of commerce responded in the same fashion. Some did not. Years later, when the U.S. Congress at long last enacted a statute outlawing the boycott, one of the activities prohibited by the anti-boycott provisions of the 1977 Export Administration Act was the answering of boycott questionnaires. Until then the Arab Boycott Committee used the questionnaire as an effective propaganda instrument.

We learned to play rough ourselves when American companies were obdurate. Dealing with hard-nosed business men, it was immediately clear many of them considered only the dollar, so we used the lever of money. If an American company submitting to boycott demands refused to desist, we publicized the company's compliance with Arab blackmail. If the company persisted we began a public "information" campaign directed to the community at large, confident that most Jews and many non-Jews would react responsibly without suggestions from us. It was enough to inform. One major American corporation, Brown & Williamson, came to us in those early years troubled about widespread rumors it was pro-Arab and anti-Israel. The rumors started because of the comany's alleged refusal to sell Lucky Strike cigarettes to Israel while other American companies were exporting large amounts of their brands to the Jewish state. Brown & Williamson satisfied us that the British-American Tobacco Company, not Brown & Williamson, owned the Lucky Strike franchise for Middle East markets. Brown & Williamson offered to make a categorical statement that although handling Lucky Strikes in the United States it had no control over distribution, sale or franchising of the product in areas controlled by British-American. Brown & Williamson volunteered to state publicly that it disagreed with the attitude and conduct of British-American. I was convinced Brown & Williamson was acting in good faith. We made the story public and quickly killed the financially damaging rumor. Unfortunately British-American Tobacco persisted in complying with the Arab boycott. Unable to prevail on them, we were out of weapons.

Another company of grave concern in these early years was Raytheon, the New England manufacturer of sophisticated military hardware. It had been selling to both Israel and the Arabs when suddenly the latter demanded Raytheon stop furnishing certain weaponry to Israel. The immediate reaction of Raytheon was to hesitate to deal directly and openly with Israel. I learned of the Arab boycott move against Israel from friends inside the company. Whatever the decision, ultimately it would not be Raytheon's alone, the Arab boycott demand having been made through the U.S. Defense Department, the traditional intermediary in matters of this sort. Under the law the United States government must approve the export of military materials although it need not share its rulings with the public. What it says, goes.

An investigation of Raytheon's program was no simple task. The giant company was building secret, sensitive, sophisticated military armament, and one could not just pick up a telephone and ask Raytheon whether it planned to boycott Israel. Rather, it was necessary to accumulate facts indirectly, gather evidence from secondary sources while making sure we were not inadvertently stumbling into U.S. Government classified information. I reaffirmed that Raytheon's giving in to the Arabs could only be with the knowledge and consent of the American Defense Department. I released a portion of our findings to the public while presenting the sensitive evidence directly to Raytheon. We then talked to officials in the American government, executives in the American military purchasing mission—the traditional conduit for the purchase of American armament by foreign nations—and the situation was resolved. Raytheon never did discontinue supplying Israel's defense needs.

We had knocked on the right doors, posed the appropriate questions, raised the correct issues and consequently Raytheon, now with the approval of Washington, categorically rejected the insistent Arab demand that sales to Israel be discontinued. The military hardware in question was very important to Israel's security.

The boycott conduct of Arab countries was purely opportunistic. The Arabs would first try to bring a firm in line. Approaching an American company whose product they desperately needed, a preliminary demand would be made to the seller that it discontinue business with Israel. If the company rejected the appeal, the Arabs then pretended to be unaware the company was trading with Israel and a deal would be made anyway. This was important for us to know. Discovering companies whose exclusive products were essential to Arabs, and who were asked to comply with boycott rules, we urged them to stand up to the Arabs. We told them they could reject Arab boycott demands without sacrificing sales, able, as we were, to exhibit a long list of companies that had done so without being penalized. The list was persuasive evidence. Although we achieved a measure of success with this case-by-case approach, a federal law would have been incomparably more effective—and in harmony with democratic principles.

Renault, the French auto manufacturer, had franchised a company in Israel for the assembling and distribution for its car. The head of the firm given the franchise, Ephraim Ilin, was a prominent and affluent industrialist who had been a successful purchaser of arms and other military equipment for Israel in its early years. Having made his fortune, Ilin was now a prominent Israeli businessman in a variety of enterprises. He said he owned a Chrysler franchise for Israel (which he never used) and moved to Renault only after the American company terminated his Israeli license. When he lost the Renault franchise, he came to see us. According to Ilin, Renault cancelled its agreement with him solely for Arab boycott reasons. The controversy between Renault and Ilin, however, did not touch any American interest directly; it was a dispute between two foreign companies operating overseas. But we rationalized an argument: Americans who cared about a friendly ally would not like to see a company in a third country boycotting it. Thus, if Renault, selling in the United States to a major market here, found it was jeopardizing its American sales by refusing to sell cars to Israel it might decide against further participation in the Arab boycott.

Arranging a meeting with Renault representatives in the United States, I said that their home office had given transparently lame reasons for cancelling its Israeli franchise, and no reason at all for discontinuing the sale of replacement parts. Renault resolved the matter by agreeing to pay Ilin one million dollars for cancelling his contract. That sum a quarter of a century ago was a handsome amount in any man's calculation. We did not admire the solution that ended the issue, but the parties themselves had determined its terms.

The Renault case established a precedent in the boycott fight. We had successfully stepped into a boycott situation in which a foreign company, because of the Arabs, ceased doing business with Israel. Our battle horizons now stretched across oceans.

* * *

From 1952 until the early seventies we were virtually alone in the fight against the Arab boycott in the United States. Other Jewish agencies did not believe the Arabs constituted a controlling or even substantial international commercial factor, and Arab oil income during that period was small. Consequently Arab threats of boycott did not impress or disturb too many people. To them it was more a nuisance than a problem.

Israeli representatives, too, seemed indifferent to our efforts. Some did try to help; there was a division of official Israeli opinion about whether the boycott should be fought publicly. One segment argued that by openly opposing the boycott I was helping to publicize it, making it *seem* more potent, and thereby increasing its effectiveness. This group feared that a noisy boycott controversy would serve only to attract attention. Business leaders, fearing trouble for trading with the Jewish State, might be prompted to avoid entanglement at all costs. Worse, companies noticing the predicament of others caught in the boycott struggle might break off dealings with Israel.

Abba Eban declared himelf among the government officials who disapproved of publicly challenging the boycott, believing it to be counterproductive. He was, at the time, ambassador to both the United Nations and the United States. I called on Golda Meir, then Israel's foreign minister, when next she came to New York. Explaining to her what had been achieved since we launched the anti-Arab boycott operation, I convinced the foreign minister that if we did nothing, failed to fight, more and more companies would surely submit to the Arab boycott. I showed her evidence that companies we had previously exposed were among those now refusing to comply with Arab boycott demands. She promised to discuss the matter with Ambassador Eban. The effort to impede my activities stopped.

Some years later the situation again reversed iself. I called on Shimon Peres, then a member of the prime minister's cabinet, and complained to him. Israeli consular officials in New York, I said, advised me they would no longer cooperate on antiboycott activities and suggested I discontinue my public compaign. I made a presentation to Peres similar to the one I had given Golda Meir—with equally good results. Peres agreed I should continue my efforts, promising to talk to appropriate Israeli officials to make certain there was no further objection. There wasn't.

But we were still virtually alone in our antiboycott efforts. And despite our successes we were discovering an ever-increasing number of major companies submitting to the boycott, including, Ford, General Motors, RCA and *all* American banks. With no expressed desire among other Jewish organizations to join in the fight, I found the going difficult and frustrating. But not always.

On January 11, 1961, the New York *Times* reported in a dispatch datelined Cairo that the local manager of Coca-Cola's bottling plant, owned and operated by Egyptians, said, "The Coca-Cola Company has not and will never allow Israel to bottle Coca-Cola." It added that the company's export corporation in New York claimed bottlers did not make such decisions and went on to say that Coca-Cola's Mediterranean-area vice president, John Talley, asserted bottling franchises were based on economic rather than political considerations. That brief, scarcely noted, news item started a chain of events that ultimately obliged Coca-Cola to stop its boycott of Israel and changed the climate of opinion in the boardrooms of a handful of giant American corporations. At the end of the following controversy many companies decided to defy the boycott—including RCA and Ford. But no American banks, not one of them.

In response to my inquiry about the New York *Times* dispatch, Roy S. Jones, senior vice president of Coca-Cola, denied knowing the source of the Cairo story. There were thirty Coca-Cola bottling operations in various Mideast countries, he noted, all privately and independently owned, and all had been required to invest one million dollars on the average per plant to qualify for a franchise. And, he added, the company's marketing surveys in more than six Mediterranean and Mideast countries, including Israel, persuaded Coca-Cola that no investment in any one of them would be successful.

I made informal inquiry of Israeli sources about its soft-drink industry. They believed the absence of Coca-Cola had been the decision of Israel's economic authorities. Israel, they told me, had discouraged the import of soft drinks in an effort to build its own domestic bottling trade. That answer held me for nearly four years from pursuing the matter. If Israel didn't want foreign soft-drink competition I thought it immaterial that Coca-Cola might be publicly disingenuous while thankful it didn't need to face the issue with the Jewish State. If the Israelis didn't want them in I could not argue with the company for not going in, no matter it might be pleased about being kept out.

In January 1963, two years after the Cairo story, Benny Navon, a young attaché in the Israeli Consulate in New York working on boycott matters, phoned me to ask if I could arrange an appointment with Coca-Cola for a Mr. Moshe Bornstein, head of Tempo Soft Drinks Co., Ltd., Israel. He explained that his government had now recognized the economic wisdom of welcoming foreign companies—including Coca-Cola—willing to invest, contributing capital, know-how, patents and franchises.

I arranged a meeting with James A. Farley, chairman of the board of Coca-Cola Export Corporation, who had been an intimate of Franklin D. Roosevelt and for years a major power broker in the Democratic Party. Ten minutes at his desk and we visitors were aware that Farley's was a ceremonial role designed to give Coca-Cola political prestige and clout. He listened quietly, picked up the telephone to ask whose direct concern the Bornstein application would be, and told us the matter was in the hands of the Coca-Cola office in Lebanon. Mr. Bornstein should make his approach to the area manager in Beirut.

It seemed embarrassingly unnecessary, but I reminded Mr. Farley why an Israeli company could not go into Lebanon—it was at war with the Jewish State. The General—as Farley was called because of a term he served as postmaster general—then suggested we reach the Beirut manager through the company's office in Rome. Farley surely knew the transparency of his deadpan advice. And we understood the game he was playing with us. I instructed Bornstein to repeat his request to Farley in a formal letter—for the record.

In September 1964, a year-and-a-half later, we picked up a brochure distributed by the Iraqi Embassy in Turkey stating that Shell Chemicals, Renault, Dow Chemicals and several other American companies had been removed from the Arab blacklist because they had "terminated all business with Israel." It said that Coca-Cola and two other corporations were "adjusting" to "conform" to the regulations, and added:

> . . . none of these firms was forced to terminate its relations with Israel. They made the break of their own volition. These firms realized that they would have much greater benefits from working with eighty million Arabs . . . would lose these opportunities in trading with Israel . . . consequently chose the gigantic Arab markets . . .

My letter to Farley about the Iraqi boast was forwarded by him to R. L. Gunnels, vice president of the Coca Cola Export Corporation. He replied that Coca-Cola had no relationships whatever with Israel and thus there was nothing to terminate. Nor was there any foundation, he said, for the Arab allegation that Coca-Cola desired the benefits of choosing Arab countries over Israel. And no Arab demands had been made of Coca-Cola. The situation, he said, remained as it had been three-and-a-half-years earlier at the time of the Cairo dispatch.

Matters may have stood still that way for Coca-Cola but not for the Arab boycott, Israel or my antiblacklist activities. The Central Arab Boycott Committee, hub around which the entire Arab League blacklisting operation turned, was on high speed. We were now confronting complaints that ships carrying goods to or from Israel, or anchored in Israel, were blacklisted; that investing money in Israel was forbidden; that using a Shield of David as a symbol on a product doomed it; that films depicting anything favorable about Israel or Jewish history were barred— as were films with actors who publicly expressed support for the Jewish State. This included Harry Belafonte, Helen Hayes, Ear-

261

tha Kitt, Frank Sinatra, Elizabeth Taylor and others, and major corporations across the United States that had not fallen in line.

Yuval Elizur was a familiar name to me. His daily economics column in *Maariv,* a popular Hebrew language newspaper in Israel, frequently dealt with the boycott. I knew about him as a comrade-in-arms fighting blacklisting, and was delighted when in November he called to see me. Yuval had taken a leave of absence from journalism, he said, to be a consultant to his government in the matter of the boycott. He added he would like to bring along Moshe Bornstein to discuss a renewed attempt for a Coca-Cola franchise. As a concentration-camp survivor, Bornstein would even be willing to battle for it, having succeeded in harder struggles in Nazi Europe. Owner now of a prosperous business, and qualified by any count to handle the product, he was willing "to go to the mat" with the Coca-Cola company. To avoid a fight and get the franchise he would even be willing to put his own Tempo drinks "on the back burner."

Bornstein accepted my suggestion to bring in an outside attorney. He agreed and I arranged an appointment for them with R. L. Gunnels, the same vice-president I had previously corresponded with. Bornstein's presentation was brief. The economic hurdles originally cited by Coca-Cola had disappeared; Israel was now enjoying a period of economic strength. Tempo was the largest soft-drink company in his country, could meet all the prerequisite financial and technical requirements, and the Israeli government would give the venture every cooperation.

The Coca-Cola executive was equally succinct: he knew about Israel's solid economic condition, its increased export trade and its fiscal resources. Coca-Cola was anxious to increase its markets, was engaged in feasibility studies and within two months would reassess the Israeli market. But, he warned, a Coca-Cola franchise frequently depended on a bottler's willingness to devote himself primarily to the company's product. This was meant to be a hint that Tempo's preoccupation with its own drinks would preclude the required "exclusivity."

Bornstein's attorney replied that his client had a *primary* interest in handling Coca-Cola, and it would be good for both sides, damping down, as it surely would, increasing rumors that Coca-Cola was boycotting Israel. The meeting ended cordially but with no commitment from Coca-Cola.

Months passed. In August 1965, Bornstein again visited New York to see Coca-Cola, this time bringing along the franchise correspondence. Coca-Cola's final reply, again from Gunnels, had been that the company would not yield to pressure. If an Israeli franchise were to be issued which turned out unsatisfactory and then withdrawn, Gunnels said, Coca-Cola would be embarrassed by the charge it had reacted on "political grounds." A curiously negative approach going in, I thought.

It was unanimous in ADL that I should undertake a world-wide investigation of Coca-Cola's franchise history to determine whether Tempo had been treated differently from other franchise applicants. Requiring seven months, it was completed in March 1966, and had taken our researchers to the Caribbean, the Mediterranean area, Europe and North Africa. The inquiry needed various kinds of specialists and cost a goodly sum of money. Our premise was simple: Coca-Cola, in all its explanations for withholding a franchise from every Israeli applicant, had set forth a tripartite criterion to win the right to manufacture and sell its drink. Aside from required experience with soft drinks and a good reputation, the applicant had to have, minimally, capital assets of a million dollars; had to be willing to handle Coca-Cola almost exclusively; and the area of operation had to pass Coca-Cola's market-feasibility test—that is, proof that the venture would be mutually profitable. Two-and-a-half cases per adult, per year, it had been suggested, would make it feasible.

We now needed to find out whether these criteria had been applied equally to other applicants in the recent past. Also, I had to learn, if possible, from inside the Coca-Cola company whether there was, in fact, a deliberate policy of rejecting Israel to retain Arab favor. I set up one final exchange with the Coca-

Cola in order to create an irrefutable record. A letter went forward from Bornstein's attorney to Gunnels saying Tempo "meets all technical, financial and reputation requirements," can institute a "mutually profitable operation, and has the enthusiastic approval of the Israeli Government, which promises every cooperation and support."

The Coca-Cola vice-president replied, "There have been no changes" of any consequence, and no "useful purpose could be served by further discussion". He suggested Tempo seek out some other leading soft-drink manufacturer.

That letter arrived on September 23, 1966. Only three days earlier there appeared in the *Wall Street Journal* a prominently placed article based on in-depth interviews in which Coca-Cola said that while its international sales led all others by far, the company was nevertheless turning more innovative and aggressive than ever. Instead of studying the "thirty Mideast franchises" Coca-Cola said it had issued, we decided to concentrate only on the handful of countries whose size, population and climate most resembled Israel's. It would be a better comparison. And we would still look at the others to determine whether they affected our conclusions. After months of legwork we had this:

COUNTRY	POPULATION	FRANCHISE INVESTMENT
El Salvador	2,721,000	$200,000–1965
Ireland (Belfast)	2,841,000	$28,000–1949
(Cork)	———	$92,000–1951
(Dublin)	———	$11,200–1938
(Dublin)	———	$14,000–1950
Kuwait	322,000	$280,000–1953
Lebanon	1,800,000	$290,000–1948
Uruguay	2,556,000	$146,000–1946

We found that credit reports and other financial information about franchise holders showed no hard evidence, in a majority of cases examined, of an average million-dollar investment.

Nothing near it. Of ten companies in eight comparable or neighboring countries—adding Norway and Iraq to those listed above—the average original investment came to about $245,-000. Yet Tempo's financial reports showed a capital, including its new bottle-making plant, of just under $3,000,000. In short, measured against the start-up capital of comparable successful franchise applicants, Tempo more than met Coca-Cola's financial requirements.

Our research on market feasibility showed "no contest" either. Comparison of business conditions in Israel with franchised neighboring countries, and comparing Israel and franchised countries generally similar in size and climate revealed Israel to have vastly better per capita soft-drink market-potential. With a prevailing nine-month hot season, Israel's dry climate made consumption of large quantities of liquid almost a necessity. Further, Israel boasted the highest standard of living outside Europe, Canada and the United States. Its total soft-drink consumption was ten times Ireland's—in dollars, five million against a half million—and this with a population a half million less than Ireland's three million.

We found the Coca-Cola requirement that the franchise applicant have a virtually exclusive concern with its product to apply only to Israel. Almost without exception, new franchise holders outside of Israel were, like Tempo, already in the business of manufacturing other brands of soft drinks as their primary product. Tempo, on the other hand, had even offered to change the name of its company to "Coca-Cola of Israel."

I now looked at the confidential reports of our investigators, who had found their way to Coca-Cola personnel qualified with firsthand knowledge to comment on the company's attitude toward Israel and the Arab boycott. A private conversation with a highly placed public relations executive in the company's export corporation outside of New York produced this statement:

We seek to get into the climate of the country where we operate. Mr. Farley is a Catholic. We recently opened three

new bottling plants in Ireland and you can be sure that Mr.
Farley saw to it that Catholic clergy were there to add dignity
to the openings . . . We recently opened a plant in Thailand.
You may be sure we saw to it that a soothsayer was there to
make the proper optimistic prediction . . . In Moslem countries
we show proper respect for Moslem procedures. We are not
in all Arab countries yet but are making good headway . . . At
home the founders of our company in Atlanta were good Fundamentalist Christians and still are.

In another confidential talk, this one with a key Coca-Cola
executive in North Africa:

We have plants in every Middle East country now except
Israel. Israel? Absolutely not. How can we sacrifice 120 million
for a market of 2 million? In addition to losing the Arab markets, we would risk having our plants confiscated, and of being
kicked out.

Tempo's application had been rejected even though it met
the three special criteria presented to it by Coca-Cola; a reason
for concluding the real cause for the rejection was the Arabs.
We asked Bornstein's New York attorney to write one final
letter seeking reconsideration of Tempo's request for a franchise. When the anticipated negative reply arrived, repeating
all the old excuses we now knew to be disingenuous, I wrote to
the company on the ADL letterhead, reciting the record of
Tempo's efforts to obtain a franchise, and said that since visiting
them I had looked carefully into the facts of the alleged
prerequisite criteria. I asked if Coca-Cola would share with us
copies of its relevant Israeli feasibility studies—without suggesting we would challenge their validity. I was turned down. In the
temporary absence of Gunnels, another senior vice president of
Coca-Cola, H.F. MacMillan, responded on March 18, 1966, that
the information was confidential, not available to outsiders.

The story, quoting a Tempo spokesman, appeared in *Maariv*,
the Israeli newspaper. It said ADL had established Coca-Cola's

submission to Arab boycott. The news report was immediately picked up by *The Wall Street Journal*, followed by The New York *Times* and by wire services telephoning to confirm that ADL had completed an investigation establishing Coca-Cola's position. I recited our findings for attribution and furnished copies of the documented study.

Coca-Cola insisted to the press the franchise had been refused for "economic and market conditions rather than political considerations," adding it had told me so, personally, numerous times. I replied the company's criteria were "obvious nonsense," asserting that while submitting to the Arab boycott, Coca-Cola "assiduously attempted to camouflage its submission as a purely nonpolitical decision." Their refusal to sell in Israel, I added, "contrasted sharply with the company's proclaimed desire for new markets," and with its aggressive attempts to do business overseas. Our study, I pointed out, showed the company had added ninety new foreign bottlers and had set up operations in fourteen new countries in the previous three years. The story was front-page news.

Deep down, I knew this fight was a dangerous one to lose. My apprehensions were confirmed when a friend phoned to warn that I had "declared war on a company whose income and assets were greater than the Israel government's budget," and I had better know what I was doing lest I commit ADL suicide. I later learned my "friend" was delivering a message, although I could never learn from whom.

As with so many prominent news stories, this one precipitated the usual calls, people dialing to congratulate or condemn, to give advice or information. One caller told me that Henry Morgenthau, Jr., with another man and Abraham Feinberg—a prominent American Jewish leader—had sought a Coca-Cola franchise fifteen years earlier but that "nothing had eventuated." Phoning Feinberg's office brought the information that he would be back from Israel in a week. I left my name.

What Coca-Cola hoped would be a one-day news sensation that could be put to rest by a straight-faced explanation began to heat up, generating man-in-the-street press interviews, editorial comment and stories about citizens emptying Coke bottles at curbsides. Coca-Cola released a statement over General Farley's signature asserting the charges to be "completely unfair and unfounded." Coca-Cola had apparently been persuaded or decided to abandon its original claim that Tempo had failed the company's tripartite test. But it added two new reasons for rejecting Tempo. In past years, said the general, the company had approved a franchise application only to have the Israeli government deny the prerequisite permit to initiate operations. Further, Tempo particularly had been refused a franchise because "in 1963 the Israeli courts found the Tempo Beverage Company guilty of infringement of the Coca-Cola trademark and bottle design."

Reading about the controversy on America's front pages, Mr. Bornstein flew to New York carrying a bottle of Tempo. We called a press conference. Exhibiting the Tempo bottle, Bornstein upset the Coca-Cola claim that it resembled Coke's design, which was said to be in the shape of an impressionistic woman's figure. Reporters could see the difference for themselves. As for the charge of patent infringement, Bornstein explained that his bottle, registered twelve years earlier, contained a cola-flavored beverage labeled Tempo Cola, similar to more than hundreds of such cola drinks across the world, including Pepsi Cola and Crown Cola. Nevertheless, he said, Coca-Cola instituted a court action which was quickly *settled* when Tempo, for reasons of goodwill, accepted a Coca-Cola suggestion that the Israeli label, when written in English, be spelled Tempo Kola instead of Tempo Cola. Never, concluded Bornstein, was there an Israeli court finding of trademark or bottle-design infringement as claimed by General Farley. Bornstein showed not only certified copies of the court documents but a letter from General Farley himself, written in the same period, saying how pleased he was to receive Mr. Bornstein in his office in connection with a possible franchise.

The day after the press conference Abe Feinberg, back from Israel, returned my call. Yes, he and Henry Morgenthau, Jr. had been part of a threesome that applied sixteen years earlier for a Coke franchise. Coca-Cola's feasibility study had been positive, he revealed, Israel was a good market for its soft drink. But Prime Minister David Ben-Gurion had told him that a Coca-Cola franchise would make Israel's hard currency exchange even more difficult, so he, Abe, withdrew the application.

"But," I said, "Farley insisted the Israeli government denied the franchisee, denied you the right to begin operations after Coca-Cola approved the applicant."

"My group *withdrew* its request for a franchise, none was issued," he answered, "so I don't know the basis on which the Israel government could have ruled against the initiation of operations."

(Months after the controversy was resolved, while tying down loose ends, I came on one Joe Jacobson, a former assistant minister of defense in the Israeli government, the man who originally put together the Morgenthau-Feinberg group that had considered the Coca-Cola franchise idea. He said that Coca-Cola was indeed enthusiastic in 1950 about issuing an Israeli franchise. It changed its mind, however, when the Arab League organized its worldwide boycott. "After that," Jacobson wrote to me, "the company was no longer interested in doing business in Israel. It was trying to placate the Arab boycott . . .")

Feinberg said he had recently been having conversations with Coca-Cola about renewing his franchise application. If I would agitate the situation no further, and Bornstein would also keep quiet, he, Feinberg, might be able to obtain the franchise. "Get lost for a while," was the way Feinberg put it. Tempo stood no chance at this time, he said; the situation was "boiling hot." When "things cool down in a month or so," the matter would be happily resolved, he assured me, for Tempo and all concerned.

Persuaded that Coca-Cola would back down if it could save face, I agreed to get Bornstein out of town and hold still while Feinberg negotiated a contract. Did Feinberg want to meet Bornstein now? Feinberg thought it unwise; Coca-Cola might conclude he was in a deal with Tempo. "I am going to get the franchise for myself. That should be clear," he said. "But I'll see Bornstein afterward to work things out."

With Feinberg's okay, I informed Bornstein of the arrangement, and he was agreeable. Bornstein would visit relatives in New Jersey until the franchise agreement was concluded. Later that day Feinberg telephoned again. He was worried his deal, which was "hanging on a thread," could be destroyed if I did not keep my promise of temporary silence. He feared I might misunderstand the release he was preparing about his taking the franchise. The substance would be that he would "not do business with a company that submits to the Arab boycott."

On Saturday morning, March 16, eight days after the story broke, Coca-Cola announced the issuance of a franchise to Abraham Feinberg of New York. The following Monday, Feinberg telephoned to say he would be signing the papers before noon and would be pleased if I would bring Bornstein to his suite at the Drake Hotel at 4:30 in the afternoon.

We were prompt—Bornstein, his son, Zvi, Jack Baker, my associate, and I—and were greeted by Feinberg and his lawyer. During the next hour, over my heated protests, Feinberg insisted I had misunderstood our previous discussions. He never intended the franchise for anyone but himself. I was amazed at Feinberg's turn but powerless to change his mind.

Bornstein and his son returned home. I went back to my desk to continue the long, difficult fight against the Arab League's boycott operation.

The failure of Bornstein's franchise fight was a defeat he could live with, a loss that could not even be compared with what he had suffered in his life. When he escaped from Auschwitz, the concentration camp in Poland, he had found his way back to his birthplace in the village of Nowy Korczyn. Digging through the ashes of what had been his home, Bornstein discovered the charred body of a sister, carried it to the Jewish cemetery and buried her with his own hands. He then searched for and found his two other sisters in hiding and successfully led them across Europe to Palestine.

Home now from New York without the Coke franchise Bornstein's business nevertheless continued to prosper and he was a Jew happy to be in Israel. But fate had not yet done with him. A short time later his son, Zvi, crashed in an airplane over Israel and was killed.

There is one tidbit that sticks out in my mind in this whole episode, something I will never forget. To my surprise I discovered a reference to it in my archive on the case, typed by my secretary on a torn piece of pink paper. I offer it verbatim:

> Y. told me that on the evening of April 15 after Morris Abram had issued his public statement about Coca-Cola, in effect relieving them of culpability, he met with our tall, thin friend and the conversation went like this: "Do you think Coca-Cola was really guilty of boycotting Israel?" Answer: "Yes, guilty as hell."

"Y" stands for Yuval Elizur, my Israeli friend from *Maariv*, who asked the question. "Morris Abram" is the prominent new York lawyer and respected Jewish leader. "Our tall, thin friend" was Abraham Feinberg, who answered the question.

In any case, not long afterward Coca-Cola was being produced and sold in the Jewish State without any untoward result. Ironically, its sales volume places the drink number one in Israel alongside Tempo, bringing deeply satisfying profits to both its franchisee in Israel and to the company in America.

In microcosm the Coca-Cola story portrays the kind of work that absorbed us for twenty-five years in fighting the Arab boycott. In one form or another it was typical of what we confronted day in and out, and makes clear why we celebrated so enthusiastically when at long last the boycott fight was won in principle, a victory worth describing.

During the sixties into the seventies a watershed change occurred in the relationship between Arab oil countries and oil-hungry nations. The oil-needy included the United States and much of the Western world, the oil-poor, all of Black Africa. Red

271

China and the Soviet Union were not caught in the Arab vise because they possessed sufficient natural resources to avoid having to bend at the knee to the oil rich. The radical transposition of power from the buyers to the sellers had been initiated in November 1960 by the creation of the Organization of Petroleum Exporting Countries (OPEC), which in a short span of years quintupled prices, thus filling Arab coffers with awesome purchasing power. Recognizing sales opportunities, American and European industrialists competing for the new Arab markets moved into the Mideast commercial market only to find themselves facing Arab blacklisting provisions they were unable to escape. As part of the price of trading, the Arabs were demanding a boycott of Israel, of anyone doing business with Israel, and of "Jewish" firms anywhere whether or not they were trading with the Jewish state. And with their new massive spending power, Arab blacklisting for the first time could be truly punishing beyond Israel itself. As a result, American-Jewish defense agencies at long last awakened to the grave economic consequences and joined in the boycott battle.

Our crusade now had welcome allies. We had been pushing for protective legislation with no success. Changing the attitudes of both big business and the federal government was a considerable task. Both were more concerned with increasing overseas sales than with the tyranny of an economic blacklist that targeted on Jews, Israel and those who did business with the Jewish State.

In 1969 Congress threw us a bone, amending the Export Administration Act to require exporters to notify the United States Commerce Department of boycott requests they received. However, the new regulation, although urging against participation in the boycott, contained no penalty for failure to file such notices. In effect, the government was saying one could speed at eighty miles per hour on a school street, and while frowned upon, there would be no penalty if the speeder *reported* his m.p.h. Anomalous and meaningless. All we could do, in the absence of a federal law penalizing participation in the boycott, was to investigate companies on a case-by-case basis, inform the media of our findings and hope the embarrassment of publicity would bring change. It was a long, hard slog.

With each passing day interest in the boycott intensified, and Jewish organizations, now alerted to its increasing dangers, were becoming more active. As a result, in February, 1975, the American Jewish Committee, American Jewish Congress and ADL agreed on a joint campaign, assigning among themselves investigations, stimulating business interests, religious leaders and other opinion molders to speak up against the boycott and seeking court challenges and corrective legislation. By inviting local Jewish councils and their umbrella organizations to join our program, we were off and running.

Almost immediately thereafter we called a national press conference to announce the completion of in-depth investigations proving major elements of American industry to be "secret partners" in an Arab conspiracy to isolate Israel economically from the United States and to purge Jews from companies doing business with Arabs. Making public the names of the major U.S. companies and two federal agencies, we charged them all with responsibility for a damaging Arab anti-Israel and anti-Jewish economic campaign. It was deliberately sensationalist but true. A few American companies were resisting the boycott, more were submitting to Arab coercion. Still others were eliminating American Jewish personnel in a scramble for a piece of the Arab new-found wealth.

Within days Congressman Jonathan Bingham, Democrat of N.Y., Chairman of the House Committee on International Trade and Commerce, initiated hearings on Arab boycott activity that targeted American industry. The ADL, now with its two partners in the campaign, presented evidence and called for the adoption of effective anti-boycott legislation.

The participation of businessmen and public authorities in discriminatory practices struck at basic Constitutional guarantees of equality. Jews were being singled out as the scapegoat for economic imperialism. Calling for an immediate government probe, and for a clear statement of federal policy, we demanded the enactment of new legislation to halt these dis-

273

honorable business practices. The guilty companies were in chemicals, engineering, architecture, banking, education and hospital supplies. They were violating the clear purposes of federal export control regulations, weak as the rules were, that discouraged boycotts against friendly nations, and violating, too, the anti-discrimination provisions of the 1964 Civil Rights Act. (Boycotting was itself not yet a violation.)

The two government-affiliated agencies participating in the boycott were the Overseas Private Investment Corporation, empowered to stimulate investments with a hundred-million-dollar credit line from the U.S. Treasury Department, and the Army Corps of Engineers, which oversaw construction work in Saudi Arabia. The Chase Manhattan Bank was refusing to open an office in Israel while doing a thriving business throughout the rest of the Middle East. This prompted us to include Chase, particularly because we believed it unconscionable that the bank, earning enormous sums doing business with American Jews and through its yearly loans of many millions to the Israel Bond Appeal, was nevertheless boycotting Israel.

Chase Bank was indignant. Here they were, one of the most prestigious financial institutions in the nation, with their top management welcome in the White House, being reprimanded by us as if they were a bunch of shoddy businessmen with scarcely an ethical notion in their heads. Which surely they were *not*.

Mr. David Rockefeller, treated by those around him with unlimited deference, was most offended. The result was a meeting between the Chase Bank and the League. It was arranged by a prominent industrialist now deceased who was both our friend and a major customer of the bank. He hoped a face-to-face meeting would resolve the dispute, unaware of the bank's mistaken concern that millions in Arab business was at stake. The Chase people never did understand that any company, if it had the will, could flout Arab boycott regulations without penalty so long as the Arabs *needed* its services. And the Arabs *needed* Chase.

The League's chairman, Seymour Graubard, Ben Epstein and

I were escorted to Rockefeller's inner sanctum and introduced to the man himself and to three other top executives. Rockefeller made it instantly clear the going would be rough; he skipped the usual preliminary amenities indulged in on such occasions as this. "What you people in ADL did to us was very shocking", he said. "The language of your press release accusing our bank of being a 'secret ally' of the Arabs was terrible. Especially because Chase has done so much for Israel, and in view of its past relations with the Anti-Defamation League. Why didn't you check with me first?"

As the one primarily responsible for our press story, I responded promptly—and bluntly, because his tone was so sharp: "You obviously fail to understand what we tried to say in our public statement. American Jews find the anti-Semitism implicit in Arab boycott procedures totally unacceptable. Barring Jews from commerce with anyone doing business with Arab countries is fundamentally wrong, and we do not intend to cease pressing the point.

"Chase has submitted to the Arab boycott," I went on. "You were invited to open an Israeli branch and refused even while agreeing to open five different branches in other Mideastern countries. You said as much openly in a speech you delivered at Harvard University."

Rockefeller broke in: "What I said at Harvard was that it would have been *economically impossible* for our bank to go into Israel, that it would have caused us a loss of position with the Arabs. And I made that speech a year ago".

"Not so, sir," I said, now interrupting him. "What I'm talking about, you said only weeks ago."

I took out a newsclipping from my attaché case. "Let me read it to you, from the February 19 Boston *Globe.* Quote. If we were to open a branch there in Israel, all of our business in the Arab world would be boycotted and it would come to an end. End quote. That, I submit, is submission to the Arab boycott. Your suggestion that we should have verified our charge with you before issuing our report is groundless since your statement was made publicly."

275

Rockefeller's face reddened. He had no idea his speech had been reported in the press. His aides looked at each other. We visitors, on the other hand, were disappointed that the meeting had started out so badly. Seymour picked up the ball. "You say, Mr. Rockefeller," he cut in, "that opening a branch in Israel would be economically unfeasible. Is there a feasibility study available?"

"It's confidential," replied the banker. "Two years ago I met with Prime Minister Golda Meir and her economic minister, Pinchas Sapir, and they understood the bank's problem and accepted its position and they approved our opening the Cairo branch. But now ADL is blackmailing us, trying to force us into Israel even though it is economically unfeasible."

"Two years ago is ancient history," said Graubard with a genial smile. "It's a very different world now that the Arabs have new oil billions. Their pressures on banks and business houses all over the world have made it different. If American banks yield to the boycott as European banks have done, Israel may be in deep trouble. And American Jews believe that they too may be in deep trouble."

Taking advantage of a slight pause by Seymour, I put in, "The simple fact is, Mr. Rockefeller, the Israeli government asked you to open an Israeli branch and you refused, and they are disturbed. And if you are talking blackmail, it's our view the Arab states are blackmailing you, forcing you to refuse to do business in Israel—"

Ben, deciding an accord with Chase was not in the cards, interrupted me. "If Chase would refuse to knuckle under to blackmail", he said, "the Bank of America and National City Bank would follow suit, and the Arabs would lose the boycott game, at least in the banking world."

One of Mr. Rockefeller's aides, apparently also recognizing that the meeting had already failed, moved in to take the heat off his superior. "The League," he countered rather irrelevantly, "was not present in January at the Chase meetings with the Israeli officials and you cannot tell us what happened there, so don't try".

Now it was my turn to be rough. "I talked with officials of the present Israeli government in Jerusalem after your January meeting, and I can tell you they are unhappy with your position. The Israeli press reported your refusal to open a branch in Israel and the government confirmed to me personally that the press reports were accurate."

Sy Graubard then made a last-ditch effort to save the meeting. In a conciliatory tone he said: "Why don't we all try to be a bit more constructive. We Jews believe we face a major problem, that we must fight the Arab boycott. Even the president of our country has agreed that submission to the boycott is wrong. Let's see what we can do together".

It did no good. One of Rockefeller's associates responded that the League had precipitated a boycott against the Chase Bank. Sy explained ADL had been careful to tell all who inquired about the subject that the League was fighting against boycott, not starting one. We have been scrupulous, he added, in advising people who ask our guidance not to close their accounts at Chase. When the executive persisted that a boycott would be the inevitable result of ADL's press release, I said that if it did happen, the boycott was the result of and a response to Chase's actions, not ours.

It was clear Rockefeller would hold fast to his attitude and position. We had succeeded in changing nothing. Sy confessed that they and we were both now obviously talking in circles and there was no purpose in continuing. He added, without visible enthusiasm, that he hoped our hosts would give some thought to what we might do constructively together, exchanging any ideas that might come to mind.

It is to be regretted that from that day to this writing, more than twelve years later, the situation remains unchanged. On its face, Chase does not appear to be violating any antiboycott law. Under the statutes, refusal to do business in Israel, freely decided and not responsive to Arab demand, is entirely legal. The absence of a trade relationship is not evidence; an agreement to boycott must be proved. Chase Bank is still Israel's main fiscal agent in the United States—presumably because the Jewish

State cannot secure a better financial arrangement elsewhere—and Chase remains without a branch in Israel.

A month afterward, in March of 1975, ADL turned its attention on more than two hundred American corporations and twenty-five major commercial banks—many in alliance with Arab-American chambers of commerce—who were participating in economic warfare against Israel in collaboration with the Arab. The group was a "who's who" of American banking and industry. They were flagrantly disregarding U.S. antiboycott policy and flouting repeated Federal Reserve Board warnings against participation in the Arab boycott. Government reliance on voluntary compliance with current U.S. policy had failed, and effective legislation banning American participation in the Arab boycott was, we thought, therefore essential.

Among the twenty-five banks processing boycott-tainted letters of credit were six of the nation's largest financial institutions—Bankers Trust, Chase Manhattan, Chemical Bank, First National City and Morgan Guaranty Trust Company, all of New York, and the Bank of America, San Francisco. Among the eighteen firms submitting to Arab restrictions were Aramco, Bausch & Lomb, Flintkote, General Mills, Ingersoll-Rand and Pillsbury. Among the corporations identified as participants in the boycott operations of Arab-American chambers of commerce were such major oil companies as Amoco International, Aramco, Continental, Exxon, Gulf and Occidental, and such other companies as Merrill Lynch, Pierce, Fenner & Smith, Inc., Uncle Ben's Rice, and the Bechtel Corporation.

We showed no hesitancy in confronting this imposing combination of political and economic power. I knew our accusations to be carefully documented, based, as they were, upon intensive field investigations. Our charges were making a substantial impact across the nation. Three months later, in May, we charged key agencies in the federal administration with having tackled the Arab boycott in an uncoordinated manner, resulting, we said, in contradictory policies, buck-passing and confusion. A parade of high administration officials had testified in Congress *against* proposals for antiboycott regulatory foreign-investment laws. They were *opposed* to proposed legislation prohibiting compliance with Arab boycott demands.

Shortly thereafter I filed charges with the Equal Employment Opportunity Commission under the 1964 Civil Rights Act accusing Aramco, the world's largest oil combine, and three other major American corporations with anti-Jewish discrimination. We needed a ruling to serve as a binding precedent against discrimination by American firms doing business with the Arabs. This was our way of initiating the first test of the Civil Rights Act's extraterritorial jurisdiction. By this step we made clear to large American corporations that they could no longer play the Arab game without suffering consequences. The result was a long series of negotiations with the companies involved that turned out successfully with several of them.

Three months later, in August of 1975, we protested that the Department of Commerce was itself cooperating and assisting in Arab boycott operations against Israel. The department, we said, was aiding the boycott even while it was reminding American firms that federal law required them to report boycott demands. In our letter of protest to Rogers Morton, secretary of commerce, we informed him that his own department was disseminating foreign "tenders"—requests for materials and equipment—that included boycott provisions against Israel. We cited a letter, nationally disseminated by the department, containing a June 1975 communication from Iraq that solicited 3,550 precast buildings. Included in these specifications was this: *"Country of Origin: The tenderer should not incorporate in this tender any material that has been manufactured in Israel or by companies boycotted officially by the Iraqi Government."*

I had arranged for one of our people to visit the Commerce Department to examine tenders it distributed from June 1974 to August 1975, spot-checking those from Iraq, Saudi Arabia, Libya, Syria, Qatar, Egypt, Lebanon, Jordan and the United Arab Emirates. He discovered additional instances in which the department had sent out tenders containing Arab boycott provisions. It had become standard government practice.

One month later we filed a federal suit to stop the department from violating U.S. law and policy in "promoting, aiding and abetting Arab boycott operations, and by restricting free trade and discrimination against Jews." The suit charged that the department was itself flouting federal antiboycott policy and was failing to comply with the Freedom of Information Act in order to shield companies ignoring the policy. What a distance we had come from the early days when my appearance in the magistrate's court was considered a bold step for ADL.

The Commerce Department had previously refused our demand that it make public the responses of American firms reporting receipt of Arab boycott requests. It held confidential, too, the identities of those who failed to report, as required by law, even those to whom the department had sent warning letters. The lure of Arab money had blinded it to its responsibility to obey and uphold American laws and policies. The Commerce Department was more interested in expanding trade with Arab countries than in enforcing declared American policy against trade boycotts.

As a result of all this activity I received a phone call inviting our National Chairman and me to meet with Rogers Morton, the secretary of commerce. He confessed he agreed with us regarding the damage being done in America by the Arab Boycott Committee. A department lawyer who was present conceded the government's controversial practices could well be ended. Information on file in the Commerce Department indicating how companies had responded to boycott requests, he said, might also be made available. The secretary promised to develop a clear position and announce it publicly.

When the department did not follow through, we took another tack, this time charging the existence of a multimillion-dollar Arab master plan for an anti-Israel, anti-Jewish propaganda and lobbying activity in the United States. Basing the statement on our own comprehensive two-year study, we revealed that a propaganda fund of thirty million dollars was marked to come from the Arab states and an additional fifteen million from OPEC. An explosive charge but, again, true.

The shocking fact was that the know-how and manpower for this pro-Arab activity were coming from former Washington, D.C. officials, from paid propagandists in academia and from spokesmen in the religious community. We called the campaign to swing both American public opinion and U.S. foreign policy against Israel "a key element in an Arab economic and political master plan against the Jewish State." Heavily financed by swollen oil profits, the Arab propaganda effort, we said, was reaching American legislators, mass media, business, labor, college campuses and churches.

In June of 1975, in an appearance before a congressional committee, our chairman called on Congress to recognize the failure of voluntary antiboycott action. He urged the enactment of strong laws to divorce American business from international politics. The administration had clearly been guilty of indifferent enforcement of the antiboycott provisions of the Export Administration Act, and of failure to use enforcement powers authorized by Congress. In part the government was influenced by companies worried about possible business losses if they resisted the boycott. More significant, the administration insisted antiboycott measures would jeopardize Middle East peace negotiations, and nothing should be done until peace was achieved. But years had passed with no resolution of that conflict, and we argued it was self-defeating to wait for "final peace" in the Middle East before halting Arab blackmail of American firms. Laws against boycotts were just as necessary as laws against bribery or blackmail.

In September 1976, ADL leaders, including Irving Shapiro of DuPont, met with George P. Shultz, then a major policy maker of Bechtel and later to become secretary of state, and his Washington public relations advisor Charles Walker. Also on hand was Walter Shorenstein, an influential San Francisco real estate man and friend of both sides who had suggested the meeting. We met in Mr. Shultz's Manhattan apartment.

A year earlier I had turned over to the Justice Department evidence that the Bechtel Company of San Francisco had been complying with Arab boycott regulations. I urged the government to take some action. Seymour Graubard and I had met at that time with Mr. Shultz in his New York City apartment and discussed Bechtel's practices. We explained why we had turned over our data on the company to the U.S. Justice Department. It had been a friendly exchange of views. The Justice Department had announced an anti-trust case against Bechtel for participating in the boycott. Bechtel was charged with boycotting companies that had been blacklisted by the Arabs. The stake was a billion dollars worth of American equipment and know-how, including commodities desperately needed by the Arabs. So Bechtel was in a position, we thought, to refuse to submit to Arab blackmail. More than a year later Bechtel settled the action, signing a stipulation agreeing to cease and desist from the disputed practices.

We now repeated our original view that Bechtel's failure to support American public policy opposing U.S. participation in a restraint-of-trade conspiracy was a fundamental violation of at least the spirit of American law. At this second meeting Shultz argued anti-boycott legislation would be counterproductive. We said it was essential to end Arab blackmail in the United States. We disagreed about the status of the boycott. Bechtel was convinced it was deescalating. We were firm that what minor changes could be detected were the result of our efforts to end the Arab campaign. Shultz believed the "personnel aspect" of the boycott had been relaxed, especially in Saudi Arabia, but that most Jews assigned to Arab lands by Bechtel did not want to work there. In Algeria, he noted, the boycott "isn't around and is not an issue." It is more of a problem, he suggested, in other Arab countries, repeating what he had told us the previous year: that the most recent Saudi Arabian-Bechtel contract contained no mention whatsoever of the boycott. We were delighted and told him so. Shultz concluded with the comment that "while Arabs don't need the U.S., they like us," and that the Europeans and the Japanese are ever-present and competitive. It was, he said, our mutual obligation to protect

American business interests. We agreed, pointing out that our efforts were directed exactly to that end.

Shultz's second thrust was that every effort should be made to slow down legislative steps that might result in tax penalties for participation in the boycott. His concern was the pending Ribicoff Amendment, denying certain tax privileges to overseas subsidiaries of American or multinational corporations that submitted to Arab boycott regulations. It was enacted into law in 1976. He worried, too, about congressional proposals for tough antiboycott statutes that included broad prohibitions and severe penalties.

These laws, he said, would precipitate a major confrontation between the Saudis or other Arab buyers and American exporters. It would surely cause the Arabs to turn to other nations for services, production and commodities. As Americans, Shultz repeated, ADL should be deeply concerned about such an unhappy development and should do what was necessary to head it off. He wanted us to "slow down the process" leading to the enactment of laws so as to give the administration more time to find satisfactory substitute approaches. We refused.

Charles Walker, Shultz's companion, indicated that it was "very late in the day." Stringent antiboycott proposals had already been adopted by House and Senate committees. This meeting with us, he said, was a last-ditch effort. Walker admitted that the legislative situation had developed because the administration had been "stonewalling," maintaining its opposition to antiboycott legislation and failing to offer any substitute.

Shultz and Walker admitted they saw us in a pivotal position in the drive for antiboycott legislation, able, at least, to slow down the process if not stop it. It was a great overstatement to say so, we told them, adding, incidentally, that while we never endorsed the Ribicoff Amendment we would surely not take a public position against it. Nor would we oppose antiboycott congressional proposals, and we thought it too late in the day for us to try to delay legislation even if we wanted to, which we didn't. If the administration was ready with some kind of workable proposal that made sense to us, we would be willing to present it to interested Jewish leaders for consideration. The meeting ended with a vague Shultz promise to be in touch again if he obtained any proposal from the administration that might be of mutual interest.

In October of 1975 the Department of Commerce finally amended its regulations to *require* an exporter to report its response to every boycott request it received. The heat was on. Congress decided to investigate the practice of boycott submission, keeping in mind that no penalties were yet attached to compliance. The congressional study of the first three months of reporting to Commerce revealed that 91 percent of the American companies filing answers admitted submitting to Arab restrictions.

Some federal departments were still disturbingly negative. It had to be stopped. We charged the administration with "contradictory policies," citing a communication from the White House released in response to ADL's praise of President Ford's "outspoken condemnation of anti-Jewish discrimination in Arab policies." His condemnation seemed to assure that the administration would correct the situation. Officials of State, Treasury, Commerce and Justice had, indeed, testified, as suggested, before a House committee "addressing many of the issues" we had raised. But most of the officials testified *against* the proposed antiboycott legislation.

Eight weeks after our meeting with Rogers Morton, the White House announced a series of antiboycott measures that we decided had the sole objective of stopping only *Arab* anti-Jewish practices on the domestic scene. The administration's antiboycott package was designed in our view only to help tighten defenses against *Arab* anti-Jewish discrimination. But *Americans* were using the Arab boycott to victimize Jews and American business. This was ignored in the new administration program.

We demanded the government take the next important

step—end U.S. distribution of Arab boycott-tainted trade-tenders among Americans. The new government program did not prohibit violations still being practiced by the government itself—actual participation of the Commerce Department in procedures aiding the Arab boycott. Our pending lawsuit against the department to halt its distribution of notices of boycott-related business opportunities had been ineffective. The presidential package had failed to prohibit federal agencies from disseminting boycott-tainted Arab trade opportunities among American business firms. But no longer were we dealing with the Administration hat in hand; that was history. We no longer were afraid to bring even the Washington administration before the courts or to the bar of public opinion. We had taken the fight to the government, and we had made a dent.

Such was the history of Arab boycott in the United States during the years of Presidents Richard Nixon and Gerald Ford. Neither one was of much help in the fight against the war on American enterprise. This was mostly due to the opposition of American companies to laws restricting in any way their perceived right of contract, that might impede the sale of products to the Arabs. American firms put last any concern that Israel, a friendly ally, might be boycotted into economic unviability—or that their own neighbors at home, American Jewish businessmen, would be unfairly hurt. They knew only that they wanted no law in the U.S. that would lessen their commercial opportunities in the Arab world, reduce their profits or, in some cases, jeopardize profitable sources of oil. No surprise, then, that we had hit a stone wall at the White House.

But this just spurred us on. We intensified our campaign against boycotting corporations and elements in the federal establishment that worried more about losing Arab trade advantages than anything else. Our fight was to protect freedom of trade, insisting on the obvious—that all American companies had the fundamental right to deal with anyone they pleased without any foreign power intruding on that right, *and* to be protected from economic reprisals for doing so. American enterprise was entitled, even if it did not appreciate it, to be protected by its government from blackmail.

We decided to sharpen even further our criticism of companies that were submitting to the boycott to win competitive advantage over others who refused to be intimidated by the Arabs. The result was we found ourselves eyeball-to-eyeball with an opposition that insisted rejection of Arab regulations gave European, Latin America and other foreign companies an advantage that, they said, would gravely damage our own economy.

Responding to this argument we accused guilty companies of venality, of aiding enemies of American foreign policy, of abandoning and betraying a friendly nation, Israel. Restraint of trade imposed from the outside was supposed to be anathema to Americans. Silence and inaction, we were sure, would ultimately divide American business into opposing camps—those who surrendered to Arab economic tyranny and those who defended genuine freedom of trade. We said a law was needed that provided categorical protection against foreign powers dictating American economic dos and dont's.

A national debate was provoked, with most of the press picking it up and editorially demanding relief for American business—which was our position.

A presidential election was upcoming—incumbent Gerald Ford versus Jimmy Carter. We were determined to make the controversy an election issue. At a press conference we charged that a triumvirate composed of administration officials, certain American oil companies and prominent Arab government spokesmen were participating in an un-American, misleading propaganda campaign defending and protecting Arab boycott operations in the United States. The goal of this tripartite force, we said, was to kill proposed legislation outlawing the Arab boycott. Our efforts to stifle the boycott had sharply intensified, yet our widespread campaign to protect the rights of American enterprise was being blocked. We disputed the claim that the United States would suffer political, economic and energy reprisals if an effective antiboycott bill was enacted. These fears had been nurtured by the Arabs. Administration spokesmen were parroting them, and major oil companies along with the others were seeking to turn public opinion around. Oil companies were explicitly identified in our press statements—Continental, Exxon, Mobil and Texaco. We identified the Arab nations involved in the conspiracy—Saudi Arabia, the Kuwait, the Emirates, along with the Arab League itself, representing the entire roster of Arab-world countries.

Arab information offices operating throughout the United States had been issuing false warnings of oil shortages. We labelled their threats of massive penalties as blackmail. We publicly identified government officials who were actively trying to prevent Congress from considering an antiboycott law—including an assistant secretary of state who had calamitously insisted that an antiboycott law would shift business to other countries. We cited an assistant deputy secretary of state for declaring antiboycott proposals to be deliberate attacks on the Arabs—a "negative situation," he said, to be avoided.

We pointed to the secretary of the treasury for his assertion that an antiboycott law would be detrimental to American interests, and to an assistant treasury secretary for arguing that our antiboycott proposal, even without being enacted, was hurting business.

We criticized Secretary Rogers Morton's successor in the Commerce Department for stating an antiboycott law would be "untimely, unnecessary and counterproductive." We said the undersecretary of commerce was the source of the government statement that an antiboycott law would force Arabs to do business elsewhere.

Our attacks on the executive branch naming names was, for the Anti-Defamation League, a bold move, but we had the evidence and didn't hesitate. Second-class citizenship, the quiet approach, behind-the-scenes negotiation, in this type of situation was for us dead and buried together with the corpses of the Nazi victims not saved by the quiet, behind-the-scenes negotiations during the war period. We had learned our lessons.

* * *

At this time the counterpart of the American secretary of commerce in the Israeli cabinet was Haim Bar-Lev. During a visit to the U.S. unrelated to the boycott controversy, the minister met with Rogers Morton, who raised the subject of ADL's attacks on the State Department and others in the administration. Morton informed Bar-Lev of our conspiracy accusations against him, Mr. Morton and others for their opposition to an antiboycott law. Bar-Lev, according to the secretary, said that the Israeli government was not especially concerned about the Arab boycott. A press release was then issued by a White House spokesman asserting that the Jewish State did not support our efforts. Having invested years of days and nights helping to create a favorable climate for an antiboycott law, I was frankly livid. Telephoning friends high in the Israeli government, I complained bitterly. But the damage was done.

To this day I do not know whether Bar-Lev understood the foolhardiness of his comment. Surely, to my personal knowledge, his remarks did not square with what we knew to be Israel's official attitude as reflected by the prime minister and by the antiboycott activities of those in the Israeli government charged with dealing with the problem. The divided attitude in official Israeli circles involving the boycott has long disappeared, Bar-Lev's comment to the contrary notwithstanding.

The Carter-Ford election campaign had heated up, and boycott was high on the list of controversial political issues. Larry Peirez, an active leader in our ranks, was invited in his personal capacity to join a small delegation to candidate Carter in Atlanta for a meeting arranged by Robert Lipschutz, a local and close friend of the man who would be elected president. (When Carter took office the following January, Lipschutz was appointed counsel to the president.)

In advance of the session, Peirez handed Lipschutz a packet of materials about the boycott with the hope Lipschutz might use it to persuade Mr. Carter to make a campaign promise: that if elected he would support the adoption of an antiboycott law.

A short time later Carter made that commitment, thereby encouraging us to believe victory was now assured. It did not come that easy.

For years, the Mobil Oil Company had been a prime target. It was, after all, the self-chosen spokesman of the oil lobby. With the controversy now escalating, Mobil prepared a series of full-page ads for major newspapers. Mobil was throwing down the gauntlet. Its advertisement argued that antiboycott legislation was counterproductive, ineffective and anti-Arab. It urged the American people to oppose the adoption of this legislation and recognize that the United States was in effect at the mercy of the Arab, and to submit to the Arab boycott. Mobil's ad effectively supported the Arab anti-Israel boycott crusade.

We sent a letter to the editor to every newspaper that carried the Mobil ad. We expressed "considerable amazement" that these papers would print an ad inaccurately excerpting editorial comments from The New York *Times* to make it seem to support Mobil's position. The New York *Times* editorial actually had referred to the boycott as a repugnant example of foreign economic blackmail and urged Congress to strengthen the Export Administration Act by making it illegal for American firms to engage in secondary or tertiary boycotts.

Despite all our efforts, in the waning days of 1976, with the congressional session fast coming to an end, various bills proposing antiboycott rules failed to pass—mostly thanks to the outgoing Ford administration's opposition. However, one antiboycott measure, the "Ribicoff Amendment," was approved and made part of the 1976 Tax Reform Act. Its penalties included loss of foreign tax credits, denial of tax deferrals on income from foreign sources, and cancellation of other tax benefits for companies complying with the boycott.

Early in January 1977, with a new president coming into office, we opened our campaign with a news conference in Washington, D.C. Two separate coalitions had, we said, organized parallel campaigns to block the enactment of newly introduced antiboycott legislation. One coalition, we further said, represented large and respectable firms in the American business establishment. The other was a potpourri of American Arab organizations and domestic extremists spreading anti-Semitism. Named in the first group were the National Association of Manufacturers, the U.S. Chamber of Commerce and the Emergency Committee for American Trade (ECAT), which included sixty-four major banks and multinational corporations as the spearhead of the first coalition. This coalition, we added, included leading oil companies and major construction firms. The second coalition, we said, was headed by Full Employment in America Through Trade (FEATT), a group created by the National Association of Arab Americans but waving the American flag. More than one hundred American business representatives, including at least ten oil company officials, were participants.

I was the designated spokesman at our press conference. Acknowledging that we had no evidence of direct interaction between the two coalitions, I pointed out that they used similar arguments, sometimes verbatim, and had a mutual goal—blocking passage of effective antiboycott federal legislation. Major oil companies, heavy equipment manufacturers, construction and engineering firms with huge stakes in the multibillion-dollar Arab market had stepped up their antilegislation advertising and public relations campaigns immediately after the passage of House and Senate bills separately in the last session. Simultaneously, an intensive lobbying program by this proboycott group had been instituted during the closing months of the 94th Congress when it appeared that passage of a congressional compromise was possible in spite of "the stonewalling resistance" of the Ford administration. In short, the anti-antiboycott forces had fielded a most awesome combination of power, money and political influence to stay the Congress' and president's hands against passage. As a result the bills died at the end of the 94th Congress.

With the new president's commitment in mind, the one made to Larry Peirez months earlier at the small Atlanta meeting, we asked the White House to support our renewed struggle for an antiboycott law. Mr. Carter let us down, stonewalling in the manner of his predecessor. It seemed his mind had been changed.

Burton Joseph, our new national chairman, realized that President Carter was caught between two opposing forces in the bitter antiboycott-law struggle. Fearing a legislative failure again in the 95th Congress, Joseph proposed a challenging approach. He would try to recruit Irving Shapiro, president of DuPont, presiding officer of The Business Roundtable and a firm supporter of the League. The Roundtable was a highly select group of business leaders from some 170 of the largest corporations in America. It included the chief executives of oil companies, banks, utilities, among others, and was accurately regarded the most powerful business-political lobby in the United States. With the cooperation of the Roundtable we just might dissuade the major corporate opposition from its fight against an antiboycott law. Perhaps an acceptable compromise could be developed that we could jointly support.

In January of 1977 we met with the Roundtable leadership. On hand were Thomas Murphy of General Motors, David Rockefeller of Chase Bank and George P. Shultz of Bechtel, with whom we were not strangers, Bruce Atwater of General Mills, Herbert Schmerz of Mobil, Reginald Jones of General Electric, Clifton Garvin of Exxon, Hans Angermueller of Citicorp, Walter B. Wriston of Citibank and Irving Shapiro of DuPont. Representing ADL were Burton Joseph, Dore Schary, Max Kampelman, Kenneth Bialkin and several others including myself.

From the outset the tone of the meeting was cordial, and while that never changed, it was also quickly evident that the two sides were miles apart. However, there was fundamental agreement that anti-Jewish discrimination within the United States must be eliminated, and that American interests were paramount. But when we discussed the business of American branches abroad, we hit a snag.

Most of the firms present had overseas offices. If the Arabs were permitted to impose boycott rules on overseas facilities, such a large loophole would render domestic prohibitions meaningless.

Mr. Shultz's initial statement was that competition for Arab customers was keen. The Germans, Italians, Japanese, Koreans and others, he said, were all eager for Middle East trade. Bechtel, he added, merely had a fraction of it, less than one third of Bechtel's business. Walter B. Wriston argued that while Negative Certificates of Origin—testaments that there was no prohibited-participation in a deal—violated fundamental American policy regarding boycotts, U.S. banks who handled them as mere messengers played only a neutral role. Clifton Garvin raised eyebrows when he declared that the U.S. was "absolutely dependent on Arab oil." The American oil-depletion rate was 5 percent annually, he said, and because other substantial sources of substitute supplies were not readily available, the "free world is stuck." We must recognize, he said, that anti-Arab legislation is hazardous. The Exxon chairman warned it would take "fifteen years" for the U.S. to solve its oil shortage, and that turning the Arabs away would create "an Amoco problem we cannot deal with." Reginald Jones contended that while we could not solve the energy crisis in this century there was a workable antiboycott legislative approach. But he did not spell it out, saying only that the major pending anti-boycott proposal was counterproductive. George P. Shultz had an additional word. He had met with the Pope in a private audience, he said, and found himself discussing the complex oil shortage. Critical of the West's failure to solve the difficulty, Shultz suggested to the Pope that mild weather was more effective than businessmen in resolving civilization's energy shortages. The Pope responded with a straight face: "Maybe the mild weather was the wrath of the Almighty."

Max Kampelman of our team revealed he had been informed the president promised to fulfill his campaign commitments. The American people resented the boycott, he said, and would not accept additional delay in achieving corrective legislation. And the administration would welcome a "deal" if our two sides could create one. The meeting ended with a consensus that despite obvious differences we should go forward together.

A six-man committee of lawyers, including myself, was

created. Maxwell Greenberg, long-time ADL leader and distinguished West Coast lawyer, became ADL's anti-boycott spokesman before Congressional committees and worked on the new team with us. The meetings were long and arduous, embroiling the legal team in complex questions, but ultimately we agreed any proposed legislation required the incorporation of four fundamental principles:

- Companies doing business with the Arabs would be prohibited from discriminating on the basis of religion.
- No U.S. entity would be permitted to furnish potential foreign buyers with data about the race, religion or nationality of anyone involved in a deal.
- No U.S. entity would be allowed to refrain from doing business with a foreign country for the purpose of complying with a foreign boycott regulation.
- No U.S. entity would have the right to refrain from doing business with any other U.S. entity in order to comply with a foreign boycott regulation.

The creation of the ADL-Roundtable group was a major news story. And the ADL had unintentionally become the single spokesman on the legislative issue for the Jewish community. In our judgment this was an unwholesome development. So we shared with other Jewish organizations, most importantly the American Jewish Committee and the American Jewish Congress, the details of our efforts with the Roundtable and invited them to join us. They did and the combined group ultimately worked out and agreed on a "Statement of Principles" with our counterparts from the Roundtable, a formula that became a reality. In its main features it followed the general principles formulated by the original six-man lawyers' committee.

Legislation compatible with the joint-formula was adopted and passed by both Houses, resulting in a bill that was signed into law by President Carter on June 22, 1977. It outlawed direct Arab boycott activities in the United States. It outlawed secondary and tertiary boycotts by U.S. companies operating anywhere in the world. Enactment also meant it was unlawful for an American citizen or corporation to refuse to do business with other companies simply because they were engaged in commercial activities with Israel. It became a violation of law for anyone to advise subsidiary, servicing or sub-production companies not to do business with another because the latter was doing business with Israel.

The statute, to be sure, outlawed the right of Americans to furnish a foreign source with information about their direct or indirect dealings with Israel, or about the religion of their employees. The "Negative Certificate of Origin," that no part of a product being sold to an Arab buyer came from Israel or from a company doing business with Israel, was prohibited. No longer was it permissible to honor a letter of credit if it included nullification language saying "in the event the debt to be satisfied by it is to a company, doing business with Israel." The Arabs had had the nerve, as mentioned, to require that American companies demand its top officers sign affidavits swearing they were not Jewish, and many did. The statute ended that outrage.

American business enterprises were mandated to disclose to the Commerce Department, with specifics, compliance with any request to participate in the Arab boycott. The law also prohibited compliance with boycott by any foreign branch controlled or owned up to twenty-five percent or more by an American company. The criminal penalties for violations (which have never yet been imposed): a first offense, one year in prison or a $25,000 fine; a second offense, a $50,000 fine; for willful violation, $50,000, or five times the value of the contract, plus five years in prison. What have been imposed are civil penalties at $10,000 for each violation.

Has the antiboycott law proved damaging to American big business? The annual increase in American exports to Arab nations, comparing favorably with U.S. trade among Western nations, establishes conclusively that the fears expressed about the counterproductive potential of antiboycott legislation have proved false.

Is the law perfect? Not by a long shot! Of course it has loopholes. To claim it has solved the problem of Arab boycott would be overstatement. Sovereign Arab nations are not bound by American laws, and while it has become uneconomic for some of them to flout U.S. regulations, others still buck them. The Arab Boycott Office openly continues its anti-Israel activities while still trying to force compliance by American companies with its rules, as the price of doing business. As recently as January 1987, the boycott office in Damascus announced that for reasons sufficient unto itself, Sears, Roebuck had been removed from the blacklist. Simultaneously, the office banned thirty-two foreign companies, including some American firms, because they were trading with Israel. Eight weeks later our own United States Department of Commerce was again caught disseminating trade opportunity notices containing information on how to abide by the Arab boycott of Israel—in violation of its own regulations.

The Bechtel Company, it will be recalled, was "burned" by the federal case against it for Arab-boycott involvement. Bechtel did not make the same mistake twice. In 1983 the Bechtel Group, while denying political reasons for what it was doing, placed Israel on a list of ten nations barred from the Group's business because of the Jewish State's alleged "unstable conditions." Other nations far less stable than Israel were not similarly precluded. Today, five years later, the Bechtel situation remains the same, according to Will Maslow of the American Jewish Congress, a recognized expert on the subject of the Arab boycott. Bechtel does not do business in or with Israel.

Yet the statute plus public opinion plus government attitude has had a real impact on the American business community. The healthy effect of the antiboycott law as a whole is far more substantial than any of its parts. Responsible American business leaders are most reluctant to deliberately flout federal regulations in order to secure an Arab contract.

It took twenty-five long years to bring the boycott fight to at least a qualified successful resolution—from 1952 when we first became active in the controversy until June 1977, when the anti-boycott legislation became American law. Unhappily, except for our own country, many nations around the world still submit to the boycott mandates of those Arab nations that persist in keeping and enforcing their blacklists.

25

"President Carter does not yet understand . . ."

We could taste the elixir of a victory, however long it took and however imperfect it might be. But at least attention had been paid, and from the highest governmental place.

No surprise on this and on a more specific count that the vice president of the United States, Walter Mondale, asked us in June of 1977 to come by his office for a serious talk. He had delivered a speech to a branch of the World Affairs Council in San Francisco only days before, and the response of American Jewry, he said, called for a heart-to-heart chat with us.

The vice president, I felt, was overly sensitive. Actually there was no major criticism from Jewish quarters about his West Coast speech. American Jews were mostly still favorably disposed toward both President Carter and Vice President Mondale. Disappointment would be a more accurate evaluation of American Jewish reaction.

In his speech Mr. Mondale had spelled out what the administration believed to be a fair approach to resolving hostilities in the Middle East. His outline seemed a well thought out plan for peace in the area. But there was no indication that the proposal had been shown to or discussed with the Israeli government. It was known the administration had talked about it with Arab leadership although nothing was said publicly one way or another. Announcing the proposal as he had, seemed to put unfair pressure on one of the two contending forces in the Mideast.

Most observers regarded the Mondale speech as supportive of continued American backing for Israel's broad position and needs. The plan, however, provided for gradual Israeli withdrawal from the Occupied Territories with an allowance for security emplacements until peace was achieved—in return for only an Arab promise of peace. In the interim, it was suggested, the Arabs were to have a "homeland," preferably federated to Jordan and presumably on the West Bank. Negotiations were to be held in Geneva with the Great Powers in attendance. All this was announced publicly without first discussing it with the Israeli government.

The mere public statement of the plan's provisions was regarded in Israel and among Israel's U.S. supporters as a victory of sorts for Arab propaganda, and so Mondale's speech was seen in some Jewish quarters as undermining Israel's negotiating position. It encouraged the Arabs to assume the United States would be making serious efforts to satisfy their demands, including the return of territories. And the cost to the Arabs was only a paper commitment—land for paper.

As a result there was disquiet in Israel and some American Jewish quarters about the drift of the Carter administration— although this was long before substantial disenchantment set in among Jews about the party in power in Washington. It was still nothing more than disquiet; President Carter had, after all, been in office only five months.

Six of us attended the Mondale White House session: our national chairman, two top officers, our Washington representative, Ben Epstein and myself. We had all met the vice president at different occasions over the years, enjoyed his public appearances on our platforms and always found his door open when we wanted his guidance on a problem. We expected the meeting would be an informal session.

After handshakes all around the vice president wasted no

time in expressing his surprise and concern about critical Jewish reaction to his San Francisco speech. He was especially disturbed, he said, by the statement—"warmed-over administration policy"—of an unidentified Jewish leader quoted in a New York *Times* front-page report.

Mondale wanted us to know the unspoken background for his West Coast remarks. President Carter had concluded from his meetings with Israeli and Arab leadership that peace negotiations had bogged down. Inaction was producing, in Washington's view, nothing more than a "continuing charade with little flexibility" on either side, and "movement was urgent." The president and other administration spokesmen, Mondale informed us, had begun to issue critical statements in order to precipitate reactions and create movement. Mr. Carter was impatient, and the vice president's San Francisco speech, Mr. Mondale explained, was the result.

Several of us spelled out the reasons for the Jewish chagrin which had disturbed the vice president; springing the plan with prior notice only to the Arabs; the inequity of the plan itself, etcetera. We said flat out but with respect that we disagreed with the administration's harsh view about the alleged intransigent attitude of the Israelis. As American Jews we had hoped for more understanding from the White House.

"The president," said Mr. Mondale, "has little knowledge and less experience with the American Jewish community. In his need for expert assistance on the subject, he brought with him to the White House two close friends from Atlanta who are Jewish." But being Jewish, Mondale added, "is not a sufficient qualification."

Our eyebrows went up at the vice president's response. He went on to say that "the president does not yet understand that American Jews perceive a personal stake in Middle East developments," and that a certain respect was due this Jewish concern. The administration, the vice president concluded, will have to give time and attention to the Jewish community, and he promised that it would.

We told Mr. Mondale why we considered the administration's

proposal for a Geneva Conference wrong, why we thought it would pull the rug out from under Israel's feet. And we expressed unhappiness at the hinted use of American aid-to-Israel as a lever to press the Jewish State into acceding to the will of the United States government instead of allowing it to follow its own inclinations. We urged that the nations of the Middle East be free to negotiate on their own and not be limited to American plans that were created without consultation.

Mondale spelled out administration positions, and it was all very cordial until we got to the subject of Carter's concept of a "Palestinian homeland." This was, we suggested, based on a false premise. It sought to imitate a genuine fact of *Jewish* history for propaganda reasons. There *never* was an *Arab* homeland in the specific area known as Palestine. We urged the vice president not to allow the administration to be taken in by an Arab political fraud.

Mr. Mondale was noncommittal, obviously reluctant to betray the administration's position and express agreement with us if, in fact, he felt that way. The vice president suggested that several of us, four or five, should meet privately with the president from time to time, just to talk, perhaps to brief him on the nature of the American Jewish community, familiarize him with its views and the persuasive reasons for its attitudes. Let Mr. Carter know our reactions to his Middle East views and plans.

If we were prepared to do this, Mr. Mondale said he would try to initiate the first session and set up others from time to time. We quickly responded that we wanted to meet with the president on the matter. (It is now nine years later and we are still awaiting the first such invitation. I suspect it was not Mr. Mondale's fault.)

We heard the vice president on two other issues. Regarding the antiboycott legislation that had recently been adopted by the Congress and signed by the president, Mr. Mondale wanted us to know that privately the Saudi Arabian authorities had surprisingly approved the concept of America's outlawing Arab anti-Israel boycott activities in the United States. He thought that was a nice thing to tell about them.

Needless to say, I refrained from sharing with the vice president what I thought about the role Mr. Carter had actually played in the boycott matter, in spite of his somewhat different public stance. Nor did I make any effort to spell out for Mr. Mondale the criticisms felt by those of us involved in the struggle against the Arab boycott in regard to the legislation finally adopted. (I wish one child went to sleep without pangs of hunger for every thousand dollars worth of business the Arab nations, the Saudis in particular, have cleverly denied those who trade with Israel. There would be no more hungry children in the world.)

In his very last remark Mr. Mondale was prophetic. He said that President Anwar Sadat was "economically on the ropes," and no one could guess "when his term of office in Egypt might suddenly end."

On October 6, 1981, in full view of world television, Sadat was murdered by the Takfir Wahigra, an underground group of extremist Arab Fundamentalists.

A tragic setback for us all.

26

"The New Anti-Semitism"

Despite setbacks, going into the seventies it was evident that traditional anti-Jewish discrimination in the United States had been substantially diminished. A war against Hitler, a democracy shaken up by the war's underlying religious bigotry followed by an inspirational Civil Rights Movement that resulted in progressive court decisions and in landmark legislation outlawing inequality of opportunity, all combined to mandate the healthy change.

The dynamics of this watershed change brought organized anti-Semitism as we had known it for more than thirty years to "a low ebb." Far Rightists were now targeting primarily on liberal opponents whose political philosophy was anathema to them, and Jews became only incidental and secondary demons. Yet, Jewish anxiety about anti-Semitism did not diminish. Jews have long believed they possess special antennae that enable them to detect ill-feelings otherwise concealed from them. Determined to understand the continuing Jewish concern, we set out on an in-depth research, and in three-and-a-half years were ready with a report—*The New Anti-Semitism.*

Released in 1974, the study created excitement and not a

little protest and resentment. Those targeted by name were deeply offended—not enough to sue for libel but sufficiently to strike back, and in tones loud enough to generate controversy. Some criticized us for "spreading too wide a net" in labeling people virtual anti-Semites. They were wrong. There was a new kind of anti-Jewishness abroad in the land, more sophisticated, more subtle and more invidious than the old, vulgar, blatant bigotry Jews had suffered for so long. It was not the hatred spewed by rabble-rousers or the polite, pseudointellectual aspersions put out by the seemingly more sophisticated. It had two aspects. A pervasive insensitivity or indifference to the rights and security of Jews, blocking their status as equals. And an antipathy to Israel that, if implemented, would cause the destruction of the Jewish State. This second kind of anti-Semitism was frequently hidden in a pretense of anti-Zionism.

Most who criticized us for defining as camouflaged anti-Semitism a malevolent anti-Israel attitude and a vindictive anti-Zionism came to learn that our definition was hard to argue with. At first the bigotry beneath these "political" Mideast positions was evidently not detected by very many observers. Today, it is widely discerned.

Rejected, too, was our charge that callous indifference to patent anti-Jewish bigotry—an indifference too often exhibited by respected community elements—was itself another form of anti-Semitism. Although we had forgotten it, I had reported the same attitudes in *Anti-Semitism '47*, a repetition I discovered doing research for this memoir. But now for the first time we were insisting the American community challenge it as anti-Semitism. We said, for example, to the good people of Eureka Springs, Arkansas, that if the town authorities, its press and leading citizens abided in silence one of the nation's most vulgar, professional anti-Semites—Gerald K. Smith—accepting him in their midst as one of their own, they themselves were anti-Jewish. We asserted to federal officials in Washington that if they persisted in making large grants to a schoolteachers' association in a period when that organization poured forth a continuing stream of anti-Semitism, then the officials themselves were suspect. We said to the Christian clergy that accusing Jews of deicide—preaching that the Jewish people are guilty in the death of Jesus—persuaded us the preacher himself was anti-Jewish. We insisted that the Radical Left's committment to the forcible liquidation of the Jewish State rendered its leadership anti-Semitic. We said the same of Arab nations committed to the death of Israel. *The New Anti-Semitism* covered a wide spectrum of indifference.

Ultimately we convinced most Jews that fatal indifference to social, political and economic mistreatment of Jews, and to malignant hostility to Israel, were forms of anti-Semitism. In doing so I think we helped bring about a fundamental change in Jewish thinking. No longer would Jews passively accept insensitive nonaction from non-Jews, a landmark correction of the relationship. Recognition also by non-Jews of our principle would mean the beginning of the end of "second-class citizenship" for Jews. Insofar as we have succeeded in persuading non-Jews of the validity of our definition of the "new" anti-Semitism, Jews in fact are no longer universally viewed as one among other minorities in our country.

Today, when a politician, civic leader, clergyman or other community leader stands mute and indifferent to blatant anti-Jewish bigotry, he is perceived by many as a passive anti-Semite. Confronting anti-Semitism in silence, without protest, is a form of acceptance, or worse still, an implication of agreement. A civilized code of behavior mandates that bigotry be challenged. The Congressional Gold Medal of Achievement awarded to Elie Wiesel in 1986 states: "Indifference to evil is evil."

What we tried to say in 1974—that anti-Zionism is often a smokescreen for anti-Semitism—was tragically and forcefully demonstrated by Arab terrorists in September 1986. Two Arab gunmen raided Sabbath-morning services at Neve Shalom, Istanbul's newly restored main synagogue, killing twenty-one of the twenty-five members of the congregation at prayer. The Arab terrorists were murdering elderly Jews as Jews, not as Israelis. But hatred of the Jewish State was the ostensible reason.

27

Golda Meir

There was a popular but vulgar apocryphal story told by Israelis about Golda Meir during her first months as prime minister. A British diplomat chatting with a member of Israel's foreign ministry commented, "You chaps are a funny lot. First you deny Moshe Dayan a chance at your top job because he has only one eye. Then you give the number-one slot to a lady."

"Right," replied the Israeli, "but what a pair of balls."

I learned the point of the anecdote the hard way, dealing with this tenacious woman over a long period that continued to the end of her life. As foreign minister she was supportive in our fight against the Arab boycott, pressuring reluctant associates high in the Israeli government to encourage the League to carry on our campaign without interference from Jerusalem. When she achieved prominence in the official establishment I made it a regular practice to stop at her office to record "Dateline Israel" radio interviews.

Only once did Mrs. Meir frustrate me. It was 1972. Scheduled to interview her for my radio program, I was asked to be at the P.M.'s desk all set to record the moment she arrived. Zev Furst, a young ADL executive in charge of Middle East matters at the

League in New York, acting as my recording engineer, accompanied me to the ministry.

The two of us were ready when the prime minister entered her office and sat down. After appropriate greetings Mrs. Meir looked at Zev fiddling with the oversized earphones on his head and at the recording apparatus spread out before her, paused for a moment and said: "Put the equipment away."

"I beg your pardon," I said, not sure I understood.

"I said put the equipment away," she repeated, now looking at Zev too. He was in a deep frown, having gotten the message twice through the earphones. He turned to me, puzzled, as we heard, "Now shut the thing off and put it aside." I nodded to Zev, and he did as she said. "Listen," she explained, "I have little time and I want to talk with you instead of making a program." I was relieved.

"Tell me, first, frankly, about your President Nixon. How American Jews feel about him. What do you think? Is he a friend?"

Quite a question, I thought, and a heavy responsibility, answering it for Israel's prime minister. I told her frankly that I did not think well of Mr. Nixon's political views. He was far too reactionary for me and not good for our democracy. I added that in this I believed I reflected a large segment of American Jews but had no right to speak for them. The President, I said, was undoubtedly well disposed toward Israel, which, of course, was of prime importance but not the sole criterion. But I qualified Mr. Nixon's pro-Israel stance that was prompted, in my view, primarily by a deep-rooted hostility toward the Soviet. He was sure Israel could be counted a reliable ally because it, too, was a Soviet target. I went on, sprinkling my opinions with some backup facts. When I finished, Mrs. Meir probed about the place of American Jews in the political scheme, our role, if any, in the administration, and national attitudes in the States toward Israel. She then thanked us cordially and led us to the door. It had taken perhaps thirty minutes. She was on a personal fact-finding mission. No radio program.

The very first time I interviewed Golda Meir for Dateline

Israel radio I was accompanied by Abe Foxman, at the time handling the Israeli desk in New York. Born in Poland, a survivor of the Holocaust, his parents took him back from the Polish Christian family in whose charge they had secretly placed him before being dragged off to the concentration camp—from which they miraculously returned. Abe's folks brought him to America, a very young child, and schooled him in Judaism, and Yiddish and Hebrew; as a result he spoke Hebrew without a hint of an accent.

Abe was now with me setting up the recording equipment in the prime minister's office in Jerusalem and I introduced him to Mrs. Meir, using my fractured Hebrew. He bowed slightly and said in flawless Hebrew how privileged he was to find himself in her presence. The prime minister immediately assumed he'd been born in Israel. But having heard him talk to me in equally unaccented English, she also concluded Abe was a *yored,* an Israeli who had emigrated to the United States. Her friendly attitude of moments earlier chilled, and I realized her misapprehension.

"I think you should know, Prime Minister," I quickly put in, "Abe is an American out of Poland who mastered Hebrew at school in Brooklyn."

The freeze melted. She smiled and said, "We Israelis are a funny lot. We want Jews from everywhere to study and speak Hebrew. But when we meet one who does, we automatically assume he's a *yored* and dislike him because he abandoned us for the fleshpots of the Diaspora."

Today Abe is the National Director of the ADL.

Mrs. Meir was still chief of state in 1973 during Israel's celebration of its twenty-fifth anniversary. I thought it appropriate to interview her on my newly instituted TV version of our "Dateline Israel" program. We set the date through an aide. It wasn't easy. The program was to be filmed in the prime minister's official headquarters in Jerusalem's *Hakirya,* the government center.

Arriving early in the morning to give our crew "setup" time in Mrs. Meir's office, we waited while she attended a cabinet meeting in a nearby conference room. Her secretary whispered that it was a rough session.

The door opened and she charged in, obviously hurried and harried. Seeing the camera, its accompanying equipment and a TV crew, she stopped, surprised. "What's all this?" she demanded without a hello or other greeting to any of us.

"We're doing a television program instead of the usual radio interview," I said.

Mrs. Meir looked at me for a long moment. "If you had let me know that in advance I would have worn a proper outfit. I look like a slob."

The prime minister was wearing a plain dress and had long before given up the use of cosmetics. Unfortunately she refused the services of our makeup person, who had just finished with me. I thought little of it until, during an interruption in the filming, the cameraman whispered, "Except for the beard, she looks like my father".

"Your father has no beard," I told him.

"No, but Golda has."

Despite the unexpected change in format, Mrs. Meir settled into her chair, readied herself for the interview and I assumed we were over the hurdle. But then: "I thought this was to be a fifteen-minute radio program. You get half an hour for this interview and that's all. Finish in thirty minutes."

Those who knew the lady will not be surprised. But those who know how half-hour TV programs are filmed will at least be sympathetic. Shot in 16mm., the cassette used in the camera runs about eleven minutes and must then be replaced. In between each change the crew may refine the position of Kleig lights, adjust reflectors, a plant, props, etc. The interview resumed, the director is never reluctant to interrupt with suggestions, holding things up further. And then he keeps the questioning going until he considers that he has enough material to cut, edit, tighten and still come out with a half-hour program. In short there is no way to do a proper half-hour film in half an hour. Two to three hours absolute minimum, unless it's a live television program in a studio. But Mrs. Meir, a determined woman, repeated: "You've got half an hour, no more. That's it."

I proceeded to do the half hour program in exactly a half hour. I asked the prime minister whether she regarded Israel as having a special role among nations.

"No, I don't think that we have to be something special for the nations of the world. We have to be a Jewish State. When I say a Jewish State I don't mean that no others can live among us, God forbid. We have a minority of non-Jews now of about thirteen to fourteen percent and always room for people who are not Jewish. But when I say a Jewish State I mean that this is where Jewish culture, the Hebrew language, the principles of Judaism are carried out and implemented. For ourselves I would want this to be a model state that would have an informed society, justice, and not too great differences between various groups in society. I would like a society where each one really has an equal opportunity, where those that come to us from societies in which they have been held back be given greater opportunities in order to reach a certain cultural or educational level. I would like a society where it's good to live for everybody—not because we want to be a model for other countries but for ourselves."

"Has Israel's presence for a quarter of a century," I asked, "changed anti-Semitism anywhere in the world?"

"That," said Mrs. Meir regretfully, "was my greatest disappointment. I believed that when there would be a Jewish State, anti-Semitism would automatically disappear. To my sorrow, that didn't happen. There is anti-Semitism in the world—in some places, very evident and very brutal, in other places, less. Anti-Semitism did not disappear."

When I asked Mrs. Meir if she thought twenty-five years of a Jewish State in any way changed the character of her country's Jews, instead of answering my question she corrected the history underlying it. "It isn't correct," she said, "to begin our existence here from the fourteenth of May, 1948. There were always Jews here. Throughout the two thousand years since our dispersion, this country was never entirely without Jews. On

November 29, 1947, the United Nations declared that there should be a Jewish State. They would never have declared it if all the elements of a state had not already been created. The basis, the foundation, was created for many, many decades. The United Nations decided on the fact that the foundation was already here and because the Second World War highlighted what happens to a people who have no place in the world to which they can come."

She went on: "I'm convinced that during the Holocaust, during the Nazi regime, if there had been a Jewish State at that time—I don't say that we could have saved all of the six million Jews, but there's no doubt whatsoever in my mind that many of them would have been saved. In the darkest, darkest hours of that period we were dependent on the number of certificates that we got from another power as to how many Jews we could bring into the country. If the doors of Israel had been open, as they are today, many of those that are not here any more would have been alive. We would have brought them here."

In the spring of 1975, two years after the TV interview, Mrs. Meir, having stepped down, was no longer the prime minister. The relationship between the United States and Israel was in one of its awkward periods. Secretary of State Kissinger was home from the Mideast, having failed in his mission to achieve a peace agreement between Israel and Egypt. Israel's succeeding premier, Itzhak Rabin, had refused to cede the Sinai Passes and the Abu Rudeis oil fields in the Southern Sinai Desert without an Egyptian declaration of nonbelligerence. This prompted the secretary to bring his visit to an abrupt halt, ending his efforts at mediation.

Kissinger flew back to the States and within a day or two of his arrival President Gerald Ford announced the administration was undertaking a complete reassessment of its Middle Eastern policy. Meanwhile it was reported by White House spokesmen that everything would be kept on the back burner, including military aid to Israel. The United States action was euphemistically called an "agonizing reappraisal" by editorial writers.

The alleged review lasted almost nine months, until, that is, the U.S. Defense Department announced the sale to Israel of F-15 jet fighters. But from its start, the American tactic of withholding military equipment had been recognized by everyone involved either as punishment or as an obvious effort to force the Jewish State into line with American policy. Secretary Kissinger on his arrival home had offered public assurances to Israel that reassessment was not a matter "of cutting off aid." "Rather", he said, "it means that we are facing a new situation of some peril and it is inevitable in such a situation that the president order a review to see what is the best policy for the United States to follow."

Several days later the secretary stressed that U.S. reassessment was "not directed against Israel" and "not designed to induce Israel to alter any particular policy." Despite such repeated disclaimers and Kissinger's firm statements about not blaming either side, press reports disclosed the secretary of state was, in fact, deeply disappointed by Israel's alleged inflexibility.

In July of that year I was back in Israel on our semiannual visit to interview for "Dateline Israel." Out of office fourteen months and retired from public life, Mrs. Meir had returned to Ramat Aviv to live in her modest little house on the northern outskirts of Tel Aviv. I telephoned her and said we, Zev and I, would like to come by and visit. I had been asked to extend an invitation to Mrs. Meir to accept an award at a League dinner, and wanted to invite her in person.

"Come for tea late Sunday afternoon", said Mrs. Meir. Then correcting herself quickly, she added, "Excuse me, you are Americans. I mean coffee".

Six P.M. on the twentieth we presented ourselves to the guard at the gate, who led us to the front door. Golda herself answered the bell, accepted a formal kiss on the cheek from each of us and showed us into the living room. Telling us to make ourselves comfortable in the cool of the parlor, Mrs. Meir disappeared into her kitchen. A moment later she was back carrying coffee on a tray filled with assorted cookies she assured us she had baked herself.

"The only luxury I allow myself here is the air conditioner," she said as we settled into chairs. "I can't stand the intense humidity of Tel Aviv. But never mind, tell me about the United States. What is public opinion like these days about Israel? What do Americans think about our trouble with Egypt? And Jews, are they uncomfortable?"

The gist of my response was that, goaded by Washington, Americans were somewhat impatient with the situation but not sure who was at fault. They tended to support the administration's critical attitude toward Israel. American Jews, I ventured, seemed divided about the truths of the controversy but were nevertheless supportive of the Jewish State.

She reacted to this with questions about Kissinger's role in the censure of Israel. He was, I thought, the prime source of the peace proposal and the consequent negotiation, and was also the major architect of the negative American attitudes precipitated by the impasse.

Then it came out, suddenly, but with controlled anger. "That man Kissinger," she sizzled, "sat in the very chair you're sitting in now, on the afternoon of the day the negotiations broke down. He stopped to see me on the way to the airport. He told me he had already given orders to the State Department that no blame was to be attached to Israel for the suspension of the negotiations. He promised me he would not blame Israel. But even before he arrived back in the United States, while still on the airplane over the ocean, he talked with members of the press and violated that promise. He told reporters specifically it was Israel's fault. I will never believe him again. I am waiting to see him again and I will ask him, 'Henry, why did you lie to me?' "

Seizing the opportunity, I said the ADL would offer her a major platform in the United States, our annual dinner, and be delighted to have her as our guest of honor. She could make whatever political statement she pleased to the American people, including her opinion of Secretary Kissinger. "No," she said, "I cannot go to the United States and make speeches. The government of Israel would regard it as interference with its foreign policy. I am out of office and must stay home for the time being."

Having peremptorily put aside the idea of a trip to express her feelings about Kissinger, Mrs. Meir went on about what she considered his betrayal. She seemed preoccupied with the subject. She reminded us that two years before, shortly after the Yom Kippur War, on November 2 and 3, she went to Washington to negotiate with the administration. She recalled that her sessions with Kissinger at the time were tense and, in her own words, she "wouldn't wish those meetings on my worst enemy." She told us that on the Saturday morning after a late meeting the previous night with the secretary of state she convened her staff and was sharing with them the content of the discussions. In walked Simcha Dinitz, Israel's ambassador to the United States, to report that Kissinger said he saw no point in continuing the confrontations with Mrs. Meir because they had reached an obvious dead-end. The Secretary, said Dinitz, recommended that Israel send its foreign minister, Abba Eban, to talk to the American under-secretary of state, Joseph J. Sisco.

Mrs. Meir told us she then instructed Dinitz to repeat verbatim to Kissinger the following message: "Tell Kissinger that as secretary of state he has the right to decide that he does not want to meet with the prime minister of Israel. But he cannot choose who will represent Israel in the negotiations."

Dinitz did as she asked and returned to report that the secretary of state of course wanted to meet again with the prime minister. Another round was then set for that Saturday morning.

During the course of the negotiations Mrs. Meir said, she proposed six points for Kissinger to take back to Anwar Sadat. But the secretary responded negatively, arguing the Egyptian president would find her ideas unacceptable and that it was unrealistic to offer them as a basis for negotiation.

Mrs. Meir was insistent that Kissinger nonetheless present

them to Sadat, who, she said, finally did accept the six points as a basis for discussion. Although ultimately those six points were insurmountable hurdles that thereafter precipitated the disengagement, each side, she pointed out, finally understood the other's position, and this was progress. Six months later, she said, Secretary Kissinger returned to her to confess he had been mistaken and would never again predict what Sadat might or might not accept as a basis for negotiation.

After the Washington meetings, Mrs. Meir went on, she thought that on her way back home she would like a meeting of the Socialist leaders of Europe. Within forty-eight hours a session was convened in London in which she as prime minister of Israel took part. Mrs. Meir opened the conference, she told us, with a speech in which she asked the assembled guests where their "Socialism" went astray in refusing Israel the use of even a centimeter of their soil, or the skies over it, during the course of the Yom Kippur War. How ironic it was, she told them, that only President Nixon, the embodiment of anti-Socialism, had responded favorably to Israel's plight, while the Socialist nations and the Socialist parties of Europe ignored the predicament of the Jewish State.

Mrs. Meir recalled describing how painful it was for her, a woman who lived her life steeped in Socialist tradition, suddenly to realize that her Socialist comrades had abandoned her and Israel. With this, she said, she stopped and waited quietly for a reply. Not a sound, she added, to be heard in the room. The silence was answer enough.

At that point, and her voice choked a little in the telling, someone behind her whispered to her. She heard it but was too embarrassed to turn around, so to this day she does not know who it was. The person said softly, "They can't answer you because they are choking on oil."

As a kind of postscript to the incident, Mrs. Meir told us that when she met with Helmut Schmidt after he assumed power in Germany the chancellor pleaded with her to be more flexible in the forthcoming negotiations with the Arabs. She requested Schmidt to take two messages back to his country from her.

First, that Israel was indeed sorry that Germany was suffering because of the oil embargo. In truth, the Jewish State ardently wished that Germany, and all of Europe, had warm and cozy homes. But, said Mrs. Meir, "Israel won't commit suicide to keep those houses warm and comfortable."

She also informed the German chancellor that if the world wanted to destroy Israel, "We will take the world to hell with us." Schmidt asked if she was threatening the use of nuclear weapons! Said Mrs. Meir: "I don't recall using the words 'nuclear weapons.' I did say if the world wants to destroy us, we'll take the world to hell with us."

Later she learned through intermediaries that Helmut Schmidt disliked her. Said she: "You can see how upset I am that Schmidt doesn't like me."

Smoking endless cigarettes, Mrs. Meir fixed more coffee for us and reminisced about her experiences with bereaved parents of Israeli soldiers lost in Israel's recurring wars. She talked about her grandson, who at the age of twelve already understood war and its inevitable death and suffering. She castigated the United Nations for its use of abstentions when a nation obviously has a clear position on a given issue but nevertheless does not want to stand to vote. Then she returned to the subject evidently still much on her mind: Kissinger.

She recalled that he once began a discussion with her by saying he was Jewish and therefore was to be trusted on Israel. "I have lost thirteen members of my own family in the Holocaust, and I won't be a party to another," was the way she quoted him. And she had answered: "That's my problem. If I didn't trust you, I would know exactly where I stand. The problem is that I do trust you, and I'm confused."

Mrs. Meir told us that for a long time she believed it was Secretary of Defense James Schlesinger who had held up the airlift for six critical days during the Yom Kipper War. But now she was not so sure it was Schlesinger. It could have been Kissinger, as many charged.

While she was extremely critical of Kissinger, nevertheless Mrs. Meir admitted she had supported him in Israel and had worked closely with him since 1969. He was not "all dark and bad. He did do some things for us in the past, and we mustn't forget them." But she now believed she had been manipulated by him and it upset her to think so.

Our visit with Mrs. Meir came to an end with the appearance of Moshe Dayan and his wife. We took a moment to say hello to the Dayans, and to convey to Mrs. Meir our deep gratitude for her candor and friendship.

28

"A Change of Pace"

1979. It was time after forty years—and yet it wasn't. A clean split from the League would have been less emotionally hurtful. Holding on partially to my ADL responsibility was punishing; withdrawal pains always are unpleasant. I wanted to stay with the League and I did, on my own terms, since nobody asked me to step away. But I was no longer totally involved in what had absorbed me for so long. In a consulting role as general counsel I was on the periphery when I still wanted to be deep inside.

I chose Shea & Gould, a prominent New York law firm, because of an old treasured friendship with Milton Gould. The two of us had worked closely together in the early forties. Once very long ago he successfully defended me, *pro bono,* in a libel suit instituted by a well-known anti-Semite. When Milton read in the press of my semiretirement from ADL, he phoned and in his characteristically gentle manner said, "We cleaned out a room in the office, told the secretaries they no longer can use it for lunch, and we shined up the desk with a little spit. When are you getting your butt over here?"

I was back in the private practice of law.

* * *

Sometimes an obsession with major social problems is supplanted by a toothache—or a lump. In a way it's a reminder of our mortality, a most democratic emotion. Besides, there's nothing that concentrates the mind as totally as fear or pain. It happened in June 1980. Drying myself after a hot shower, I saw a bulge protruding from the right side of my groin below the hip. The next morning Elie Stoller, lifelong friend and first-rate physician, confirmed the diagnosis he had made over the telephone. But the hernia, he added, was only a secondary problem. Now just past my sixty-eighth birthday, treatment for an enlarged prostate had been a regular part of my routine for many years. Elie advised against prostate surgery unless and until I first underwent hernia surgery. I was in and out of the hospital in a few days, the rupture repaired. A month afterward I checked into the hospital, went under the knife and returned home in ten days, the prostate problem resolved.

Preoccupied with juggling law practice at Shea & Gould and responsibilities at ADL, it was easy to dismiss any lingering thoughts of my recent bouts with medicine. Doctors were forgotten as I sat at a large conference with several other lawyers quietly probing a legal question. Leaning back in my chair, hands resting in my lap, I slowly became aware of a hard lump in my right groin. Five days later I came awake in my hospital room after the operation, yet not fully alert. Ben Payson, the surgeon who performed the excision, was standing at my bedside. He seemed at ease, his hand resting gently on my wrist. "I'm sorry to tell you, my friend, I removed a malignant tumor. Not a bad one. We can deal with it." He patted my hand.

The sedative was apparently still very much with me. "Could you be mistaken?" I asked without feeling real concern.

"It's no mistake." "You had a lymphoma. But get yourself healed, and in a few days we'll meet with some other doctors and talk about it".

During the next five weeks my first stop each morning was at the radiation center of Beth Israel Hospital, and then to my office. There was damage from the cobalt treatment. Three years later my leg began to show the fallout of radiation, from

318

the hip to the ankle. The doctors were not surprised. They had suspected from the beginning that cobalt might injure the lymph system in the area of treatment, a penalty they assured me I should be willing to pay for continued life. The right leg is half again larger than the left one, and during the day I wear an elastic sleeve on it from the toes to the hip. But it's now nearly nine years since the surgery and I am satisfied. No, gratified. No, lucky.

29

From Kibya to Beirut

Early in October of 1987 a truck loaded with Gaza Arabs crashed through a roadblock and Israeli guards shot three of its occupants. Days later a Jewish salesman was gunned down in the Gaza town square. Shortly thereafter an Israeli truck driving along the strip smashed into an automobile, killing several Arabs. In November a PLO terrorist armed with a machine gun overflew the Lebanese border in a motorized hang glider and landed near an Israeli military encampment. Shooting his way past the sentry, the guerrilla killed six soldiers, wounded seven others before being shot dead.

With each incident following closely after the other, tensions increased and intermittent Arab demonstrations, already endemic on the West Bank and in Gaza, escalated into bitter violence. To the traditional stones, epithets and burning tires, protesters numbering in thousands added rocks, lead pipes and gasoline bombs. In turn, the Israeli military brought in live ammunition besides their rubber bullets and tear gas. By December the territories, racked with turmoil and torn asunder, saw Israeli soldiers, themselves frightened of being killed, shooting at rampaging Arab youth. A crackdown was ordered by the

Senator Henry Jackson and playwright Paddy Chayefsky sharing
a speakers platform with the author in New York City, February 1980.
(Photo: Whitestone Photo)

Author with his wife and Dore Schary at ADL dinner at the Waldorf-
Astoria in New York City, February 1980. *(Photo: Mort Kaye Studios, Inc.)*

Author against a montage of himself, enjoying a joke at his expense by Toastmaster Dore Schary at dinner celebrating thirty-five years with the ADL, May 1974. *(Photo: Whitestone Photo)*

Yosef Tekoah, Israel's Ambassador to the United Nations, at a dinner in honor of the author, at the Waldorf-Astoria, May 1974.

Author delivers address on receiving Honorary Doctorate in Philosophy at Ben Gurion University of the Negev in Beersheba, Israel, May 1984.

Arnold Forster honors his close friend Meyer Levin, prominent Jewish author of *Compulsion* and other best sellers, March 1974.

Author speaks at a dinner (above) in Westchester County, New York, honoring opera singer Robert Merrill, June 1982. From left to right, Alfred B. DelBello, Joey Adams, Mrs. Jan (Alice) Peerce, author, Mrs. Robert (Marian) Merrill, Robert Merrill, Mrs. Frank (Barbara) Sinatra, Frank Sinatra. With Frank and Barbara Sinatra (below).
(Photos: H & H Photographers)

Famed violinist Isaac Stern and wife, Vera (at left), at a Washington, DC dinner with the author in June 1983. Stern and Zubin Mehta were honored for winning an Emmy in the author's film, "Zubin and the IPO."

Henry Kissinger and wife Nancy share the speakers platform with the author and his wife, at annual dinner of Ben Gurion University of the Negev, New York, September 1981.

Author (with Congressman Herbert Tenzer looking on) congratulates
General Ariel (Arik) Sharon on his court victory in libel case against *Time*
Magazine, January 1986. *(Photo: Camera Arts Studio)*

Author shares a speakers platform in June 1987 with Benjamin Natanyahu,
Israel's Ambassador to the United Nations.

Prime Minister Yitzhak Shamir confers with the author at ADL Executive Committee meeting in New York City, June 1988.

army to bring quiet from chaos, and by Christmas twenty-two Arab youths were dead.

William Safire, columnist for The New York *Times*, wrote: "Demonstrators know that the heaving of a Molotov cocktail is rarely if ever caught by the camera, but the subsequent subduing of the bomb-thrower makes the authorities look cruelly repressive on front pages and television." TV commentators and crews, given total freedom by Israeli authorities, competed with each other in condemning Israel, showing pictures to match, while newspapers enflamed its readers with hyperbole. The U.S. government admonished Israel for being excessively harsh and then voted in the United Nations to support censure of the Jewish State for ordering nine Arab ringleaders deported. The character of the criticism would have been more appropriate had it targeted on the murder of ten thousand rebellious civilians killed in a single day by Syrian government troops a few years ago in the city of Hama. Except that those killings were not to be seen at the time on television while only a few newspapers gave the story as much as one full paragraph.

It was March 6, 1988, a time of ever enlarging West Bank and Gaza riots that had by then become a virtual Palestinian revolution. The Arabs now counted nearly ninety dead among the protestors. Israeli soldiers, frustrated and infuriated with orders not to use live ammunition no matter the provocation, had violated belated but strict rules in unmercifully beating captured culprits, during one incident even covering four of them in a shallow ditch with dirt up to their necks—an outrage, no question, but not, as reported, being buried alive.

When thirty United States senators, all proven friends of Israel, joined together in a letter to Secretary Shultz, expressing support of his newest peace proposals, the nation's television and newspaper headlines uniformly distorted the content of the communication—to support their own disapproval of Prime Minister Shamir's position. Except for Egypt, the Arab leaders to whom Secretary Shultz had appealed with his revised plan, like Israel's prime minister, had tentatively rejected his proposals in one manner or another. The joint senatorial letter therefore berated both sides for intransigence, laying it on the Arabs somewhat more than on Israel's Shamir. But no television viewer or newspaper reader who failed to see the full text of the letter, unavailable nearly everywhere, could possibly know that the missive meticulously blamed *both* sides, rather than simply expressing "dismay" at the obstinance of the Israeli leader.

It is no answer, just hogwash, that criticism of the media for thus mishandling this urgently important story is tantamount to blaming the messenger for the message. When the messenger, either deliberately or for simple lack of conscious objectivity, distorts the message, he *is* blameworthy.

The civilian murders at the hands of the Syrian military in Hama in 1982 referred to above have become the classic case to cite as evidence of the double-standard treatment. But Hama was only one of a myriad number of similar killings that daily went unreported by the very press that gave regular front-page space, like daily baseball scores, to each individual West Bank death. The virtual absence of reports on the countless other such civilian deaths is a test of the accuracy of the double-standard charge against the media. For example, on July 12, 1988, three car bombs were detonated by suspected Soviet terrorists in the Pakistani city of Karachi, killing 72 civilians, wounding 260 others. The incident was only a small part of the eight-year-long terrorist campaign that targets on the Pakistani population. How many Americans know of this? Careful readers of Lally Weymouth's reports in the Washington *Post* are among the small number of Americans who remember the story. Nightly television and daily newspapers have paid but small attention to this costly Soviet war on a civilian population. How to explain the difference in the media's treatment of the West Bank Gaza story?

On March 19, 1988, a Jerusalem *Post* reporter wrote that he had been surprised to learn that in January of the year, in one month, 950 persons had been killed by terrorists in the Indian state of Punjab alone. He should not have been surprised; the media had kept it a virtual secret.

With the daily press front-paging each single death in the

continuing West Bank riots, during the third week of March, Iraqi forces, warring on the Iranians, showered cyanide and mustard gas on the Iraqi city of Halabja. Five thousand civilians were killed, according to Iran's representatives at the United Nations, five thousand others critically burned. Several days later, The New York *Times,* in an editorial criticizing Iraq said only five hundred had been killed. Simultaneously, The Washington *Post* reported Iraqi's grave violation of international law. But it was only a one-day news story for most of the American media, with little if any critical editorial comment to be found in the sea of American newspapers.

In short, bias and the double standard used in holding Israel to rules and standards that apply nowhere else was once again at work. No sufficient background explanation was offered to put events in accurate perspective. Never mind that the Gaza strip had been abandoned by Egypt, leaving impoverished Arabs to rebel under the reluctant authority of Israel. Ignore that other Arab nations had deliberately kept West Bankers sealed in for years as tinder to enflame the area against the Israelis. All the media could find to say was that no matter the dangerous conduct of the rioting Arabs, no matter the injuries sustained by young Israeli soldiers, no Arab rioter should be shot, even unintentionally, by Israeli troops trying to restore order. The treatment accorded Israel was a replay of the critical reaction to its attempt in 1982 to end the PLO destruction of Lebanon at Israel's expense. And for the same reason: civilians were getting killed. Now again Jewish efforts to win fair, unbiased coverage from Israel's critics of these tragic events went for nought, and the damage to Israel's image abroad was the worst since its Lebanese invasion.

Tragically, the almost worldwide condemnation of Israel's actions was wide of the relevant issue; the uprising was only symptomatic of the far more profound underlying problem. What governments and opinion-makers everywhere should have been dealing with were the fundamentals. Why was this killing happening? Was it because Israel had been intransigently rejecting genuine peace negotiations by its relentless grip on the West Bank in spite of Camp David? Or because the Arabs had been frustrating honest movement toward peace by refusing to negotiate directly with Israel without preconditions or the participation of supportive outsiders? Did Israel have the right to refuse to deal with Yasir Arafat, head of the terrorist PLO that has avowed its destruction? Or was the basic problem the Arab refusal to come to terms with Israel's presence in the Mideast? Or Israel's refusal to consider Arab rights? Or both?

Faced with the magnitude of the Mideast turmoil and killing, is not in-depth analysis a basic responsibility of a free press? What is learned from the Mideast's forty-year political history since the reestablishment of the Jewish State? Can four decades of Arab rejection of Jews as a sovereignty in their midst be forgotten? Are interminable wars to wipe out the Jewish State to be erased from memory? May a defeated aggressor unilaterally discard a thousand-year-old international law that an attacked country is entitled to retain lands in dispute that in defending itself are successfully occupied? Should a group of prejudiced nations impose themselves as impartial arbiters in peace negotiations between warring enemies? How absolute are Israel's sovereign rights to decide its own security needs and detiny, or is the Jewish State bound to heed the advice of armchair generals, Jews and non-Jews alike?

These and other questions were the real issues at least begging for considered attention. The primitive, sensationalist coverage of the seemingly insoluble tragedy, the distortion of daily events to justify predetermined attitudes was outrageous. For it should have been clear that the solution to the fatal riots had nothing to do with the riots themselves. The refusal of the United Nations and its individual members to deal with these and other such issues while journalists made a punching bag of Israel was typical. The history of such bias and unfairness goes back almost to the beginning of the Jewish State.

When Israel declared itself a sovereign state in 1948 its borders, except for the area reaching to the Mediterranean Sea, became most dangerous places. Between 1948 and 1953 armed gangs from surrounding Arab countries succeeded in crossing their frontiers to kill or wound hundreds of Israelis. Unwilling to accept the presence of a Jewish State in their midst, and lacking an Arab government prepared to make war on Israel, segments of the Arab community resorted to individual forays into the territory of the new nation. Quietly encouraged by Arab governments to engage in these activities, and frequently furnished arms and funds by Arab authorities, these intruders did a great deal of damage. They were forerunners of the highly organized, militarized terrorist movements of later years. In the first ten months of 1953 alone more than 130 Israeli civilians, including many women and children were murdered or seriously injured.

Ten miles south of Tel Aviv, the small border town of Yahud situated on the edge of Israel's narrow waist faced the Arab village of Kibya in Jordan just across the line. Since the beginning, Yahud had been the target of incessant raids by armed Arab trespassers intent on catching Jews off-guard. In late 1953, on the night of October 12, Arab intruders stole into the Jewish town to murder and pillage, killing a mother and her two children asleep in their beds. Forty-eight hours later an Israeli military team paid a reprisal visit to Kibya and some fifty Arabs were slain. Asked to explain the raid and loss of life, Prime Minister Ben-Gurion answered that "the patience of the Jewish settlers had been exhausted, and crossing into Kibya was to cauterize 'the main center' of the Arab murder gangs." He stated that "Israel would never agree to allow its citizens to go unprotected from armed marauders."

The administration in Washington, fearful that increasing hostilities were lessening the chances for peace, was annoyed with Israel and not satisfied with Ben-Gurion's explanation. The State Department protested that "at least forty-two defenseless persons," Jordanians, had died, and announced that the United States would delay several millions in grants to Israel. It would take the distressing matter to the United Nations Security Council, it said, to determine how to deal with border tensions, and it immediately requested the UN to provide a firsthand report from Major General Vagan Bennike, the UN's truce team chief-of-staff. Simultaneously the Arab states, denouncing the murders of sixty-six Jordanians, accused Israel of using six hundred troops to carry out the deadly raid. Ben-Gurion denied the charge as an "absurd, fantastic allegation."

According to newspaper stories, there were recurrent reports in Washington that the Kibya incident was being used by the administration as an excuse to reorient American Mideast policy in a renewed effort to woo the Arabs at any price. One newspaper described the tactic as a "moral cover for a cynical deal by the United States and Great Britain with the Arab nations."

Within days independent investigators confirmed that Kibya was indeed Israel's swift response to a whole succession of Arab attacks, more than eight hundred in number, which culminated with the killing of the mother and her two youngsters in Yahud. John Glubb, popularly known as Pasha Glubb, the Britisher who had commanded Jordan's Arab Legion, conceded that Israel had been provoked by Arab infiltrators. Among other border incidents were the murder of several American tourists in Jerusalem including a woman and children, and an armed attack on a youth village for retarded children. The UN's Major General Bennike reported his findings on Israel's counteractivities: Between 250 and 300 Israelis were involved in the Kibya attack, and fifty-three villagers died in the raid.

On October 26 of 1953, two weeks after the Yahud murders that triggered Kibya, Time magazine led off its foreign affairs section with a report captioned: "Israel—Massacre at Kibya." Painting a picture of what happened that night, it printed a dramatized version of the event, selecting facts to fit the version, and choosing adjectives and statistics different from most other reports available to interested observers. These excerpts from the article are an example:

> At 9:30 one night, most of the people were just going to bed in the Jordanian village of Kibya—a light still burned in the village coffeehouse where a few late gossipers were preparing to depart. On this quiet night, as usual, everyone put his trust

in the UN 'Truce' and thirty skimpily armed Jordanian National Guardsmen. Suddenly, Israeli artillery previously zeroed onto target opened up, and a 600-man battalion of uniformed Israeli regulars swept across the border to encircle the village . . . the town shuddered under shell bursts . . . the villagers, screaming and milling, rushed out to the surrounding fields and olive groves . . . the Israelis moved in with rifles and Sten guns. They shot every man, woman and child they could find, then turned their fire on the cattle. After that, they dynamited forty-two houses, a school and a mosque. The cries of the dying could be heard amid the explosions. The villagers, huddled in the grass, could see Israeli soldiers slouching in the doorways of their houses, smoking and joking, their young faces illuminated by the flames. By 3 A.M. the Israelis' work was done, and they leisurely withdrew.

At dawn the villagers crept out of the grass and made for the smoldering ruins, looking desperately for a husband, a wife, a child. They crowded around a young girl whose body sprawled grotesquely, forefinger raised to heaven as Moslems do when they say, "There is only one God, and Mohammed is his Prophet." An old man dug furiously in the debris, occasionally looked up, terror in his eyes, then laughed hysterically. Once he shouted to the sky, "Allah, I have no relations. Why didn't you leave me one person?" It was the bloodiest night of warfare since the 1949 armistice . . .

Time, in describing the British, Washington and Arab reaction to the Israeli raid, said "cold-blooded murder," "distress," "horror," "shocking." For the Israelis it reserved the words, "defiant and unapologetic," continuing with this:

"When I heard the news, my heart swelled with pride," said one Israeli. In the Mosaic tradition of an eye for an eye, the Israelis produced statistics to show that since May 1950, 421 Israelis had been killed or wounded by Jordanian murderers.

To make certain that readers clearly understood Time's point of view about the Kibya event, the magazine, for a last sentence, declared: "Israel made peace harder than ever to obtain."
We were shocked by the hyperbole and the fictionalized style

of this news reportage. It was a description we could find nowhere else in the American press. Our switchboard lighted up with protesting calls. One complainant commented sarcastically that Time magazine obviously must have had a reporter on the scene either accompanying the Israeli raiding party or hiding in Kibya waiting for the appearance of the "Jewish stormtroopers." If its story was to be believed, Time even knew the precise number of ammunition rounds allotted to each Israeli soldier.

Time had deliberately depicted the Arab village as a simple pastoral scene filled with innocent, harmless, home-loving farm folk. Not a hint of the Arab murderers long holed up there, always ready to choose the strategic moment to cross the border and kill Jews. The defenders of Kibya had been only "skimpily armed" Jordanian troops. Its terrified villagers had "huddled in the grass", crawled around dead bodies, watched Israeli soldiers "smoking and joking." After all, wrote Time, the Jews were only following the "Mosaic tradition of an eye for an eye." Even the magazine's friends were surprised at that shot, convinced that Time's trained researchers must have known the biblical phrase meant to Jews only "let the punishment fit the crime," not revenge.

It was typically lively Timese, even if less than accurate. But Jews were angered and up in arms. They had long been complaining to the Anti-Defamation League about the character of the magazine's coverage of Israeli and Jewish affairs, never with any apparent result. They could not know, of course, that in response to their previous protests, a year and a half before the Kibya incident I had requested from our own research library an analysis of Time's treatment of Jewish and Israeli subjects. After reading the resulting memorandum I had decided to wait and allow the magazine's record of objectionable items to grow and thereby avoid any doubt about the validity of our case if the day came to make it.

The Kibya story in Time broke the back of our patience. Our leadership met to determine a course of action. In the meantime I asked that our file memorandum on the magazine be

brought up to date and that it incorporate a study of Life magazine, the pictorial weekly published by Time, Inc. A look at the
additional data made evident that a meeting with responsible
executives of the magazine was long overdue. One of our key
laymen was asked to meet with his friend, Roy Larsen, president of Time, Inc., to confer about it.

Within days our updated memorandum analyzing four years
of Time magazine's coverage of Israel was ready. In my opinion
the new material together with the old, plus some items from
Life magazine, represented a convincing document that
demonstrated unfair attitudes toward Jews and Israel. The data
was redrawn in the form of a letter to Mr. Larsen and was
forwarded with the reservation that "we do not believe Time
or Life is in any sense anti-Semitic"—put in to avoid a charge
that the League was begging the question it seemed to be raising.

The result was an invitation to a luncheon, which we accepted. On January 21, 1954, we were greeted on our arrival at
Time's executive dining room by Henry Luce, the publication's
owner-founder, and James Linen, its publisher, and the managing editor, along with three other executives. Our group consisted of Philip Klutznik, president of *B'nai B'rith*, Henry
Schultz, ADL chairman, Barney Balaban, chief executive officer
of Paramount Pictures and a Jewish elder statesman, along with
Ben Epstein and myself.

Lunch and the amenities over with, Phil Klutznik began the
serious part of the meeting by stating that we intended neither
to exert any censorship pressures or to charge Time or Life with
anti-Semitism. Our purpose was to inform them of the increasing concern among Jews about the treatment in the periodicals
of Jews and Jewish problems. For more than two years, he said,
we had been receiving critical comments from our constituency
about articles in both publications.

Luce immediately interrupted Klutznik's introductory remarks with the impatient observation that we would not be
meeting at this very moment, would not even have asked for
the meeting, if it were not for Time's editorial policy on Israel.

He dismissed the notion that his publications were anti-Semitic —ignoring Klutznik's waiver of that question in his introductory remarks—adding a guess that we did not believe it either. Suggesting greater candor on our part, Luce recommended that we ought frankly to admit that the real purpose of our delegation was to protest Time-Life's anti-Israel attitude.

Listening to Luce was quite painful for several reasons. First, he was afflicted, unfortunately, with a most disturbing and disconcerting stutter. And then, of course, we had not planned on a fight; we wanted peace with these powerful publications. Our goal was to create some empathy among Time's policymakers for American Jews so troubled by the magazines' attitudes. We were eager to convey a clearer understanding of Israel's predicament in the Middle East. None of us, though, was prepared to accept being told that we were deceptive about the reasons for our presence. But we held our tempers, assuring Luce in polite if firm terms that our motive for the meeting was exactly as stated—a primary concern for American Jews. Luce's associates were clearly uncomfortable with the way he had phrased matters. It was evident, too, that if Luce was in the habit of dealing with others in brusque and blunt terms, he could do so with us but expect no less in return.

Our responses to his comments modified Luce's tone a bit, and during the next few minutes he acknowledged that Time magazine had, in the past year or two, been anti-Zionist. I looked around at our people. It was obvious we all thought it a startling confession. He quickly added that in the early years of Israel's existence, Time had published laudatory articles about the Jewish State.

Luce then sent us into mild shock with an explanation of his approach to what appeared in the pages of his magazines. He welcomed, he said, the creation of Israel but resented the American government's partiality toward the Jewish State, "at least until Eisenhower's assumption of the presidency." The general press, he continued, was afraid of "criticizing Israel because of the sensitivity of American Jews," and he "resented" that fact because it denied Americans a balanced picture of events in the Middle East. He was determined, he said, to "equalize" the quantity of information reaching the American people. For this reason, he said, he had "instituted a policy of partiality to the Arab cause." This was why, he added, James Bell, Time's correspondent in the Near East, had been "pursuing a pro-Arab policy."

The chagrin and surprise we shared must have registered on our faces, because Luce then hurried on to sing the praises of Ambassador Abba Eban as "the single most brilliant representative that any government had in Washington." Luce apparently thought this opinion helped offset Time's admittedly slanted reportage on the Middle East. The founder of the magazine then, in our view, fumbled the ball. "America's interests and Israel's are separate and distinct, and Time and Life," he said, "must remain impartial." Hardly what he had told us only moments before.

We pressed Luce with the obvious question about how Time could be both "impartial" and "anti-Israel" at the same time. His rejoinder was that the weight of pro-Israel editorial opinion across the United States was not really offset by Time's editorial treatment of its news stories.

In an effort to move onto a more constructive track we stressed Israel's repeated pleas for a permanent peace in the Mideast and its unsuccessful efforts to meet with its Arab neighbors. Luce seemed somewhat unfamiliar with Israel's efforts for peace. But he did think, he said, the Arab refugee problem needed more attention, sparing us an explicit statement about whose responsibility he believed it was.

We brought him back to the subject of American Jews, pointing to the dangers inherent in falsely equating Jews with Communism. In this connection we questioned the fairness of Time's identifying culprits as Jews in articles about Communism. And we named names, the same ones identified in our letter which he and the others had seen. Several of Luce's associates spoke up in explanation of this problem. The religious or ethnic factor, they told us, was an essential part of some news stories about people, and Time writers were powerless to change it in view

331

of "reporting policy." They did not explain why "reporting policy" could not be changed.

Toward the end of the luncheon Luce switched somewhat. He said that in the future his magazines would try for impartiality and we would likely not have any reason for criticism. If we did we should not hesitate to bring it to his personal attention. We had had some impact after all, I thought. It was these last statements from Luce that persuaded Ben Epstein, after the meeting, to write a note of appreciation to him.

I was wrong. In the long years since that meeting, and until the Sharon v Time case, there was little if any evidence of any real change in Time's approach to the Middle East story. (In my view their continuing partiality toward the Arabs was what led thirty-two years later to the Israel General Ariel "Arik" Sharon's libel action against the publication. More of that later except to say that by its writing style Time suggested to readers that it knew the details of the Kibya raid inside and out, including, as I have said, the ammunition rounds allotted each Israeli soldier. Evidently at the time it did not know the identity of the Israeli lieutenant who commanded the special antiterrorist unit that carried out the raid. They learned it at the libel trial. But at his trial, as the first actual eyewitness to what happened in Kibya, Sharon put the matter in context and perspective.)

In May of 1982 Britain engaged the Argentine in a shooting war over the Falkland Islands, and insinuations persisted in British government circles that Israel was selling arms to the Argentinian forces. Speaking out in anger, Shlomo Argov, Israel's ambassador to England, asserted his country "neither wished nor needed to apologize to anyone for anything," and added that it was useless to hope he could effectively correct distorted media reports. When Britain shortly thereafter severely condemned Israel's air actions in Lebanon, Argov took the platform of an Anglo-Jewish Society in London to express sarcastic surprise at British hypocrisy, pointing out that the English had not hesitated to seek recourse in the UN Charter to justify its own military action in the Falkland Islands as self-defense. "The UN Charter, Article 51, was not meant," he declared, "to be invoked or put into practice selectively."

No wonder Ambassador Itzhak Rabin in 1968 had personally selected Shlomo Argov to be his minister in Washington; Shlomo's brilliance made him a special asset. Tall and thin, stooped, physically awkward, he was a knowledgeable and highly skilled diplomat whose government career began in 1955 after eight years of service in the Israeli army. His skills also caused him problems. Argov argued against his embassy's deliberate policy in Washington of avoiding confrontations in the face of repeated evidence of what Shlomo regarded to be anti-Israel attitudes in some American government circles. When three years later he stepped down from the post somewhat disenchanted with his assignment he was by no means finished with government service.

After returning home Shlomo was named director of information in the Foreign Ministry in Jerusalem, a job in which his talents showed to advantage as he supervised the projection of Israel's image to the world. In rapid succession he was then picked as ambassador to Mexico, to The Hague, and in September 1979 a prize assignment—ambassador to Great Britain.

After almost three years in this post Shlomo was considered tops among the highly respected members of the foreign diplomatic service at the Court of St. James. And this despite his candor at public meetings, where he never hesitated to blast Israel's detractors while offering cogent arguments in support of its actions. As a guest in the country Shlomo's caustic and frequently stinging criticism of British Israel-haters would normally have rendered him *persona non grata*. But his painful honesty brought him respect on all sides. (It had also protected him from criticism eleven years earlier when he helped me with information ADL needed in its fight against the Arab boycott, a fight frowned on by some of his own superiors in the Israeli government.)

Our close personal relationship did not end when Shlomo returned to Jerusalem and was later posted to Mexico, The

Hague and finally London. On the contrary, instead of frequent but hurried phone calls and brief visits, now we had the advantage of a continuing, in-depth correspondence.

In May 1982, my wife and I were on our way to a Ben-Gurion University board meeting in Israel with dear friends Joan and Robert Arnow, he, the chairman of its board, and stopped overnight in London. Invited to the ambassador's home for a Sabbath evening dinner, the four of us stayed well past midnight talking with Shlomo and his wife about Israel's difficult position regarding the PLO occupation of Lebanon. How long, we asked each other, could Israel be expected to tolerate the continuing deterioration of the Lebanese government infrastructure and its growing helplessness at the hands of a terrorist army planning and working on Israel's destruction.

Several days later Shlomo was attending a formal dinner in the line of duty. The function took place at the Dorchester Hotel on Park Lane in London's fashionable West End, not too far from Buckingham Palace. The street outside was crowded with traffic as guests poured out of the ballroom entrance and into limousines. Shlomo among them. He walked about a hundred feet toward his auto, but before its door could be opened a burst of machine gun fire ripped into his brain. He slumped to the ground as a Scotland Yard bodyguard brought down the Arab assailant with a bullet in the neck while two accomplices escaped in their car, to be captured a short time later.

Shlomo was paralyzed in every limb and muscle, able only to move unfocused eyes. The last time I visited him at his bedside he labored slowly to form his words into a coherent message. "Arny . . . my . . . dear . . . friend. Please . . . have . . . them . . . put . . . me . . . to . . . sleep . . . for . . . good."

On June 6, 1982, three days after the attempted assassination of Shlomo, the Israeli Defense Forces invaded Lebanon. In justification the government of Israel recited a list of anti-Israel attacks: the assault on its ambassador to Britain; the killing a few weeks earlier outside his home of Israel's second secretary at its French embassy; the murder of five local embassy employees;

a long string of deaths and injuries of Israel's diplomatic personnel in previous years—all attributed to the PLO. This carnage,
said Jerusalem, had to be stopped once and for all.

From the perspective of time it seems fairly clear that Israel
had by then determined to end the PLO's growing power to
control Middle Eastern destiny. In Lebanon the Palestine Liberation Organization had become a government unto itself, the
duly constituted authorities unable or unwilling to restrict its
actions. Led by Arafat, the terrorists were a fully equipped army
financed by the Saudis and other wealthy Arab nations. They
maintained a countrywide tax-collecting structure. They dic-
tated policy to television, radio and most of the press by machine guns at the heads of management. All of this was accompanied by a never disavowed determination to destroy Israel.

Out of fear or sympathy, other Arab nations—Syria, Jordan,
Saudi Arabia, Libya, to identify a few—were in effect pandering
to the PLO and turning their backs on Israel's repeated pleas
for them to cease financing, encouraging and justifying the Arab
terrorist forces. Western Europe, unwilling to sacrifice lucrative
Arab trade and its sources of oil, and likewise feeling either fear
or sympathy for the PLO, was openly ignoring Israel's requests
to close ranks with the Jewish State against the well-organized
guerrilla movement. The U.S. administration, reluctant to offend friendly Arab nations, was also still trying to persuade
Arafat to cease his terrorism against the Israelis, recognize their
right to exist and join the peace table. But beyond talk Washington was doing little to discourage the PLO. As a result Israel
concluded that only at the risk of its future could it delay any
longer a military effort to free itself from a pro-PLO steel trap.
And so it invaded Lebanon.

At the outset of Israel's sudden move across its northern border, the Western world seemed content to stand aside and
watch the Jewish State's armies invade its neighbor for the
purpose of establishing its announced *cordon sanitaire* against
the PLO in southern Lebanon. But as the Israeli forces, moving
into Arab land, discovered a greater PLO military machine than
they had thought to exist, a decision was made to press forward,

335

to Beirut if necessary, in order to crush the entire PLO army. The outside world, shocked at this, took a 180-degree turn, bitterly criticizing Israel for what it was doing, intensifying the criticism with each additional mile Israel's tanks and men moved forward. The Israeli army in turn was stunned at the strength of the PLO, the amount and quality of its gun emplacements, deliberately set up within occupied, residential buildings and churches, its use of mortars from inside hospital and school grounds, its practice of compelling Arab youngsters to precede its shooting tanks—all in the hope Israeli soldiers would withhold fire.

The Israeli forces pressed on in spite of numerous casualties and arousing much criticism within Israel itself: an unnecessary thrust beyond the security belt; too many Israeli soldiers dying; destroying the PLO was too costly; saving Lebanon was not worth the sacrifice. This was followed by a groundswell of furious protest from the very governments that in the first place had done the least to relieve the difficult Israeli dilemma. Media elements seemed to take special satisfaction in critical overstatement about the character and manner of Israel's fighting tactics. Fury tends to feed on itself. By the time Israeli armies reached the capital city of Beirut, news reports of Lebanese events had become uniformly distorted, accompanied by hostile editorial commentary. It all made headlines. It did not reflect the truth or provide perspective. It was not, however, popular for Jews to say so.In light of the obvious harm being inflicted on the Jewish State's good name, it was suggested I fly to Lebanon, see for myself and report my findings on the air.

I was in for a surprise. From the moment the invasion began, like so many others at home, I had been scrutinizing every press story out of Lebanon, careful to see and hear morning and evening network news programs. What I witnessed and learned at the actual scene had little resemblance to what had been described in the press and on TV. My observations and reports after returning home were a desperate although small effort to project some truths to the American people. An exercise in frustration against a massive backdrop of blatant anti-Israel reportage. Typically, John Chancellor on NBC had said to his audience of millions: "What will stick in the mind about yesterday's savage Israeli attack on Beirut is its size and its scope . . . Nothing like it has ever happened in this part of the world!" *The Christian Science Monitor* compared the Israelis with the North Vietnamese, while another newspaper equated them with Hitler. Other journalists actually described Beirut as resembling Auschwitz, the Nazi concentration camp where over a million Jews were gassed and cremated. *Holocaust, genocide, Warsaw Ghetto, blitzkreig* and other gruesome synonyms were used freely and repeatedly in countless reports. President Reagan appeared on television to agonize over a news photo of an armless infant, an alleged victim of Israeli guns.

Only a few of us who had been eyewitnesses troubled to report southern Lebanon's entire population was a hundred thousand less than the number reported to be homeless, and the alleged ten thousand dead a gross exaggeration. Unknown to the American public, the original source of such exaggerations was the Red Crescent of Lebanon, in no way a counterpart of our Red Cross but a PLO operation controlled by Yasir Arafat's brother, Fathi.

The American people had to be told these truths along with others that had been given equally little notice. Several days after the publication of the picture that upset the president, the UPI apologized for distributing the misleading photograph; the baby, both arms in place, was safely at home with its mother. Contrary to the claimed wholesale destruction of cities along the southern Lebanese coast, those of us who walked its streets found ourselves among teeming residents going about routine daily chores. Housewives on busy sidewalks carried shopping bags, men toting leather portfolios and children pedaling bikes. Shops and restaurants bustled with customers.

As for John Chancellor's description of the Beirut devastation, an inch-by-inch scanning of entire Western Beirut through field glasses from the Baabda hills above it showed only scattered ruin pocking the central city, with no severe damage except on the city's edge in the Burj al Brajneh neighborhood and at the airport beyond. It is worth noting that in the years since the August 1982 departure of the PLO from Lebanon precipitated by the Israelis, the utter destruction of the city once regarded as the Paris of the Mideast was actually committed by the Lebanese themselves, who to this day carry on the ruthless, insane tribal warfare that has afflicted that benighted little world for hundreds of years.

From this distance in time one might seek an explanation of the media's conduct during the Israeli invasion. Each of us has his own answer. Elie Wiesel, foremost philosophical historian of the Holocaust, suggests the world blew out of all proportion Israel's role in Shatila and Sabra in order to stop Jews from reminding others about the ghastly extermination of the Six Million. Rabbi Emanuel Rackman, chancellor and until recently president of Israel's Bar Ilan University, speaking generally and without any particular person or institution in mind, suggested it was plain, unvarnished anti-Semitism at work.

When the Israeli armies finally occupied Beirut itself, Western Europe and the United States joined in demanding that Israel permit the main PLO forces, still in Beirut and northern Lebanon, to leave the country safely, taking only small arms with them. The television pictures of American marines lining both sides of the roads leading to the "rescue" ships in Beirut harbor while the armed PLO legions, fingers held high in "V for victory" signs, shouting "Death to the Israelis," marched by is a memory difficult to erase from one's mind.

In any case Arafat and his PLO leaders betrayed their promise to evacuate Lebanon. Instead they arranged to hide ten thousand of their number in and around Tripoli in the north, and two thousand in the two contiguous Beirut neighborhoods of Shatila and Sabra. When Bashir Gemayel was elected president of Lebanon, only to be assassinated before he could take office, it seemed to be a signal for the enemy Palestinians purposefully still within the country to rise up in one last effort to take control again.

It required little foresight to predict Bashir's assassination. When, after lunch one day in Beirut in late August of 1982, I saw

Bashir drive off, his bodyguard in the backseat, I predicted he would be assassinated within twenty seconds of his scheduled inauguration on September 23, 1982. I was wrong only by days.

The Christian Lebanese forces believed that unless the hidden Palestinian terrorists were rooted out and destroyed a disastrous insurrection would be inevitable. The Israeli generals on the scene agreed with the decision, and when General Sharon, then Israel's minister of defense, arrived by helicopter in Beirut to pay a condolence call on the Gemayel family, he approved the Israeli commander's consent to the Christian Phalange forces to search out PLO terrorists left behind hiding in Shatila and Sabra with heavy arms in considerable supply.

The Phalange went into Shatila and Sabra and hundreds died. The PLO terrorists had been hiding in underground connecting tunnels throughout both neighborhoods. The world was up in arms. Israel had pledged quiet and instead it had permitted killings. If the press had been intemperate before, now it unleashed a torrent of reportorial invective that aroused international fury against Israel. Later, careful research revealed that there were approximately thirty-five noncombatants—men, women and children—killed; the hundreds of others were armed PLO guerillas. However, Israel's ethical reputation was considerably damaged.

The widespread criticism of Israel was aggravated within Israel itself when popular anger at the own high army death toll triggered huge protest meetings demanding investigation of the tragic events in Beirut. Great numbers of Israelis earnestly believed that failure to exercise sufficient caution to prevent civilian deaths—at the hands of the Christian Phalange—even among the enemy was wrong, and if it were true that Israeli military leadership was responsible, someone should be punished.

An *Israeli* Commission of Inquiry took many months—from September 1982 to February 1983—to investigate the tragic incident. Its final report found a number of highly placed military and civilian leaders culpable in varying degrees, though none willful, for the terrible events in Shatila and Sabra. General Sharon, the defense minister, was found to be among those "indirectly responsible" for what occurred in the two Palestinian neighborhoods. Under all the circumstances, said the commission, he should have anticipated what might happen if the Phalangists were allowed into the PLO neighborhoods so quickly after the murder of their president-elect.

Much of the foreign press recognized the high ethical character of Israel's soul-searching examination of its own conduct during the course of the war, and paid its genuine respect to the Jewish State for this instance of self-critical integrity, a rarity in the history of any government. But for other elements of the press, media exaggeration was still the order of the day. Journalistic assassination of Israel was in style, and publications seemed to compete with each other for the most punishing story they could hang on the Jewish State. Accuracy was the other victim in the race for readers and, if the reports were to be believed, Israel no longer had a right to hold its head high among nations.

Time magazine, not satisfied with the commission's finding of Sharon's "indirect responsibility," reached for its own "exclusive" fillip—that there was more Sharon actual responsibility and guilt than even the Commission of Inquiry had dared to reveal. Referring to a secret appendix to the commission's report, which it said was treated as confidential because it contained the names of Mossad agents and other similar information, the magazine portentously reported that *Time has learned that it contains further details . . . Sharon reportedly told the Gemayels that the Israeli army would be moving into West Beirut and that he expected the Christian forces to go into the Palestinian refugee camps. Sharon also reportedly discussed with the Gemayels the need for the Phalangists to take revenge for the assassination of Bashir . . ."*

It had remained for Time to concoct the worst story of the war. The startling revelation, touted by Time in a news release, was headlined in much of the world press, giving the magazine due credit for its exclusive "discovery." If the charge were accurate, no one could possibly argue that the Jewish State had any conscience or ethical principles. Israel's foremost living military hero, "Arik" Sharon, had allegedly participated in a conspiracy to commit mass murder of women and children. Time's report could be fairly interpreted to mean that Sharon had obviously perjured himself in his testimony before the commission of inquiry in testifying that he did not anticipate the tragic turn of events in Shatila and Sabra. Also that the Commission of Inquiry had covered up Sharon's active encouragement of the mass murder of civilians. The State of Israel had appointed Sharon head of military activities and he should have been made to bear the blame for his deeds. But according to Time, Israel's official Commission of Inquiry had suppressed the outrageous truth. These were the inevitable conclusions to be drawn from Time magazine's alleged revelation. The hurt to Israel was incalculable.

Uri Dan, Israeli newspaper reporter and in this period General Sharon's press representative, was a friend. Our paths had crossed many times over the years in the course of our work. Discussing the Time story with him on a transatlantic phone, and knowing Sharon was still an Israeli minister although no longer in Defense, having resigned his defense post following the Report of the Commission of Inquiry, I wondered what impact the magazine's charges would have on the general in his own country. "Terribly damaging. He's in a rage," said Uri, "and justifiably so. The story is full of hatred and typical of Time magazine."

I recalled to myself the meeting with the magazine's late publisher, Henry Luce, in January 1954—the one arranged with Luce and his associates—when he conceded he had instructed his Middle East correspondent to file pro-Arab, anti-Israel stories. I could not now argue with the Israeli journalist, understanding his reaction and the general's outrage. "The newspapers here report that Sharon has started a libel suit in Israel," I said. "What impact will that have on his situation?"

"Not much," said Uri Dan, "but it's important for the record. Except that people in your country will say it's to be expected if he wins in Israel. An American court would be much more effective if that were possible. Can you find out?"

"It is possible if we can initiate a seperate case here even though you have already instituted action in Israel," I told him. "Let me look into it and I'll let you know."

As it turned out, Time maintains two separate publishing corporations, one in Europe for its Time and Life publications there and in the Mideast, and another in New York for circulation and sale of Time magazine in this hemisphere. The lawsuit in Israel was against the European corporation. Printing the story in the United States was a separate act because the publisher was a different legal entity, an American corporation. A litigation in an American federal court in tandem with the Israeli case was perfectly in order.

I took the matter to Milton Gould, founder and senior partner in our law firm. We called in several other trial men in our office, also experts in libel law, for an in-depth examination of the facts at hand and an analysis of the applicable law: Richard Goldstein, Bernard Fischman and Adam Gilbert. We all agreed a good course of action could be set forth against Time magazine, and in light of the damage done to General Sharon, to the cause of truth and to the State of Israel, we should be willing to undertake the responsibility if Sharon wanted it.

I telephoned Uri Dan and told him our reaction. Not long afterward Sharon appeared at our offices, accompanied by Dan. Gould, Fischman and I listened to Sharon's story firsthand and questioned him at length. The facts clarified, Gould then proceeded to explain to Sharon the extraordinary difficulty, virtually insuperable, of winning a libel case under American law. If, said Milton, a plaintiff complaining he was damaged by libel is a "public person" (well known and active in communal life), he must establish that the false and defamatory statement about which he protests was uttered in malice. And the definition of malice, he added, is a legal one, not simply the ordinary dictionary meaning of the term.

Milton went on to explain to General Sharon that from our preliminary understanding of the matter we believed that, assuming the availability of certain essential documentation, we might be able to establish the presence of malice, within its technical, legal connotation. Sharon agreed to return to Israel, examine his files and return with critical material.

At the second meeting we brought in Richard Goldstein, who was to become second in command to Milton at the trial. Again we went over the details of the case, examining the data that Sharon now spread before us. After hours of discussion our team concluded Sharon had a good (provable) cause of action if there was sufficient evidence to find that Time magazine or the reporter responsible for the objectionable story published it "with knowledge of its falsity or with reckless disregard of its truth or falsity"—that is, the legal definition of malice. In addition, said Milton, it would be important to produce two vital documents: the minutes which had been made of the Sharon condolence call at the Bikfaya home of Pierre Gemayel, father of the slain president-elect, and a copy of the secret appendix from the Israeli Commission of Inquiry that Time had reported contained the conversation it attributed to the Israeli general. Were they available?

Sharon's Israeli lawyer, Dov ("Dubi") Weisglass, who accompanied him to this consultation with us, telephoned the Defense Ministry in Israel. The Bikfaya minutes were read to him while he made notes on a pad. In addition, Weisglass had with him his own notes, based on his own earlier reading of the secret appendix. That seemed to satisfy everybody in the room.

Sharon asked that we take his case to court. We knew that the undertaking would be extraordinarily costly and the stakes extremely high, involving the reputation of Israel itself and, in the nature of things, of Jews generally. When Sharon said he was unable to commit himself to pay for our services, Gould invited our other senior founding partner, William A. "Bill" Shea, to join the deliberations. Explaining the matter to Bill, Milton said that our team believed that we, as Jews, owed it to Israel to take the case. Bill Shea, a prominent Irish-Catholic American, did not hesitate for a moment. If we who studied the matter felt that way, he was all in favor of doing it. If we believed exoneration of General Sharon was of importance to Israel and to Jews everywhere, he would be pleased for us to undertake the matter and be paid only if we achieved a substantial money verdict for General Sharon, an unlikely possibility.

Sharon was appreciative. He assured us that he would assume full responsibility for actual out-of-pocket expenses in the case, recognizing that Shea & Gould could not do so under the Code of Professional Responsibility regulating lawyers. With this, we were off and running, never dreaming that out-of-pocket costs would reach well beyond a half-million dollars, and that the fees for our services, never paid, would be in excess of a million and a quarter dollars.

The only concern I felt about Shea & Gould representing the general was that some might mistakenly conclude the litigation was an Anti-Defamation League matter. After all, as both the League's general counsel and a partner in Shea & Gould, the connection would seem close. In fact, however, I shared nothing about the case with anyone in ADL while our law firm was studying the subject and until just before it would agree to represent Sharon. Both Kenneth Bialkin, ADL's national chairman and Nate Perlmutter, its national director, were surprised to learn of my connection with the matter but expressed no objection whatever to my involvement in it.

The Shea & Gould decision gave me heart. There was no doubt in my mind, reading Time across the years, that the magazine, in spite of the promise of Henry Luce in the long ago, seemed mostly to support the Arab position. By its own admission Time incorporated its editorial view in its news reports, believing that its readers want and expect interpretation, not just straight bare facts from the magazine. Again and again I would become angry at the character of its coverage. On rare occasions only was the magazine able to find anything positive in Israel's presence in the center of the Arab world. I realized much would be accomplished for Israel in the court of world opinion if an American jury found Ariel Sharon, former defense minister, innocent of the dreadful charge of instigating the murder of women and children levelled at him by the magazine. His alleged culpability for the crime of Shatila and Sabra had surely

344

also stained his country, and a finding of his innocence would therefore also lift that mark of Cain from Israel's reputation.

Yet as we organized our case I was aware that Time's attitude toward Israel would not be an explicit issue before the court. We urged our client to exclude it from his complaint when we drafted our initial papers. We did not want to encumber with extraneous charges our legal task of proving that Sharon had been personally libeled—a burden that was already difficult enough under American standards of libel law.

For the same reason we had no intention of charging Time magazine with anti-Semitism in the lawsuit. Gould wisely determined to keep the issue narrowly on the solitary legal question he was raising: had Time told the truth when it reported, in essence, that Israel's minister of defense had encouraged, instigated or condoned the massacre of Palestinian civilians in West Beirut?

Inevitably, when the lawsuit came to trial the controversy was an immediate matter of international interest. Most recognized Israel's stake in the outcome, aware that a verdict for Sharon would work to the benefit of Israel's reputation. There was understandable but mistaken disappointment in some pro-Israel circles that our legal papers did not include anything about Time's attitude toward Jews or Israel. However, we recognized that some evidence relevant to the narrow issue of libel would be admitted into the record which might inevitably reveal Time's attitudes.

With rules of evidence in our federal courts these last years changed as they have been, courtroom surprises are kept to a minimum. The objective is to be sure both sides are fully aware of the intended testimony of the other's witnesses, and of the factual evidence in the hands of the other, *before* the litigants get to the courtroom for actual trial of the issues. This means that at an opponent's request, when subpoenaed for pre-trial examination under oath, the other side must produce any planned witnesses, or submit copies of any documents to be offered in evidence, or have them excluded at the trial.

Getting a good portion of the pretrial testimony or the documentation we requested from Time magazine was like pulling a wisdom tooth of a rhinoceros, although the defendant would likely make the same claim about the plaintiff. In any case, after a good deal of legal maneuvers, Time turned over to us for examination, as part of Halevy's personal file, an exchange of correspondence involving its Israeli correspondent, David "Dudu" Halevy, the reporter primarily responsible for the controversial paragraph.

It was an exchange between Halevy and Dick Duncan, his superior in New York, the chief of Time correspondents throughout the world. Significantly, the correspondence touched on more than the specific issue in the libel case, revealing in addition the respective personal views of the two newsmen about Israel and Jews. And it is not unreasonable to wonder what role those views may have played in what they wrote for and printed in their magazine. In reproducing the exchange of letters—grammar and all—between Time's Israeli correspondent and his New York chief, Duncan, I have italicized the statements that significantly reveal attitudes about Israel and Jews.

May 17, 1984

To: Dick Duncan
Fm: David Halevy

whenever i feel like writing or even when i am forced to write, i seem to have some kind of problem with the opening lines. so, in order to make it simple, basically there are two reasons for this note: one, i felt like writing to you and sharing some of my personal feelings and two, there are practical reasons.

i have to admit that the last weeks have taught me a lesson. *apparently journalistic "victories" only leave a sour taste. Almost four years after publishing the story on the Jewish terror network, after telling the story of Begin halting the investigation,* etc., the facts are finally proving the accuracy of the story published by the Washington *Star* on August 7, 1980. but then i found asking myself—so what? So the *Star* was right, i was right and who really give a f——?

and while saying this i don't mean Time. being right or wrong in our profession has little meaning. it is the personal professionalism, self-integrity and self-confidence that counts. the rest is actually irrelevant and this includes all the rough times—you know—i went through, the names and the suspicion.

aside from the personal point of view, *there are some developments—to which jewish terrorism should be attached—that seem to me to be very worrying. these are the actual vindication of arik sharon, the cabinet minister's statement justifying the bombing of the west bank mayors (professor yuval ne'eman) and other signs of mysticism, fascism, and radicalism. i don't want to draw historical analogies but it seems to me that the difficulty in recording these trends is as complicated as it was in the twenties and thirties in europe and mainly germany.* one thing is clear and this is that the deteriorating economic fabric, which will only become really clear after the general elections on july 23, will only add to the frightening reality.

the involvement of IDF soldiers and officers is another factor leading to a general feeling that someone has pulled the rug from under my feet. as far as i know the facts, i wonder whether the investigation will actually dig to the end. a few days ago, when harry interviewed amos oz, the writer, he said he used this phrase—speaks for itself. yet, i cannot share his feelings. the gap between my generation's dreams and the day to day reality is too big.

strange as it may sound, the result of all this is boredom. *there is nothing here to cause enthusiasm, nothing rates as a challenge anymore. the political developments are running in a pattern that is easy to predict. the military-defense establishment is taking a route that at best will lead nowhere. and the intelligenzia is taking such a non-ideological approach that no sparks are lighting up the darkness that is engulfing us all.*

if these statements lead you to believe that I have lost the ability to analyze, you will be wrong. *i know this country and its people, i was once part of it and them. this tunnel is going nowhere and there is no light at the end.* i might be wrong from A to Z, but i may also be right.

whatever the case my own personal point of view is irrelevant. someone else has to sort it out. harry and others should find the answers and make the judgment. i managed to survive mrs. meir and mr. begin. i have done it all. i had my victorious moments and weeks. i had my first rate stories and i had a bigger share of suffering for being first, for spelling it all out. i have established my reputation from here and whatever is here i have already done it. i want to spend some time in a place where the level of my personal involvement will be less acute.

i can no longer become enthusiastic over here and i will not regret what i have written, nor have i said it all because i am in a bad mood. i will not change my decision when the weather improves or when shimon peres will (if at all) become prime minister. cutting a long story short i'll stay as long it suits you, harry and the magazine. i would love to hear from you about the timing of my next assignment.

David

PS: *an israeli publisher and also an american agent have approached me and asked me to write a book on jewish terrorism. harry—and i share his view—thinks it is a bit too much to handle for us and myself right now.* please let me know your feelings."

May 25, 1984

Dear Dudu:

Thanks for your letter. I can certainly see how you must feel let down that justification doesn't really come in kind, for the story that got you into so much trouble. On the other hand, I have always felt that the trouble you were in was not so much a matter of truth or falsehood; plenty of stories can be wrong or half-wrong. The heart of the trouble was politics.

And even when the facts now tend to vindicate you, the politics are the same. Perhaps not quite the same in the Begin sense, *but the politico-cultural atmosphere which makes an outcast—or worse—of those who dare to criticize the Central Myths of Israel (some of them the finest myths in the west, some pretty damn debased and self-serving recently); that atmosphere is unchanged and seems to be stifling you. As it must stifle many.*

Your German analogies frighten me. I know what you mean, I think, but I hope you are not proved right.

My timetable for your departure is still the same. I'll have word for you by later this summer, at the latest, of a move to be instituted late this year. There are a few things I want to clean up first. But I'm quite clear in my own mind, as I think you are, that this is the right way.

Perhaps you could come to the States and rub elbows with all the nice liberals, intelligent devout Jews here and pick up a little much-needed rosy nostalgia for Israel. You know, singing songs together down on the Kibbutz, that sort of thing.

In a funny way there is an American parallel. The Moral Majority is fighting for a return to the rural and small-town Protestant cultural (into which I was born) which is lost forever, except in Ronald Reagan's speeches.

Please cover the elections for us and get us through the formation of government, and then we'll get you a mover for your furniture.

Also please do not do any books on terrorism, especially Israeli. And lie low on Sharon. You will be rewarded, although I'm not sure I'll ever see another Bureau Chief as good as Kelly. Love to Nikki.

Dick

Although Duncan wrote that he understood Halevy's references to Europe and Germany, and to the analogy with Israel, an outsider may find the comment vague and puzzling. But a reading of a short excerpt from Halevy's Examination Before Trial serves to clarify. Those of us on the plaintiff's trial team had been obliged to surmise what was in Halevy's mind in his reference to the thirties in Germany, until he answered some questions for us at his pretrial deposition in our offices.

Q. Do you recall, sir, the testimony that you gave on the first day when I asked you about materials that you reviewed in preparation for your deposition and you responded that one of the things you saw was—or reviewed a portion of William Shirer's book, *The Rise and Fall of the Third Reich?*
A. Correct.
Q. Do you remember what portion you reviewed?
A. If I am not mistaken, I said I was looking for the Lidice incident and for the assassination of the chief of the German security forces and Gestapo Heydrich.
Q. Do you recall whether or not you found that piece when you were looking for it?

SQUARE ONE

A. I did not. I didn't have a lot of time. I went quickly through the book and I did not find that piece.
Q. Why were you looking for the piece on Lidice?
A. Because I think there is a lot of similarity. Unfortunately there is a lot of similarity.
Q. Between what and what?
A. The assassination of Bashir Gemayel and the assassination of Heydrich, and what resulted from the two assassinations.
Q. What happened as a result of the assassination of the German Heydrich?
A. A massacre in a Czech Village.
Q. What happened as a result of the death of Bashir?
A. A massacre in a Palestinian village.
Q. What benefit did you see in reviewing the William Shirer book in preparation for this deposition?
A. I didn't see a benefit, but you gentlemen, you kept me occupied and you kept all of us occupied with the subject of Sabra and Shatila. It's not a subject which I am very proud of as an Israeli. It's a subject I am really ashamed of.

I don't like very much the IDF, to whom I belong, standing around camps and looking the other way when something is happening inside the camps.

I don't like to see my chief of staff and—my chief of staff offering the Phalange more bulldozers and tractors to cover up their operation, so-called, inside the camps. It doesn't give me a lot of comfort. And you kept me busy and occupied with this matter.

The more you think about it, the more some historical analogies come to your mind. And one of them which came to my mind—and I told you that before in an off-the-record conversation—I am a student of *The Rise and Fall of the Third Reich*.

You asked me a question and I gave you an answer. I tried to locate it, to find if the circumstances were the same.

Here was a German commander assassinated by the Czech underground or by Czech freedom fighters, and, as a result, a massacre in a Czech village.

Here you have a Lebanese warlord, Bashir Gemayel, and, as a result, his buddies, his bodyguards, his intelli-

gence unit goes and carries out a massacre in a Palestinian
refugee camp.

The similarity is almost on the wall . . .

Making an analogy between the Christian Phalangist's actions
in Shatila and Sabra, and the unspeakable Nazi murders in Lidice, and then connecting both to Israel on the basis of General
Sharon's "indirect responsibility," showed Halevy for what he
was. Especially when one recalls some of the Lidice details. Had
Halevy, the self-proclaimed "student of *The Rise and Fall of the
Third Reich,* found the section of William Shirer's book that he
searched for, this is what he would have read:

THE DEATH OF HEYDRICH AND THE END OF LIDICE

"Midway through the war there was one act of retribution
against the gangster masters of the New Order for their slaughtering of the conquered people. Reinhard Heydrich, chief of the
Security Police and the S.D., deputy chief of the Gestapo, this
long-nosed, icy-eyed thirty-eight-year-old policeman of diabolical cast, the genius of the 'final solution,' Hangman Heydrich,
as he became known in the occupied lands, met a violent end.

"Restless for further power and secretly intriguing to oust his
chief, Himmler, he had got himself appointed, in addition to his
other offices, Acting Protector of Bohemia and Moravia. Poor
old Neurath, the Protector, was packed off on indefinite sick
leave by Hitler in September 1941, and Heydrich replaced him
in the ancient seat of the Bohemian kings at Hradschin Castle
in Prague. But not for long.

"On the morning of May 29, 1942, as he was driving in his
open Mercedes sports car from his country villa to the Castle in
Prague a bomb of British make was tossed at him, blowing the
car to pieces and shattering his spine. It had been hurled by two
Czechs, Jan Kubis and Josef Gabeik, of the free Czechoslovak
army in England, who had been parachuted from an R.A.F.
plane. Well equipped for their assignment, they got away under
a smoke screen and were given refuge by the priests of the Karl
Borromaeus Church in Prague.

"Heydrich expired of his wounds on June 4 and a veritable hecatomb followed as the Germans took savage revenge, after the manner of the old Teutonic rites, for the death of their hero. According to one Gestapo report, 1,331 Czechs, including 201 women, were immediately executed.[1] The actual assassins, along with 120 members of the Czech resistance who were hiding in the Karl Borromaeus Church, were besieged there by the S.S. and killed to the last man. It was the Jews, however, who suffered the most for this act of defiance against the master race. Three thousand of them were removed from the "privileged" ghetto of Theresienstadt and shipped to the East for extermination. On the day of the bombing Goebels had 500 of the few remaining Jews at large in Berlin arrested and on the day of Heydrich's death 152 of them were executed as a 'reprisal.'

"But of all the consequences of Heydrich's death the fate of the little village of Lidice near the mining town of Kladno not far from Prague will perhaps be longest remembered by the civilized world. For no other reason except to serve as an example to a conquered people who dared to take the life of one of their inquisitors a terrible savagery was carried out in this peaceful little rural place.

"On the morning of June 9, 1942, ten truckloads of German Security Police under the command of Captain Max Rostock arrived at Lidice and surrounded the village. No one was allowed to leave though anyone who lived there and happened to be away could return. A boy of twelve, panicking, tried to steal away. He was shot down and killed. A peasant woman ran toward the outlying fields. She was shot in the back and killed. The entire male population of the village was locked up in the barns, stables and cellar of a farmer named Horak, who was also the mayor.

"The next day, from dawn until 4 P.M., they were taken into the garden behind the barn, in batches of ten, and shot by firing squads of the Security Police. A total of 172 men and boys, over

[1] According to Schellenberg, who was there, the Gestapo never learned that the actual assassins were among the dead in the church. (Schellenberg, The Labyrinth, p. 292.)

sixteen, were executed there. An additional nineteen male residents, who were working in the Kladno mines during the massacre, were later picked up and dispatched in Prague.

"Seven women who were rounded up at Lidice were taken to Prague and shot. All the rest of the women of the village, who numbered 195, were transported to the Ravensbrueck concentration camp in Germany, where seven were gassed, three "disappeared" and forty-two died of ill treatment. Four of the Lidice women who were about to give birth were first taken to a maternity hospital in Prague where their newly born infants were murdered and they themselves then shipped to Ravensbrueck.

"There remained for the Germans the disposal of the children of Lidice, whose fathers were now dead, whose mothers were imprisoned. It must be said that the Germans did not shoot them too, not even the male children. They were carted off to a concentration camp at Gneisenau. There were ninety in all and from these, seven, who were less than a year old, were selected by the Nazis, after a suitable examination by Himmler's 'racial experts,' to be sent to Germany to be brought up as Germans under German names. Later, the others were similarly disposed of.

" 'Every trace of them has been lost,' the Czechoslovak government, which filed an official report on Lidice for the Nuremberg tribunal, concluded.

"Happily, some of them, at least, were later found. I remember in the autumn of 1945 reading the pitiful appeals in the then Allied-controlled German newspapers from the surviving mothers of Lidice asking the German people to help them locate their children and send them 'home.'

Actually Lidice itself had been wiped off the face of the earth . . ."

Suffice it to say, whether or not we included in our complaint any reference to Time's attitudes toward Israel and Jews, whatever they were, it was now clear, at least, that the Time reporter who was responsible for the false and defamatory paragraph was himself intensely hostile to Sharon and to the present State of Israel. During the pretrial period the magazine resisted public disclosure of parts of Halevy's personal file until ordered to do so by the court. The file revealed that he had previously been placed on probation by the magazine for another "scoop," one about the health of Prime Minister Menachim Begin.

Halevy's hostility had apparently led him to renounce identification with his native land and its people—*I was once part of it and them*—and to compare his people with the Nazis. The "similarity" which Halevy saw between Lidice and Shatila/Sabra existed only in his mind. No longer wishing even to live in the land of his people, Halevy had asked Time to reassign him to a post outside the Jewish State *"where the level of my personal involvement will be less acute."*

We had our own pre-trial problems, one of which was quite revealing about Arik Sharon, who is reputed to be the toughest of all Israeli leaders. In preparing the case for trial it was crucial we know exactly with whom our client talked, and in whose presence and where, during the few days of events at Shatila and Sabra. Every minute had to be accounted for with utmost precision. It could be disastrous to be caught unprepared by a credible witness or a memorandum attesting that Sharon actually did encourage the massacre. Putting together all the data that our staff was able to accumulate, we discovered a three-hour lapse in the chronology—the hours before noon on Friday morning, September 17, immediately preceding the start of the Holy Day of Rosh Hashanah, the Jewish New Year.

We laid before General Sharon our five-day "calendar" and asked him please to try to remember in detail what he was doing, and where, at that critical juncture Friday morning. To our surprise he responded that he well remembered, adamantly insisting, however, that under no circumstance would he share the information with us. Milton Gould, informed of the impasse, was equally adamant that Sharon must do so.

"Tell the general we will withdraw from the case if he holds out on us," said Gould. "I will simply not go to trial and leave myself open to fatal surprise. No way."

Told of Gould's attitude—that he would have to retain new lawyers or abort the case if he insisted upon remaining silent—Sharon consented to fill in the gap. But only for us, and in absolute confidence, not to be used in the court. He warned that if the Court insisted on an answer he would refuse and ask that the trial be ended with him paying whatever penalty was imposed, and go home.

He explained: Many years earlier, on the eve of the Jewish New Year, his twelve-year-old son, playing at home with a friend, discovered one of Arik's hidden guns. The gun went off and Arik's son was dead. Every year since, on the anniversary of the boy's death, as is the custom among Jews, Sharon visited the grave to offer the traditional prayer of mourning, the Kaddish, for his boy. It made no difference to him, Sharon said, that the Commission of Inquiry had succeeded in learning of his visit to the cemetery. He himself nevertheless did not want the fact to come out at a public trial, lest anyone conclude that he was using his son's death to win sympathy. He would rather pack up and accept defeat.

Fortunately, Sharon was never questioned about that Friday morning.

The case came on to be tried before Judge Abraham D. Sofaer in the federal court, Southern District of New York. Judge Sofaer was a former professor at Columbia University School of Law and a respected jurist. With so many questions about Israel and Jews, it was all but inevitable that the story Time had printed about Kibya thirty years earlier would surface during the course of the trial, and it did. In his opening to the jury Tom Barr, defendant's trial counsel, read from various periodicals several reports of purported atrocities attributed to General Sharon *not on the question of their truth—they were inadmissable, as evidence, for that purpose—but as proof of Sharon's public reputation.* Gould, well prepared about the truth regard-

ing Kibya, believed it worthy to draw from the plaintiff what
actually happened:

Q. General Sharon, did there come times in your life when
you were accused of killing Palestinian or Arab civilians?

A. I was hearing here yesterday, maybe ten times, the story
of Kibya . . .

Q. You tell us, General, in your own way, what Kibya was all
about.

A. Kibya is in Samaria, about 20 miles northwest of Jerusalem
and about a mile and a half, maybe, from the '67 boundaries that were created after the War of Independence,
after the invasion of the Iraqis, the Jordanians, the Egyptians. These were the cease-fire lines in 1949 . . . Kibya is
a village, about two miles from those frontiers, from a small
Israeli town called Yahud.

Between the tenth and the fifteenth of October of '53,
Arab terrorists who came from Kibya went into this small
town of Yahud, threw hand grenades into a bedroom of a
civilian family, and a mother and two children were killed.
It was a deliberate attack. It was not shelling . . . Here, they
came, opened the window, threw a hand grenade into the
room. A mother and two small children were killed. One
of them was a girl. Her name was Shoshana.

But that was not the only case. I am not going to speak
about thousands of cases that took place, but I would like
just to emphasize, some of those events . . . I would like just
to give you the atmosphere in Israel in the fifties.

In March 1954, a place called Scorpion Pass—on the
road from Beersheba which one may call the capital of the
Negev—is in the southern part of Israel. The Scorpion Pass
was on the main road to Eilat. And there were people
coming from a celebration in Eilat . . . They were am-
bushed and twelve people were killed, among them children. A girl five years old . . . stayed alive because an Israeli
soldier was sitting there in the car. When he got hit he fell
over her body, or maybe he protected her. He was killed.

In April 1954, near Tel Aviv . . . in a place called Shafrir,
a religious village . . . there is what is called a Yeshiva, a
religious school. While praying—they were eight boys
around ten years old—hand grenades were thrown into
this room. They were praying their evening prayer. Four

were killed, three wounded. Among those four, I think, one was a teacher.

In April 1955, in a village called Patish . . . close to the Gaza district, at a wedding . . . hand grenades were thrown into the celebrating people there. A girl twenty-two years old was killed, a big number of casualties.

In October 1956, in a place called Kadima, not far from the place where I was born, two workers in an orange grove were killed and their ears were cut and taken . . . Arab terrorists did quite a lot of that.

In 1955, in order to travel from a place called Gedera, twenty miles from Tel Aviv, the traffic was organized in convoys. I was stationed there . . . There were nights when you could not have gone to Jerusalem . . . convoys were formed and were protected against terrorists who used to cross the border to commit their terrible crimes and to withdraw, disappear, run away, the same night . . .

Now I would like to come to Kibya. This is what happened after that murder, the murder of that family in Yahud. I was instructed—and you have to know Israel is a state of law, Israel is democracy, no one initiates operations on his own—I was instructed—

Q. At that point, at the time of this Kibya incident, what were you?

A. I was then the commander of the 101 unit, a special unit formed to fight terrorists. One of the purposes of forming this unit was that terrorists those days, like later in Lebanon, used to find shelter among the civilian population . . . So my unit was formed in order to find those terrorists.

I was instructed to carry out a raid on Kibya, where we knew—first from tracks that were moving, that took us to the border, to the direction of this place, and from other intelligence sources—that those terrorists came from Kibya.

Kibya, a village on a hill, on a mountain had several dozens, maybe thirty or forty, fifty maybe, armed people. They were a civilian part of what used to be called the Home Guard, the Jordanian Home Guard . . . We were instructed to go there. I commanded that operation.

Q. How many men took part in the operation?

A. In Kibya itself around seventy people . . . we had a small deception operation because Jordanians used to protect the terrorists. When we were going into a place where

357

terrorists were, they used to come and act against our forces. So we had to put some roadblocks and make a deception operation. Altogether, with all the deception operation together, there were about 100 soldiers . . . I led those forces . . .

We were armed with light weapons. We had one section of mortars, single mortars, one section of two mortars. We did not shoot even one shell into this place. They were prepared . . . to be used against a Jordanian military position that could have prevented us from withdrawing. We came there in surprise . . . entered and captured the defensive positions surrounded with barbed wire fence, thick and high, and trenches. In these trenches, I believe that about around eight people were killed in fighting.

Q. Male?

A. Males, armed males that were there . . .

Q. What happened next?

A. Another, maybe four, were killed when a Jordanian reinforcement managed to enter the village in the middle of the operation . . .

Q. The Jordanian reinforcement, were they uniformed Jordanian troops?

A. Yes. It was not a Jeep. It was a Land Rover that moved in during the operation. Maybe they used one of the roads that we did not block to this place. We went into this place. It was at night. And we found the place empty. We did not hear anything. We did not see anything besides some, I will say, in maybe two places. In one place we found a boy, a child. So we took him to a safe place. In another place, after fusing—

Q. What do you mean by fusing?

A. When you put demolition, when you put explosives, in order to operate that you fuse them—you light them. After that, we heard a cry of a girl, and I was standing there with the officer that put those explosives which were already lighted. He moved in, he moved in. He took this girl. We found the girl, maybe between eight to ten years old. We took this girl out. We have not heard not a cry. We did not see.

We checked as much as we could have checked. If you asked me could we check, could we check every hole, every cave, every cellar, my answer will be no. It was impossible. We were . . . it was war. We were in an area

358

occupied by Jordanian forces since 1948. So we made our best effort. I don't know if anybody else would have done it.

And I remember this officer taking this girl out, and believe me, Mr. Gould, we took all possible precautions, all possible precautions. We endangered ourselves by staying several hours. After doing that we left. When I came back . . .

Q. Did you blow up the houses?

A. Yes, we did.

Q. Was it the purpose of the mission?

A. Yes, that was the order we got.

Q. Was it the purpose of the mission to blow up the houses to discourage Arab terrorists from making murderous raids into Israel?

A. Yes.

Q. What was the purpose of your mission?

A. Mr. Gould, the purpose of the mission was to enable our people—Jews and Arabs—to live without being threatened day and night by those Arab murderers . . .

When I came back, I was met on the border by a representative of the Central Command, an officer, and I reported to him that we accomplished our mission, that a number of casualties—and I reported what I saw myself—casualties to the enemy, was between ten and twelve. That was what we saw there . . . Later I heard on the Jordanian radio that they were talking about sixty-nine people killed. We did not see them. We took every effort. I think we were around a hundred men there . . . If you ask me could we have checked every hole where people found shelter there, was it possible. It was impossible . . .

Q. It says here in this paper, this Time magazine, that: "Israeli artillery zeroed on to this target Kibya, and a six hundred-man battalion of uniformed Israeli regulars swept across the border to encircle the village. Was any artillery zeroed in on the village?

A. Never.

Q. Were there six hundred Israeli regulars?

A. No . . .

Q. It says here that for the next two and a half hours the town shuddered under shell bursts. Were there any shell bursts?

A. No . . .

THE WITNESS: Your Honor, with your permission, I just

359

	want to say one sentence with your permission.
THE COURT:	If it has anything to do with this article, my permission is denied. If it has to do with what happened that evening, etcetera, I will permit you to say what you want to say.
THE WITNESS:	I want to say a sentence about what could have happened. If I could have had Your Honor put Time magazine to trial then, believe me I would not have been here today . . .

Sharon's testimony under oath was a far cry from the atrocity story Time offered its readers in October 1953. Ordinarily a self-serving version is what one might expect from a person accused of perpetrating a heinous crime. But Time had no reporter on the scene even though its previously quoted, imaginative eyewitness style of writing made it seem so. The magazine's inflammatory report was second hand, composed, at best, from information furnished by Kibya villagers or the Jordanian military; hardly impartial witnesses.

As I sat listening to the cross-examination of General Sharon about the character of Time's description of the event, my head pounded with the memory of Henry Luce's instruction to James Bell, his Middle East correspondent in that period. I had an urge to stand up and shout to the jury Luce's instruction to Bell—*pursue a pro-Arab policy*—so that they too would know the truth, and the world would know that the magazine's story of Kibya was the tainted acorn that gave life to the tree of hatred for Sharon. The jury would understand my point, I thought, because Time's lawyer had already emphasized to the jury that the story of Kibya had been publicized over and over again in 1981 when Sharon was appointed defense minister, and then published again and again when Shatila and Sabra were invaded by the Lebanese Christian Forces. But evidence of Time's attitude toward Israel then or now was irrelevant to the narrow legal question of libel. The only issue was Sharon's alleged complicity in the Shatila/Sabra deaths; if he knew what I remembered about our meeting with Henry Luce he might well have blurted it out and caused a mistrial.

When the evidence-taking was over the jury returned with findings that made clear to the world Sharon's innocence of the charge made by Time. There had been no evidence introduced during the trial that the minutes by the Israeli note-takers of the Sharon condolence call at Bikfaya on the father of the assassinated president-elect contained any corroboration of Time reporter Halevy's accusation. And there was proof developed at the trial that the secret appendix of the Israeli Commission of Inquiry made no reference to the matter.

The jury told the court it found Time's accusations false and defamatory of the Israeli general. Asking the court's permission, the jury added to the findings its conclusion *"that certain Time employees, particularly David Halevy, acted negligently and carelessly in reporting and verifying the information which ultimately found its way into the published paragraph of interest in this case."*

Several weeks after the trial Judge Sofaer, in an interview done by The American Lawyer, endorsed the jury's finding in much stronger language, saying Halevy was "the kind of reporter who was a bad apple" and that there was "quite a bit of evidence that Halevy was lying."

Under American laws of libel, to win a judgment a public person must prove not only that the accusation was false and defamatory but that it was made with malice. Not personal, actual malice, for Lord knows, that was amply demonstrated during the course of the trial, but *legal* malice, an entirely different concept—that is, with knowledge that it is false or with reckless disregard of whether it is true or false. The jury did not find such legal malice, and so Sharon could not be awarded a money judgment. But the general had already declared publicly that if the jury did allow him an award of money he would give half to the organization of Disabled Israeli Veterans, the rest to Jerusalem's Anti-Terrorist Organization.

Clearly Sharon wanted vindication in the matter of the terrible charge made against him, and equally clearly he had achieved what he wished. But Time magazine, refusing to accept the jury's decision graciously, publicly insisted that it could have proved its case, could have won total victory except for the refusal of the Israeli government to open its files to the magazine for the nonexistent material.

Few observers were deluded. The press was almost unanimous in reporting Sharon to be the victor, and Time magazine arrogantly stubborn. The Los Angeles *Times* headlined the result: TIME WINS IN LAW BUT LOSES TRUTH, and wrote that it was "a victory that damaged the reputation of American's most powerful news magazine." John Kuhns, Washington *Post* executive and former libel lawyer, called the verdict "an unequivocal moral victory for Sharon. The issue is truth or falsity. Time's story was false." Richard M. Clurman, former chief correspondent for Time magazine commented that "in journalism, there is only one sin worse than being found wrong: an unwillingness to admit it." The New York *Times* summed up editorially: "The jury found an absence of malice but no shortage of arrogance."

Time magazine—its European corporation—still had to face the problem of Sharon's case pending against it in Israel, where there was no requirement to prove malice. The magazine there asked the Israeli judge to accept the findings of the American court on the basis of the "full faith and credit" treaty between the two nations, in the hope that this would cause a dismissal of the Israeli case. Time's request was a mistake. The Israeli court agreed to accept the New York federal court finding that Time had defamed General Sharon. It then concluded that by doing so it remained only for Sharon to prove the amount of damages he had sustained. Malice was irrelevant.

The Israeli decision at long last broke Time's intransigence and the magazine settled the matter by acknowledging on the Israeli court record that its report of General Sharon's discussion with the Gemayels about the need for revenge was erroneous. No longer was Time contending the State of Israel had withheld essential evidence. And Time agreed to contribute to Sharon's Israeli court and attorney's costs.

That is "Arik" Sharon's satisfaction.

Looking back at the entire picture, some facts stand out: If Henry Luce's promise of objective reporting was kept for any period of time, it surely was abandoned by Time magazine in May, 1977, when Menachem Begin won election as Israel's Prime Minister. The rhyme in the magazine at the time declared: "Begin Rhymes with Fagin" (the scoundrel in Charles Dickens' *Oliver Twist.*). Time did not publish a responsive letter to the editor, a copy of which I received in the mail, which was captioned: "Time Rhymes With Slime." From the moment Menachem Begin became prime minister, to read Time magazine was to learn that the Jewish state could rarely do right. Israel's head of state, said *Time,* "was a terrorist" who was "totally insensitive to any problems beyond those of Jewish Israel."

What happened after the trial may or may not have had a direct connection with the trial, but subsequent changes in the magazine's slant and in its personnel seem worth noting. Henry Grunwald and David Halevy both departed the weekly. Grunwald, its editor-in-chief, not quite reaching his scheduled retirement age, resigned on August 17, 1987, to become US Ambassador to Austria. Halevy, having been transferred to the Washington, D.C., offices of Time, did not stay long in his new assignment. A phone call to the magazine in April, 1988, brought this information: "Mr. Halevy doesn't work here anymore. If you want to reach him, he's living in Chevy Chase, Maryland." Another apparently significant change was reported by Dr. Yoel Cohen, professor of political studies at Israel's Bar-Ilan University, in a round-up of scientific research into media coverage of Israeli events. Dr. Cohen, himself a journalist who has written extensively on mass communications, reported his findings in the Jerusalem *Post,* no friend of Sharon's, in March of 1988: "An examination of the moderate attitude and tone of Time magazine's reportage of Israel over the past three years contrasts with the lecturing stance which characterized reporting during the Seventies and up to the Sharon trial."

Confirmation of Cohen's study was to be found only a month later, in the April 4, 1988, issue of Time itself. Covering Israel's fortieth anniversary, the magazine printed a balanced, pene-trating, in-depth analysis that revealed sensitive understanding of the Jewish state's central political and military problems—its legitimate concern for survival and its justified fear that the Arab enemy has not genuinely accepted Israel's right to exist in the Middle East.

When Milton Gould made his opening statement on the first day of the trial he asked the jury rhetorically why in the first place it believed the Sharon case was brought to an American court. And he answered his own question this way:

> . . . We will prove that they were telling the world that this Jewish soldier, this revered hero, this man who had risen from the most abject poverty to the highest command in the Israeli army, this man had conspired with Phalangist leaders to mur-der civilians, women and children. That is the way the world understood it . . . Unless it is repudiated in this room, that is the way the world is going to understand it . . . Why are we suing in a New York court? Why are we trying to get an American jury to give the lie to this terrible defamation? We are doing it because if we don't do it, history will record that an Israeli general, a great hero in Israel, did such a horrible thing. And when the historians record that, there will be a footnote at the bottom of the page, and it will say "See Time Magazine February 21, 1983. That's the proof of it." And our job here is to persuade you by the evidence that there should be a *second* footnote, a second footnote that says, "By the way, an American jury, having heard all the evidence, said no, it did not happen, no Israeli general did anything like that.

That history will know the truth is Israel's satisfaction.

30

United Nations

Late in 1983, nearly forty years after the evening with Walter Winchell when we speculated about the future of the newborn infant, the United Nations, our former ambassador to the U.N., Jeanne Kirkpatrick, addressed an Anti-Defamation League luncheon. Declaring that the "U.N. record on human rights has been perverted," she noted that the international body had repeatedly and selectively remained silent in the face of abounding human-rights abuses of one particular group. Mrs. Kirkpatrick pinpointed the continued U.N. silence in face of "shocking resurgence of attacks against Jews in the world" and the concomitant denial of civil liberties to hundreds of thousands of Russian Jews.

This was not the first time Mrs. Kirkpatrick had spoken out in this fashion. Some months earlier the ambassador delivered a similar attack on the U.N. She complained about "the approach taken toward the Arab-Israeli conflict at the United Nations," which, she charged, had "nothing to do with peace but is quite simply a continuation of the war against Israel by other means."

One would have thought she would have shown a higher

regard for the international organization, or at least be as tactful and conciliatory as possible so that her diplomatic colleagues would accept her as a peer, at least within its precincts. But Mrs. Kirkpatrick knew what she was saying. With the avowed support of President Reagan, she had obviously concluded that her views should be made public, in the hope that some otherwise silent nations might speak up and urge culpable members to mend their ways.

There can be little doubt anti-Semitism has tattered the moral fabric of the United Nations. Bigotry is undeniable when a majority of its members ignores the plight of Jews whose rights and lives are trampled on. "All that is necessary for the triumph of evil," reasons the aphorism, "is that good men remain silent in the face of it."

Israel is more than a Jewish nation; it is the heart and soul of the Jewish world. Snuffing out Israel, the primary Jewish physical, cultural, religious, ethnic and political center, means destroying the core of international Jewish life. As we've observed, the destruction of the State of Israel is the ultimate anti-Semitism—and could be the epilogue for Hitler's "Final Solution." Yet anti-Jewish prejudice is openly voiced by many member states of the United Nations who want to see Israel disappear as a formal Jewish entity in the Mideast. And some member delegates and ministers are willing, no, eager, to work tirelessly for that goal, hoping thereby to bring Israel to a violent end.

As a result the United Nations in recent years has been the world center of anti-Semitism. Only a simpleton would not recognize Israel's position as both its scapegoat and *bête noire*. The record plainly demonstrates the Jewish State is the primary target of an anti-Western coalition that virtually controls the international structure, its agenda, propaganda and decisions. In the 1980 term exactly one-half of all resolutions adopted by the Security Council condemned Israel. Since then there have been more than one hundred resolutions of a similar character passed by the U.N. General Assembly.

For their passive acceptance of this political poison, the majority of Western nations stand revealed as refusing to resist an anti-Zionist, anti-Jewish, anti-Israel campaign long coordinated by an Arab-Soviet, Third-World coalition. A decade ago its manipulators won approval of a resolution recognizing the PLO as the sole legitimate representative of West Bank Palestinians. This in the face of the PLO's Constitution, which declares the "Zionist" state in the Mideast must be brought to an immediate end—in direct contradiction of the chartered United Nations purpose.

Hiding behind the word "Zionist" instead of candidly saying "Jew" when that's what is meant, has long been a tactic of professional anti-Semites and Arab propagandists. Interchanging the nomenclature comes as no surprise to those of us who long ago learned that people who hate Jews try to attach to the three words Jews, Zionist and Israel precisely the same meaning. But it still remained for the United Nations to become the world instrument for the classic misuse of the term "Zionist" to convey both an anti-Israel and anti-Jewish meaning. Before Israel came into being "Zionist" meant a belief in the need for the reestablishment of a Jewish State in Palestine. After Israel's birth in 1948 the word took on additional meaning: a conviction that the Jewish State has a right to exist in peace and security. Which means, of course, that one does not have to be Jewish to be a Zionist.

"Zionism is Racism" is false and mindless. Turned into an official United Nations Resolution in 1975 by a coalition of communist and Arab nations, the phrase became another weapon in the Arab propaganda arsenal. In winning approval for the resolution the Arab-Soviet bloc was supported by a handful of Black African countries seduced by promises of massive financial grants, military arms and oil, which, ironically, they never received. More than a dozen resolutions have reaffirmed the anti-Jewish position since its adoption, and it is unceasingly used by Arab, Soviet and Chinese propagandists to justify hatred of the Jewish State.

Acceptance of the resolution bespoke anti-Semitism, since the essence of Zionism is a love of Jerusalem, its other name.

Zionism's core purpose is the quest for freedom and the right of Jews to live as equals among sovereign nations. It is a liberation movement. Racism is the antithesis, arguing as it does the inherent superiority of one human species over another. It was diabolical for the U.N. to have officially adopted the false slogan. A U.N. objective, as stipulated in its charter, is to rid the world of racism. So the vicious syllogism goes: posit that Israel is inherently racist; its presence in the international organization is anathema; it is, therefore, to be expelled and destroyed. Q.E.D. This is the most hurtful in a long list of anti-Semitic assertions made at the U.N. Another is that the Jews are an "imaginary people" who never in fact existed, do not now exist, never experienced the Holocaust and—since they are a nonpeople— are not entitled to the rights accorded real nations. An Iraqi representative at the U.N. willingly joined the campaign to obliterate from history the murder of the Six Million. He urged the U.N.'s Palestinian Committee to oppose a television film entitled "The Holocaust" on the ground that its content "was undoubtedly Zionist propaganda."

To this day such undisguised anti-Semitism is easy to find in the publications of the U.N. Special Unit servicing the Palestinian Committee. It's to be seen also in documents of the United Nations, typically in the Commission for Western Asia, which, incidentally, accepts the PLO as a member-state while denying Israel's right to sit as a recognized member of the United Nations.

The litany of anti-Jewish U.N. prejudice begins in whispered corridor conversations, and then bursts forth on the open floor. In the exclusive halls of the Security Council, the late Saudi Arabian Ambassador Jamil Barody once declared the Holocaust was simply fiction and Anne Frank's diary a forgery. Only the Netherlands ambassador, in whose occupied country the Dutch girl hid until discovered, rose to challenge the lie.

On December 8, 1980, the Jordanian ambassador, Hazem Nusseibeh, asserted in the General Assembly that the Arab world had long been "held in bondage and plundered" by the Jewish people's "cabal," which controls and manipulates and exploits the rest of humanity by controlling the money and the wealth of the world. During this "debate" Ambassador Falilou Kane of Senegal added that news organizations are "dominated by Jews," a fabrication given currency by the Nazi propaganda machine almost fifty years ago. This provocative falsehood was also received without objection.

The proponents of Arab anti-Semitism counter, disingenuously, that "Arabs cannot be anti-Semitic because they themselves are Semites." It is a semantic quibble, without real meaning. The phrase "anti-Semitic" long ago lost the connotation of being against Semites. It means anti-Jewish, and everyone knows it. Professional bigots have long used the dodge on the premise that their followers are ignoramuses who don't know any better.

Jews, as such, have no position or role in the United Nations and must rely on the State of Israel and the intermittent decency of Western bloc members to speak out against anti-Semitic calumnies. Jews can't withdraw or resign as a religious community from the international body. Some observers wonder why the Jewish State doesn't retire from the U.N. Benjamin Netanyahu, Israeli ambassador to the U.N. in mid-1985 had an answer: Membership in the world body, he said, gives the Jewish State international legitimacy, providing it with essential diplomatic channels otherwise denied it by countries that refuse its recognition. The United Nations, he added, is the only worldwide political forum available to the Jewish State for making its own case. Surrendering its membership, he concluded, would allow gloating enemies to assert Israel is a "second-class state" unworthy of belonging.

If Yasir Arafat's Palestine Liberation Organization or its offshoots have more than the cat's proverbial nine lives, it's due less to the terrorist leader's capacity to survive, or to the passionate following of his army of murderers, than it is to the failure of some so-called civilized nations to end their direct or covert support of these elements. Certain Western nations keep shoring up Arafat on the groundless conviction it will lead to a

369

genuine Mideast peace while the Soviet Union and the stronger Arab nations, financing and arming the PLO, use him for their own ulterior purposes.

The PLO's organized cruelty against a background of open support by many reputable states tempts one to update a Karl Von Clausewitz maxim. The nineteenth-century political scientist and military strategist argued that war is a natural and proper extension of diplomacy. In our time terrorist warfare is accepted by some as a "natural and proper" extension of political action. What better example than the explicit support of Egypt, Italy and Yugoslavia for the PLO after the aborted terrorists' effort to seize the Italian cruise ship, *Achille Lauro,* on a Mediterranean voyage in October 1985? It made no difference to these nations that the Arab hijackers had unlawfully seized a ship on the high seas. Nor that the terrorists were planning to use it for a commando-style raid into Israel when it reached Ashdod, where they planned to kill every Israeli in sight until they themselves were gunned down.

Discovered at sea before the ocean liner docked at the Israeli port, four heavily armed PLO gunmen took control of the vessel. Vacationers from nearly a dozen countries were caught in the mass abduction. Brutalizing the crew and guests, the four terrorists selected Jewish passengers for special assault, killing Leon Klinghoffer, a sixty-nine-year-old American tourist who had been confined to a wheelchair because of heart attacks and strokes. They shot him and threw his body overboard, wheelchair and all.

Before the world learned about the murder Yasir Arafat had stepped into the picture on the pretense that he wanted to rescue the passengers and ship from the four hijackers. A sympathetic Egypt had requested his act of "mercy," Arafat said, and he agreed to help because Italy had been friendly and supportive. He pretended that he had no advance knowledge of the hijack conspiracy and was not aware of the terrorists' identities or the particular organization they represented. In fact, because of advance publicity the hijack was becoming counterproductive to Arafat's purpose and had to be aborted. Nations friendly to his cause were being critical.

So in the initial period of this misadventure, Arafat succeeded in appearing as some sort of savior and his effort was uncritically reported by important sections of the American press and television, accepted and believed by a willing world. Until, that is, it was discovered the terrorist who conceived and personally masterminded the seizure of the *Achille Lauro,* one Abdul Mohammed Abass, was the same political thug who had been appointed only a few months earlier by Arafat to membership on the PLO's highest national council.

When the PLO quartet, at Arafat's reluctant instruction, brought the ship into the Cairo harbor, the American government leaned hard on the Egyptians to turn over the culprits to the U.S. Arafat, his deception exposed, moved back into the shadows, relying on the Egyptian government to rescue his captured murder squad. Mubarak thereupon announced he was unable to surrender the captured terrorists in his custody to the U.S., that he had already handed them over to Arafat for punishment.

But Mubarak had bungled the rescue scenario, entangling himself in an embarrassing lie. The murderers, it was revealed, were still in Cairo. Some hours later they were actually put aboard an Egyptian commercial aircraft to be flown to Tunisia. Because of surveillance, an American air force squadron was able to catch up with the plane and force it to land in Sicily. The terrorists were then flown to Rome. The United States asked the Italian government to hold Abass prisoner along with his squad in order to allow our Justice Department time to submit conclusive proof of Abass' culpability in the hijacking of the ship and the murder of an American citizen. Italy said no.

Ironically, Italy itself was a primary victim of the terrorists— the *Achille Lauro* had been flying the Italian flag. It made no difference. Rejecting the American request, Italian Prime Minister Bettino Craxi ordered his police to take Abass back to the airport and put him safely on a commercial Yugoslav airliner to

Belgrade, and freedom. Craxi then accused the United States of piracy and invasion of Italy's sovereignty. Mubarak in Egypt added that Washington had stabbed him in the back.

In the unlikely event the role that was played by Jordan, Egypt and Italy failed to make it abundantly clear that each of them implicitly endorsed terrorism as a legitimate political tactic, and the PLO as an exemplary means of implementing the tactic, the three nations made their positions further explicit in the aftermath of the *Achille Lauro* affair: King Hussein welcomed as a "positive step" Arafat's announcement that he was renouncing terrorist acts *outside Israeli occupied territory.* Egypt's President Mubarak made plain his approval of Arafat's actions by posing alongside the terrorist leader while reading a prepared statement to the press outside the palace in Cairo. Italy's Prime Minister Craxi declared on the floor of his Chamber of Deputies that while he opposed Palestinian armed struggle as counterproductive, "I don't contest its legitimacy." To top these three, France, in the wake of the Klinghoffer murder, gratuitously pledged continued support of the Palestine Liberation Organization. And to underscore his attitude President Mitterand instructed his spokesman to convene a press conference to share this intelligence with the world.

The three captured terrorists were sentenced in Rome to jail terms ranging from fifteen to thirty years. Those still at large, including Abass, the ringleader, were given life terms; an exercise in futility. Lino Monteverde, the sentencing judge, told reporters his leniency was because of the youth of the defendants and on the ground that they had "grown up in the tragic conditions which the Palestinians endure." He added that he had dropped the charge of "armed terrorism" inasmuch as the PLO "has as its goal the restoration of a homeland to the Palestinian people." In short, the Italian court used the trial to reaffirm the legitimacy of the PLO and its acts of terrorism.

The Arabs—Saudi Arabia, Kuwait, Libya, Iraq, United Arab Emirates, Algeria and Qatar—watched the unfolding events in silence; they had decided to contribute $300 million a year to the PLO over the next ten years. Before one concludes that the

PLO is exclusively dependent on this not inconsiderable stipend of $300 million a year, despite his vague gangster-style secrecy Yasir Arafat is known to control somewhere between two to fourteen billion dollars.

As for the Soviets, a month after the *Achille Lauro* they showed their attitude toward the PLO by having a spokesman in Geneva declare the Soviet would renew ties with Israel only if the Jewish State agreed to the PLO's participation in Middle East talks.

Many naive Americans, hardened to the Soviet position, were shocked at the conduct of Egypt, Italy and Yugoslavia in aiding the escape of a band of cold-blooded terrorists and its leader. But it should have come as no surprise in light of the record. The two European countries, along with others, have long been friendly and helpful to Arafat and his organized killers. Governments on the continent, large and small, have long openly submitted to the demands of the Palestinian terrorists while piously indulging in mind-boggling rationalizations to avoid fitting punishment for the culprits. Some nations sympathetic to terrorist activities have even decorated perpetrators with medals for valor, along with donations of huge sums of reward money. Our own State Department vacillated about the PLO before George Shultz became secretary of state. When Yasir Arafat accepted an invitation in 1974 to address the U.N. Assembly at its New York headquarters, the terrorist chief planned to take advantage of the trip for other purposes. The PLO leader would, he thought, travel around the United States and share his political views with the most representative American groups that would welcome him.

There was no way the U.S. government could refuse Arafat a visa for the journey to the world body on Manhattan Island. The U.N. headquarters on the East River represents several acres of international diplomatic territory over which the United States has waived its right to bar entry. However, our State Department was not obligated to grant the PLO chief a visa beyond the U.N. confines. It has the power to limit an official U.N. visitor to a visa restricting him to a twenty-five-mile radius from the U.N. hub—enough to get to and from the airport. It may do this when there is good and sufficient reason— criminality, for example—for such a ruling. But at Arafat's request our State Department decided to issue a less restrictive visa permitting him to travel to Harvard for a scheduled lecture, then to Washington for a TV appearance on an influential talk show.

On March 1, 1973, the PLO murdered Cleo A. Noel, Jr., U.S. ambassador to the Sudan, and George C. Moore, his charge d'affaires. In June 1972, an arm of the PLO kidnapped and murdered the U.S. ambassador to Lebanon, Frances E. Meloy, Jr., and our Foggy Bottom officials apparently could not comprehend that Arafat's extensive record of terrorism was more than sufficient reason to deny him the relaxed visa classification he had so easily obtained. In effect the State Department ruled that Arafat was the legitimate spokesman of an authentic political entity. Other governments had made the same tortured rationalization.

We petitioned the U.S. Federal court, Eastern District of New York, to compel a change of Arafat's visa status to the twenty-five-mile limitation. Unwilling to confront an adverse ruling and an angry public opinion, the U.S. State Department appeared in court to inform the judge that it had itself reduced the visa as we had demanded. Our action evidently caused the Department to realize it could not justify classifying Arafat's record as lawful political action. Hearing from its attorney that the Department would now issue only C-2s to Arafat and his entourage of eight, with our consent the court dismissed our petition. When Arafat arrived his travel was limited to the United Nations—from Kennedy Airport and back.

It is not unfair to record this 1974 State Department/PLO incident at this late date for the insight it provides. On October 23, 1986, Secretary Shultz met in Washington with three top ADL executives to discuss the plight of Soviet Jewry and other matters of mutual concern. Burt Levinson, the League's national chairman, raised the subject of the PLO offices operating on American shores, pointing out that even King Hussein had closed them down in Jordan, and urging the same action here.

The secretary responded that a question of free speech was involved. It was then suggested to him that since the PLO-observer office at the United Nations was not staffed by U.S. citizens, under the U.N. Headquarters Agreement our government could close the office as a security threat. The discussion ended inconclusively. Levinson then wrote a letter for the record urging that the office be closed. When the State Department's passive attitude became known in Congress, an effort was begun to force its hand. Under this pressure, and much against its will, the Department ordered the PLO Information Office in the nation's capital closed. But it balked at closing the PLO's Mission to the U.N. in New York City, citing a U.N. Headquarters Treaty, in spite of an internal department memorandum to the contrary. A Senate amendment to the State Department budget mandating closure precipitated a counter-drive by pro-PLO elements as well as the American Civil Liberties Union in behalf of the PLO's free-speech rights. As if there is some constitutional right, protected by the First Amendment, to be organized for the purpose of killing Israelis and other Jews if necessary to liquidate the Jewish State.

In March 1988, U.S. Attorney General Edwin Meese III cut the Gordian knot, serving notice on the PLO Mission that it must close its offices or risk the federal court doing it for them. Congress, he said, left him no choice, and his spokesman made it clear that a United States statute overrides any contrary international legal commitment. But Secretary Shultz condemned the anti-PLO provision as "one of the dumber" things the American Congress had done. Only days later, on March 26, Shultz invited two members of the Palestine National Council to confer with him about his proposed Peace Plan—Edward Said, a Columbia University professor of English and comparative literature, and Ibrahim Abu-Lughod of Northwestern University. The PNC was widely known to be the legislative body of the PLO and Said, admitting that he had informed PLO chairman Arafat of the planned Shultz meeting, publicly said: "It should be clear that we reflect the view of the PLO." Yet Shultz, to justify the session with Arafat's two spokesmen, held to the fiction that the Palestine National Council was separate and distinct from the PLO. By holding the meeting Mr. Shultz softened the American position toward Arafat's terrorist movement.

This from a secretary of state who has proved beyond question his sure and incisive understanding of terrorism and the many good reasons why the United States should never, ever submit or surrender to the efforts of terrorists. This from a secretary who has demonstrated time and again in recent years a keen analysis of Middle East issues, and his loyal friendship, sympathy and support of the State of Israel, the PLO's single sworn enemy. All of which underscores, too, Jimmy Carter's announcement made after his March 1987 Middle East visit. The PLO leadership, said the former president, should be part of the peace negotiations, to which its chairman, Yasir Arafat, would be "welcomed by me."

From day one in the life of Arab terrorism, back in the fifties, Jews have been part of the forefront of efforts to expose the organized killing of innocent noncombatants. Admittedly our ox was the first to be gored, the PLO targeting from the beginning on Israel as such, and on Jews as Jews.

Much of the world—in addition to the Jimmy Carters of our nation—accepts the PLO as the legitimate representative of Palestinian Arabs. The United Nations, set up to promote and safeguard international peace and security with justice, is not concerned that the PLO murders Jews, at least not concerned to the point of closing ranks against these gangsters. In fact, the United Nations closed ranks *in behalf of* the PLO when in the same month of March 1988 it voted overwhelmingly—143 nations in favor, the United States abstaining—to take every possible legal step to frustrate American efforts to force the PLO U.N. Mission out of business. The world's leading terrorist organization thereby received an official stamp of approval from the world's most representative body. This is the significant fact—

the U.N.'s acceptance of the PLO's killing of Jews as a tolerable means of eliminating Israel from the face of the earth in order to establish the PLO's own sovereign state in its place. A benign or passive attitude toward this fact increases the clear and present dangers to Israel and peace in the Middle East.

31

Square One?

Has any genuinely fundamental change in American anti-Semitism been achieved since the middle thirties?

Simply put, yes—if the criterion is the extent of anti-Jewish discrimination in our daily lives and the magnitude of professional bigotry around us.

There has been a significant relaxation in restrictions against Jews in housing, education and employment. Prejudice in social accommodations—private clubs, some fellowship organizations, private resorts—a revealing measure of attitudes, has changed only in part. Private club barriers against Jews continue to stand high, and even in a small number of otherwise altruistic, national service organizations. One should not be misled by museums, symphonies, "good government" groups who overwhelmingly welcome Jews. They are not "social" in the sense the word is used. Such communal endeavors cannot very well exclude members of the Jewish faith while accepting their beneficence. And Jews are generous in these areas.

The really meaningful correction in the traditional pattern of social discrimination has been in the operation of resort hotels, but that is at least in part because religious discrimination in public facilities was outlawed by statute (along with similar racial barriers). Which means, of course, that it is not all prompted by sociological change but by legal necessity.

And there has also occurred a major change in the size and strength of *organized* bigotry. Studies spell out the shrinking number of professional anti-Jewish movements and in the memberships of those few groups still active in America. The far-right anti-Jewish fanatics calling themselves The Order have been decimated by long prison terms given to their revolutionary leadership. The Order's end is implicit in the judicial punishment it has suffered. Aryan Nations, Posse Comitatus, Identity Churches, and others like it, little-known hate groups, traveling the same road of violent bigotry are today more a police matter than a sociological phenomenon requiring community counteraction.

One bellwether is the Ku Klux Klan. The largest KKK membership that can be documented in recent years is about six thousand compared to more than a million in the thirties. The John Birch Society, disturbing exemplar of the sixties' anti-Semitic wing of the Radical Right, which once counted its membership near a million, admitted in 1986 to its being below fifty thousand and having a nine-million-dollar debt. There was also the so-called Christian Front, an anti-Semitic movement fifty years ago whose membership was then put at over five million. The Christian Front is long dead.

Today's comparatively small amount of *organized* bigotry is a welcome change in spite of such an aberration as Lyndon LaRouche's much criticized The National Democratic Policy Committee, Louis Farrakhan's misnamed Nation of Islam, and several other less-publicized groups of similar character. The central fact that needs to be kept in mind about these organized manifestations of bigotry, insubstantial as they may be, is that just by existing they undeniably reflect adverse attitudes toward Jews. And, of course, even such scant evidence of bigotry is too much.

However . . . against the comforting truth that institutions of discrimination and organized hatred have faded, there is little persuasive evidence of any similarly convincing change in *attitudes*. Collectively, polls on anti-Semitism all lead to one conclusion: anti-Jewish attitudes among Americans are very much and very disturbingly present.

In July 1981, the American Jewish Committee, reporting on a national survey it had commissioned, found "nearly one fourth of the non-Jews in the United States to be still anti-Semitic." Six months later *Present Tense*, a publication of the same agency, noted that polls conducted over many years showed a spread of 15 to 30 percent endorsing negative Jewish stereotypes. At the same time, a Yankelovich-Skelly national study of attitudes toward Jews concluded that "23 percent of non-Jews can be characterized as prejudiced. In September 1983, a Gallup test found that 12 percent of Americans would not vote for a Jew for president. And according to national opinion polls done by Gallup, Harris and Yankelovich in the two years from 1981 to 1983, there was a marked increase (10 percent) in those who felt Jews have too much power in the United States, while 40 percent were "tired of Jewish concerns about the Holocaust."

It is, of course, true that every step forward, no matter how small, is significant, since even standing still means a retreat of the "anti" forces. Even so, the statistics reflect a prejudice over and beyond negative attitudes generally found in pluralistic societies where groups raise walls of exclusivity. To sum up, there is no absence of anti-Semitic attitudes, whatever the depth or extent of them. And we must sadly recognize an abundance of current instances in our everyday lives that arguably stem from at least subconscious unsympathetic and even hostile feelings toward Jews in America.

Sometimes this mind-set reveals itself in insensitivity or indifference to the rights of Jews or to offenses committed against them. Perhaps the most egregious example of recent years is President Reagan's visit on May 5, 1985, to the Kolmeshohe Military Cemetery in Bitburg, where forty-nine soldiers of the Waffen SS are buried. The controversial trip offended and frightened Jews across the world. Two weeks earlier, Nobel Laureate Elie Wiesel, receiving the Congressional Gold Medal of Achievement in a White House ceremony, literally implored Mr. Reagan to cancel the cemetery visit, saying, "That place, Mr. President, is not your place. Your place is with the victims of the SS."

The president's voyage followed Wiesel's plea and congressional resolutions in opposition to the trip adopted only days earlier. The House of Representatives by a great majority asked the president to "reconsider" the journey; the Senate, in a resolution sponsored by eighty-five members, asked him to "reassess" his planned itinerary. He made the trip anyway. And yet no intelligent individual would suggest Ronald Reagan is in any way or degree tainted with anti-Semitism. But the act can be just as hurtful, even if without malice.

Mr. Reagan fumbled when he attempted to justify his decision to pay his respects to the new Germany at this cemetery by asserting many young Nazi soldiers "were victims, just as surely as the victim in the concentration camps." It was further argued by his aides that the small number of SS Troops buried in the same ground did not render its soil less hallowed.

More troubling was the evident failure of our president to have comprehended the profound meaning of the Holocaust to world Jewry. With all possible goodwill, he was simply unresponsive to Jewish feelings and, if as America's choice for top leader, he failed the test, heaven only knows how badly the American people would flunk. Some cynic once said that the will of Americans to sacrifice in order to protect the natural human rights of the Jews is about a hundred miles wide and a half inch deep. Such a view, I believe, underestimates the basic decency of Americans, but who can say by how much?

If one regards this evident cynicism as an unfair reflection on basic American decency, one needs also to look at some examples of domestic responses to sectional economic difficulties. In the first half of the eighties, due to a series of national and worldwide economic factors, our Midwestern farm belt was financially devastated. Farmers in wholesale numbers were forced into bankruptcy, compelled to sell off their lands and become destitute unemployables. A 1986 ADL survey to determine whom the farmers faulted for their harsh plight found 27 percent believed they had been exploited by "international Jewish bankers." Nine percent thought Jews "a great deal" to blame, while an additional four percent said, "yes, but much less so." Such perceptions frighteningly belong with the old Protocols of the Elders of Zion libel against the Jews.

American blacks have the worst of both worlds. Within their own ghettoes, life can be a nightmare—broken homes plagued with rats, roaches, battered walls, leaking toilets, open ceilings, rooms that freeze in winter and suffocate in summer. Crime, drugs and murder are on their streets. Outside of black areas they suffer lower-level jobs, are resented and resisted in white schools, denied decent housing, all the while widely regarded as inferior to whites. Among the few groups of Americans who have tried to be friends and allies of victimized blacks in their disenfranchisements, Jews can be counted in disproportionately high number. Yet the same 1981 survey that found almost 25 percent of Americans to be anti-Jewish also disclosed that 37 percent of the nation's twenty-six million black people were similarly minded. And in June 1984, Louis Harris, the respected pollster, reported more blacks than whites believed Jews to be slum owners, choose money ahead of people and are more loyal to Israel than the United States. Add to this the ugly phenomenon of preacher Louis Farrakhan and the huge following he boasts in his Nation of Islam. An avowed racist and anti-Semite, Farrakhan has the absolute loyalty of supporters who seem impressed by his incredible accusations against Jews.

Another instance of popular indifference sticks out in memory: Reverend Jesse Jackson's appearance in July 1984, as an invited speaker to the National Democratic Party Convention in San Francisco, after he had hugged and kissed Yasir Arafat on one of his trips to the Mideast. In September 1979, Jackson echoed anti-Semitic claims of alleged "Jewish control of the media and the banks." Later he requested American recognition of the PLO as a "government in exile"; blamed Jews for the ouster of Andrew Young as U.S. Ambassador to the U.N. when Young's secret meetings with Zehdi Terzi, the PLO's U.N. representative, were discovered; attributed to Jewish influence the Democratic Party's failure to condemn Israel; charged black progress was blocked not by the KKK but by the American Jewish community, and announced he was "sick and tired of hearing about the Holocaust."

Among some other of Jackson's more egregious public statements were these, culled from his speeches, interviews and articles recorded as a presidential aspirant over the years:

- "... The conflict with Jews began when we Blacks started our quest for power ... Once we began the push for our share of universal slots in institutions, Jews called these quotas and opposed us. Even as we were expected to support jets for Israel, Jews had no problem with an expanding relationship with South Africa ..."
- "Jewish intellectual and legal opposition to Black upward mobility ... made popular the demagogic terms 'reverse discrimination' and 'preferential treatment' ..."
- "The scheduled heavyweight fight between John Tate, a Black American, and Gerrie Coatzee, the White South African champion ... represents humiliation to Blacks and concerned Whites around the world. It is sponsored by two Jews ..."
- U.S. policy toward the PLO is "an international absurdity and a crime against the civilized community ..."
- "We cannot become limited by some of the paranoia of Israeli leadership."
- "Irish-Americans do not dictate policy to Washington. Neither do Mexican-Americans. The United States must be free of all ethnic influences in order to successfully resolve the problems in the Mideast ..."
- "The PLO is not merely a terrorist gang, even though it has engaged in some terrorists acts. It is a government in exile."
- "Few Jewish reporters have the capacity to be objective about Arab affairs." His media critics, Jackson said, "were all Jewish." And he suggested he had not received favorable editorial comment because "there are no Arabs and no Palestinians writing for a major newspaper or television stations ..."
- Condemning President Nixon's alleged insensitivity to the poor, he charged that of Nixon's top advisors, "four out of

five of them are German Jews." (He falsely identified John
D. Ehrlichman and H. R. Haldeman as 'German Jews.')

- "Zionism is a kind of poisonous weed that is choking Judaism."
- "I think that Israel is, in fact, a nation, however illegiti-
mately it was conceived."
- The Democratic Party's positions were "perverted by a reaction . . . to the Jewish element within the party . . . a kind
of glorified form of bribery."
- "There's been an overreaction to Farrakhan, as if Farrakhan
has state power. He does not. So there's been a certain
exaggeration in the reaction."
- On the Pope's audience with Waldheim: "That was a decision the sovereign head of the Catholic Church . . . had to
make . . . He had some moral obligation because Waldheim
was a Catholic . . . You could not very well demand of the
Pope whom he should meet with and whom he should not
. . . The Pope has ties to Catholics in South Africa. So he
maintains his relationship to his Church and tries to use his
church to change the system. Israel has ties to South Africa
diplomatically, sells arms to South Africa in substantial
quantity, though the whole world is trying to isolate South
Africa."
- On Israel functioning as a U.S. tool: "Some of what America
cannot do in South Africa directly because of the laws, it is
doing through Israel as a conduit."
- Syria, Saudi Arabia, Iraq, Libya and Iran "already accept
the State of Israel as a fact . . . There is no evidence of
them using, for example, their collective might in a contrary way . . ."

In the face of such views, many of them uttered by Jackson
more than once in different forms, his repeated calls for recon-
ciliation between blacks and Jews, his 1984 Convention plea for
"healing and unity," coupled with his declaration that Jews and
Blacks "are copartners in a long and religious history," sharing
a "passion for social justice at home and peace abroad," and his
denials of prejudice, all had a very hollow ring.

Months before the 1984 Democratic Convention Jackson
topped his own long record of disturbing statements with his
use of the phrase "Hymie Town" to describe New York City.

Square One?

Because of the honesty of Milton Coleman, a Black journalist, in reporting the story in the Washington *Post,* Jackson's secret comment was made public. The media quickly followed up and there was nationwide criticism of the black leader.

At no point during the 1984 primary campaign did Jackson categorically retract or apologize for his remark. Yet he nevertheless polled three-and-a-half million primary voters, of which over 20 percent were White. The National Democratic Party, long the favorite choice of a majority of Jews, honored Jackson with a prominent place at its nominating convention, also hoping he would use the opportunity to repudiate his own remark. This was, I believe, one of the reasons for inviting him, although the National Democratic Committee would deny it—as would the Party's standard-bearer of the day, Walter Mondale, himself certainly no anti-Semite.

It was the committee's way of saying to the Blacks of America that Jackson was still one of the Party's leaders. This interpretation would appear borne out by the withdrawal, reportedly prompted by fear of upsetting Jackson's followers, of a proposed convention resolution condemning anti-Semitism. Apparently it was sufficient that during his speech Jackson had asked forgiveness from anyone in the land whom he had "discomforted" or caused "pain."

It is not too much, then, to conclude that if the committee had to choose between their much larger numbers and the far smaller group of Jewish voters, it seemed to prefer the larger vote of Blacks. And Mr. Mondale, titular leader of the Party at the moment, held his tongue . . . to hold the Black vote for himself and the Party.

For the moment at least, opportunism won, integrity lost. And in the process some of the will to stand up against anti-Semitic expressions had vanished. But apparently the lesson was not lost on Jackson; he understood there had been no need for him to declare he had abandoned his questionable attitudes.

As a result, in 1987, three years later, again a Democratic candidate for the presidential nomination, Jackson's stated positions remained constant. Nor did his popularity among Democrats, despite that he was anathema to most Jews, suffer any discernible dent as a result of his November–December 1987 interview in Tikkun, a prestigious Jewish magazine, in which he still was insisting that Jews overreacted to Farrakhan, still faulting Jews for allegedly obstructing Affirmative Action in behalf of blacks, still refusing to frown on the papal audience granted Kurt Waldheim or the unmitigated praise His Holiness, John Paul II, bestowed on the unrepentant Austrian president, and still castigating Israel for trading with South Africa. (Actual international trade with South Africa released in August 1987, in billions: U.S., 3.4; Japan 2.9; German, 2.8; United Kingdom, 2.6; Israel, 0.2.)

In spite of the character of these Jackson statements and positions, the nation at large and Democratic Party ranks in particular remained fairly indifferent. Such indifference was documented early in March of 1988 on so-called Super-Tuesday when millions went to the polls and voted Jackson second place in the Primaries.

Early in April, during the New York State Primary, in which Jews and blacks were a significant proportion of the vote, Jackson rejected an invitation to meet with the Conference of Presidents of Major American Jewish Organizations, the most representative umbrella agency of American Jews concerned with Israel's welfare. On April 15, four days before the Primary, when asked by Barbara Walters on ABC's "20-20" television program about his relationship with Farrakhan and his "Hymietown" comment, Jackson said he had apologized for it, adding: "Any statement I may have made to offend or hurt anybody, I'm sorry. Because that's not good. And that's not my highest, truest and best self."

Credit must be given him for consistency. On the same day, when interviewed by The New York *Times,* Jackson said that his problem with Jews continued to be their refusal to share power with blacks. ". . . we must talk with the PLO sooner or later," he said, adding that the mandate prohibiting it "should be changed because it is an ineffective law and it has weakened our ability to help Israel." (Israel never sought, always rejected, this particular help.) He also said, as he had so frequently, that he resented the "Israel-South African connection." (He did not mention that South-Africa trade in 1986, among those black African nations that alone had no formal trade agreement with it, totalled a billion-and-a-half dollars, and only Guinea Bissau of all African countries did no business with South Africa. Others did untold millions more.)

Many have asserted that Jewish opposition to Jackson in fact had nothing to do with the color of his skin; American Jews had too long been loyal friends of the black community in its struggle for equality. Experience indicated Jews would overwhelmingly oppose *any* candidate—white, Jewish or otherwise—with a record like Jackson's. And they would have supported Jackson in overwhelming numbers regardless of his color had his record been even neutral. But by his charges against Jews and Israel it was felt by critics that he had added racism to the campaign even while attacking the alleged racism of others. The pity of it is that many of Jackson's progressive political views are attractive to many Jews who would have liked to support him because of such views but would not in the light of his other tainted positions. I myself would have derived sheer joy from being able to vote for a black president, my personal knife in the belly of American racism, but not a candidate with the record of a Jesse Jackson.

The point is: Anti-Jewish expressions and hostility to Israel did not cause the Democratic Party wing of the American electorate to oppose Jesse Jackson. Judging from the vast reportage on the subject, the anti-Semitic factor simply played no appreciable role in the American mind. If, in the future, Reverend Jackson fails in his reach for political stardom it will evidently be for reasons other than his comments about Jews and the State of Israel.

Some social scientists believe that opinion-testing procedures have advanced enough to uncover human attitudes even when the subject would prefer to keep his true feelings concealed. For some, an empirical, non-scientific test can suffice. A drunkard who venomously labels me "Jew bastard" cannot convince me after sobering up that he is free of anti-Semitic prejudice; nor can an angry man whose tongue slips in similar fashion. I can also accept the validity of a test of attitudes where no time is allowed for cautious reflection.

Such an opportunity provided itself in December, 1985, when an American Jew was accused of committing a most heinous crime—betrayal of his country. Jonathan Pollard, a civilian intelligence analyst for the navy, was charged with selling classified U.S. government documents to Israel, and after pleading guilty was sentenced to life imprisonment. In addition to appropriate news and fair editorial coverage in most of the press about Israel's complicity in the crime, a number of newspapers printed syndicated editorial cartoons on the subject. Among the artists who crossed the line of mere insensitivity were, I thought, Dana Summers and Ed Gamble, cartoonists for Orlando and Jacksonville newspapers, respectively, in Florida. Summers' drawing depicted President Reagan dressed as a cleric sitting in a confessional listening to an Israeli whose private thoughts, shown above him, are about losing U.S. grant money. The president is commenting that he is "surprised that confession comes this easily to someone of the Jewish faith." Gamble's cartoon shows an Israeli seeking a loan from Uncle Sam, telling him that he's "had some extra expenses this year," while outside the office a spy is standing with a wad of American money in his hand. The Israeli is drawn in the style of the traditional anti-Semitic stereotype—old, bald, bearded and with a large hooked nose.

Whether it is absence of prejudice and simple decency, or fear of losing readers and advertisers, with some exceptions the American press normally is careful not to offend religious, racial or ethnic components of the population. Except for cartoonists who seem somehow licensed to be blatant at will, such material is rarely found on editorial pages. But the affirmative exercise of such cartoonist freedom can show a disturbing attitude, more so because some of the cartoonists are widely syndicated or employed by large metropolitan newspapers.

Square One?

In this context I put aside as actually crossing the line into anti-Semitism the matter appearing in the publications of such propaganda mills as Willis Carto's Liberty Lobby, that operates in the nation's capital. It is not his bigoted junk mail or foul-mouthings that perturb as much as his ability to win allotted time to present them to congressional committees presumably concerned with serious legislative matters of state. What attitude underlies the congressional indulgence—indifference, insensitivity, prejudice?

Most people of good will would say that Lyndon LaRouche's movement is unimpressive evidence of any widespread, organized hatred. I agree. But what of the unconcern of the general public to the movement's divisive activities until at least 1986? The ex-Trotskyite-turned-rightist and his disciples had been around for more than a decade trying to spread their lunatic ideas. But the community at large reacted to the well-financed and cleverly organized group as if it were little more than an innocuous band of political eccentrics.

Not until two of LaRouche's representatives in March of 1986 won the Democratic Party nominations for lieutenant governor and secretary of state in Illinois did the nation's press target in. But by then LaRouche's minions had already fielded hundreds of candidates in local and state elections across the nation. Only after the damage was done did authorities move in under the criminal statutes.

It was conventional wisdom that the two LaRouche candidates won their preliminary skirmish in the primaries because the Democratic Party machine and the electorate were both asleep. But how about the previous decade? Few people apparently gave enough of a damn to stand up to these extremists when they first appeared among us demanding the heads of the Queen of England, Henry Kissinger, the Rockefeller family and the World Zionist Movement for their alleged leadership in an international drug conspiracy.

Worse still was the reaction when the Illinois victory of LaRouche's NDPC candidates precipitated an intensive month of national media coverage spelling out his propaganda, including comments about Jews. With this information, only 20 percent of Americans subsequently queried in a New York Times/CBS national poll expressed an unfavorable opinion of LaRouche. One percent regarded him with approval while nearly 80 percent had no opinion. Most of those interviewed were obviously not very troubled by the nature of LaRouche's propaganda. Perhaps some were fooled by the Jewish background of one of the Illinois candidates. But the 20 percent who rejected him gave as their first reason his "extremism" or "radicalism," and their second that he was "strange" or "crazy" or "weird." No reference to his comments about Jews except as some may have preferred the euphemism "crazy." In microcosm, a classic instance of domestic indifference. If LaRouche and some of his followers are ultimately brought down by the alleged misdeeds for which he and they have been put to trial in the federal courts, it will not be because the community exhibited any serious concern about his bigoted propaganda. It will be because the short-lived primary election "success" of several of his leadership group sent up warning signals that the American political fabric was being endangered. In short, it is not just LaRouche and his followers who are of concern here; more alarming is the lack of responsible reaction to them and to what they say.

Except in degree, this was the same sort of indifference that on an incomparably large scale trapped Germany fifty-five years ago. That was a time, please remember, when our own country also counted dozens of bigoted groups, large and small. Then, too, domestic indifference was the norm until Americans looked up to find themselves awash in an orgy of bigotry from which they were saved mostly by the onset of World War II, and then only because so much of the propaganda seemed to border on treason.

Attitudes evocative of the early thirties are evident all along the political spectrum. Among the handful of so-called leftist publications is The Nation, a weekly magazine published in New York City that once could justifiably boast a genuine liberal philosophy and independence from mainstream political thought. But during the Vietnam War period when millions of Americans were in intellectual or actual rebellion over the role of the United States, The Nation's editorial pages, together with other forces on the port side of the political center, veered into a pattern of hostility to Israel and sympathy for Palestinian revolutionaries.

On the subject of Israel, anti-Semitism aside for the moment: When the Oxford-educated Alexander Cockburn was suspended by *The Village Voice* as its political columnist in January of 1984 The Nation took him on. His removal from the *Voice* had followed the discovery of a $10,000 grant he had quietly accepted from The Institute of Arab Studies of Belmont, Massachusetts, to underwrite a book he planned about Israel's invasion of Lebanon. In the pages of the *Voice,* and in the highly respected and fair *Wall Street Journal,* Cockburn had shown himself to be a strident critic of Israel. The institute funding him, now defunct, was an offshoot of one of the more militant, pro-PLO groups in America—The Association of Arab American University Graduates.

In the pages of The Nation Cockburn compared Israel's invasion of Lebanon to a "Nazi blitzkreig," accused the Jewish State of behaving like a war criminal. In an article entitled "Israel's War Against Foreign Journalists," Cockburn accused Israel of lying about the deaths of two CBS newsmen in Lebanon. But a CBS News vice president, Ernest Leiser, assigned to investigate the matter, contradicted Cockburn and reported the fatalities as inadvertent. And in July 1985, Cockburn charged the United States with "lashing itself into a state of incoherent paranoia" about terrorism. The Nation is the same publication that later asked for less name-calling in the controversy it precipitated by printing the *ad hominem* words of Gore Vidal in its 120th Anniversary issue.

(Gore Vidal is the same writer who in another day collided with William J. Buckley during a national television broadcast while the two were co-commentators at the 1968 Democratic convention. Buckley, in response to Vidal's referring to him as a "crypto-Nazi," responded with: "Now, listen, you queer, stop calling me a crypto-Nazi or I'll sock you in your goddamned face and you'll stay plastered." The mutual lawsuits were settled out of court.)

Vidal's attention was now focused on the spokesman of so-called neoconservatism, Norman Podhoretz, editor of the prestigious Commentary magazine, and his wife, the very able polemicist Midge Decter, along with their firm support of Israel. In The Nation's March 22, 1986 issue, Vidal accused the Podhoretzes with having a dual loyalty, and called them the "Lunts of the right wing (Israeli Fifth Column Division)" and even hinted that they might be unregistered foreign agents. As for them having moved away from liberalism, Vidal wrote: "The reason for that is simple. In order to get Treasury money for Israel (last year three billion dollars), pro-Israeli lobbyists must see to it that America's 'The Russians Are Coming' squads are in place . . . to frighten the American people into . . . support of Israel in its never-ending wars against just about everyone . . . it is necessary for the pro-Israel lobbyists to make common cause with our lunatic right."

He went on about Podhoretz: ". . . his first loyalty would always be to Israel. Yet he and Midge stay among us, in order to make propaganda and raise money for Israel . . ." Of Ms. Decter, he wrote: ". . . like most of our Israeli fifth columnists, Midge isn't much interested in what the goyim were up to before Ellis Island . . . Midge is not [ashamed of what the United States did in the Philippines] because in the Middle East another predatory people is busy stealing other people's land in the name of an alien theocracy. She is a propagandist for these predators."

At this point Vidal moved from the particular (Podhoretz) to the general (Jews): "In order to get military and economic support for Israel, a small number of American Jews, who should know better, have made common cause with every sort of reactionary and anti-Semitic group in the United States . . ."

Toward the end of his piece Vidal came to his central point. Addressing Midge Decter, an American citizen, he wrote: "I've got to tell you I don't much like your country, which is Israel."

When a magazine of demonstrated intellectuality and some respectability publishes and thereby disseminates such statements about people of the Jewish faith, those of us whose memories and age cast long shadows are reminded that in the twenties, too, such articles—and cartoons—stained the pages of the left-wing journals. With the American Left now seemingly back to its post–World War One comments about Jews, the practice has resurfaced. It is a device that, incidentally, was also the hallmark of the extremist Right.

The Nation's claims of commitment to the survival of Israel fall, at least in this corner, on disbelieving ears. And when the magazine, answering critics, says that its writer has only "violated the taboo that forbids discussion of the relationship of the American Jewish community to the State of Israel," it forgets, I suggest, that the taboo at issue is bigotry, not legitimate argument. The Nation's underlying attitude seems clear.

Yes, prejudice against Jews is alive and well in the United States even if today there is far less anti-Jewish discrimination and organized bigotry evident across the nation. The extent of the problem may never be susceptible to mathematical calculation or any other such measure, but there is surely something to worry about if the youth of our country show signs of falling victim to it. In March of 1986, as only one example, members of a fraternity and a sorority on the campus of the University of Southern California chanted anti-Semitic doggerels and daubed "Jew Week" on the walk in front of Sigma Alpha Mu, a mostly Jewish fraternity house. The two chapters had lost to S.A.M. in a sports-for-charity competition during Greek Week exercises.

Bigotry is the enemy of education. Prejudice on the campus, or its absence, is a reasonable caliper for measuring the attitudes brought to the school by its students. And if the university's civilizing impact is so negligible, how deep are the built-in prejudices?

Isolated, the University of Southern California incident would not count for much. But 1986 witnessed an appalling eighteen

393

more such incidents on American college grounds—among them a rash of anti-Jewish graffiti at Rutgers, a wave of anti-Semitic hate mailings at Oregon State, swastika vandalizing at the University of Maryland, burning of a Jewish student newspaper stand at UCLA, and at Yale, Vanderbilt, C.W. Post and Philadelphia College, four *sukkahs* (thatched huts symbolizing the Jewish harvest holiday) were destroyed, toppled or otherwise vandalized.

Overt acts of anti-Semitism obviously mirror inner feelings, and if there are so many instances of anti-Semitism, one must conclude anti-Jewish attitudes prevail at least in direct proportion to their numbers. Put it this way: If the very young desecrate Jewish institutions, and college youth perpetrate anti-Jewish violence on campus, and professional anti-Semites murder Jews to show where they stand, are community attitudes not suspect?

There may be disagreement among political scientists and Jewish agencies about the extent and character and measurability of hostility toward Jews. But there is at least agreement that anti-Semitism is indeed alive in America—and elsewhere.

Elsewhere? Near to home. In Canada, for example. There, disturbing anti-Jewish attitudes evidently linger just beneath the surface. In March, 1988, Joe Clark, Canada's foreign minister, severely criticized Israel at a large public gathering, provoking an outraged Jewish reaction that in turn prompted the Toronto *Star*, the nation's largest circulation daily, to accuse Canadian Jewry of dual allegiance. The donnybrook precipitated anti-Semitic mail and anti-Jewish invective over the radio. By happenstance, almost simultaneously an opinion poll was released indicating that Canadian anti-Semitism was appreciably greater than in the United States. Available evidence shows the situation to be similar abroad. But as in the United States, *organized* bigotry against Jews overseas appears to be substantially lower than it has been during the last fifty years. In France, for example, the one meaningful formalized activity of rightful concern to those who worry about such things is the politically oriented National Front, led by former paratrooper Jean-Marie LePen.

It is of small comfort to French Jews that France's immigrant Arab population is as yet the only victim of violent attacks by LePen's forces in the fifteen years since he founded it. While his adherents in the extreme right wing of the political spectrum insist their leader is "calling the shots correctly" and that the issue is "immigration and societal discipline," others have labeled LePen, and not without reason, a demagogue whose racism incorporates a discernibly anti-Jewish component. His party publications have expressed racist and anti-Semitic viewpoints and some National Front leaders have Nazi or neo-Nazi connections. At a luncheon table in a Manhattan restaurant in February 1987, he protested to a small group of us that no one could "find anything I have ever said or done that is anti-Semitic." In March 1986, the National Front showed a strong-enough electoral strength, 10 percent of the vote, to be entitled to a coalition role in the new Mitterand administration. In September 1987, LePen settled the question of his attitude toward Jews, at least in the minds of most French Jews, when in answering a question about French propagandists who argued that gas chambers were a figment of Jewish imagination he said: "Do you want me to say it is a revealed truth that everyone must believe? I say there are historians who are debating these questions."

Pressed, the National Front head compounded his slander of the Six Million Dead with this: "I am not saying that gas chambers did not exist. I could not see them myself. I have not studied the question. But I believe it is a minor point in the history of World War II."

The unexpected outcry to this gem precipitated another of LePen's often repeated denials of anti-Semitism and assurances of his high esteem for the State of Israel. But Jews, knowing for certain that the nationalist leader's power base included a large number of France's Jew-haters, were more troubled that LePen had become a candidate for the nation's presidency, and that

395

countrywide surveys indicated he had increased his support to perhaps fifteen percent of the French vote. Their concern was justified. On April 24, 1988, in the first round of the French presidential elections, LePen's once "fringe" party, much ignored by the press from the party's inception in October, 1972, startled experienced observers by winning four-and-a-half million votes, only a fraction less than fifteen percent of the total in a four-way contest with President François Mitterand, Prime Minister Jacques Chirac and Raymond Barre, a former prime minister.

All this against a blight of synagogue bombings causing death, as elsewhere in Western Europe, with small-time anti-Semitic outfits comparable to those in our own country and with the sale of such anti-Jewish frauds as the *Protocols of the Elders of Zion*—French edition, printed in Kuwait.

West Germany's organized anti-Semitism should also be noted. Like its forerunner, neo-Nazism is by definition anti-Jewish. In June of 1986 the Interior Ministry reported seventy-eight neo-Nazi groups operating within the country, with a combined membership of 22,500. Not much if one keeps in mind the nation's sixty-one-million population. And while it does disturb because it is Germany, the comparatively low figure confirms the impression that European *organized* anti-Semitism fits the current pattern.

The organized structure of anti-Jewish bigotry across all of Western Europe needs not be gone into further, except for some telltale signs. The French political experience is also to be found in one form or another, to a lesser or greater degree, at one time or another since the mid-forties in England, Belgium, Italy, Sweden, Spain and Germany. Go southeast to Greece and learn that in the spring of 1988 its Jews reported a five-month wave of anti-Jewish incidents—anti-Semitic daubings, property vandalism, telephone threats, desecration of Jewish monuments. Move westward to Italy, where in May of 1988 Chief Rabbi Elio Toaff said the growing number of anti-Jewish incidents "are reminiscent of those that occurred fifty years ago and which preceded the legislation of the fascist racial laws against

Jews." The rabbi told of walls near Jewish stores scrawled with "Jews back to the ovens. Re-open Auschwitz."

In the Soviet Union the government itself has long been the inspiration for anti-Semitic feelings. The free world's initial impression has yet to be borne out with conclusive evidence that Mikhail S. Gorbachev's *glasnost,* his policy of openness, meant Soviet relaxation of government-managed anti-Semitism. The chairman's actual purpose in granting a limited right of criticism to the Soviet people was to create a ground swell of support for *perestroika,* his internal campaign to restructure the collapsing Communist economic system. Mr. Gorbachev had to prove to Politburo doubters that protracted national dissatisfaction with the inferior quality of Soviet life demanded relief through basic change. Central planning and pricing had to end in favor of local and regional flexibility. Food had to be more plentiful and in greater variety; housing more adequate. To make those needs clearer to his associates it was necessary to ungag moderate voices of discontent; they would make the case for the chairman. One may assume the Communist chief and his supporters also realized that widening the right of speech could soften up the United States in its dealings with the USSR. An extra dividend.

But none of this had anything to do with Soviet Jews. *Glasnost* was not for them, not designed to expand their human rights, certainly not to extend to their right of emigration. Yet the Soviets knew that the release of a handful of prominent, articulate Jewish leaders would put a silencer on the controversy within Soviet borders. Meanwhile, in January of 1987, they ordered an official *narrowing* of conditions under which Jews would be permitted to leave the country. Regulations now provided that only those with "first degree" relatives abroad could apply, thereby reducing eligible applicants to 10 percent of the four hundred thousand who had tried or wanted to get out. In 1988 only insistent American pressure brought some relaxation of this tightened restriction.

Glasnost did indeed have one effect on Jews—in reverse. The enlarged right of speech drew out from under the rocks the

Pamyat movement—a political group of anti-Semitic activists wanting to cut back whatever rights remained to Jews. Now its membership had legal permission to agitate openly. Seventy years of state-enforced secular life with an overlay of religious suppression did not end anti-Semitism within the Soviet Union.

Incidents behind the Iron Curtain indicate that Soviet satellites in Eastern Europe understand USSR anti-Jewish signals well enough, if indeed, signals are needed. In Rumania in October 1986, a synagogue in the Moldavian town of Bohush was burned to the ground following the stabbing of the Jewish caretaker by four masked men. In Poland, in March of 1987, a heated controversy about Polish guilt in the murder of millions of Jews was brought on by an article in Tygodnik Powszechny, the nation's most important Catholic weekly. The magazine asked the nation to confess its special responsibility for the Nazi crimes and shame for its anti-Semitic past. The resulting flood of protest letters was so heated and so terrible the editors refused to print them. According to the New York *Times,* which reported the story, the Polish editors said: "... the letters testify that anti-Semitism continues to exist in the country, even though today there are practically no Jews left in Poland."

In Latin America, anti-Jewish propaganda is still widespread in the Argentine, where it is used to frustrate the nation's shift toward democracy. The press there plays its usual role. In January 1986, it published as news an alleged "Jewish plot" to turn the country's Patagonian area into a Jewish State to be populated by tens of thousands of Soviet and Israeli Jews.

In Brazil the Methodist University of Piraeicaba signed a cultural exchange agreement with the PLO in August of 1986 "dedicated to the democratic, antiimperialist, anti-Zionist struggle." Two months later in Paraguay there were anti-Jewish outbursts. Defacing Asunción, the nation's capital, was a series of posters, one calling for a boycott of Jewish shops that "rob the country and send the money to Tel Aviv and Moscow." Another that said: "Wanted: Jews. Dead or Alive for killing Christ, for establishing the Communist Party, for causing two world wars, for bombing Libya and killing children . . ." Symptoms and symbols of a similar character can be found in other countries of Latin America.

In short, patent or implicit attitudes that don't express themselves in organized anti-Jewish movements seem to resemble the U.S.'s latter-day experience. Feelings about Jews across Europe, the Soviet Union and in the "westernized" nations of Latin America are, by all available evidence, still infected with anti-Semitism.

In some of these places the *political* base of anti-Semitism runs far deeper than in our own country and can be more hurtful. This, of course, is particularly true in the Arab world, where the antagonism is overt because of the Jewish presence in its midst. Dr. Bernard Lewis, Professor of Near East Studies at Princeton University, summed it up in his *Semitism and Anti-Semitism,* saying that since the end of World War II "certain Arab countries have been the only place in the world where hardcore Nazi-style anti-Semitism is publicly and officially endorsed and propagated."

Supporting the professor's basic finding was the wildly anti-Jewish book, *The Matzoh of Zion,* written by Syria's defense minister, Mustapha Tlas. According to the American Jewish Congress, that volume retrieved from the Middle Ages the charge that Jews murder Christian children to use their blood for baking unleavened bread to eat on Passover. The AJC reached too far back. Hitler resurrected this same "blood libel" less than fifty years ago. And I was held in "contempt of court" by a New York City magistrate in the late thirties for arguing against the right of a gutter hoodlum to scream out the very same obscenely false accusation from a soapbox at Columbus Circle.

In Malaysia, in November 1986, an Islamic Party youth leader, Mustapha Ali, charging "Zionist interference" in the nation's affairs, accused the American-based Asia Foundation with "fronting for the Jews." *Watan,* a Malay weekly, reported that Ali declared, "Our determination is to destroy the Jews." In South Korea, in February of 1988, according to Seoul's English-language newspaper, the Korea *Times,* otherwise respectable businessmen blamed Korea's trade war with the United States on the "Jewish Mafia's" control of American commerce and its communication media.

In recent years, too, Japan has shown serious symptoms of the anti-Jewish disease. Several of its popular authors, infected with the Western world's virus, write that Jews are responsible for most of the nation's woes. Blaming American Jews further, for everything from the Great Depression of 1933 to Watergate, these best-selling writers have borrowed Hitler's anti-Semitic propaganda, claiming that Jews control the world through "international conspiracies." The New York *Times* story in March of 1987, reported Japanese propagandists also adopting post–World War II anti-Jewish cliches—Jews exaggerate the Holocaust; Jews hold the United States captive through their alleged control of such giants as IBM, General Motors, Exxon, Standard Oil, and so on.

Among the anti-Semitic Japanese books are such titles as, *If You Understand Judea, You Can Understand the World, The Secret of Jewish Power to Control the World, The Jewish Plan for Conquest of the World.* The authors include Eisaburo Saito, a member of the Japanese parliament, and the well-known writer, Masomi Uno, who regards himself a Christian. Here, too, the seriousness of the situation moved Elie Wiesel to urge Japanese leaders to speak up against anti-Semitism and for human rights.

Back to Germany, Europe's special case: twentieth-century history has already marked Germany as the demon of European Jewry. Inevitably, then, Germany, even divided, is perceived as the continental bellwether of the Jewish condition. It's fitting that we look briefly in these closing pages at the overt attitudes revealed there in its post–World War II period.

In December of 1982 Colonel Hans-Ulrich Rudel, the most decorated officer in Hitler's air force, died in the small West German village of Dornhausen. More than two thousand mourners gathered in this out-of-the-way place, dressed in their old uniforms, mostly former Nazi officers alongside neo-Nazis—

all on hand to pay their last respects. As the body was laid to rest in the grave, from the ranks of the mourners came the Nazi hymn, "Song of Germany," sung with right arms lifted high in the Nazi salute.

A month later a collection of young Nazis, sixty of them, heads shaved, went on a melee, roughhousing their way through Frankfurt's downtown area. A few days afterward the finance minister of Stuttgart allowed contributions to the SS Panzer Veterans' Association to be tax-deductible as a charitable gift. And in May of 1983, several hundred former Nazis held a reunion in the Hesse town of Bad Hersfeld while the mayor claimed he was powerless to stop the rally.

In October of 1983 Jewish protestors prevented R. W. Fassbinder's play, *The City, Garbage and Death,* from being presented at Frankfurt's municipal theater because of its alleged anti-Semitism. Many in the audience agreed that the play was objectionable but argued that freedom of speech was more important and the play should go on. Angered by the protest, the theatre manager argued that the "no-hunting season on Jews was over."

In December of the same year West German police reported that neo-Nazi activists were increasing their penetration of sports-fan clubs, inciting anti-Semitism, and that these elements were particularly active in soccer and football clubs in four West German cities, including West Berlin and Dortmund.

By May 1985 Interior Minister Freidrich Zimmerman reported there were thirty-four known organizations in West Germany that advocated a return to Hitler's Third Reich. In January of 1986 a Christian Democratic member of the Bundestag, Herman Fellner, declared that former Jewish slave laborers had neither a legal nor moral basis for demanding reparations. "Whenever there is money to be had from German coffers," he said, "the Jews are there to grab it." According to Der Speigel, Chancellor Helmut Kohl, the Christian Democratic leader, criticized Fellner while admitting that the vast majority of Germans think like his Bundestag deputy.

The readiness with which some normally sensitive German

politicians allow themselves to indulge in such anti-Semitism would seem to confirm Kohl's opinion. In mid-March of 1986 Count Spee, the mayor of a Munich bedroom community, while engaged in a heated debate in the town council about budget difficulties blurted out that the only way to solve the problem was by "killing a few rich Jews."

In April a two-year-old parlor game reappeared in Hesse and was distributed widely to schools and other institutions in Germany. It consisted of a pressed board made in the shape of a Star of David on which pawns were moved on squares according to the throw of the dice. Each pawn represented a million Jews and on each square was the name of a former Nazi death camp in Europe. So-called "Auschwitz jokes" are popular.

Less than twenty-five thousand Jews live in Germany today, yet in 1983 EMNID, a well-respected polling agency, reported in a survey that 30 percent of the population showed clear anti-Semitism. Godesburg's Reverend Eberhard Bethge, commenting on the study, said: "For decades, Germans were sensitive about the treatment of Jews. In recent years there have been more and more 'slips of the tongue'—or, at least, that's what they are called."

On April 5, 1988, the State Interior Minister of North Rhine-Westphalia, Herbert Schnoor, publicly declared that "the increased provocative and violent activities of neo-Nazis in some towns have become unbearable." Whether the underlying character of German or other such harsh European attitudes toward Jews is substantially different from its American counterpart is of little importance. In these percentages each can lead to the same terrible result.

Even Switzerland, that paragon of political neutrality, has not escaped the anti-Jewish virus. According to the Jewish Telegraphic Agency, a secret poll completed in March of 1988 by a responsible minority-rights organization showed thirty percent of Zurich's population to be anti-Semitic. The findings revealed that nine percent of the city's population admitted being anti-Semitic, eleven percent confessed similar tendencies, while another eleven percent acknowledged intermittant hostility.

Square One?

* * *

Moving over to Austria: On May 4, 1986, Kurt Waldheim, former secretary general of the United Nations, ran for the presidency of Austria and won 49.6 percent of the national vote against his opponent's 43.7 percent. Short of the required majority by half a point, a run-off election was required, and on June 8, Waldheim was elected to a six-year term, winning 53.9 percent of the nearly five million votes cast, compared to 46.1 percent for his Socialist opponent, Kurt Steyer.

Despite Waldheim's documented Nazi background, more than half the voters of Austria endorsed him for their highest elected office. The fact that he kept secret for years his record of involvement in Nazi atrocities with a false story, and then flatly lied about it when confronted with the evidence, made no material difference to the Austrian voter.

During the election campaign The World Jewish Congress brought to international attention documented evidence that Waldheim had been a German intelligence officer for a Nazi military command that had brutalized Yugoslav partisans and had carried out mass deportations of Greek Jews, sending thousands of them to their deaths. For his "heroic" activities, according to the newly discovered evidence, Waldheim was awarded a Croation medal as a member of a Nazi unit that had been accused of killing thousands of civilians in 1942.

To appreciate the enormity of Waldheim's futile lies about his actual role in the intelligence branch of Army Group E is to understand the real reason he hid his past. Frank Gervasi, author of several major works on the World War II period, was a reporter for Collier's magazine at the time. He had in his files a document from British intelligence summarizing the orders of Waldheim's Salonika-based Army Group E, and released it in a letter to The New York *Times.* It said:

"When large numbers of persons have to be dealt with, they are to be distributed for shooting among your various units . . . Bodies are to be buried in sufficiently deep graves. Burning of bodies is to cease. Placing of flowers on graves by the populace is to be prevented. In order to avoid unnecessary contact

403

with bodies, persons are to be led directly to the edges of graves. In cases of mass executions, it is allowable to cause hostages to kneel with their faces toward graves. Shooting of large numbers is to be carried out in groups of from five to eight—those to be shot must have their legs tied."

Gervasi then offered the following as "a partial list of the outrages committed by Army Group E between 1941 and the summer of 1943: "German troops followed the procedure scrupulously when they shot 550 Yugoslavs at Krusevac; executed 250 more on the fairgrounds at Zenum, near Belgrade; murdered 2,000 in Belgrade itself between June 10 and June 20—on the pretext the hostages were Communists, although only seven were; shot one hundred men and seven women, three of them with small children, at Kraljevo, and killed at the same place thirty teenage boys by order of the local Gestapo chief, Josef Eckert."

The recitation brings a shudder. For the guilty it must be worse. To achieve peace of mind one is tempted to cast it from memory. Perhaps this explains Waldheim's alibi for his deception: "There were atrocities on both sides," he said. "Who can remember everything from the war period?"

Israel, the American government and Austria asked to examine a secret United Nations War Crimes file on Waldheim, and copies were furnished to each. The file contained seven pages of documentation that had been provided by the Yugoslav War Crimes Commission, and it confirmed the World Jewish Congress' revelations. Documenting further that the head of Waldheim's army group, Gen. Alexander Lohr, had been hanged for war crimes, it concluded with a demand for the extradition of Waldheim himself.

When these facts were made public, The New York *Times,* in the middle of April 1986, in an interview two weeks before the election, confronted the former U.N. Secretary General with the information at hand. Faced with the documentation, Waldheim at last conceded that as a German army lieutenant preparing daily battlefield situation reports in the Balkans he was aware of the Nazi atrocities and the execution of captured

Yugoslav partisans. "I knew that," he said, "but I also knew that many German soldiers were trapped and executed in a similar way."

Waldheim obviously also knew his Austrian constituency.

But what the former U.N. secretary general strangely still failed to understand was that, inevitably, cover-ups are rarely effective for public figures. One does not become a world-known personality without a minutely detailed record accumulating along the way, as well as witnesses to record it on every side. Three days before the May 4 Austrian election, German war documents ending all doubts in the matter were turned up by a history professor, R.E. Herzstein of the University of South Carolina, who had been assigned to the research task by the World Jewish Congress. Waldheim had kept his army group's day-book from July 19 to August 21, 1943, and he recorded messages that passed from unit to unit within his group. Marked "top secret" and sent to the so-called Parga area, Waldheim wrote that a "mopping-up operation" would begin in two days, and was to be "combed most severely and the male population is to be shot and/or seized in entirety" in accordance with the Fuehrer's orders. His August 7 message notation was that the division "complied with the orders," rounding up all able-bodied males between the ages of sixteen and sixty.

At the outset of the 1986 campaign for the presidency, candidate Waldheim was well behind. Most pollsters agreed that he had only a slim chance of winning, perhaps none. But the exposé of the former U.N. secretary general's Nazi record radically changed the picture in the middle of the campaign. The wrong way; it put him in the lead.

After the May 4 vote Mr. Waldheim and his Socialist opponent agreed that the dispute about Waldheim's Nazi past had helped him win a major triumph, a conclusion reaffirmed by the June 8 run-off that gave the victor nearly 50 percent of the vote, far more than anticipated by early election polls.

Some cynics suggest Waldheim might well have won an even larger majority had the Austrian constituency known before election day that resting in the U.S. national archives was a Nazi intelligence document bearing the candidate's own handwritten notations that directly refuted his repeated denials that he was a German intelligence officer. WJC researchers came on it too late. Political analysts described the swing to Waldheim as the *mitleid factor,* the factor of pity. His election committee seized the opportunity to flood the country with posters declaiming, "NOW MORE THAN EVER".

Little surprise that as the campaign sharpened between Waldheim's conservative People's Party and the opposition Socialist Party, the Jews of Austria were flooded with hate mail. And even less surprising that in the final weeks West Germany's Chancellor Kohl came to Waldheim's side to help him achieve his victory. The Austrian state radio carried Kohl's voice from Vienna strongly defending the former United Nations chief: "I have known Kurt Waldheim for many years . . . He is a great patriot . . . Those who make accusations about him come from a later generation . . . I sense an arrogance of the late-born which I find hard to bear . . . I would know how to vote if I had the right to vote in Austria." Kohl also obviously knew *his* constituency. Not to be left out, Saudi Arabia's government-controlled press added to the campaign's anti-Jewish fallout. The expose on Waldheim, said *Arab News,* an English language daily published in Jedda, was "nothing short of a witchhunt" conducted by Jews in a "grotesque Zionist campaign of slander." Among the nearly thirty anti-Jewish cartoons drawn in support of news items and editorials in Saudi newspapers in the month of June were six depicting Jews in a fashion reminiscent of Hitler's house organ, Der Steurmer. One cartoon showed the Statue of Liberty being borne to her grave while a hook-nosed Jewish gravedigger waited in gleeful anticipation of burying the Lady.

Somehow it does not shock that Waldheim won the presidency of Austria despite his Nazi record. On the contrary, it seems to confirm the suspicion that in the country that gave birth to Hitler's anti-Semitism, underlying attitudes have not basically changed in the last fifty years. The American government's action in barring Waldheim from the United States sharpens the contrast to the shameful election victory Austria handed the former U.N. chief.

Austria's postelection criticisms of Waldheim, and its embarrassment at having made him president even though—because?—he was revealed to have been a Nazi participant in the Holocaust, did not suggest that the community suddenly had turned against the former U.N. secretary general. It meant only that the Austrians were now worried more about the damaging impact of the Waldheim victory on its foreign and trade relations than about its own preference for the man. The international commission of six military historians funded by the Austrian government—with the endorsement of Waldheim's backers—to study and report on the president's wartime involvements resulted in some damning findings. This, despite their having been watered down by government pressures before being released. The commission report concluded that Waldheim was "in close proximity" to and aware of Nazi crimes being committed, yet remained silent, doing nothing to stop it. Waldheim at this writing remains in office.

And so it goes, not to mention the September 1986 synagogue bombing in Istanbul that killed twenty-one Jews at prayer, and the many bombings and consequent deaths in recent years of European houses of worship, Kosher restaurants and the many other Jewish gathering places on the continent—not to mention Latin America and the United States itself.

The point is made. It would seem a fair conclusion that in many countries the contemporary attitude toward Jews remarkably resembles the attitudes toward them at the beginning of the thirties. The unspeakable anti-Semitism most recently the hallmark of Adolph Hitler's National Socialism, a recurring phenomenon across two millennia, is gone although not out of mind, but we may be back where we were before the birth of Nazism. The political and constitutional restraints existing today in some nations to protect against a repetition are of little significance. Such barriers have *never stopped a world gone mad.*

* * *

During the half-century since Nazism a fundamental switch has occurred in the Christian world's attitude toward Jews. International Protestant leadership, centered in the United States, changed places with the Catholic hierarchy in their relationships with world Jewry. In the thirties Jews in the West felt a chill from the Catholic Church while the Protestant church extended a hand of friendship. Previously there had been no significant rapport between Catholics and Jews; the abyss seemed unbridgeable. In the early forties we visited *The Tablet* officials in the Brooklyn Archdiocese to discuss their support of the Christian Front and their repeated attacks on Jews whose liberal mindedness they somehow equated with disloyalty to America. The late Jacob Grumet, a prominent New Yorker and in the early years a General Sessions judge, accompanied me to the meeting. As we walked out he said, "When we entered, I felt I had walked into the fourteenth century. Now I feel I am returning to the twentieth century."

Today, with some reservations, the Roman Catholic Church is the friend, having made something like an 180-degree turn when the Second Vatican Council of 1962–65 issued *Nostra Aetate,* (Our Times). *Schema Four* of that declaration proclaimed, in effect, that hostility toward Jews based on the Crucifixion story was a misreading of Catholic doctrine and should end. In 1975 the Vatican supplemented the declaration with a "Guideline" that categorically denounced anti-Semitism. The positive impact in Catholic articles was extraordinary.

The relationship between the Catholic Church and Jews is now better than cordial. Friendship, mutual understanding, hands clasped in the struggle against religious hostility would more accurately describe it. And lest there be any doubt about the Catholic change, the visit of Pope John Paul II in April 1986 to Rome's central synagogue, where he joined together with the congregation, sealed it in history. While there His Holiness reemphasized that no ancestral or collective blame could be laid at the doorstep of Jews for what happened in "Christ's passion." So that none might misinterpret his message, he repeated the thrust of *Schema Four:* "The Church deplores the hatred, persecutions and displays of anti-Semitism directed against the Jews at any time and by anyone. I repeat, by anyone."

But at the same time, if America's number-one leader, President Reagan, evidenced an extraordinary callousness toward Jewish feelings in his insistent visit to Bitburg, so the Catholic world's number-one leader, Pope John Paul II, did the same on June 25, 1987, in granting an audience to Kurt Waldheim. Jews were deeply disappointed and many were offended by the Pope's praise for the Austrian president, who came as an intransigent and unrepentant sinner denying his proven guilt. Both acts dealt blows to the Jewish sense of well-being, and yet neither was anchored to any *discernible* anti-Semitism, although the decision in each case seemed to reflect indifference and insensitivity, and to raise a question about deep-seated unconscious, unspoken beliefs.

It should be said that on the surface, at least, the Pope was more likely motivated by what the Vatican regarded to be its overriding obligation to honor Catholic Austria's chosen representative. No doubt this same "political necessity" is what has long mandated the papal refusal of diplomatic relations with Israel—millions of Arab Christians, many of them Catholics, who have traditionally looked to their religious leaders for support and guidance as much as to their governments.

Paradoxically, though, in the case of the Vatican and the Jews, both sides have agreed that the donnybrook served, in the end, to strengthen rather than weaken the bond of friendship that had been built up in the two decades since Pope John XXIII. And this despite the papal refusal in September of the year to discuss with Jewish leadership, both at Castel Gondolfo and in Miami, Florida, either John Paul's audience with Waldheim or the absence of diplomatic relations with the State of Israel. Most significantly, it is probably the first time in history that representative spokesmen of world Jewry met with the Papal Nuncio

409

on an equal footing, engaged in candid dialogue on the differences that had broken out between them, left dissatisfied, *and yet came away still good friends.*

In the same period, with the exception of most American evangelists who are unswerving in their support of Israel, Protestant leadership in the Christian world underwent an unsettling transformation. Their good feelings toward Jewry, evident before World War II, are now diluted by a disturbing harshness. A major segment of the Protestant religious establishment is preaching a new concept. Before it only said that Judaism has no place in God's plan of salvation. Today its religiopolitical criticism of Israel denies Israel has become the determining factor in the equation. The change is often expressed overtly in criticism of Israel itself and of Diaspora Jews for their support of the Jewish State in its struggle with its neighbors. It is especially evident in the highly politicized National Council of Churches, an American umbrella agency representing about eighty percent of organized Protestantism.

A momentary look at the Protestant establishment is in order, lest my generalization unfairly stain innocent constituent members within the N.C.C. umbrella: Baptists, Methodists, Episcopalians and Lutherans are not all equally antagonistic; some could not be friendlier. The Quakers, for example, are not very sympathetic, at least in their leadership. On the surface, pacifism seems the basis of their partiality to the Arabs, but their lopsided application of pacifism somehow always results in disadvantage to Israel and then spills over on Jews. Quaker missionary history in the Arab world is probably an important factor in bringing them to the side of the Arabs. Even today there remain in positions of leadership members whose initial training and field experience was in the Arab Middle East. The Christian Science Monitor, which represents to speak for Christian Scientists generally, is perhaps more unsympathetic to Israel than the Quakers. Again, it would seem to be a matter of the background of its personnel. *If* the National Council of Church's antagonism toward Israel is less than representative of the Protestant masses in America, and some informed circles believe it so, this unfortunate situation can be corrected—given a group will strong enough to express its disagreement with the leadership of the National Council of Churches.

Some may conclude from reading this that Protestant hostility toward Jews is no greater than Catholic antipathy, considering the Vatican's refusal to recognize Israel or maintain diplomatic relations with the Jewish State, and even more by the church's evident partiality toward the Arabs in their forty-year dispute with the Israelis. And then again there is Pope John Paul's granting an audience to Kurt Waldheim.

Some political scientists might also argue that a second shift has occurred over the last half-century, with the extremes of the political Left and Right exchanging positions vis-à-vis the Jews. The Far Left, they suggest, has taken over anti-Semitism from the Far Right, which in turn has become a political "friend" of the Jews. Not quite. As indicated earlier, the Far Left in the twenties contained an anti-Jewish quotient (one need only review issues of the *Daily Worker* for those years) which has been revived and intensified by today's Communists. They charge Israel with being a reactionary imperialistic power dominated by the United States and accuse its supporters in the Diaspora with being Rightist reactionaries. It's true that a segment of the contemporary Right supports the Jewish State, and seems also far less hostile to American Jews than it was in earlier years. But this change has likely come about because the Soviet government, openly anti-Israel, is a priority enemy of the Right. The enemy of my enemy is my friend, says the proverb. Also there remains in America an extremist, lunatic Right that has never surrendered its anti-Jewish hostility. So one feels this purported shift is not all that substantial or firm.

The Protestant/Catholic shift possesses a far more solid base. In the last fifty years the three religious groups have apparently completed a semicircle. And with the essential reversal of positions by the two major Christian communities, in spite of the extra strength of the better-organized Catholic Church, Jews are probably in the same situation they were before the Holocaust, other than the change of partners.

SQUARE ONE

To use the cliché, we may be back to Square One.

Except for one player—Israel.

The Jewish State that appeared in May 1948 does make a difference. Just as the Holocaust was a watershed event in Jewish and human history unlike any other event, so was the establishment of the State of Israel a monumental happening that cannot be compared in its importance to any other. How much significance remains to be seen in the years ahead. But that it will be a major defense factor is certain if ever the anti-Semitic monster typified by the Babylonian Exile, the Spanish Inquisition or Hitler's Germany reappears on the world scene.

On the other hand, the reality of a Jewish State among the family of nations may make little real difference to traditional anti-Jewish hatred. Israel is not and cannot be a protective policeman in lands near or distant from the Jewish State, and therefore is able to be of little aid in diminishing built-in anti-Semitism. The Soviet Union and other Eastern European countries are examples of Israel's limited power and influence. In Helsinki, Finland, where the Soviet Union and Israel met in September of 1986 to discuss possible diplomatic reapproachment, the meeting ended abruptly after only ninety minutes because Israeli representatives raised the plight of Soviet Jewry to a high place on the agenda. In this respect the United States may be of more help than Israel. For the time being there seems relatively small movement in this area.

Mr. Gorbachev's December 1987 visit to the United States to sign an antiballistic-missile treaty was the occasion for President Reagan's second attempt to achieve some wider freedoms for Soviet Jews as Jews; he failed in Reykjavik a year earlier. He failed again. In an interview the Soviet leader granted NBC's Tom Brokaw at the time, Mr. Gorbachev stated his position, mincing no words: The Soviet Union would not grant Jews the fundamental right to emigrate where its "security" was at stake (where the applicant had been employed in some kind of sensitive position at any time in the past), or if it resulted in a brain-drain from the USSR. (Jews, in the view of the Soviets, are apparently proportionately smarter than non-Jews; a reverse form of anti-Semitism.) But the saving grace for Soviet Jews may rest in the dynamics of change—that is, *Glasnost* may eventually spill over onto Jews. Or so one hopes.

However, if Jews face a catastrophic situation any place, any time, Israel will assuredly play a major role. How, when or where no one can prophesy in advance. That Israel would sit still and do nothing in face of a major, organized calamity is unimaginable. Some thoughtful but militant-minded Israelis articulate the difference between 1938–1945 and post-1948 this way: If a potential Holocaust looms, before the dust settles, the Hamanlike nation, large or small, would suffer for it dearly— even, as Golda Meir stated, if Israel were destroyed in the process.

But for now we put aside this unlikely cataclysm.

If my analysis is essentially accurate, are we then back to Square One? If so, it might be argued that the last fifty years were an exercise in futility for those who engaged the anti-Jewish enemy. Cynics say that history teaches us that we learn nothing from history. If true, the axiom is equally true about the history of anti-Semitism.

But if by just posing the question I appear a pessimist and cynical about the struggle against anti-Semitism, allow me the expression of a countervailing thought: As we face the facts directly, without rose-colored glasses, the view gains depth and perspective, and with these the chances improve perspective, the approaches to a better world may be seen that all of us will perceive the common identity and common cause of all human beings. Coming to this startling rational truth can consign civilization's gigantic conflict today to its last stages. Either through the blinding flashes of nuclear bombs—or the stronger light of understanding—we will perceive our true identity and each other. What we have refused to do for the good of our souls in past ages, we will have to do to keep ourselves alive in the ages to come.

Index

415

INDEX

Jackson, 382–86; in Korea, 399–400; lack in U.S. of defense organizations to fight, 41–42, 77–78; in Latin America, 398, 407; "low ebb" of, in seventies, 302; in Malaysia, 399; in The Nation, 390–93; nationalism, role of, in, 74; in Nazi Germany, 217–18, 225; new forms of, 303–304, 338, 340, 366; persisting attitudes of, 38–85, 387–91, 393–94, 399–411, 413; police, apathy toward preventing, 100–103; political patterns of, 98, 399; in post-WWII forties, 83, 85–88, 94, 97, 98, 103; in press, 48, 52, 97, 338, 388, 398; in sixties, 174–78; social indifference to, 99, 303–304, 389–90, 409; in Switzerland, 402; in thirties, 40–44, 47, 390–91; on U.S. campuses, 393–94; violent aspects of, 70, 130–33, 407; in Western Europe, 396–97. *see also* Anti-Defamation League; Jews; *under names of individual nations.*
Arab boycott 252–61, 265–96; attempts of, to prevent growth of Jews in Palestine, 252; early response of Israel to, 258–60, 288; banks, submission of, in U.S. to, 259, 274–78, 290; bans films of pro-Israel actors, 261–62; role of oil supply in, 271–72, 285, 287, 289, 292; compliance of federal agencies with, 279–81, 284–85; use of, by Americans against Jews, 284; compliance of U.S. corporations and oil companies with, 278–79, 281–82, 285, 287, 289–91
Arab League 287
Arabs: anti-Jewish terrorism by, 304–305, 320–21; 325, 335, 372–73, 376; economic warfare of, against Israel, 278–90; in Israel, 249, 321–23; peace initiatives, frustrations of, by, 324; political master plan of, against Israel, 107, 138, 173, 223, 247, 249, 281, 304, 324, 335, 367, 373, 376, 399; propaganda movement, 98, 173, 253, 280–81, 286, 298, 300, 367; proposed peace plan by U.S. rejected by, 321–22; Soviet influence on, 247; U.S. support of Palestine homeland for, 298, 300
Arad, Bela 136
Arad, Shimshon 136, 143
Arafat, Fathi 337
Arafat, Yasir 324, 335, 337–38, 369–73, 376, 382; speaks before U.N., 373
Arendt, Hannah 194, 196; Eichmann in Jerusalem, 194
Argentina 187–90, 202, 210, 222, 332; anti-Semitism in, 398; protests abduction of Eichmann, 192
Argo, Shlomo 332–34
Aryan Nations 379
Asher Court 88; *X-Ray*, 88
Association of Arab-American University Graduates, 391
Austria 403–407; anti-Semitism in, 403, 406–407; Jews in, 406
Avenue of the Righteous Gentiles (Jerusalem) 241–43
Avi Yonah, Prof. Michael 238

Baker, Jack 270
Balaban, Barney 329
banks: Bank of America, 278; Bankers Trust, 278; Chemical Bank, 278; Citibank, 278, 298; Citicorp, 278, 291; First National City Bank, 278; Morgan Guaranty Trust, 278
Bar-Lev, Haim 288
Barody, Jamil 368
Barr, Tom 355
Barre, Raymond 396

Bechtel Corporation (San Francisco) 278, 281–83, 291–92, 295; anti-trust suit filed against, 282; bars business with Israel, 295
Begin, Menachem 354, 363
Belafonte, Harry 261
Bell, James 360
Belth, Nat 151, 155
Ben-Gurion, David 105–106, 135, 137, 139–44, 187–88, 199, 204, 244–51, 269, 325–26; and emigration to Palestine, 248–50; failure of, to resist Holocaust, 25–51; and media, 247; views on Middle East, 246–47
Ben-Gurion, Paula 139–40, 142–43; death of, 244
Bennike, Maj. Gen. Vagan 326
Bethge, Rev. Eberhard 402
Bialkin, Kenneth 291, 344
bigotry *see* anti-Semitism; discrimination
Bilbo, Sen. Theodore 56, 58–59, 75; member of KKK, 58–59
Billingsley, Sherman 94
Bingham, Rep. Jonathan 273
Birch, John 113–14
blacklisting 163–72; exposed by Cogley Report, 164–67, 169; investigated by Fund for the Republic, 163–64; role of CBS in, 166
Blacks 21, 58–59, 61, 83, 86, 96, 174–75, 385; anti-Semitism of, 382–83; and Jews, 21, 86, 97, 382–87; voting rights of, 58–59
Blueprint for Freedom 109–11, 148
B'nai B'rith 46, 88, 146, 329. *see also* Anti-Defamation League
Bormann, Martin 187
Bornstein, Moshe 260–63, 266, 268–71
Bornstein, Zvi 270–71
Boston *Globe* 275
Brandeis University 180, 185
Brandt, George 41
British-American Tobacco Company 255
Brokaw, Tom 412
Brookhart, Lt. Col. Smith 207–208
Brown & Williamson Tobacco Company 255
Buckley, William F., Jr. 176–78, 391–92
Burack, Zahava 242–43
Business Roundtable, The 291

Carter, Pres. Jimmy 286, 288–92, 297–301, 376; commits to antiboycott legislation, 288–90; Jewish community in U.S., understanding of, 299–300; Jewish disenchantment with, 298–99
Carto, Willis 389; *Liberty Lobby*, 389
Catholics and Catholic Church 71, 82, 88, 96, 101–103, 174, 384, 408, 411; anti-Semitism among, 66, 72, 74, 101–102, 148; anti-Semitism as part of anti-Soviet sentiments among, 74; changes in relationship with Jews, 408–11; denounces anti-Semitism, 408–409; Jewish deicide repudiated by *Nostra Aetate*, 408–409; meetings with Jews, 103, 408–409; repudiates Coughlin, 69, 71, 82–83; as target of Soviet Communism, 66–67
Chancellor, John (NBC) 337
Chandler, Douglas 203
Chaplin, Charlie 168
Chase Manhattan Bank 274–78, 291
Chayevsky, Paddy 106–108
Cherry Lane Theatre 35
Chicanos 174
Chirac, Jacques 396
Christian Front, The 50, 70, 82, 89, 379, 408

416

Index

Christian Educational League, The 62, 87
Christian Frontier 97
Christian Mobilizers 70
Christian Nationalist Crusade 86
Christians and Christian churches 232, 234,
    242, 410; against anti-Semitism, 56, 66, 180;
    and anti-Semitism, 304, 410–11; change of
    attitudes of Jews by, since WWII, 408,
    410–11; resistance of, to Nazis, 242–43
Christian Science Monitor 337; unsympathetic
    to Israel, 410
Churchill, Winston 51, 246
Citizens Protective League 70
City Patrol Corps (NYC) 103
Civil Rights Act (1964) 274, 279
Civil Rights Movement 302
Clark, Joe 394
Close, Upton 85, 120–21
Clurman, Richard M. 362
Cobb, Lee J. 147
Coca-Cola Company 259–70; submits of Arab
    boycott, 265–67, 269–71; and Tempo
    franchise, 262–65, 268–70
Cockburn, Alexander 391; "Israel's War
    Against Foreign Journalists," 391
Cogley, John 163–68
Cogley Report 166–70
Cohen, Dr. Yoel 363–64
Cohn, Justice Albert 46, 158–60
Cohn, Roy M. 46, 158–62, 172
Coleman, Milton 385
Columbians of Georgia 97
Committee to Keep America Out of War 81
Commoner Party of the United States 97
Commonweal, The 69, 164, 171
Communism and communists 51–52, 62, 66,
    68–71, 73, 86, 112–13, 145, 170–71;
    anti-Catholic policies of, 66–67;
    anti-Semitism of, 411; feigned support of
    Jews, 52–53, 71; infiltration of Civil Rights
    movement by, 159; paranoia against, in
    U.S., 112–14, 117, 119, 123, 126, 145–50,
    163–64, 170–71, 177–78; reaction of, to
    Eichmann trial, 211–12, 217; and
    Rosenbergs, 52–53, 126–28. *see also* Soviet
    Union
Communist Party International 170–71
concentration camps 206, 212–13, 215,
    220–21, 223–24, 229, 235–36, 238, 381;
    children in, 229–30; Auschwitz, 206, 223,
    229, 270; Belzek, 206; Buchenwald, 206;
    Gneisenau, 353; Maidanek, 215; Ponar,
    235–36; Ravensbruck, 206, 353;
    Thereseinstadt, 238, 352; Treblinka, 206;
    Wolzek, 206. *see also* Final Solution; Jews;
    Holocaust; Nazis and Nazism; Third Reich
Conference of Presidents of Major American
    Jewish Organizations 386
Constitution Christian Party 97
Conte, Richard 145
corporations: Aramco, 278–79; Bausch &
    Lomb, 278; Dupont, 291; Flintkote, 278;
    General Electric, 291; General Mills, 278,
    291; Ingersoll-Rand, 278; Merrill, Lynch,
    Pierce, Fenner & Smith, 278; Pillsbury, 278;
    Uncle Ben's Rice, 278
Coughlin, Fr. Charles E. 67–73, 75, 82–83,
    126; attacks FDR, 68; campaigns against
    Jews, 68–69; draws on Nazi propaganda, 69;
    forced out of public life, 83; and Radio
    League of the Little Flower, 82; and Shrine
    of the Little Flower, 82; and Social Justice
    Publishing Company, 82; supports Christian
    Front, 70; *Social Justice*, 67, 69, 73, 82

Coughlin Movement, The 67. *see also*
    National Union for Social Justice
Craxi, Bettino 371–72
Crusaders for America 70

Daily Worker, The 145, 411
Dalton, Harry 44
Dalton, Leo 44
Dan, Uri 341–42
Davies, Marion 117–18
Davis, Sidney 151, 155
Dayan, Moshe 305, 316
De Aryan, C. Leon 88; *American National
    Weekly, The*, 88
Deatherage, George 70
Decter, Midge 392–93
De Gaulle, Charles 246
Dekker, Albert 146
Democratic Convention (1984) 384–85
Democratic Party 382–87, 389; indifference
    of, to anti-Semitism, 385–86; Jewish
    community and, 385
Dennis, Lawrence 61–62, 70; as racist, 61–62;
    black heritage of, 62; *Appeal to Reason,
    The*, 61; *Awakener, The*, 61–62; *Coming
    American Fascism, The*, 61
Dilling, Elizabeth 88; *Octopus, The*, 88;
    Patriotic Research Bulletin, 88; *Red
    Network*, 81, 88
Dinitz, Simcha 313
discrimination: broadens in U.S., 174; decline
    of, in recent years, 378–79, 393–96;
    institutions of, 78–79, 174, 284. *see also*
    anti-Semitism
diShalit, Memi 105–106, 135
Dow Chemical Corporation 261
Draper, Paul 148
Duncan, Richard 346–51
Dupont, Irénée 85
Dupont, Lamont 85

East Germany 216–17
Eban, Abba 189–91, 258, 313, 331
Edelsberg, Herman 158, 160–61
Egypt 173, 239–40, 246, 259, 301, 321, 323;
    peace efforts of, with Israel, 310; role of, in
    Achille Lauro affair, 370–71
Eichmann, Adolph 186–94, 198–236; children,
    orders killing of, 228–30; seizure of, by
    Mossad, 190–92, 211, 213, 215; capture of,
    incitement to anti-Semitism, 192–93;
    description of, 232; Holocaust, emotional
    response of, to, 233–34; in hiding, 210–11;
    role of, in Final Solution, 206–208, 223,
    226, 229–30, 233–34; not guilty plea by,
    232–33; as symbol, 219–22, 224, 231, 233,
    235
Eichmann trial 194–236; legal and moral
    aspects of, 201–204, 211, 213, 215, 234;
    letters in response to, 209–10; media
    coverage of, 201, 204, 211–15, 227;
    revelations of Holocaust at, 219–20; role of
    U.S. response to, 221; world response to,
    217–28
Eichmann, Vera 188
Eisenhower, Pres. Dwight D. 113–14, 246,
    330; administration of, attacked as
    pro-communist, 114, 177
Eitan, Rafael 189–91
Elizur, Yuval 262, 271
Emergency Committee for American Trade
    (ECAT) 290
Emory University (Atlanta, Ga.) 175
Engberg, Ed 163, 166, 171

417

Index

Gilbert, Adam 342
Glasnost see Gorbachev, Mikhail S.
Glubb, John "Pasha" 326
Gods of the Lightning (play) 35–36
Goebbels, Joseph 69, 71
Goldstein, Richard 342–43
Goldwater, Barry 175
Gorbachev, Mikhail S. 397, 412–13
Goren, Shlomo 239–41
Gould, Milton 317, 342–43, 354–56, 364
Goulet, Robert 176
Graebe, Herman Friedrich 195
Graubard, Seymour "Sy" 274, 276–77, 282
Grauer, Ben 109
Great Britain 74–75, 80, 86, 332; seen as pro-Soviet, 74; and Falklands War, 332–33
Great Depression 36–38, 71–72, 76–78; rise of anti-Semitism during, 38, 71–72
Greenberg, Maxwell 293
Greenfield, Bob 45–47
Greenglass, David 126
Grotius, Hugo 202
Grumel, Judge Jacob 408
Grunwald, Henry 363
Gunnels, R.L. 261–64, 266
Gutstadt, Richard 96

Halevy, David "Dudu" 346–51, 353–54, 361, 363
Harris, Louis 382
Hart, Merwin K. 61–62, 85, 87
Hatfield, Sen. Mark 176
Hausner, Gideon 195–96, 213, 223, 225–29, 235–36
Hayes, Helen 261
Hearst Corporation 117–18, 159
Henried, Paul 145
Hepburn, Katherine 145
Herzog, Chaim 137–39
Herzog, Rabbi Isaac Halevi 137
Herzog, Yaacov 137–39
Herzstein, R.E. 405
Heydrich, Reinhard 229, 351–53
Hill, George 81
Himmler, Heinrich 207, 351, 353
Hindenberg, Pres. Paul von 226
Hitler, Adolf 23, 38, 42, 44, 51, 54, 69, 71, 75, 94, 138, 186, 199, 207–208, 212, 216, 218, 222, 228, 231, 234, 302, 351, 399, 405
Hoffman, Rep. Clare 56, 62, 87
Hoffman, Irving 110
Holliday, Judy 147
Hollywood Reporter, The 110
Holocaust 79, 83, 95, 138, 186, 192, 194–96, 199–200, 206, 210, 217–19, 221–24, 228–29, 231, 233, 236, 250–51, 270, 380–81, 383, 407, 411–12; attempts to prevent, 78–79, 234–35, 287; denials of existence of, 368, 395, 400; lack of international resistance to, 235, 250, 310, 315, 338; revealed by Eichmann trial, 227–30
Holocaust, The (film) 368
Horne, Lena 145
House Committee on Un-American Activities (HCUAA) 145–47, 150–51, 153, 164, 167, 169, 172
Hudson, Charles B. 88; *America in Danger*, 88
Hussein, King of Jordan 373, 375
Hutchins, Robert M. 166–67
Hutton, E.F. 86

Identity Churches 379
Ilin, Ephraim 257

Ingalls, Laura 80
Institute of Arab-American Affairs 98
Institute of Arab Studies, The 391
International Communist Conspiracy 113, 117, 126, 177
Internationalists 86
International Jewish Conspiracy 88, 117, 126, 382, 400
Iraq 261, 279, 323, 372
isolationism 59–62, 70–71, 74–76, 83, 85–86, 113
Israel 23, 38, 86, 93, 98, 104–107, 135–44, 188, 245–51, 383–84, 386–88, 392, 394; and anti-Semitism, 309; Argentina, sale of arms to opposed, 332; boycott of, by U.S. businessmen, 252–61, 272–73; capital punishment in, 200–201; censured for abduction of Eichmann, 192–93, 199, 201–205, 211, 213, 234; and Chase Manhattan Bank, 276–78; and Coca-Cola franchise, 268–69; Commission in, investigates invasion of Lebanon, 339–41, 343, 355, 361; conflicts with Arabs, 320–21, 324–26, 376; declares independence (1948), 104–105, 138, 324; as defense against international anti-Semitism, 412–13; and Eichmann trial, 199–236; ethical reputation damaged by Lebanese invasion, 339–41, 343–45; Kibya, alleged massacre by, at, 326–28, 332, 356–60; Lebanon, invasion of, by, 334–39, 391; Mossad, establishes (1960), 186–89, 211, 340; opposition of Arabs to, 107; opposition of, to antiboycott efforts, 258–59, 305; opposition to existence of, 106–107, 144, 394; opposition to, in press, 107, 321–23, 326, 332, 390–93; and peace efforts with Egypt, 310; and Pollard incident, 388; reaction of youth in, to Eichmann trial, 194–96, 212, 218; subjected to double standard in media, 321–24, 332, 336–38, 340; U.S. admonishes, for Arab policy, 321; U.S. policy toward, changes in, 311–12, 391; U.S. support and aid to, 298, 300, 310–12; U.N. attacks on, 366–69; Waldheim, requests U.N. files on, 404; West Bank, policies in, censured, 321–23 *see also* Arabs; Jews; Middle East
Israel Anniversary Committee 154
Israel Bond Appeal 274
Israel Philharmonic Orchestra 241
Italy 370–72

Jackson, Rev. Jesse 382–87; Jewish opposition to, 387
Jacobson, Joe 269
Jerusalem Post 322, 363
Jewish Agency 104–105, 252
Jewish Defense League 249
Jewish War Veterans 42, 44
Jews: accusations against, for deicide, 408; and "blood libel," 45–46, 49, 159, 399; and communism, 72, 76, 126–28; confused politics of, 76, 78; Diaspora, relationship of to Jewish state, 105, 410; failure of, in U.S. to aid European Jews, 52, 77–78, 96; identified with communists, 51, 62–63, 66–69, 71–74, 85, 112, 119, 126, 128, 331, 398; immigration of, to Palestine (*aliyahs*), 248–50, 252; insecurity and poor self-image of, 53, 73, 78, 128; resistance of, in WWII, 228–29, 234–35; role of leadership among, in U.S., 52–53, 76, 83, 98, 140; and Rosenberg case, 126–28; in Soviet Union, 374, 397–98, 412; treated as second class

419

INDEX

Index

421

422

Index